Go for Java Programmers

Learn the Google
Go Programming Language

Barry Feigenbaum, Ph.D.

Apress®

Go for Java Programmers: Learn the Google Go Programming Language

Barry Feigenbaum, Ph.D.
Austin, TX, USA

ISBN-13 (pbk): 978-1-4842-7198-8
https://doi.org/10.1007/978-1-4842-7199-5

ISBN-13 (electronic): 978-1-4842-7199-5

Managing Director, Apress Media LLC: Welmoed Spahr
Acquisitions Editor: Steve Anglin
Development Editor: Matthew Moodie
Coordinating Editor: Mark Powers

Cover designed by eStudioCalamar

Cover image by Ricardo Gomez on Unsplash (www.unsplash.com)

Distributed to the book trade worldwide by Apress Media, LLC, 1 New York Plaza, New York, NY 10004, U.S.A. Phone 1-800-SPRINGER, fax (201) 348-4505, e-mail orders-ny@springer-sbm.com, or visit www.springeronline.com. Apress Media, LLC is a California LLC and the sole member (owner) is Springer Science + Business Media Finance Inc (SSBM Finance Inc). SSBM Finance Inc is a **Delaware** corporation.

For information on translations, please e-mail booktranslations@springernature.com; for reprint, paperback, or audio rights, please e-mail bookpermissions@springernature.com.

Apress titles may be purchased in bulk for academic, corporate, or promotional use. eBook versions and licenses are also available for most titles. For more information, reference our Print and eBook Bulk Sales web page at http://www.apress.com/bulk-sales.

Any source code or other supplementary material referenced by the author in this book is available to readers on GitHub via the book's product page, located at www.apress.com/9781484271988. For more detailed information, please visit http://www.apress.com/source-code.

Printed on acid-free paper

To my wife Martha who sustains me.

Thank you for putting up with all the time
I spent working on this book.

This book was developed during the Covid-19 pandemic.
Many thanks and kudos to all the health-care workers that served so
many that became ill and to the essential workers that keep the country
going during this time of crisis. My heart goes out to the many who lost
friends and loved ones due to Covid-19. May time reduce your pain.

Personally, the stay-at-home nature of this crisis offered me the time
needed to author this book, so in some way is it a, hopefully, positive
by-product of the pandemic.

Table of Contents

About the Author

Barry Feigenbaum, Ph.D., has decades of software engineering experience. During his career, he has worked for major industry-leading companies, such as IBM and Amazon, and is currently at Dell where he is a Senior Principal Software Engineer. He has worked on mainframe and midrange servers and many applications for personal computers. He has developed software products, such as assemblers for multiple hardware architectures, in many key industry languages such as C/C++/C#, Python, JavaScript, Java, and now Go. He has extensive experience in the full software development life cycle. Most recently, he has committed himself to leading teams developing mission-critical microservices, most often written in Go, that operate in large clustered environments.

He led the early development of the LAN support inside Microsoft Windows (he defined the SMB protocol that is the basis for both the CIFS and the SAMBA technologies). He has served as a software tester, developer, and designer as well as a development team lead, architect, and manager on multiple occasions. He was a key contributor as a developer, architect, and manager to several releases of PC-DOS and OS/2. In these roles, he worked extensively with Microsoft on joint requirements, design, and implementation.

Dr. Feigenbaum has a Ph.D. in Computer Engineering with a concentration in object-oriented (OO) software design and other degrees in Electrical Engineering. He has published multiple articles in technical magazines and juried journals. He has coauthored several books on IBM PC-DOS. He has spoken at numerous technical conferences, such as JavaOne. He has served on industry standard bodies. He has taught multiple college-level courses on data structures, software engineering, and distributed software as an adjunct professor at several universities. He has over 20 issued US patents.

He is married, has one son, and lives in Austin, TX.

About the Technical Reviewer

Ronald Petty, M.B.A., M.S., is founder of Minimum Distance LLC, a management consulting firm based in San Francisco. He spends his time helping technology-based startups do the right thing. He is also an instructor at UC Berkeley Extension.

Acknowledgments

To my son Barry, Jr., for his careful review of the drafts of this book. He provided a perfect example of the book's target audience: a professional Java programmer wanting to learn Go.

A hearty thanks to all the other reviewers that made helpful comments, suggested additional content, and/or made errata corrections: Charles Stein, Divya Khatnar, Rosish Shakya, and Sharath Hegde.

I especially want to thank Ronald Petty for his thorough technical review of this text. Also, for his numerous suggested content improvements and code samples, several of which were included.

I wish to thank Jason Isaacs at Dell who supported me during the creation of this text and allowed me to go forward with this effort.

To the developers of Go and to the Go community in general, many thanks for building such a powerful tool. I learned much from the extensive Go documentation and the many articles, blogs, wikis, tutorials, and books provided by the community.

Introduction

Since its debut in the mid-1990s, Java has enjoyed huge success. Arguably more so than other languages, Java is a major player in the web application space and key data processing areas such as Big Data tools, among others. Among other aspects, Java's high level of portability across operating systems and hardware architectures, its rich and improving over time language and library of functions, as well as its good performance contributed to this success.

But Java comes with some drawbacks. Java was created at a time when *Object-Oriented Programming*[1] was the norm and network delivery of code was advantageous. The resulting Java runtime footprint is quite large, and it is resource intensive. The Java developers are trying to address this to some degree with the use of Java *Modules* along with standard library subsetting and the Graal[2] Virtual Machine, but typical Java code, for the same functionality, often uses more resources than typical Go code does.

As time is passing, the Java language and runtime is no longer an optimal fit for many modern, especially cloud-based, applications. Also, the Java language is continuously growing and can be a challenge to fully master. Go is deliberately a simple, thus easy to master, language.

The Go language and runtime is relatively new and designed to meet the needs of modern cloud computing systems and other system[3] programming tasks. It is considered by many to be a "better C than C" and thus a potential replacement for the C[4] programming language, the language it most closely resembles. Go is also likely to take over a large fraction of the Java server and application space. Thus, it is the *raison d'etre* for this book.

Many new applications and reengineering of existing applications are now being developed in Go. For applications previously written in Java, Kotlin[5] or Scala[6] JVM

---

[1] https://en.wikipedia.org/wiki/Object-oriented_programming

[2] www.graalvm.org/java/

[3] Oriented to operating the computer system rather than achieving business tasks.

[4] https://en.wikipedia.org/wiki/C_(programming_language)

[5] https://kotlinlang.org/

[6] www.scala-lang.org/

(both available as Java Virtual Machine–based languages) might be the more expected language to use, but often Go is winning out over them. As an example of a redo into Go, Khan Academy[7] is using Go to reengineer[8] its previous Python site implementation. This often happens because Go exhibits many of the ease-of-use features common to scripting languages with the efficiency of compiled languages.

The original Go lead designers, Robert Griesemer, Rob Pike, and Ken Thompson, all at Google, wanted to define a language and associated runtime with these key features (some also provided by Java):

- High developer productivity – Go offers a consumable and reasonably complete runtime. It also offers a one-stop shopping toolchain. It has widespread high community support.

- High readability and developer usability – The language itself is small, so it is easy to learn, and its code is both easy to read and understand vs. easiest/fastest to write. It has a targeted ease of use comparable to nonstatically typed languages like Python. Often, the language is opinionated (sort of take it or leave it).

- Go uses memory garbage collection (GC) which reduces programmer effort and makes for more reliable programs.

- Go is statically linked (vs. dynamically linked, as Java is); this makes it easier to manage deployment and execution of Go programs.

- Static typing – Generally supports safer, more performant, and more predictable programs; helps with high reliability and long duration execution critical for servers.

- Runtime efficiency – The code efficiently uses the processors it runs on, comparable to what is achievable in C/C++[9] applications.

---

[7] www.khanacademy.org/
[8] https://blog.khanacademy.org/half-a-million-lines-of-go/
[9] https://en.wikipedia.org/wiki/C%2B%2B

- High network performance – Distributed/cloud use cases are now common, and the code needs to be performant for them. For the same level of function, Go is often less resource intensive than Java typically is; this helps with reducing resource footprint and improving scale in modern cloud distributions.

- High utilization of multi-processor systems – The code needs to allow easy and safe exploitation of multi-processor (core) systems that have become the norm. Go excels at this.

Robert Pike summarized[10] this as follows:

> *… we wanted a language with the safety and performance of statically compiled languages such as C++ and Java, but the lightness and fun of dynamically typed interpreted languages such as Python. It was also important that the result be suitable for large systems software development on modern, networked, multicore hardware.*

The *Go Brand Book*[11] (GBB) states:

> *Go is an open source programming language that enables the production of simple, efficient and reliable software at scale.*

The GBB further states that Go has these benefits for new programmers:

> *Developer productivity of a dynamic language with the speed, safety, and reliability of a static language*

- *Easy to learn & readable*

- *Has a vibrant, welcoming community, spanning open-source developers, startups, large companies, and universities*

- *The language for the Cloud*

And these benefits for experienced programmers:

- *Solves big engineering problems*

- *Backed by Google, who understands and supports needs specific to open source communities and Go*

- *High demand for Go programmers*

---

[10] www.red-gate.com/simple-talk/opinion/geek-of-the-week/rob-pike-geek-of-the-week/
[11] https://storage.googleapis.com/golang-assets/Go-brand-book-v1.9.5.pdf

In many ways, Go is a lot like *Node.js*,[12] a popular JavaScript[13]-based application development platform. Node.js makes it easy to develop lightweight servers very quickly and thus is popular as a microservices platform. Node.js and Go have similar capabilities, history, and community support. Go, because of its type safety and goroutines (vs. Node.js's event loop), is likely to be able to provide more scaled and reliable solutions than Node.js can. In the author's opinion, Go will also consume a significant number of the Node.js use cases.

As a result, many applications previously done in Java can instead be implemented in Go with some advantages, especially in cloud environments.

So, in summary, here are some Go advantages relative to Java:

- Go is a smaller language that is clean, maintainable, and easy to learn.

- Go is better suited to support multi-core processors and high levels of concurrency.

- Go has a smaller but strong set of standard libraries, especially for building servers, that comes bundled with the standard installation.

- Go is well suited to cloud execution, especially in a containerized environment.

- Go is well suited to any constrained environments where large code and runtime footprint can be issues.

Go is open source, has an active developer community, and is sponsored by Google; it will not go away. Future Go evolution will retain backward compatibility;[14] this is a Go community promise. This makes Go a great language for commercial development.

Hackernoon[15] says: "*Go is on a trajectory to become the next enterprise programming language.*"

---

[12] https://en.wikipedia.org/wiki/Node.js, https://nodejs.org/en/
[13] https://en.wikipedia.org/wiki/JavaScript
[14] https://golang.org/doc/go1compat
[15] https://hackernoon.com/go-is-on-a-trajectory-to-become-the-next-enterprise-programming-language-3b75d70544e

They further say:

Go—a programming language designed for large-scale software develop-
ment—provides a robust development experience and avoids many issues
that existing programming languages have. These factors make it one of the
most likely candidates to succeed Java as the dominating enterprise soft-
ware platform in the future. … Taken as a whole, they (Go's design choices)
position Go as an excellent choice for large development projects looking
for a modern programming language beyond Java.

InfoWorld[16] says:

Google's Go programming language has certainly made a name for itself.
Lightweight and quick to compile, Go has stirred significant interest due to
its generous libraries and abstractions that ease the development of concur-
rent and distributed (read: cloud) applications. … But the true measure of
success of any programming language is the projects that developers create
with it. Go has proven itself as a first choice for fast development of network
services, software infrastructure projects, and compact and powerful tools
of all kinds.

Open source projects they mention that use Go include Docker, Kubernetes, Fedora
CoreOS, InfluxDB, Istio, Traefik, Hugo, Terraform, CockroachDB, and Gravitational
Teleport.

Note that Docker and Kubernetes are the foundation technologies for the
containerization of many modern applications. Many organizations depend on them to
be rock solid and performant. This is a testament to the maturity of the Go language and
its runtime.

Brainhub[17] list some major companies using Go and the advantages they see:

- Simple code

- Created for large projects

- Easy to learn

- One problem – one solution

- Ease of maintenance

---

[16] www.infoworld.com/article/3442978/10-open-source-projects-proving-the-power-of-
google-go.html
[17] https://brainhub.eu/library/companies-using-golang/

- Similar to C

- Designed for multi-core processors

- Designed for the Internet

- Quick compilation

- Small application size

- Open source model

They mention companies using Go including Google (of course), Uber, Twitch, Dailymotion, SendGrid, Dropbox, and SoundCloud.

Awesome Open Source[18] lists over 15,000 (and growing) projects that use Go.

Sandra Parker[19] projects[20] Go has a winning future where she emphasizes: *"Because it is made by* Google."

She indicates why it's currently popular: *"Go is different from other languages. It is young but so powerful that it was able to bring up geek's engagement from the very start."*

In summary:

- *It is convenient, fast, and secure to write code with Golang, and it provides cross-platform support...*

- Google *cares about the user.*

- *Golang has cloud infrastructure.*

- Google *has money.*

And why it is going to get more popular as time passes:

Applications written on Go are highly performant. Golang is very efficient like C/C++, handling parallelisms like Java, and has easy code readability like Python, Perl, and Erlang. ... This is why many companies migrate to Golang from other languages. Golang is the future.

---

[18] https://awesomeopensource.com/projects/go

[19] www.quora.com/profile/Sandra-Parker-34

[20] https://medium.com/@Sandra_Parker/why-golang-is-the-future-part-1-ed7dd4f419d and
https://medium.com/@Sandra_Parker/why-golang-is-the-future-part-2-1f984ae8f1a4

In 2020, Ziff Davis[21] showed that Go is the most desired new language to learn, as shown in Figure 1.

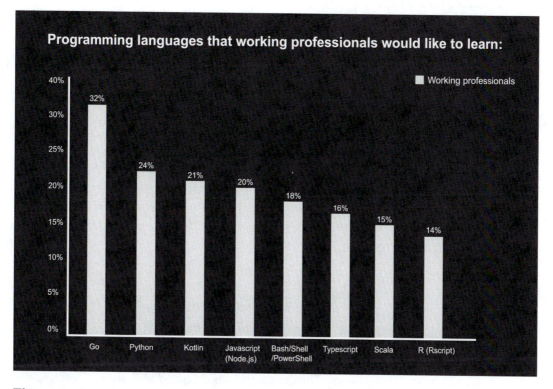

Figure 1. *Programming languages professionals want to learn*

Other sources extol the virtues of Go and indicate it has a growing future. For example, *Towards Data Science*[22] states these as key features for Go's success:

1. *Go has language-level support for Concurrency. It offers a CSP[23] based message-passing concurrency via Goroutine (lightweight Green thread) and Channel.*

---

[21] https://en.wikipedia.org/wiki/Ziff_Davis, www.zdnet.com/article/developers-say-googles-go-is-most-sought-after-programming-language-of-2020/, and www.hackerearth.com/recruit/developer-survey/

[22] https://towardsdatascience.com/top-10-in-demand-programming-languages-to-learn-in-2020-4462eb7d8d3e

[23] Communicating sequential processes – https://en.wikipedia.org/wiki/Communicating_sequential_processes

2. *The biggest USP[24] of Go is its language design and simplicity. It has successfully combined the simplicity and productivity of* Python *and the power of* C.

3. *Go has embedded Garbage Collector (albeit not as mature as JVM garbage collector). Go developers can write* system programming *with the safety of Java,* Python.

Go is ranked as one of the top five most loved languages by *GeeksforGeeks*,[25] which describes Go as follows:

Go is a statically typed, open-source programming language designed at Google that makes programmers more productive and helps to build simple, reliable, and efficient software very easily. This language ... is syntactically similar to C, but with memory safety, garbage collection, structural typing, and CSP-style concurrency. Go is well known for its high-performance in networking and multiprocessing.

They cite these key virtues:

1. *Concurrency: provides greater* concurrency *with the help of goroutine which makes it extremely easy to implement in a concurrent system. ...*

2. *Simplicity and Consistency: This language was designed with a very minimalistic approach and it is well known for its simplicity. ... The standard library and the packages are consistent.*

3. *Object-oriented: Go is an Object-oriented programming language and supports the useful features of OOPs. ...*

4. *Tools: Go provides many useful tools for building, testing, and analyzing code...*

5. *Compiler: Its compiler is super-fast and easily compiles a large go program within a few seconds. ...*

---

[24] Unique selling proposition – https://en.wikipedia.org/wiki/Unique_selling_proposition
[25] www.geeksforgeeks.org/top-5-most-loved-programming-languages-in-2020/

Note that this author disagrees with point 3. In his opinion, Go is object-based,[26] not object-oriented.

The popular TIOBE[27] index shows that Go use is growing at a fast rate. A late 2020 survey shows this:

- Current Year Rank: 13

- Previous Year Rank: 20

- Growth Rate: High

Few languages have seen such high year-over-year growth. TIOBE twice named Go as the "language of the year." The future need for Go programmers is expected to continue to grow rapidly.

A look at Go Users[28] shows hundreds of organizations, including some of the world's largest companies, using Go around the world. This list is likely to omit many actual users.

Go is used, and in many ways proven effective, in many complex programs. The Docker[29] container system and the Kubernetes[30] container orchestrator are prime examples of industry-leading programs written in Go. Also, the Go compiler, builder, and most of the standard libraries are written in Go.[31] They are an important test case in themselves.

In 2020, *StackOverflow* has ranked (https://insights.stackoverflow.com/survey/2020) the most loved languages. Go is among the top of the top 25 listed well-known languages, and it ranks higher in that list on the desired ("loved") scale than Java. Note how well it compares to Python; this is remarkable for a compiled language.

---

[26] https://en.wikipedia.org/wiki/Object-based_language

[27] The Importance of Being Earnest – https://en.wikipedia.org/wiki/TIOBE_index

[28] https://github.com/golang/go/wiki/GoUsers

[29] www.docker.com/

[30] https://kubernetes.io/

[31] Originally bootstrapped from a C version of these tools.

Table 1. *Most Loved Languages Survey*

Language	Loved Percentage (Using and Want to Continue Using)
Rust	86.1%
TypeScript	67.1%
Python	66.7%
Kotlin	62.9%
Go	*62.3%*
Julia	62.2%
Dart	62.1%
C#	59.7%
Swift	59.5%
JavaScript	58.3%
SQL	56.6%
Bash/Shell/PowerShell	53.7%
HTML/CSS	53.5%
Scala	53.2%
Haskell	51.7%
R	44.5%
Java	*44.1%*
C++	43.4%
Ruby	42.9%
PHP	37.3%
C	33.1%
Assembly	29.4%
Perl	28.6%
Objective-C	23.4%
VBA	19.6%

All this should make learning to program in Go highly interesting to experienced Java developers looking to broaden their skills and marketability. In the author's opinion, Go will emerge as the go-to language for multi-core computing over networks, especially for servers.

Of course, for a complete analysis, we need to contrast the mascots of Go and Java. In the author's opinion, Go's mascot is both simpler and cuddlier, as, arguably, is the language itself.

Figure 2 shows the Go logo and Gopher mascot.

Figure 2. *Go mascot and logo[32]*

Figure 3 shows the Java mascot (Duke).

Figure 3. *Java mascot[33]*

---

[32] The Go gopher was designed by Renee French. (http://reneefrench.blogspot.com/) and is licensed under the Creative Commons 3.0 Attributions license.

[33] https://wiki.openjdk.java.net/display/duke/Main

INTRODUCTION

Gophers, welcome aboard! In this book, we will briefly explore the concepts behind Go and why it was created. This overview will be followed by an introduction to Go's various features and a look at if/how they differ from Java. Then comes a presentation of most of the Go language statements and data types. This is followed by a brief look at some potential future Go enhancements. A capstone example Go program is then presented to unify the Go experience. Next comes a review of the Go standard libraries as they compare to similar Java libraries. Finally comes a survey of a subset of the various Go standard libraries as an introduction to their usage. Deeper and more comprehensive descriptions are available at the Go site.

More precisely, this book's content is broken down into three parts with several chapters within each part.

Some background on Go:

- A brief look at Go vs. Java comparing key features of both languages

- Summary of features Java has that Go does not have

A description of the Go language and its key features with a look at using Go in practice:

- A brief side-by-side comparison of Go features with Java

- A survey of Go key features

- A more detailed view of important Go characteristics (like Go keywords, etc.)

- A detailed view of Go data types

- A discussion of Go's error reporting mechanism

- A broader discussion on Go's interface data type and how it is applied

- A description of each Go statement

- A more detailed discussion on applying Go data types

- A look at testing Go vs. Java programs

- A brief look at possible future Go enhancements

- A *capstone* program illustrating many Go and Go library features

An introduction to the Go standard libraries in comparison with Java libraries combined with a survey of key Go standard libraries:

- A discussion of key Java library packages with similar Go packages.

- A brief side-by-side comparison of commonly used Java methods with similar Go functions.

- A brief discussion of formatting data values in Go.

- A brief discussion of file input/output in Go.

- This part includes chapters covering compression/decompression, image processing, input/output, cryptography, relational database access, network access, and Go runtime access.

- It is intended to bring awareness of the various Go libraries and not a complete understanding of all the available functions.

- This is the largest part of the book.

In addition, there are five appendixes with supplementary information such as how to install Go, as well as some summary and reference information.

Note   In some of the code examples in this book, long source lines are wrapped into multiple lines. This wrapping may not be allowed in actual Go source.

The source for the capstone programs, as well as for some of the other listing samples in this book, is available at the book website: `www.github.com/apress/go-for-java-programmers`.

Before we dive into Go, let us consider why Go exists. Rob Pike summarized[34] the language and why it was created this way:

> *The Go programming language was conceived in late 2007 as an answer to some of the* problems *we were seeing developing software infrastructure at Google. The computing landscape today is almost unrelated to the environment in which the languages being used, mostly C++, Java, and* Python, *had been created. The **problems introduced by multicore***

---

[34] `https://talks.golang.org/2012/splash.article`

processors, networked systems, massive computation clusters, and the web programming model *were being worked around rather than addressed head-on. Moreover, the scale has changed:* ***today's server programs comprise tens of millions of lines of code, are worked on by hundreds or even thousands of programmers, and are updated literally every day.*** *To make matters worse, build times, even on large compilation clusters, have stretched to many minutes, even hours.*

Go was designed and developed to make working in this environment more productive. *Besides its better-known aspects such as built-in concurrency and garbage collection, Go's design considerations include rigorous dependency management, the adaptability of software architecture as systems grow, and robustness across the boundaries between components.*

Go is a compiled, concurrent, garbage-collected, statically typed language *developed at Google. It is an open source project: Google imports the public repository rather than the other way around.*

Go is efficient, scalable, and productive. *Some programmers find it fun to work in; others find it unimaginative, even boring. In this article we will explain why those are not contradictory positions. Go was designed to address the problems faced in software development at Google, which led to a language that is not a breakthrough research language* ***but is nonetheless an excellent tool for engineering large software projects.***

Wikipedia[35] defines Go as follows: "*Go is a statically typed, compiled programming language.... Go is syntactically similar to C, but with memory safety, garbage collection, structural typing, and CSP-style concurrency.*"

Wikipedia[36] describes Java as follows:

Java is a class-based, object-oriented programming language .... It is a general-purpose programming language intended to let application developers write once, run anywhere (WORA), meaning that compiled Java code can run on all platforms that support Java without the need for recompilation. The syntax of Java is similar to C and C++, but has fewer low-level facilities than either of them. The Java runtime provides dynamic capabilities (such as reflection and runtime code modification) that are typically not available in traditional compiled languages.

---

[35] https://en.wikipedia.org/wiki/Go_(programming_language)
[36] https://en.wikipedia.org/wiki/Java_(programming_language)

These descriptions cover some of the key similarities and differences. In the author's opinion, the relative brevity of the Go description reflects the relative simplicity of Go vs. Java.

Go addresses the needs of modern system and application software development in cloud environments on modern multi-core machines. In the author's opinion, it meets these goals very well. As you explore Go more within these pages, you will see its features and functions and how they match and support the goals stated earlier. By the time you finish this book, perhaps you will also agree.

Go was not designed to replace (cover all use cases of) Java. It is more targeted toward the use cases of the C (and to some extent C++) language. It is primarily a system programming language well suited toward implementing servers and tools such as compilers. Java also supports these types of programs.

One of the reasons Go is popular is it is lightweight relative to many other languages. Go is arguably more lightweight than Java in many areas. This is one of its most attractive attributes.

Go's threading model, provided by *goroutines* and *channels*, certainly is lighter weight. Because it lacks Object-Oriented Programming (OOP) features, its data model and error processing are also more lightweight. Even more lightweight is the set of standard libraries. Perhaps most critically, Go's single executable (vs. a JRE and many JARs) deployments and resulting fast program launching are most attractive.

Go is also arguably easier to master than Java. The language is simpler and has fewer constructs to learn. The runtime libraries are, while functional, generally more basic and approachable.

This is not to say that Go is necessarily better than Java (or the reverse), but that it is often more approachable and easier to master and use. Both languages and their runtimes will extend over time; Go is more likely to continue its more approachable style.

Assessments

Divya Khatnar: *If one knows Java, they will surely enjoy learning Go using this book. The author makes sure that each topic uses Java as a baseline to explain Go. Not only does this book teach you Go, but it also sharpens your understanding about Java.*

Charles Stein: *As Go becomes a staple language, Java users need a clear guide to help them make the transition. This book thoroughly covers the basics and exciting applications of Go from a Java-analogous perspective.*

Sharath Hedge: *This book covers all the comparisons of Java and Go exhaustively. Also, it covers important packages provided by Go. As a developer if I want to start a project in Go, this book will offer ready reckoner for the many questions I have. This book offers examples for the majority of the cases, which helps a lot.*

PART I

First Look at Go

Welcome, future Gophers! Prepare for a journey of discovery and enrichment.

This is a book to help you learn the *Go* (aka *Golang*[1]) programming language and many of the Go standard libraries in order to become successful Gophers. This text assumes no prior knowledge of Go and is oriented for use by experienced Java programmers. This book is generally organized using a comparison between Java features and if/how these similar features exist in Go.

This book assumes the reader knows Java already; it is not a Java tutorial. This book also assumes the reader has basic competence in fundamental programming concepts and procedural programming techniques.

As it is generally the case for any programming language, it is nearly impossible to introduce language topics/features in a strictly linear order (all topics fully described before any are used). Most languages interdepend on their features in such a way as to make this impossible. Go is no exception; in fact, such interdependence between features is a key Go design aspect.

This book does not achieve such a perfect topic order. Topics will sometimes be mentioned before they are fully described. Some background information will be provided at the point of reference, but it may sometimes be necessary to jump ahead to scan the more detailed presentations that come later. This ordering can result in limited repetition of content throughout the book. Limited repetition is also employed throughout the text to help reinforce key concepts.

Learning by comparison and by example are powerful and effective techniques. In this book, we will be comparing Go and some of its standard libraries to Java and some of its standard libraries to teach basic Go programming. The book will often use examples to illustrate both similarities and differences. This is the major purpose of this book.

---

[1] As apart from the Go game and other uses. Also, the official website: `www.golang.org`

This book will not cover every detail or option of the Go language, but most of its features are described or at least shown in examples. Certainly, Go will be described at a useful level of detail. The Go Language Specification can be used to get a full and complete description. The same goes for many of the standard Go libraries.

Most references and comparisons will be against Java. But, as the Go language and runtime are targeted strongly to the use cases of the C language and the C standard library, this book will also compare Go to C at times. Since C++ is a derivative and superset of C, at times this book may compare Go to C++ as well. In no case will knowledge of either C or C++ be a prerequisite to use this book effectively. Occasionally, this book will compare Go to other languages.

While typically what the term "Go" means, Go is more than a language, a set of runtime libraries, and a set of developer tools. "Go" also represents a community of users and contributors. Like with Java, the community is a rich source of functions beyond the standard Go capabilities as well as a vast source of training and support for Go developers. Many of these extensions are easily accessible via the Go toolchain and repositories such as GitHub.

Go was first announced in November 2009. Release 1.0 came in September 2012. Prior to version 1.0, the language and runtime changed often, sometimes incompatibly. Post 1.0, there is much more stability.

Each release after 1.0 has a goal of complete backward compatibility (all older source programs continue to compile and run after being rebuilt), but there have been a few exceptions. The change in the default for GO111MODULE environment option from auto to on in Go 1.16 is an example. Such version-to-version incompatibilities are rapidly reducing over time.

As of the date of this book's publication, Go has had more than a dozen major (XX of 1.XX) releases and numerous point (yy of 1.XX.yy) releases. Each major release introduces new tools, language and/or library features, performance improvements, and often bug fixes. Detailing them in a book is a form of planned obsolescence and thus will not be done. A detailed summary can be found at `https://golang.org/doc/devel/release.html`.

Before we begin learning Go, we will first look at some key features of the Java language that Go does not provide. On the surface, this may make Go look inferior compared to Java, but as you go further into the text, the author believes you will see that this is not the case.

The first part of this text has a few samples of Go code; it is mostly background information. That will change in the subsequent parts of this text.

Note in the text, especially in the capstone sections, source file names are mentioned. Often, these names are not the literal operating system file names but may be shown in different cases. Some operating systems require file names to be entered in their exact case, and others do not.

CHAPTER 1

A Brief Look at Go vs. Java

There are many obvious and subtle differences between Java and Go. They can be compared as a language and as a runtime. This survey concentrates mostly on a language comparison. It is intended to present a broad-stroke comparison. Much deeper comparisons are done throughout the text.

Some of the text in this chapter might be read as disparaging Go. That is not the intent. Go is a powerful language, and it can easily hold its own against Java. But Java does have features Go does not, and they will be summarized later.

Note the descriptions here can require deeper knowledge of Go that has been presented so far for a full understanding. You may want to revisit this chapter after becoming more familiar with Go later in this text.

The Go language and its associated runtime have both many similarities and many differences from the Java language and its associated *Java Runtime Environment* (JRE). This chapter will attempt to summarize them at a high level. These similarities and differences will be discussed in greater detail later in this text.

Both Go and Java are *Turing-complete*[1] environments, which means (almost) any possible program can be written in either of them. It is just a matter of the relative development effort expended and the resulting program size and performance.

It should be noted that the Go language and the Go development experience more closely matches that of C than it does of Java. The style and semantics of the Go language more closely resemble that of C than Java. The standard Go libraries also more closely resemble those that come with C.

---

[1] Alan Turing described a universal computing engine, now called a *Turing Machine*, that can compute any possible calculation. Any programming language that can be used to author a Turing Machine is referred to as "Turing Complete."

© Barry Feigenbaum 2022
B. Feigenbaum, *Go for Java Programmers*, https://doi.org/10.1007/978-1-4842-7199-5_1

One exception with the comparison to C is that of the Go program building experience. In C, this is typically driven by the *Make*[2] (or a variant) utility. In Go, it is driven by the Go *builder* tool. In the author's opinion, the Go approach is superior and easier to use (no make files are needed).

Note some Go developers use make file–like approaches, especially in complex projects that have more than just Go source files as components and thus need other artifacts to also be constructed. Make files are often used to script multistep processes beyond what the Go builder can do. This is similar to using Ant[3] or Maven[4] in Java.

Go Is a Compiled (vs. Interpreted, As Java Is) Language

Like C and C++, Go programs are completely built before execution begins. All source is compiled into the machine language of the target computer architecture. Also, all code is compiled to the target operating system. In contrast, Java is compiled into a virtual machine language (aka *bytecode*), and that is interpreted by the Java Virtual Machine (JVM). For improved performance, that bytecode is often compiled into machine language dynamically at runtime. The JVM itself is built for a particular operating system and hardware architecture.

Once built, Go programs require only an operating system to run them. Java programs require, in addition, that a JRE (of the required version) exist on the computer before they can be run. Many Java programs may also require additional third-party code to be present.

The Go approach often results in faster program startup and a more self-contained program, both of which make it more suitable for containerized deployments.

---

[2] https://en.wikipedia.org/wiki/Make_(software)
[3] https://en.wikipedia.org/wiki/Apache_Ant
[4] https://en.wikipedia.org/wiki/Apache_Maven

Go and Java Share Similar Program Structure

Both languages support the notion of data structures that contain methods and fields. In Go, they are called *Structs*, while in Java they are called *Classes*. These structures are collected into groupings called *Packages*. In both languages, packages can be arranged hierarchically (i.e., have nested packages).

Java packages contain only type declarations. Go packages can contain base declarations like variables, constants, functions, as well as derived type declarations.

Both languages access code in different packages by importing it. In Java, imported types can be optionally used unqualified (`String` vs. `java.lang.String`). In Go, all imported names must always be qualified.

Go and Java Have Some Code Style Differences That Influence How Code Is Structured

- Java declarations put the type first, while in Go the type comes last. For example:

  Java – `int x, y z;`

  Go – `var x, y, z int`

- Java methods can return only a single value. Go functions can return many values.

- Java methods and fields must be declared inside the type that they belong to. Go methods are defined outside the owning type. Go supports functions and variables that are independent of any type. Java has no true static shared variables; static fields are just fields of some class (vs. an instance). Go supports true static (global) variables that are allocated in the executable image.

- Go has full closures (can capture mutable data), while Java only supports partial closures (can capture only immutable data). This can make first-class functions in Go more powerful.

7

- Go lacks user-defined generic types. Some built-in types (e.g., slices and maps) are generic. Java supports generic types of any reference type.

  Note there is an approved proposal to add generic types to Go in the future.

- Java allows type extension of only other types (classes, enums, and interfaces), while Go can base new types on any existing type, including primitive types (such as integers and floats) and other user-defined types. Go can support methods on any of these custom types.

- Go and Java interfaces work very differently. In Java, a class (or enum) must explicitly implement an interface if it is used (methods called) through that interface. In Go, any type can implement an interface simply by implementing the methods of that interface; no declaration of intent to implement the interface is needed, it just happens as a side effect of the methods being present. Many standard (inherited) behaviors in Java (such as the `toString()` method) are provided in Go by a type implementing a common interface (equivalently the `String()` method of the `Stringer` interface).

Both Go and Java Are Procedural Languages

Imperative programs are those that work by explicitly changing state over time and testing that state. They are a direct reflection of the ubiquitous *von Neumann*[5] computer architecture. Procedural programs are imperative programs that are composed of *procedures* (aka functions in Go and methods in Java). Each language provides the following key capabilities of procedural languages:

- Can execute an expression, often with an assignment to a variable.

- Can execute a sequence (0+) of statements (often called a basic block).

- Often also a single statement can implicitly act as a block.

---

[5] https://en.wikipedia.org/wiki/Von_Neumann_architecture

- Can make one-way (`if`), two-way (`if/else`), or n-way (`if/else if/ else`, `switch`) conditional branches in code flow.

- Can loop over statements.

- Java has `while`, `do`, and `for` statements; Go combines them all into just `for`.

- Can define reusable code that can be invoked from multiple locations.

- Java has methods; Go has functions, some of which are methods.

All[6] programs can be written using only these constructs.

Java Is an Object-Oriented (OO) Language, While Go Is Not Fully OO

As is true of all OO languages, Java is a class-based language. All code (methods) and data (fields) are encapsulated in some class implementation. Java classes support inheritance in that they can extend a super-class (starting at `Object`). Go allows composition (a struct can be embedded in another struct) that can often get some of the code reuse benefits of inheritance, but not all.

Java provides full control over the encapsulation (through visibility: public/ protected/package private/private) of methods and fields. Go does not provide all these options. Go structs are like classes in how they have fields and can have associated methods, but they do not support subclassing. Also, Go only supports the equivalent of public and package private visibilities.

In Java, both classes and interfaces support polymorphic method dispatch. In Go, only interfaces do polymorphic method dispatch. Go has no equivalent of an abstract base class. Again, composition can provide a subset of this feature.

Note Java, while generally considered to be OO, is not a perfect example of the OO style of programming. For example, it has primitive data types. But this text is not about being critical of Java's design.

---

[6] https://en.wikipedia.org/wiki/Structured_programming#Elements

Java Is a Highly Functional Language, Go Is Less So

Java, since version 8, has well supported *functional programming* (FP). FP is programming with only functions that have local data; no global and mutable state exists. Java supports the ability to create first-class function literals (called *Lambdas*) and pass them to other code to be invoked. Java also allows external (or explicit) looping (while, for, etc.) to be replaced by internal looping (inside methods). For example, the Java *Streams* support provides this.

Go also has first-class function literals, but it lacks similar support for internal looping; looping is typically external. First-class functions supply lambda-like functions, often in a superior way. The lack of internal looping is considered a virtue in Go as it produces more obvious code.

Java FP support strongly depends on generic types. Currently, Go lacks these.

Java Is a Highly Declarative Language, Go Is Less So

Through a combination of *Annotations* and features such as Streams, Java code can be written in a *declarative* style. This means the code says what is to be done, but not explicitly how it is to be done. The runtime converts the declarations into behaviors that achieve the intended results. Go does not promote an equivalent style of programming; code must be written to explicitly say how to achieve a behavior. As a result, Go code is more obvious but sometimes larger and more repetitive than typical Java code is.

Many Java Features Are Annotation Driven

Many Java libraries (especially those called frameworks), such as *Spring*, make strong use of Java's Annotations. The annotations provide metadata, typically consumed at runtime, to modify the behaviors provided by the libraries. Go does not have annotations, so this capability is missing. As a result, Go code is often more explicit; this is generally considered a virtue. Go can use code generation to get similar results to annotations. Go does have a simple form of annotation, called a *tag*, that can be used to customize some library behavior, such as JSON or XML formatting.

The use of annotations can bind configuration decisions to the source code. Sometimes, this is a disadvantage as the decision needs to be delayed until runtime. When this is so, Go and Java often use similar approaches (such as command-line or configuration file parameters).

Go Does Not Support Exceptions

Java has *Exceptions* (really *Throwables* which are Exceptions or Errors) that can be raised to report unusual conditions. Exception usage is widespread in Java and often used to report both predictable and unpredictable failures. Error returns as values from methods are rare.

Go makes a stronger separation of these roles. All failures are reported by function return values that a caller must explicitly test for. This works well because Go functions can more easily return multiple values, such as a result and an error.

Go has *Panics* that have a similar role as Java Errors. They are raised much less frequently. Unlike in Java, panic values are not a hierarchy of types, just a wrapper on a value of the developer's choice, but often an instance of the error type. One never declares the type of a panic value that a function can raise (i.e., there is no equivalent to Java's throws clause). This often means less verbose code. Much Java code follows this pattern by only throwing instances of RuntimeException that do not need to be declared.

Both Java and Go Use Managed Memory (Garbage Collectors)

Both languages use a stack and a heap to hold data. The stack is mostly used for function local variables, the heap for other dynamically created data. In Java, all objects are allocated on the heap. In Go, only data that can be used beyond the lifetime of a function are allocated on the heap. In both Java and Go, the heap is garbage collected; heap objects are explicitly allocated by code but are always reclaimed by the garbage collector.

Java has no notion of pointers to an object, only references to objects located in the heap. Go allows a pointer (or address of) to any data value to be accessed. In most cases, Go's pointers can be used like Java references.

Go's implementation of garbage collection is simpler than Java's. Unlike with Java, there are a few options available to tune it, it just works.

Go and Java Both Support Concurrency but in Different Ways

Java has the notion of *Threads*, which are paths of execution provided by libraries. Go has the notion of *Goroutines* (GRs), which are paths of execution provided by the language itself. GRs can be looked at as lightweight threads. The Go runtime can support using many more (many 1000s) GRs than the JRE can support threads.

Java supports synchronization controls in the language. Go has library functions that are similar. Both Go and Java support the notion of atomic values that can safely be updated across threads/GRs. Both support explicit locking libraries.

Go offers the notion of *Communicating Sequential Processes* (CSP) as a major way for GRs to interact without explicit synchronization and locking. Instead, GRs communicate over *Channels* which are effectively pipes (FIFO queues) combined with the `select` statement to query them.

There are other differences in concurrency approaches that will be discussed later in this text. GRs and threads are typically managed in different ways, as is passing state between them.

Go's Runtime Is Simpler Than the JRE

Go has a much smaller runtime than that provided by the JRE. There is no JVM equivalent, but similar components, such as a garbage collection, exist in both. Go has no bytecode interpreter.

Go has a large set of standard libraries. The Go community provides many more. But the Java standard and community libraries arguably far exceed the current Go libraries in both breadth and depth of function. Still the Go libraries are rich enough to develop many useful applications, especially application servers.

All used libraries (and nothing more) are embedded into the Go executable. The executable is everything needed to run the program. Java libraries are loaded dynamically upon first use. This makes Go program binaries (as files) generally larger than Java binaries (a single "main" class), but when the JVM and all dependent classes are loaded, the total memory footprint of Java is often larger.

As Java is interpreted, it is possible to dynamically create bytecode and then execute it. This can be done by writing the bytecode at runtime or dynamically loading prewritten bytecode (i.e., classes). This brings great flexibility. Go, being prebuilt, cannot do this.

The Go Program Build Process Is Different

Java programs are an amalgamation of classes, often from multiple sources (vendors), that are constructed at runtime. This makes Java programs very flexible, especially when downloaded across a network, a prime Java use case. Go programs are built statically and in advance of execution. All code is available in the executable image at startup. This provides greater integrity and predictability at the cost of some flexibility. This makes Go more suitable for containerized deployments.

Go programs are typically built by the "go builder" which is a tool that combines a compiler, a dependency manager, a linker, and an executable builder tool, among others. It is included with the standard Go installation. Java classes are compiled separately (by the *javac* tool, provided with *a Java Development Kit* (JDK)) and are then often assembled into archives (JAR/WAR) that hold related classes. Programs are loaded from one or more of these archives. The creation of archives, especially including any dependencies, is generally done by programs (e.g., *Maven*) available independently from the standard JRE.

Go and Java Have Similar Release Cycles

Go has adopted a biannual release cycle[7] for 1.xx releases. It is best summarized in Figure 1-1 (from the Go site).

---

[7] https://github.com/golang/go/wiki/Go-Release-Cycle

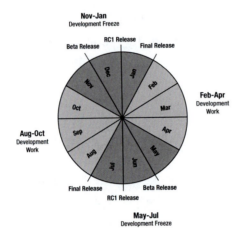

Figure 1-1. *Go biannual release cycle*

The Go team supports the last two releases.

Java has adopted a similar biannual cycle[8] for 1.xx releases. Java has an additional notion of *Long-Term Support* (LTS) releases. Non-LTS releases are supported until the next release (LTS or not) is offered; LTS releases are supported at least until the next LTS is offered. LTS often come every 18–24 months. Java also has the notion of *experimental* features that are released but subject to change (or withdrawal) in future releases; they provide previews of future support. Go has less of this, but, for example, the generic type feature is being previewed in a similar way.

---

[8] https://dzone.com/articles/welcoming-the-new-era-of-java

CHAPTER 2

What Java Has That Go Does Not

Java has some features Go does not and vice versa. So, before we look at the Java features that have some equivalent in Go, let us look briefly at the ones Go does not have. Not every possible feature Java has that Go does not have can be listed, but some key ones are summarized in the following.

Note that many of the Go "missing" features were omitted deliberately to keep the language simple and efficient, not because they were hard to provide. This is considered a virtue.

Multiple Assignments

Java can assign multiple variables to the same value in a single statement. For example:

```
int x, y, z;
x = y = z = 10;
```

The closest Go can do is

```
var x, y, z int = 10, 10, 10
```

In Go, the assigned types and values can be different.

Statements and Operators

Go and Java operators have different precedence. Go has fewer, and in the author's opinion, more natural precedence levels. When in doubt, use parentheses around an expression to be sure.

© Barry Feigenbaum 2022
B. Feigenbaum, *Go for Java Programmers*, https://doi.org/10.1007/978-1-4842-7199-5_2

A key difference is that in Go x++ (means: x = x + 1) and x-- (means: x = x - 1) are statements, not operators. And there is no --x or ++x expressions at all.

Go does not support *Ternary Expressions*. The use of the if/else statement is required. For example, the Java expression, which gets the larger value

```
var z = x > y ? x : y;
```

needs to be something like the following in Go:

```
var z = y
if x > y {
    z = x
}
```

which is similar but not the same. You can also do something like this:

```
var z int
if x > y { z = <some expensive int expression> }
else { z = <some other expensive int expression>}
```

Note the preceding if/else must be entered on one source line.

Go does not support assignment expressions, only assignment statements.

Assert Statement

Go has no assert statement. Generally, Go has *panics* which can be used to achieve a similar function, but they cannot be disabled at compile time like asserts can be. Because of this, such use of panics is discouraged.

While and Do Statements

The Java while statement is replaced by the Go for statement (i.e., for acts like while). There is no direct equivalent of the Java do statement, but the for statement can be used to replace it.

Note that the Java for statement can be used as a while statement too.

For example:

```
var x = 0; for(; x < 10;) { ... ; x++; }
```

is the same as

```
var x = 0; while(x < 10) { ... ; x++; }
```

Throw Statement/Throws Clause

Go has no throw statement (or throws clause). The Go panic(...) function serves a similar role as the throw action.

Strictfp, transient, volatile, synchronized, abstract, static

Go has no equivalent of these Java modifiers. Most are not needed as the issues that made them necessary in Java are solved in different ways in Go. For example, the equivalent of a static value is achieved by making the declared value a top-level (aka package) value.

Objects and Classes (OOP) and Inner Classes, Lambdas, this, super, Explicit Constructors

Go does not fully support *Object-Oriented Programming* (OOP) as Java does. As a result, it does not support these Java constructs. Go has features described later in this text that can be used similarly to most of these OOP features. As such, Go is better described as an *object-based* language. Go does allow one to achieve the key goals of OOP, but in different ways than a strictly OOP language normally would do them.

Go does not support true *Classes* (i.e., the Java class declaration). Go does support *Structs* which are like classes but without inheritance. Go does allow nested structs, which are somewhat like inner classes.

Go has no extends or implements clauses on type declarations. Go has no inheritance as these clauses provide. Go does have an implied form of implements for its interface types.

Go does not support Java *Lambdas* (function signatures compiled into class instances). Instead, Go supports *first-class functions* (often literals) that may be passed as parameters. Go does not support *Method References* (simple names for lambdas passed as parameters).

Go supports interfaces in a different way than Java. Go's interfaces allow *Duck Typing*. Go's interfaces do not require that they be implemented explicitly (no `implements` clause is needed in Go); any type that has methods that match all the methods of the interface implicitly implements the interface. In general, Go's approach is more flexible.

Java 8 and beyond allows implemented (concrete) methods in interfaces. Go does not. Java allows constants to be declared in interfaces; Go does not. Java allows subtypes to be declared in interfaces. Go does not.

Consider these tenants of OOP:

1. An object has an identity (it can be distinguished from all other objects).

2. An object may (typically does) have state (aka instance data, properties, or fields).

3. An object may (typically does) have behavior (aka member functions or methods).

4. An object is described/defined by a template, called a class.

5. Classes can be arranged in an (inheritance) hierarchy; instances are compositions of the classes in the hierarchy.

6. Object instances are encapsulated; the state is typically visible only through methods.

7. Variables can be declared at any level in the class hierarchy; instances of subclasses can be assigned to these variables (polymorphism).

Java supports (but not necessarily enforces) all the preceding tenants. Go does not. Go supports these tenants as follows:

1. A struct instance has an address, which can generally serve as its identity (but may not always be distinct); a struct instance is like but not identical to an object instance.

2. A struct instance may (typically does) have state.

3. A struct instance may (often does) have behavior.

4. Like a class, a struct instance is described/defined by a template, called a struct type.

5. Not directly supported; structs can embed other structs offering similar composition.

6. Supported but often not used (struct fields are very often public).

7. Not supported.

Historically, OOP languages grew out of computer simulation[1] and a desire to improve man/machine interactions.[2] OOP languages were conceived to implement message passing between simulated objects to effect behavior. As the improved behavior reuse possibilities (i.e., inheritance) of OOP became well known, it grew in popularity as a style of programming. Most modern languages provide this capability.

To many, Go's lack of full OOP is probably its greatest shortcoming. But the author expects that once you get used to doing idiomatic Go programming, you will not miss the OOP features as much as you would first think. Go is a well-designed and functionally rich language with characteristics that make it support the goals of OOP without including all the complex OOP characteristics of other languages, such as Java.

Please consider that OOP is not required to write good programs. All the existing C programs, some large and rich, such as operating systems[3] and web browsers, prove otherwise. In fact, at times OOP thinking can force inappropriate structure on a program. Again, Go is a C-like language.

OOP is not required to achieve high levels of reuse. Functions can fill that role well, especially if they are first class as they are in Go.

---

[1] https://en.wikipedia.org/wiki/Simula

[2] https://en.wikipedia.org/wiki/Smalltalk; Smalltalk introduced the Graphical User interface (GUI).

[3] www.toptal.com/c/after-all-these-years-the-world-is-still-powered-by-c-programming

Generic Types and Methods

Go currently does not support *Generic* types and methods on arbitrary types. Here, generic means being able to hold/use multiple types. In Java, a variable of the `Object` type is generic in that it can hold a value of any reference type. In Go, a variable of the `interface{}` type is generic in that it can hold a value of any type.

Java 5 refined this concept in that a declared type (say a container class) can be specified to support only specific (vs. all) types (say just strings or numbers) as a modifier on a container type, for example, a `List<String>` (vs. just `List`) type. Go's built-in collection types (slices, maps, and channels) are generic in this way.

Originally, Java did not support type-specific Generic types. They were introduced in Java 5, mostly to ease certain usability issues with collections that existed in the language. Java's generic design has some undesirable characteristics/compromises forced on it by backward compatibility.

Currently, there is an approved proposal for adding Generics to Go for much the same reasons as it was added to Java. It looks like Go will follow in Java's footsteps here.

Generic types as Java (and Go) defines them are mostly syntactic sugar to remove repetitive coding. In Java, they do not impact the runtime code at all (because of runtime type erasure). In Go, they may cause more binary code to exist in an executable, but not any more than if manually emulated.

Extensive Functional Programming Capabilities

Go does support first-class functions but not the typical generalized utility functions (map, reduce, select, exclude, forEach, find, etc.) that most functional (strongly supports the *Functional Programming* paradigm) languages and Java (via its Lambdas and Streams support) provide. This omission was a deliberate decision by the Go language designers. Go will likely add some of these utility functions when generics are included.

Boxing of Primitive Values

Java collections (arrays excepted) cannot contain primitive values, only Objects. So, Java provides wrapper types for each primitive type. To make collections easier to use, Java will automatically wrap (box) a primitive into a wrapper type to insert it into a collection and unwrap (unbox) that value when taking it from a collection. Go supports collections that can hold primitives, so such boxing is not needed. Note the need to use boxing is an area where Java is less efficient at memory use than Go is.

Source Annotations

Go has no *Annotations*. Go Struct fields can have *tags*, which serve a similar but much more limited role.

Annotations, along with function streams and lambdas, make Java (at least partially) a declarative language.[4] Go is almost purely an imperative language.[5] This is by choice. This tends to make Go code both more obvious and more verbose.

Note Go has a similar concept to Java compile-time annotations where a source file can include special comments (called *build constraints*) that the builder interprets to change how code is processed. For example, the target operating system to generate code for can be specified by a comment like this at the very start of a source file:

```
// +build linux,386
```

that will cause the file to only build for the Linux operating system (OS) and 386-based architectures.

There is an alternate (and generally preferred) syntax; the previous comment can also be written as

```
//go:build linux,386
```

Note some constraints, such as the target OS and/or hardware architecture, can be embedded in the Go file names. For example

```
xxx_windows.go
```

will only be built for a Windows OS.

---

[4] https://en.wikipedia.org/wiki/Declarative_programming
[5] https://en.wikipedia.org/wiki/Imperative_programming

Multiple Visibilities

Java supports four visibilities:

1. Private – Only the code in the containing type can see it.

2. Default – Only the code in the same package can see it.

3. Protected – Only the code in the same package or a subclass of the type can see it.

4. Public – Any code can see it.

Go supports only the equivalent of default (often called private or package in Go) and public visibilities. Gophers often refer to public visibility as "exported visibility" and private visibility as "unexported visibility."

Overloaded/Overridden Functions

In Java, functions with the same name but with different signatures (a different number of and/or types of arguments) can be defined in the same scope. These are called (via a form of parametric polymorphism) *overloaded* functions. Go does not allow overloading.

In Java, functions with the same name and signature can be redefined lower in the inheritance hierarchy. Such redefined functions are called (via inheritance polymorphism) *overridden*. As Go does not support inheritance, such overriding is not allowed.

Formal Enums

Java has formal *Enum* types which are special-purpose class types that have discrete static instances to facilitate comparison with the sameness (==) operator. Go does not. It uses the `iota` operator on constants of integer types instead. In Java, enums values can be based on several types (but integers are common); in Go, only an integer type is allowed.

Note that Java enums are classes and can have fields and methods just like any other class. They also support inheritance. Go enums have no similar features.

Built-in Binary Data Self-Serialization

Java offers the ability to serialize (convert to a sequence of bytes, often called *octets*[6] in this use case) data and objects in a binary form. The `Data{Input|Output}Stream` and (subclasses) `Object{Input|Output}Stream` types offer APIs to do this. Serialized data is often written into files or transmitted across networks and sometimes stored in databases. Serialization can offer a form of persistence to otherwise ephemeral objects. Serialization is also fundamental to most *Remote Procedure Call*[7] (RPC) mechanisms.

Java supports serialization of primitive values, arrays, and any data structure (class instance) containing primitive types or any type marked with the `Serializable` interface and any collections of these types. Java even supports structures with reference loops.

Go offers no direct equivalent to this full object serialization. Often in Go one serializes data to some text format (say JSON or XML) and saves/sends that form instead. Using text is often less efficient (more bytes and time needed) than a binary representation. These text forms generally do not support reference loops inside the data structure.

Go offers community support, such as Google *Protocol Buffers*,[8] for binary data. With standard Go libraries, one can, somewhat tediously, create custom binary formats.

Concurrent Collections

Java has many collection implementations, where each offers, often subtle, optimizations for different use cases. Go takes a simpler approach, like other languages such as Python and JavaScript, where a single collection implementation, say for a list or map, is used in all use cases. This can be suboptimal at runtime, but it is far easier to learn and use.

Java has several concurrent (that perform well (low contention) when used in multiple threads) types and collections in addition to standard equivalents. `ConcurrentHashMap` is probably the most popular example. Go has a few standard library equivalents such as the `sync.Map` type. In general, such concurrent types are less frequently used in Go. Alternatives, such as channels, are frequently used.

---

[6] https://en.wikipedia.org/wiki/Octet_(computing)

[7] https://en.wikipedia.org/wiki/Remote_procedure_call

[8] https://en.wikipedia.org/wiki/Protocol_Buffers

CHAPTER 3

A Deeper Comparison of Go and Java

This chapter drills down on the earlier introduction of Go vs. Java. It describes in greater detail the significant differences between Java and Go. By comparing Go to Java, one can absorb the Go features more readily.

Go is (in the author's opinion) a much simpler language than Java; Go is arguably even a simpler language than C. For example, the *Java Language Specification* is currently around 800 pages long, while the *Go Language Specification* is currently around 85[1] pages long. Clearly, Java has a lot more language complexity than Go does.

This is also true of the Go standard libraries. They are much smaller, in terms of the number of types and functions provided and sheer lines of code, than the Java standard library. In some ways, the Go libraries are less functional, but even so they are generally functional enough to write many useful programs.

As with the Java community, capabilities not included in the standard libraries are often provided by community members. In the author's opinion, the Java libraries, especially community-provided libraries, are, in general, often more mature than many of the corresponding Go libraries.

The Java libraries are also often more heavyweight (do more) and are arguably harder to learn and use than the corresponding Go libraries. In general, the Go libraries are more "right sized"[2] for the typical Go use cases, and, as a result, Go is not lacking in its applicability. Consider that the large codebase size of the standard Java libraries forced Java 9 into splitting them into selectable modules so the Java runtime footprint can be reduced. Also, many older libraries have been deprecated (and some now removed) to further reduce the runtime's size.

---

[1] Using Save as PDF on the current HTML form.

[2] Some might say the libraries are *lean and mean*.

© Barry Feigenbaum 2022
B. Feigenbaum, *Go for Java Programmers*, https://doi.org/10.1007/978-1-4842-7199-5_3

The Go community is mostly made of Google and many individuals or small teams. It has fewer vetted organizations like *Apache Software Foundation*[3] and *Spring*[4] that make key third-party libraries and frameworks for Java.

Go and Java[5] support similar but different statements and data types. They are summarized in the following. They will be described in much greater detail later in this text.

Both Go and Java support Boolean values and characters, integers, and floating-point numbers. In Go, a character is called a rune and is 4 bytes; in Java, it is called char and is 2 bytes. Both use Unicode encoding. Go's use of runes is, in general, better[6] than Java's char type, as any character variable can represent any legal Unicode character.

Both Java and Go support string types which are effectively arrays of characters. In Go, a string is a primitive type. Go's use of *Unicode Transformation Format*[7] (UTF-8) in strings allows many strings, especially for English text, to use fewer bytes than an equivalent Java string would.

The operators on these types are similar in each language. Go also supports complex floating-point numbers, which Java does not. Java supports big forms of integers and decimal floating-point numbers. Go supports big forms of integers and binary floating-point numbers. Both Go and Java support arrays of homogeneous values. Java aggregates heterogeneous values in classes; Go uses structs.

Java supports references to class instances. Go uses pointers, which can locate a value of any type.

Java and Go share many similar statements.

Both have assignment statements. Both have augmented (operator involved) assignments. Go has multiple (aka tuple) assignments.

Both have conditional statements such as if and switch. Go adds select. Both support looping. Java has while, do, and for statements. Go only has for.

---

[3] www.apache.org/

[4] https://spring.io/

[5] A good summary of Java can be found at www.artima.com/objectsandjava/webuscript/ ExpressionsStatements1.html

[6] See this article for the issues involved: www.oracle.com/technical-resources/articles/ javase/supplementary.html

[7] https://en.wikipedia.org/wiki/UTF-8

Both have variable declaration statements. Go adds a convenient declaration and assignment combination for local variables. Go provides generalized type declarations based on any existing type. Java can only declare class, interface, or enum types.

Both Go and Java have exception capabilities. Java can throw and catch `Throwable` instances; Go can raise and recover from panics.

There are some ways that Go is different in philosophy than Java:

- Go tends to follow a "less is more" philosophy.

  An initial motivator for Java's creation was to simplify the complexity of C++. Go can be looked at from that view, but to simplify C (and thus Java). For example, there is generally only one way in the language (vs. often several with Java) to do something in Go.

  Note that much of Java's syntax was derived from C++ syntax and that C++ syntax is a superset of C syntax, so Java syntax is also based on C syntax. To a lesser extent, much of Java's semantics is based on C++ semantics. Go is more targeted toward C functionality and its supporting libraries.

- Go was created to fit a niche like that of the C language.

  Go has more in common with C than with the C++ language (C++ is a large superset of C from which Java was derived). It is intended to be a "systems programming" language like C but with improved safety and semantics to match the needs, particularly with improved ease of utilization of multi-core processors, of modern computer systems. Java is all this but is intended to support a broader set of use cases.

  Go is like C (and thus Java) in its source syntax and formatting (use of symbols, operators, punctuation, and whitespace). As Java is also based on C, Go and Java are quite similar in this regard as well.

- Go has simpler syntax.

  For example, Go allows most use of the semicolon (";") statement terminator to be elided (not present) when it can be implied. Note that using elided statement terminators is idiomatic and preferred.

This can result in cleaner and arguably easier to read/write code vs. Java. Also, many uses of parentheses ((. . .)) in Java are eliminated in Go. Having methods defined outside of the associated type can make the code more readable.

- Go has different optimization points/targets than Java does.

    Java is more of an application (especially for business) language. Go is more system oriented. These optimization points strongly influence the design/nature of the Go language. Like all Turing-complete languages, Java and Go have areas of overlapping suitability where either can be an appropriate choice.

- Go is generally more imperative and explicit than Java.

    Java, especially if Java 8 (and beyond) features are used, can be more declarative and abstracted than Go. In some ways, Go resembles more the first (1.0) release of Java than the current definition of Java.

- In Go, most behavior is explicitly (and hopefully obviously) coded.

    Behavior is not hidden inside functional programming features like supported with Java Streams and Lambdas. This can make Go code more repetitive in style. Errors are handled explicitly (say at each function return) vs. remotely/systematically with Exceptions as in Java.

    Except for (limited in function) struct field *tags*, Go has no notion of Annotations as Java has. Again, this is to make Go code more transparent and obvious. Annotations, as does any declarative/postprocessing (vs. imperative) approach, tend to hide or defer behavior.

    A good example of the Java annotation–driven approach is how *Spring MVC* and *JAX-RS* define REST API endpoints in web application servers. Often, the annotations are interpreted, not at compile time, but at runtime, by a third-party framework.

Another example is how database *Entities*[8] are typically defined for *Object-Relational Mappers*[9] (ORM). In such limited cases, Go provides options via struct tags which are often used to advise these tools. The community-supplied *GORM*[10] ORM is an example. The built-in JSON and XML processors, among others, also consume tags.

- Go supports the concept of (source) *generators.*

  A generator is Go code that writes Go code. Generators can be conditionally run by the Go builder. There are many use cases for generators. For example, it is possible to use generators to mechanically create collection types (say a generated type for each needed T/K of List<T>, Stack<T>, Queue<T>, Map<K, T>, etc.) that mimic Java generic types but done via a preprocessor. The Go community provides such options.

- Go supports *Pointers* and Java supports *References.*

  To the computer, pointers and references are similar, but to humans they are different. References are a more abstract concept than pointers are. Pointers are variables that hold the machine address of some other value. References are variables that hold a locator (could be an address or something else) for another value.

  In Java, references are always automatically dereferenced when used (except in assignments). Pointers may or may not be. With pointers, it is possible to get the address of some data and save it in a pointer variable and to convert the pointer to some other type, say an integer. This is not possible with references.

  Unlike in C (or C++), both Java and Go restrict pointers/references to address a specific type of data. There is nothing like the "void" pointers of C. Also, there is nothing like the "pointer arithmetic" allowed in C. Therefore, Go, like Java, is (arguably much) safer (less likely to fail due to addressing errors) than C.

---

[8] https://en.wikipedia.org/wiki/Entity%E2%80%93relationship_model
[9] https://en.wikipedia.org/wiki/Object%E2%80%93relational_mapping
[10] https://gorm.io/index.html

PART II

The Go Language

In this part, some of the key and fundamental features of the Go language will be introduced. When we are done with this part, you should be able to characterize the key features that make Go different from Java.

The following chapters refer to some Go topics not yet well described. You may need to read ahead to Chapter 5, "Go Basic Features," to get the needed basics to fully grasp all the content of this part.

This and the remaining chapters of this text have numerous code examples. In general, runnable code is labeled with listing captions. This code may not be completely stand-alone (compliable and executable literally as shown) as it often needs a package statement and some imports added as well as a wrapping in a `main()` function, as described later in the text, to be complete.

CHAPTER 4

Key Go Aspects

Like in Java, at the most basic level Go source is a stream of characters often viewed as a sequence of lines. Go files are written (as is typically true in Java) in UTF-8 encoding. Go does not have a preprocessor like Java has to process Unicode escapes into raw characters; all Unicode characters are treated the same, and escapes can only appear inside of string or character literals, not in identifiers or elsewhere.

Like in Java, the characters are grouped into constructs called *whitespace* (sequences of spaces, tabs, new lines, etc.) and *Tokens* that the Go compiler parses to process Go code. Go often uses whitespace as token separators.

Except for new lines, a sequence of whitespace is treated like it was a single space character. In Go, a new line can implicitly generate a semicolon (";") statement ender so it is somewhat special. The Go lexical analyzer automatically adds a semicolon when a line end is encountered, and a semicolon is allowed after the prior token. In general, lines can be split after a comma (",") in some brace ({...}) or parenthesis ((...)) enclosed lists.

While convenient, this also restricts where certain tokens must appear relative to each other. Go is thus stricter about source statement arrangement into lines than Java is. Most significant is the block-introducing open brace ("{") must be on the same (vs. following) line as any prefix statement. You will see lots of examples of this in this text.

One generally thinks of Go programs as a stream of tokens, often arranged in a sequence of lines of code. Tokens are commonly identifiers, some of which are reserved words, delimiters, and punctuation or operators.

A simple Go source file (based on the common *Hello World* example) in a file typically called main.go in a directory typically called main:

```
1: package main
2: import "fmt"  // a standard Go library
3: func main() {
4:   fmt.Println ("Hello World!")
5: }
```

© Barry Feigenbaum 2022
B. Feigenbaum, *Go for Java Programmers*, https://doi.org/10.1007/978-1-4842-7199-5_4

Here, we have a complete program in one source file. The program entry point is specified to be in the (1) main package (as all Go program entry points must be). Like in Java, the (3–5) main() function is the required entry point. Here, main is like a Java static method. This method uses the imported (2, 4) Println standard library function to display the message. Like in Java, Go has string literals (4). One difference in Go is that a string is a built-in (vs. the library java.lang.String) type.

The preceding numbered form of listing will not be used further in this text as it tends to disrupt the sample. Source comments will be used instead to point out special details.

Note in Go and unlike in Java, the command-line arguments to main are accessed by a library function call, not as main function arguments; they are not accessed in this example.

To the Go parser, this file looks like

```go
package main;
import "fmt";
func main() {
        fmt.Println("Hello World!");
}
```

after the lexical analyzer injects semicolons at the end of lines where they are missing but expected. This form is a legal Go code, but it is not idiomatic. In idiomatic Go, statement ending semicolons are generally omitted except when multiple statements are entered in a single line, which is quite rare.

The equivalent Java program (likely in Main.java) is similar:

```java
public class Main {
  public static main(String[] args) {  // or String... args
    System.out.println("Hello World!");
  }
}
```

Note that in Java main() is public, but it is not in Go. As Go does not require functions to be members (aka methods) of some type (such as *System*), like Java does, the printing function is used directly, but instead of being qualified by the owning class, the owning package (fmt in this case) must be indicated instead. In Go, many functions behave like static functions (have no associated instance) in Java.

Java does not require code to be in a package (a default package can be used), but one is strongly recommended and is typically provided. So, the Java example would more commonly be something like

```
package com.mycompany.hello;
public class Main {
  public static main(String[] args) {
    System.out.println("Hello World!");
  }
}
```

Had the `java.lang.*` package not been automatically imported by the compiler, this would be

```
package com.mycompany.hello;
import java.lang.*;
public class Main {
  public static main(String[] args) {
    System.out.println("Hello World!");
  }
}
```

Except for the enclosing `Main` class, this looks much more like the Go version.

Note that in the Go code there is no need for an enclosing class (`Main`) to create a running program. This can reduce the number of lines needed for a basic program, but it does have a significant disadvantage. The `main` function must be in a `main` package, and there can be only one `main` package in a program (or source tree). In Java, each class can act as a distinct program if it has a `main` method.

Simple Go Program Example

As an example of a simple Go program that outputs the command-line arguments, consider this set of example variants, contrasting Java with Go. These examples can give you a deeper understanding of the similarities and differences between Java and Go coding styles. The examples use the Go `if` and `for` statements. While quite like their Java equivalents, you may want to look ahead to their descriptions.

In Go, the first program argument (Args[0]) is the program name (always present), followed by any space-separated arguments entered on the command. Note that in Java args[0] is not the program name (which would be either "java" or the name of the class being run), like it is in Go, but we will pretend it is for the sake of simplicity in these examples.

Note in the following Go examples, the expression <variable> := <expression>, often called a *short declaration*, is used. This is a short form of

```
var <previously undeclared variable> <type of the expression>
<variable> = <expression>
```

Note the preceding lines are two distinct source lines, not a single wrapped line.

Short declarations can often be embedded into other statements, such as if and for. More than one variable can be declared and assigned if at least one is newly declared.

First in Java:

```java
package com.mycompany.args;

class Main {
  public static void main(String[] args) { // or String... args
    var index = 0;
    for (var arg : args) {
      if (index++ == 0) {
        System.out.printf("Program: %s%n", arg);
      } else {
        System.out.printf("Argument %d: %s%n", index, arg);
      }
    }
  }
}
```

Then in Go:

```go
package main
import "fmt"
import "os"

func main() {
    for index, arg := range os.Args {
        if index == 0 {
            fmt.Printf("Program: %s\n", arg)
        } else {
            fmt.Printf("Argument %d: %s\n", index, arg)
        }
    }
}
```

Run (on Microsoft Windows) as: ...\go_build_main_go.exe 1 2 3
It produces this output:

```
Program: ...\go_build_main_go.exe
Argument 1: 1
Argument 2: 2
Argument 3: 3
```

Note the executable name can be (and often is) different; here it is defined by the IDE used.

Here, multiple Go packages are imported. The os.Args top-level variable is used to get the command-line arguments.

Consider this slightly different alternate (showing only the main function from this point on):

```go
func main() {
    for index, arg := range os.Args {
        if index == 0 {
            fmt.Printf("Program: %s\n", arg)
            continue
        }
        fmt.Printf("Argument %d: %s\n", index, arg)
    }
}
```

This code is formatted in the more idiomatic Go style where the use of the `else` clause is rare; instead, short-circuit actions (like `break`, `continue`, or `return`) are used. The Go style is to left-align code (or avoid deep code block nesting) as much as possible.

An alternate implementation, first in Java, is

```java
public static void main(String[] args) {
  System.out.printf("Program: %s%n", args[0]);
  for (var index = 1; index < args.length; index++) {
    System.out.printf("Argument %d: %s%n", index, args[index]);
  }
}
```

Now in Go:

```go
func main() {
    fmt.Printf("Program: %s\n", os.Args[0])
    for index := 1; index < len(os.Args); index++ {
        fmt.Printf("Argument %d: %s\n", index, os.Args[index])
    }
}
```

Either approach (for loop type) is commonly done; in the author's opinion, the first form is more desirable.

Another alternate, first in Java, is

```java
public static void main(String[] args) {
  for (var index = 0; index < args.length; index++) {
    switch (index) {
      case 0:
        System.out.printf("Program: %s%n", args[index]);
        break;
      default:
        System.out.printf("Argument %d: %s%n", index, args[index]);
    }
  }
}
```

Now in Go:

```go
func main() {
    for index, arg := range os.Args {
        switch {
        case index == 0:
            fmt.Printf("Program: %s\n", arg)
        default:
            fmt.Printf("Argument %d: %s\n", index, arg)
        }
    }
}
```

or

```go
func main() {
    for index, arg := range os.Args {
        switch index {
        case 0:
            fmt.Printf("Program: %s\n", arg)
        default:
            fmt.Printf("Argument %d: %s\n", index, arg)
        }
    }
}
```

Either of which could be considered the best form. The second Go form more closely resembles the Java code.

Note the strong similarity between the Java and Go code. Most of the differences are in the statement syntax. Go generally uses fewer delimiters. Note that no break is needed in Go's switch statement.

Another example is a complete but simple web application shown in Listing 4-1. An equivalent[1] Java example, especially using only standard JSE libraries (vs. (say) a JAX-RS framework), would be quite large and is not included.

---

[1] There is no direct Java equivalent as the JSE JRE provides no standard support for HTTP servers. Third-party code like Spring or a JAX-RS server is needed.

Note that in Go declarations, the type comes after, not before, the declared name (or names). Often, the variable's type is implied by the initial value's type and is thus omitted.

Listing 4-1. Sample Complete but Minimal HTTP Server

```go
package main

import (
        "net/http"
        "log"
        "math/rand"
)

var messages = []string{
        "Now is the time for all good Devops to come the aid of their servers.",
        "Alas poor Altair 8800; I knew it well!",
        "In the beginning there was ARPA Net and its domain was limited.",
        // assume many more
        "A blog a day helps keep the hacker away.",
}

func sendRandomMessage(w http.ResponseWriter, req *http.Request) {
        w.Header().Add(http.CanonicalHeaderKey("content-type"),
                "text/plain")
        w.Write([]byte(messages[rand.Intn(len(messages))]))
}

var spec = ":8080"   // means localhost:8080
func main() {
        http.HandleFunc("/message", sendRandomMessage)
        if err := http.ListenAndServe(spec, nil); err != nil {
                log.Fatalf("Failed to start server on %s: %v", spec, err)
        }
}
```

Here, we launch an HTTP server (via ListenAndServe) that returns a random message on each request to the "/message" path (for any HTTP method, which is not typical). The server runs (ListenAndServe does not return) until terminated by the user. The server returns many error (like 404) and success (like 200) statuses automatically. A browser on this site might show what you see in Figures 4-1 and 4-2.

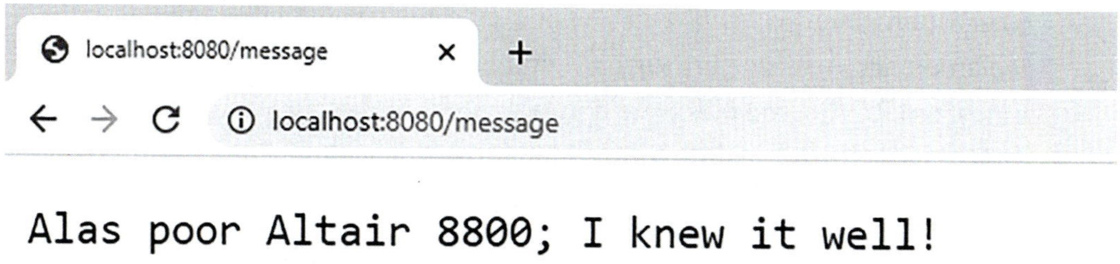
localhost:8080/message
localhost:8080/message
Alas poor Altair 8800; I knew it well!

Figure 4-1. *HTTP GET to random message server 1*

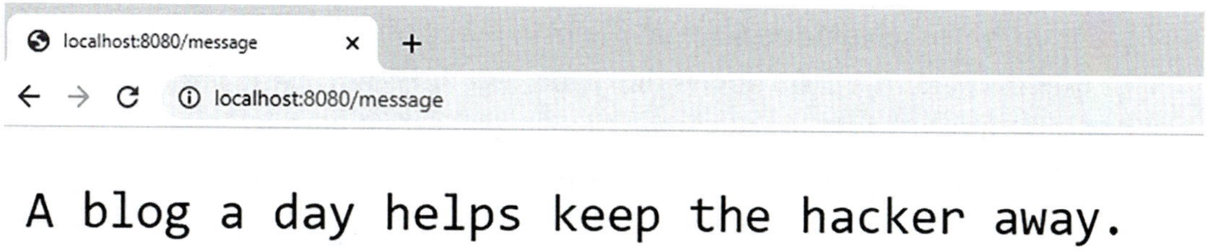
localhost:8080/message
localhost:8080/message
A blog a day helps keep the hacker away.

Figure 4-2. *HTTP GET to random message server 2*

Note the brevity of this example. The core of the server function takes only four lines of code. Such brevity is not possible with most Java libraries or frameworks.

In all these examples, the code is generally self-explanatory, and for the Go code, even with little pre-knowledge of the Go language, it is hoped that you can follow it. This is a testament to the simplicity and transparency of the Go language and its runtime libraries.

Go Packages

Go code, like Java code, is organized into *Packages*. In Go, a package is not just a collection of types (class, interface, enum) but also a collection of variables, constants, and functions. A Go package can be empty. All Go code must be in some package.

Go packages are like Java packages:

- A Go package also represents a physical structure, typically a file system directory.

All Go source files within the same package directory with the same declared package name are logically combined into the package, almost as if the source files were concatenated. All such source files need to be in the same directory, which is generally named (except possibly for a case) the same as the package.

Note a package directory may contain non-Go files. At least one `.go` source file must exist for the directory to be considered as a package.

- A Go package can also contain child packages. Go uses a forward slash ("/") to separate package names in import paths, while Java uses the period ("."). Go quotes the name; Java does not. Like in Java, each child package is independent from its parent (i.e., the child has no special ability to see the content of the parent package and vice versa). The arrangement is entirely for convenience.

- To be used by code not in the package, the package needs to be *imported* by the `import` statement. There is no equivalent, as Java provides, of using a fully qualified (e.g., `java.util.List`) name without importing it. Go has no equivalent of the Java automatic import of `java.lang.*`.

  Importing generally makes all the public members of the imported package visible to the importing package. Private members of a package cannot be imported into other packages.

  Go does not support importing of a single identifier of a package; all public identifiers in a package are always imported. This is not a conflict problem because to use these identifiers the package alias must always be used as a qualifier.

It is conventional to sort imports by the last name in the import path, but this is optional. The Go formatting tool (`gofmt`) and some IDEs will do this for you. Therefore, this order will be redone to put `rand` at the end:

```
import (
        "net/http"
        "math/rand"
        "log"
)
```

It is common that the Go tooling will edit your source when it is processed. This is generally not true with Java tooling.

Go does not allow the same import to exist more than once in a source file. It also does not allow an import that is not used in a source file. This can be annoying. Many IDEs will add any missing imports and remove unused imports for you.

The package declaration and any imports must come first in each source file; the other members can come in any order and in any file of the same package, but structure declarations should come before any associated (method) function definitions.

In Java, the types in a package can be spread across many source files, but each type must be complete in a single source file (for any type's declaration). The general structure of a Java source file is

- Package declaration

- Any imports

- Top-level type ("class," "interface," "enum") declarations, including all members

Java source files consist of one or more top-level type definitions with associated commentary. Java allows only one public top-level type per source file, but any number of default visibility top-level types. Most sources have only one type declaration. The generated class files will be logically combined into a namespace, also called a package.

Go source files consist of one or more top-level (public or package private) variable, constant, function/method, or type definitions with associated commentary. In Go, the content of the package, including types defined in the package, can be spread across many source files. The general structure of a Go source file is

- Package declaration

- Any imports

- Top-level variable ("var") declarations

- Top-level constant ("const") declarations

- Top-level function ("func") declarations

- Top-level type ("type") declarations

Note the top-level items can come in any order and can be intermixed.

Go Comments

Go, like Java, allows comments in source code. The Go comments are much like C and thus Java comments.

Like Java, Go has two styles of comments:

- Line (aka remarks) – Starts at "//" until the line end.

- Block – Starts with "/*" and ends with "*/". This style of comment can and often does span lines. Nested block comments are not allowed.

Go does not have *JavaDoc* ("/**...*/") comments. Instead, the Go documentation tools pay special attention to comments before the package statement or any top-level declaration. As a package can have many source files, it is conventional to create a document-only source file (often called doc.go) which has only the package statement prefixed with the package comment.

The best practice in Go is to comment any public declaration. For example:

```go
// PrintAllValues writes the formatted values to STDOUT.
// The default formatting rules per value type are used.
func PrintAllValues(values... interface{}) {
       :
}
```

or as:

```go
/*
PrintAllValues writes the formatted values to STDOUT.
The default formatting rules per value type are used.
*/
func PrintAllValues(values... interface{}) {
       :
}
```

Note there is no asterisk ("*") along the left side, as is often seen in Java.

The Go "doc" server creates HTML documentation from these comments in Go source much like the JavaDoc tool does for Java source. This comment text is plain text (not HTML as in Java). In this text, indented text is taken as is (like <pre>...</pre> in HTML). Left side–aligned text is wrapped.

The first (or only) sentence of each comment is special as it is included in summary documentation. This should be enough to determine the purpose of the commented item.

Refer to the Go package documentation to see samples of the general style and detail of Go code documentation.

Go Build/Run Process

The Go development experience is much like that of all compiled (vs. interpreted) languages, including Java. It generally consists of these steps:

1. Edit source files – Use some editor.

2. Compile source files – Use the Go builder.

3. Fix any compiler errors – Use some editor.

4. Build runnable – Use the Go builder.

5. Test changes – Use the Go builder and/or third-party testing tools.

6. Release the code.

Many internal loops can occur in this sequence. The entire sequence can repeat. Assuming no compiler errors occur, steps 2, 4, and 5 can be done by one command.

Note as far as building is concerned, Java is a compiled language. That the generated bytecode is often interpreted at runtime is not relevant here.

Many tools exist to assist the developer with each step. The most basic approach is to use a text editor and a command-line compiler for steps 1–3. Then some sort of program builder for step 4. Step 5 can be done with a debugger and/or a test case runner.

Often, these tools are combined into an *Integrated Development Environment* (IDE). Typically, steps 1–3 are assumed by the IDE code editor (i.e., the code is compiled as typed (interactively) in and errors are shown immediately).

Numerous options exist for Go. IDEs for Go include IntelliJ *IDEA* (or the equivalent but independent IntelliJ *Goland* IDE) and some Eclipse-based offerings. Some editors, such as Microsoft's *Visual Studio Code* (VS Code), can also act as IDEs to some degree. IDEs are convenient as they often combine an editor, compiler, formatter, vetting tool, builder, debugger, and often deployment tooling all in one. IDEs often reduce the need to use command-line tools, which is often helpful.

Note that almost all the code in this text was developed using IDEA and not via editors and Go command-line tools. Still Go code can be successfully developed without an IDE using just the Go runtime tools and an editor.

Because there is such a variety of ways to develop Go code, this book will not provide much guidance in this area. Each tool typically provides good guidance on how it is set up and used. Go itself ships tools that help with steps 2, 4, and 5.

Go Playground

If you do not have Go or a Go IDE installed yet, the author suggests you use the *Go Playground* (play.golang.org), an interactive website that lets you enter and run most Go code.

The Playground describes itself (*About* button) as follows: "*The* Go Playground *is a web service that runs on golang.org's servers. The service receives a Go program, vets, compiles, links, and runs the program inside a sandbox, then returns the output.*"

The playground is Go's logical replacement for a REPL (Read, Evaluate, Print, Loop) process, typical of many languages, including Java.

Often, the preceding sequence takes only a few seconds. Considering the extra network overhead involved, this is a testament to how fast the Go build and program launch process is.

Figure 4-3 shows the Playground screenshot just after running the displayed code.

Figure 4-3. *Go Playground Hello World run*

One can enter Go code and run it. Here, we see the results of running the sample program (in the yellow/shaded pane) in the output pane (in white) at the bottom. The playground is restricted; some Go library functions are not supported. See the *About* button text for more information.

The playground provides several samples/contexts. For example, it can run Go test cases, as illustrated in Figure 4-4.

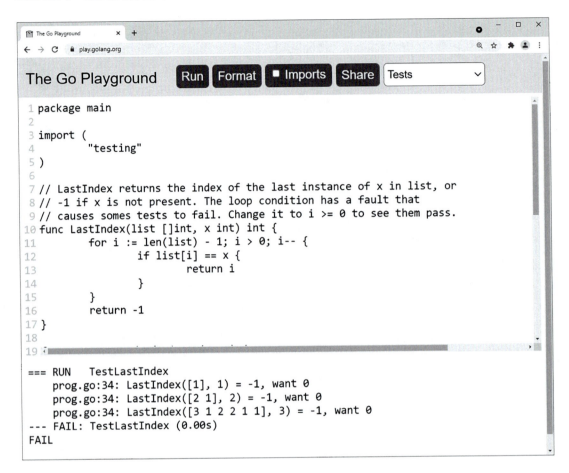

Figure 4-4. *Go Playground test case run*

The playground will allow you to run code (generally copy/pasted from some editor if complex) as if from multiple source files. For example, look at Figure 4-5.

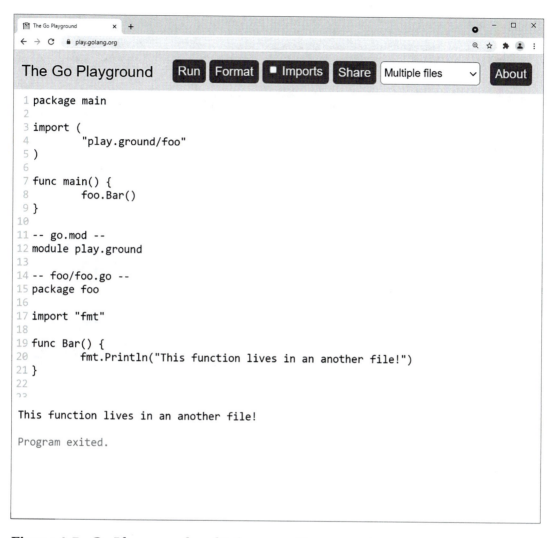

Figure 4-5. *Go Playground multiple source files example*

Note thus this example shows the use of Go modules (it has a go.mod file).

The playground offers a limited ability to share work. The active code (maximum size of 64KiB) can be saved in a Google-hosted database and its URL shared via the *Share* button. Once shared, the snippet URL can be loaded into another browser for others to see it, as shown in Figures 4-6 and 4-7.

Figure 4-6. *Sharing a code example*

Figure 4-7. *Accessing a shared code example*

Go Integrated Development Environments

An IDE can give a richer experience, such as the following IntelliJ IDEA screenshot. For example, it allows multiple source files to be open at a time in different windows. Note this sample shows a source from the capstone program. In general, the error reporting is better in an IDE.

This IDEA screenshot has many views (tabs), including a console and navigation hierarchies. It has a built-in debugger. It has a direct integration with the *Git*[2] (and possibly other) source code control system (SCCS). It can do the equivalent of many "go ..." commands and much more. So often, when using an IDE, a little direct use of the "go ..." commands is needed.

Notice the button bar on the top right in Figure 4-8 (enlarged in Figure 4-9). There is a green arrow (right-facing triangle) *Run* button that builds and runs the program. It has a green {de}*Bug* button next to the Run button to build and launch the program in a debugger. Both act much like using the "go run" command.

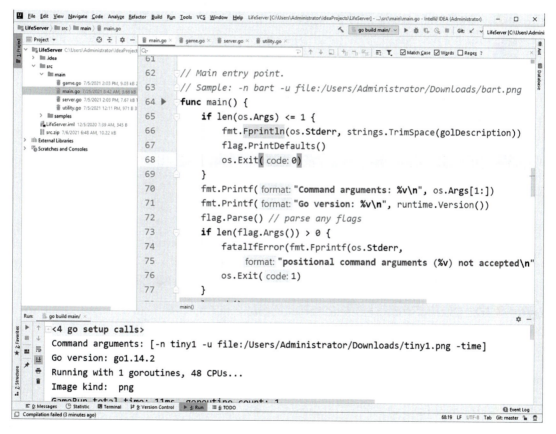

Figure 4-8. *IntelliJ IDEA Goland view*

Figure 4-9. *Enlargement of the IDEA menu bar*

Visual Studio Code (VS Code) is an alternate IDE-like tool you can use. Figure 4-10 shows a variant of the classic *Hello World* example and the output it creates when it is run.

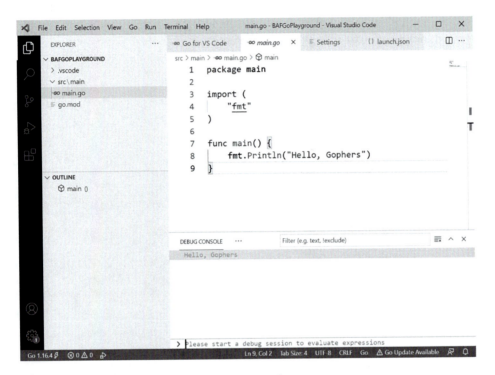

Figure 4-10. *Visual Studio Code for Go sample*

VS Code is using a Go 1.16 runtime, and thus a go.mod file is (by default) expected. This program has a minimal one in the BAFGoPlayground directory:

```
module hellogophers
go 1.16
```

A similar experience, as shown in Figure 4-11, is available for Java developers. So, if you use IntelliJ IDEA, or Eclipse, or any other major IDE, moving from Java to Go should be straightforward.

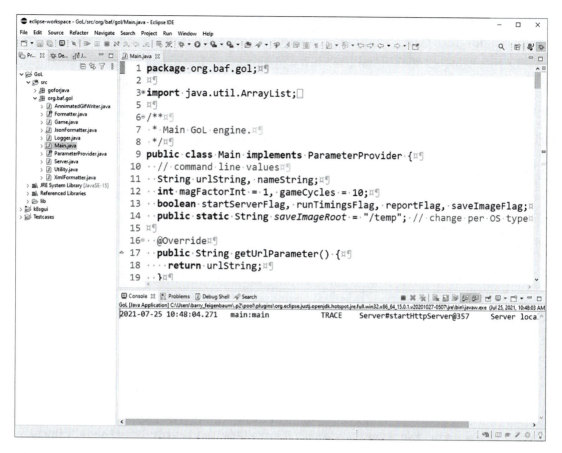

Figure 4-11. *Eclipse IDE Java view*

Some IDEs detect and present all compile-time errors in the source view as the code is entered. If no errors are shown, the code will launch. Other IDEs can only detect a subset of possible errors. Any other errors will be detected only when the code is launched.

This happens because each IDE has its own Go compiler (or just Go parser) which is different than the one used by the go command. These different compilers may detect errors differently. In general, the code generated by the Go compiler at launch time (not code from the IDE compiler, if any) is what is run.

Upon drilling down on the Go program launched in IDEA, as shown in Figure 4-12, you can see how the IDE Console shows the Go environment, the commands used to build the program (marked by the IDE with #**gosetup**, not part of actual values), and the program that is built before it shows any program output. This was launched by the Debug button:

GOROOT=C:\Users\Administrator\sdk\go1.14.2 *#gosetup*

GOPATH=C:\Users\Administrator\go **#gosetup**

C:\Users\Administrator\sdk\go1.14.2\bin\go.exe build -o C:\Users\ Administrator\AppData\Local\Temp\2___go_build_main_.exe -gcflags "all=-N -l" . **#gosetup**

C:\Users\Administrator\.IntelliJIdea2019.3\config\plugins\intellij-go\ lib\dlv\windows\dlv.exe --listen=localhost:58399 --headless=true --api-version=2 --check-go-version=false --only-same-user=false exec C:\Users\ Administrator\AppData\Local\Temp\2___go_build_main_.exe -- -n tiny1 -u file:/Users/Administrator/Downloads/tiny1.png -time **#gosetup**

API server listening at: 127.0.0.1:58399

Command arguments: [-n tiny1 -u file:/Users/Administrator/Downloads/tiny1. png -time]
Go version: go1.14.2
:
Starting Server :8080...

Figure 4-12. *IntelliJ IDEA Console view*

The preceding bold lines are from the program itself. They come from this source:

```
fmt.Printf("Command arguments: %v\n", os.Args[1:])
fmt.Printf("Go version: %v\n", runtime.Version())
:
fmt.Printf("Starting Server %v...\n", spec)
```

Running Go Programs

The Go compiler (nominally run via the "go build," "go run," or "go test" commands) creates executable binaries (EXE[3]). The resulting EXE can be run from an operating system (OS) command line. Unlike with Java, there is no prerequisite *Java Runtime Environment* (JRE), with its *Java Virtual Machine* (JVM), that must be present to run the program.

The Go EXE is self-contained and requires only standard OS functionality; all other required libraries are embedded in the EXE. Also embedded in the EXE is the *Go Runtime* (GRT). This GRT is like, but much smaller than, the JRE. The GRT is not formally defined, but it includes, at least, built-in library functions, a *garbage collector*, and support for *goroutines* (like lightweight Java threads).

This means there is no equivalent to a Java `.class` (aka object) file containing *bytecode* (object code) for the source code. It also means there are no *Java Archives* (JAR) files containing collections of these class files.

Given a Go program is built into an EXE (in this example for Windows), say `myprog.exe`, to run it one simply does ($> is the OS command prompt):

```
$>myprog arg1 ... argN
```

While, assuming the class was compiled into `MyProg.class` in the current directory, in Java one would need to do:

```
$>java -cp .;<jar directory>... MyProg arg1 ... argN
```

Here, a JVM (`java.exe`), which must be included in the OS path, is launched, and the location of any required class directories and/or JAR files is provided to it. Like with Python and other interpreters, the JVM takes the developed program (a `.class`) as a parameter and runs it, not the OS.

---

[3] EXE is the Microsoft Windows name (based on the file extension used) for an executable. Other operating systems use different terminology.

Building Go Programs

In general, any Go code is built from source including all needed source files (your code and any other libraries). This ensures all changes (edits) to any source files are included into the generated EXE. It also allows for potential cross-source file optimizations to occur.

In C/C++, the *Make* utility is generally needed to make sure all code dependent on changes in other files gets recompiled. The Java compiler conditionally (based on source file timestamps) recompiles classes other classes depend on. Both Go and Java depend on the package structure to find all referenced source files.

While the Go way may seem less efficient and potentially slower, the Go compiler is generally so fast that, except for large programs, one rarely notices the time it takes to compile all the sources each time. The compiler can create precompiled package archives that are like Java JAR files to improve build times when it can detect that the source files of a package have not changed since they were last compiled.

Some development environments may include a means to precompile some sources (especially for library types) into "object" files to improve build time, but this is generally not used by Go application developers. It is most often done to libraries from community developers. The "go install" command can do this. It creates *archive* files (with an ".a" extension) that contain precompiled code. Often, these archive files are placed in the "pkg" directory.

Like in Java and most compiled (vs. interpreted) languages, all Go source is processed in these phases by the Go compiler:

1. Lexical analysis – The source is read character by character, and tokens are recognized.

2. Parsing and validation – The source is read token by token, and the *Abstract Syntax Tree* (AST) is built.

3. Optional (but typical) optimization – The AST is rearranged to make the structure better (generally faster to execute but possibly take less generated code).

4. Code generation – The machine code is created and saved into object files; in Java, the bytecode (machine code for the JVM) is written into class files.

Note that it is in phase one that any missing statement ending semicolons are added.

The Go builder acts much like the third-party Java *Maven* or *Gradle* build tools in that it resolves dependency libraries (for both the Go compiler and code linker) and creates complete runnable code sets (in Java, often in the form of one or more JAR/WAR files; in Go as EXEs). The Go builder adds these phases:

1. External reference linking – All just compiled sources and external libraries used in the code are resolved and integrated together.

2. Executable building – An operating system–specific executable is built.

3. Optional execution – The executable is launched in a production or test context.

The source that is built can be application code and/or any dependencies (or libraries). The dependencies are often fetched (as source or, more typically, archives) as a manual pre-step (i.e., using the go get or go install commands) to the preceding sequence. Go modules can make the selection of dependency versions more predictable.

The Go builder is arguably more complete than the Java compiler (javac). The Java compiler assumes programs are assembled *just-in-time* (JIT) at runtime by the JVM, so there is no static linking and program building phase. Because of this runtime linking, it is possible that with Java different libraries are used at compile time vs. runtime, which can be problematic. This cannot happen in Go.

Go allows code to be built for many operating system (OS) types. The exact set changes with the Go versions over time, but here is a sample set:

- aix
- android
- darwin
- dragonfly
- freebsd
- hurd
- illumos
- js
- linux

- nacl
- netbsd
- openbsd
- plan9
- solaris
- windows
- zos

Go allows code to be built for different hardware (HW) architectures. The exact set changes with the Go versions over time, but here is a sample set:

- 386
- amd64
- amd64p32
- arm
- armbe
- arm64
- arm64be
- ppc64
- ppc64le
- mips
- mipsle
- mips64
- mips64le
- mips64p32
- mips64p32le
- ppc
- riscv

- riscv64

- s390

- s390x

- sparc

- sparc64

- wasm

Some of the OS and/or architecture list members may not be included in the standard Go install package.

Bytecode vs. Real Code

The Go approach is in marked contrast to Java's, where the compiler produces *bytecode* object files that are both OS and HW agnostic. It is up to the JVM to either interpret the bytecode or convert the bytecode into OS- and/or HW-dependent code. This conversion is generally done at runtime (vs. compile/build time) by *JIT* (just-in-time) or *Hotspot* (optimized by usage) bytecode compilers that are part of the JVM.

This difference accounts for one advantage Go has over Java. When a Go program is built, all code is resolved in runnable form into its image. The OS simply needs to read the file into memory, and it can start execution immediately afterward. In Java, the code is built up in memory incrementally (many smaller file reads) plus the code needs to be both JITed and linked at runtime. This incremental read and JIT behavior can slow down program startup significantly. But once this startup is finished, Java code can run just as fast as Go code can. Also, in Java, some of the needed class file may not be available, resulting in abrupt failure of the program. This cannot happen with Go.

So, one can ask: Which is faster? Java or Go?

The answer is, as is true for much in life: *It depends!*

Go programs tend to start faster for the preceding reasons. Once loaded, the picture is not so clear.

Go is statically compiled, which means it is also statically optimized. All optimizations are done by the Go compiler based only on information in the source itself. When using a Java JIT compiler, this is similar, but the optimization is done at runtime. But Java can also have a Hotspot compiler, which uses runtime information to do improved optimizations. It can even reoptimize the code as the runtime conditions vary over time. So, over the long haul, one can expect Java code to be better optimized and thus have the potential to run faster.

However, a program runtime is not always dependent on its own code. Many times, third-party services (such as database systems and remote servers) can dominate the program's execution time. No amount of optimization can compensate for this. But the better use of concurrent programming patterns may.

One of Java's initial advantages over prior languages like C/C++ was its relatively easy-to-use and built-in support of operating system threads. Go, with its goroutines, essentially does Java one better. So, in a circumstance where highly concurrent programming is possible, one should expect Go to outperform Java in the general case.

Java provides runtime access to the Java compiler (javac). This allows Java code to create Java source code and then compile it. Because Java can load classes at runtime, this allows for a form of self-extending Java programs.

Go has some similar support to process Go code through the various go package standard library sub-packages, but Go cannot reliably extend a program at runtime.

Go does have a limited (OS dependent) and incomplete library support for dynamic *plugins* where dynamic code is possible. It is to be determined if this will eventually become a fully supported feature. Go code can be compiled and built dynamically, and then the resulting executable can be launched (as a separate operating system process). This provides some similarity to the Java approach, but the plugin must run in a different process.

Java's javac compiler also allows some external code to be run during compilation, allowing modification of the *Abstract Syntax Tree* (AST) that is the compiler's internal representation of parsed Java classes. This allows for compile-time annotation processing. For example, the *Lombok*[4] tool, which can automate some common Java coding actions, uses this capability.

Go has similar support. It is used, for example, in the built-in Go formatting and linting tools, but any developer can take advantage of it to build powerful Go language processing tools.

---

[4]https://projectlombok.org/

While Go is generally operating system (OS) agnostic, it is not necessarily unbiased based on the OS type. Like Java, Go is designed to run on Unix-based systems. Go supports Microsoft Windows (and others) but not as the primary OS type. This bias shows up in several areas, such as command-line processing and file system access. Go provides access to the runtime OS type and hardware architecture so your code can adjust to them as needed.

Both Java and Go can instrument (measure/profile) code as it runs. *Java Management Extensions* (JMX) generally allow for both static and dynamic measurements to be added. Go's options are more static (but they can be enabled/disabled at runtime). Both allow remote access to these measurements. See the Go documentation for more details on this feature. Third parties extend this support. For example, *Prometheus*[5] (which is written in Go) can be used to instrument Go code.

Go Command-Line Tools

Somewhat like with Java, Go can be built into *modules*. Java modules allow packages to explicitly announce the types that are exposed for other packages to consume and to also explicitly control the packages visible to import. Most Java code developed today does not explicitly use Java modules, but it implicitly does as all the JRE libraries are modularized. Java modules make it possible, but still not commonly done, to generate Java programs in the self-contained EXE form that Go programs are.

Note that since Go 1.16, the use of modules (i.e., go.mod and related library resolution) has become the default (a small breaking change). To get the prior behavior, as commonly employed in this text (because any examples tend to be small and self-contained), modules need to be explicitly disabled by setting the GO111MODULE environment value to auto. Future Go versions may fully remove the auto mode entirely.

Go has a similar option where developers can control which packages and what version of the package get imported. Like in Java, life is a bit simpler if modules are not used, but they become important when including libraries from third parties. Unless you are creating such libraries for others to use, you can often ignore modules for your own code. Still modules allow you to better control the libraries you use, and they make it easier to expose your code as a library later, so using them is recommended.

---

[5] https://en.wikipedia.org/wiki/Prometheus_(software), https://prometheus.io/

Go without using modules assumes that all source to be built together (i.e., generates a single EXE) is included in one set of source trees (set by the GOROOT and GOPATH environment values). With modules, downloaded dependencies can be also found in a Go builder–maintained local cache.

Go only allows a single entry point (the `main` function) per EXE, so each program requires its own source tree (or main package branch if you are building multiple EXEs). In contrast, Java allows each type (class) to have its own entry point (`main` method), so each type can be its own program, independent of package structure. In Go, often multiple executables are placed in a `cmd` (by convention, an alternate to `src`) directory containing multiple child directories, per independent program, each of which typically contains a `main` directory and a `main` package of that executable.

Many Go tools assume this structure. Go with modules allows each module to optionally have its own independent source tree. This can be easier to manage (say because the source is in distinct source code repositories). We will discuss modules a bit more later in this book.

Tools Bundled in the Go Command

The "go" command has many options beside the various "build" actions. This single command replaces a whole host of distinct Java build tools. The following is a summary of the key actions available through the "go" command:

- bug – Opens a browser on a new bug report.

- build – Compiles code (by package) and any dependencies and produces an executable.

- clean – Removes any generated object files (generally done automatically).

- doc – Like the "Javadoc" command in that it creates HTML forms of package API documentation.

- env – Displays OS environment values used by the Go builder and other tools.

- fix – Rewrites Go source to replace removed features with any replacement features. As Go now promises full backward compatibility, this tool is rarely needed.

- fmt – Rewrites Go code to conform to standard (idiomatic) Go source formatting rules. Often, an IDE will do this as code is entered/saved.

- generate – Typically used to generate new Go sources based on directives (special comments) in Go source. Can be used to replace function Java offers through Generics and Annotations. It is used as a pre-step before "go build."

- get – Gets (downloads and installs) a dependency (something imported) from a (generally) public repository (such as GitHub) and builds it.

- help – Displays help on the available actions.

- install – Related to Get, Install installs and compiles code referenced via imports.

- list – Lists the installed packages.

- mod – Downloads, installs, and manages modules. It has several sub-actions.

- run – Builds and runs a Go program (EXE).

- test – Builds and runs Go tests. Tests are like programs, but there can be multiple tests defined in a single source file; Go tests are much like Java *JUnit* tests.

- tool – Lists the tools (actions) that can be run.

- version – Displays the Go version of a generated EXE or its own version.

- vet – Looks for likely issues in Go code. Much like the Unix *Lint*[6] tool and the various Java code quality checkers, this can avoid errors at runtime. Examples of Java vetting tools include *Checkstyle*[7] and *FindBugs*[8]/*SpotBugs*.[9] Often, an IDE will do this as code is entered/saved.

---

[6] https://en.wikipedia.org/wiki/Lint_(software)
[7] https://en.wikipedia.org/wiki/Checkstyle
[8] https://en.wikipedia.org/wiki/FindBugs
[9] https://github.com/spotbugs/spotbugs

For the latest list, use the "go" (no arguments) command.

The "go build," "go run," and "go test" are frequently used. See the Go documentation for more details.

Other Tools

There are also some independent tools not listed earlier. A few of high utility are listed in the following. Also, many of the preceding actions can be run as independent tools. Often, the independent tools have broader scope, say a whole source tree vs. a single Go source or package.

The "cgo" command creates a linkage between Go code and code in a foreign language (generally C). It is used much like the *Java Native Interface*[10] (JNI) is used to call foreign language (generally C) code from Java code.

Today, JNI-style code is rare; most Java functions are implemented by pure Java offerings. CGo code is more common in the Go world as a bridge to existing non-Go offerings. In the author's opinion, over time, Go will follow Java in this regard, and CGo code will fade away.

The "cover" command is used to get code coverage reports by analysis of statistics generated during a "go test -coverprofile" run. In Java, third-party (say in an IDE) tools must be used to get code coverage.

There are other Go tools. See the Go documentation for more details.

Go Runs Programs Instead of Classes

Go has no direct equivalent of a *Java Virtual Machine* (JVM) or a *Java Runtime Environment* (JRE – a JVM plus the standard Java class libraries). Go has a runtime that provides the needed function to support Go semantics. This includes libraries for its collection types and goroutines. It also includes a garbage collector to manage heap resident memory allocations. This runtime is much smaller (typically a few MB vs. 100s of MB) than a JRE.

---

[10] https://en.wikipedia.org/wiki/Java_Native_Interface

Your code, any libraries, and the runtime are built (linked) into a single executable which an operating system (OS) runs. This contrasts with the *just-in-time* (JIT) means by which Java programs are assembled and linked. Go uses early (static) linking at build time. Java does late (dynamic) linking at runtime.

The Go approach resembles the approach used in the C/C++ (and other older) languages. It is more traditional but less flexible (in particular, one cannot easily add new code to an EXE at runtime, which Java servers (and previously applets) often do (i.e., download code at runtime over a network)).

The Go approach results in an executable that is self-contained (no other prerequisites, such as a JRE, must be installed). This can make deployment easier than with typical Java. This is one reason Go is so popular in containerized (e.g., Docker, Kubernetes) environments. Other use cases also can benefit from this more self-contained characteristic.

Go is evolving to be even more self-contained. For example, Go 1.16 added the ability to embed literal content (say directories of text like HTML, CSS, or JavaScript files) into the EXE body that in the past would require independent files to be delivered. If fully utilized, a complete solution, such as a web server, can be delivered as a single binary. This embedding is done by prefixing a declaration as follows:

```
//go:embed <path to file>
var text string  // string data
```

or

```
//go:embed <path to file>
var bytes []byte  // binary data
```

or

```
//go:embed <path to directory>
var fs embed.FS  // file system
dirEntries, err := fs.ReadDir("<path to directory>")
:
```

or

```
//go:embed <path to file>
var fs embed.FS  // file system
bytes, err := fs.ReadFile("<path to file>")
:
```

The <path to ...> value can include wildcards. See the embed package description for more details.

This self-containment has the additional benefit in that there is no chance that a missing library or data is discovered only at runtime. It does mean the executable can be considerably larger than a Java program delivered only as an archive (JAR) and assuming a usable JRE is already present. Even minimal Go executable images can be a few megabytes in size. This can be reduced by building the code without debugging information, but this is not recommended.

Because the Go program is preassembled, it often loads up and starts faster (often in only a few seconds) than a typical Java program can. This also helps in containerized environments and in serverless cloud environments.

The Go approach requires that the executable be built for each target OS. In Java, class files are portable across OSes (they get JITed (compiled) into native code at runtime). This results in the famous Java *Write Once, Run Everywhere* (WORE) characteristic that Go does not have. In Java, it is the JVM, and not the program itself, that is OS and HW architecture dependent; a version of the JVM is built for each supported combination.

Fortunately, the Go language itself is generally OS and hardware architecture agnostic, and most of its libraries are also. Very few libraries are architecture dependent. The few standard libraries that are OS dependent are delivered for a set of popular OSes, such as Linux, iOS, and Windows. Often third-party libraries that are OS dependent (a small percentage) are also. Thus, most Go programs are portable across many operating systems at the cost of being built multiple times, once for each operating system.

Go Memory Management

Go can allocate space for values in several locations:

- Code image[11] – For top-level values

- Call stack[12] – For many function or block locals

- Heap[13] – For dynamic values or values accessible via closures or of dynamic size/length

---

[11] https://en.wikipedia.org/wiki/Executable

[12] https://en.wikipedia.org/wiki/Call_stack

[13] https://en.wikipedia.org/wiki/Memory_management

One of the biggest sources of errors (aka bugs) in computer programs that use dynamic memory allocation is improper memory management. Many failures, such as memory leaks, improper reuse of memory blocks, premature memory release, etc., can often cause catastrophic program failures. Like with Java, Go avoids most of these issues by providing automatic memory management.

Like with Java, Go provides an automatic (aka managed or garbage collected) heap memory management capability that offers these key functions:

1. Allocation of space for objects (instances of any data type in Go)

2. Automatically reclaiming space of any unreferenced (often called dead or unreachable) objects

Objects are dynamically allocated on either the function call stack or, as in Java, in the heap. Like with Java, Go provides *garbage collected*[14] (GC) heap memory allocation/ deallocation.

All heap-based objects are GC'ed. All stack-based objects are freed when the owning function returns or owning block exits. For either, there is no programmer accessible way to deallocate them. Like in Java, the only control one has on heap objects is to set pointers to an unneeded object to `nil`.

The Java GC implementation will call the `finalize()` method on each about to be reclaimed object. For many types, this function does nothing, but it can do cleanup activities. Go offers a similar capability, but it is not universal to all allocations. Any allocated object that needs cleanup at GC time must be explicitly registered with the Go runtime so it will be cleaned up. To do this, one uses

```
runtime.SetFinalizer(x *object, fx(x *object))
```

where `object` is of any type, which takes a pointer to x and runs fx against it in a goroutine. The x value is automatically deregistered and can be freed on the next GC.

Like in Java, a heap object is typically allocated using the new function. The object can also be placed on the heap by taking the address of an object literal or variable.

Like with Java, Go having a GC mechanism subjects code to pauses when the GC is running. A GC can potentially happen on any heap allocation and when it happens is typically unpredictable. This is the key downside to using garbage collection.

---

[14] https://en.wikipedia.org/wiki/Garbage_collection_(computer_science)

One of the reasons Java has several GC implementations is to try to tune these pauses to the nature (batch/command line, interactive, server, etc.) of the program. Note Go, like Java, has an API, `runtime.GC ()`, to allow one to force a GC, typically when a pause can be better tolerated; this can create more predictability.

The simplest GC approach, which a Go implementation may (and typically does) use, is called *mark-sweep*. It has two phases:

1. Mark – All objects are marked unreachable, then all objects accessible from each reference root are marked reachable.

    The roots are any top-level pointers or objects (structs) that have pointer fields and any similar pointers and structs in any active call stack. A reference tree walk from each root is done.

2. Sweep – All objects still marked unreachable are freed (or reclaimed).

See Appendix D for more details on mark-sweep collectors.

To prevent changes in any of these roots during GC, all the active goroutines may need to be suspended. This is often called *stop-the-world* (STW). So effectively, the Go program is doing no work during this time. The Go team has worked hard to reduce STW pause durations; most are now under a millisecond, and thus generally acceptable, on modern machines.

GC algorithms are rated by

- The maximum stop-the-world time – This should be as small as possible.

- The percentage of the total runtime that is consumed by the GC – This should be as small as possible.

- Often, it is difficult to optimize both values together.

It should be noted that the Go GC uses a different mechanism than the several (varies over time and runtime context) Java GCs do. Because Go supports pointers (vs. references as Java does), it cannot easily move objects around in the heap. So, Go does not use a scavenging (aka compacting) collector as is common in Java. Go's approach can result in higher heap fragmentation and thus less efficient use of memory.

As mentioned earlier, Java allows one to select among several GC implementations. Go does not. The Java GC options have evolved (collectors removed and added) over time (indicating the JVM cannot seem to provide a "one-size-fits-all" option) as the JVM use cases have evolved over time.

An object on the Go heap generally has two parts:

- A header – Contains at least the mark-sweep hit indicator and often the size of the data. Other values, such as type and/or debugging/profiling information, may also be present.

- The data – The actual data.

Because the headers exist, most systems have a minimum size for all heap objects, often 8 or 16 bytes, even if the data is smaller, say a single Boolean value. Memory is generally allocated in chunks at least this minimum size. So, for best heap usage, one should avoid placing many small (say scalar) values individually (vs. say as part of a large array) on the heap.

In Java, the stack vs. heap location of data is obvious. Anything created by the new operator is on the heap. All else is on the stack. In general, this means all primitive scalar variables are on the stack, and all objects are in the heap.

Note that because of boxing, Java can be less memory efficient for primitive types in collections than Go typically is.

In Go, where data lives may not always be apparent. Data can live[15] on the stack or in the heap, depending on how they are referenced and on how the Go runtime works. Stacks are optimal for function locals that live only for the lifetime of the function that creates them (i.e., have no external pointers to them or are not used by closures). Heaps are generally needed for other data. Heap allocation is also needed for large data values.

Note Go allocates goroutine call stacks from the heap. Each goroutine has its own call stack. The stacks start out small and grow as needed. In Java, thread call stacks also come from the heap, but they start out much larger (often several megabytes); this severely limits the number of thread call stacks that can exist relative to the number of goroutine call stacks.

---

[15] https://dougrichardson.us/2016/01/23/go-memory-allocations.html

The mix of stack vs. heap allocations can impact the performance of Go programs. Go provides profiling tools[16] to help determine this ratio and guide any tuning.

The way Go and Java manage the usage of memory, especially in the heap, is quite different. As the details are often implementation dependent and subject to change, they are not well documented. These differences can mean similar Go and Java programs with similar data structures can consume significantly different amounts of runtime memory. It also means out-of-memory conditions can occur differently. The JVM has more options to manage memory usage than Go currently has. Go's higher memory block fragmentation can also impact this.

Many objects are allocated by the Go new function which allocates space to hold the value (often, but not always, on the heap, as they would be in Java) and initializes it to binary zeros (interpreted as the "zero" value based on the type). The new function always returns a pointer to the allocated value (or panics if insufficient memory is available).

Many scalar values (e.g., numbers and Boolean) and structs of only scalars are allocated on the stack. Most collections (such as slices and maps) are allocated on the heap.

Often, any value that has its address taken must also be allocated on the heap. This happens because the address can be saved and used long after the block where the value was declared has returned. For example:

```go
func makeInt() *int {
        var i int = 10  // a local, can be on the stack
        return &i       // now can live beyond this function; now on heap
}
```

or the effectively equivalent:

```go
func makeInt() *int {
        var pi = new(int) // on heap
        *pi = 10
        return pi
}
```

---

[16] https://blog.golang.org/pprof

Consider this struct example:

```
type S struct {
      x, y, z int
}
```

then:

```
func makeS() *S {
      return new(S)   // x, y, z = 0
}
```

Or equivalently:

```
func makeS() *S {
      return &S{} // or &S{1,2,3} if fields initialized
}
```

Go also creates built-in struct, map, and channel types with the make function. The built-in make functions differ from new in that they initialize (somewhat like a constructor call in Java) the value based on its arguments, and it returns the value itself, not a pointer to it. For example, consider a slice-like struct which might be defined as (conceptually, not a true Go slice; not legal Go)

```
type Slice[T any] struct {
      Values *[Cap]T   // actual data; can be shared
      Len, Cap int     // current and maximum lengths
}
```

where (say) make(new(Slice[int]), 10, 100) creates and returns this struct and the backing array and sets all the fields.

Go Identifiers

Go, like Java, uses identifiers to label programming constructs. Like in Java, the Go identifiers have a set of syntax rules. Go's rules are like Java's, so use your Java experience here (any issues will be reported by the compiler). See the *Go Language Specification* for the specific rules.

In Go, the named constructs that can be identified are

- Packages – All top-level types, functions, and values are included into some package.

- Types – All variables have some type; all functions have parameter and return values of some type.

- Variables – Variables are named values that have a storage location and can be changed over time.

- Fields – Fields are variables included into structures (struct).

- Functions (declared or built-in) – Functions are blocks of code that are stand-alone or are structure or interface (prototype only) members; functions can be invoked by other functions.

- Constants – Constants are named values that cannot be changed; they are known to the compiler but generally have no runtime existence.[17]

- Statement keywords – Statements are either declarations or nested groupings of statements or represent actions that can be expressed in the Go language; most statements (except for assignments) are introduced with a keyword.

Note in Go, like in Java, every variable must have a declared static type. This means that the type is known at compile time and cannot change as the code runs. Go, like Java, allows the dynamic (runtime) type of a variable of an interface type to change to any type that conforms to (implements) the interface type. Go has no equivalent of a class type variable that can be set to instances of subclasses.

Java has a feature, which Go only partially supports, where a variable can be assigned any type (or subtype) that implements the type of the variable. This is often referred to as inheritance *polymorphism* (a key Object-Oriented Programming feature). This works for both class and interface types.

---

[17] Some Go implementations may convert constants into the equivalent of read-only variables.

In Go, such polymorphism is only available for interface types. There is no notion in Go of inheritance for struct types. So, if a Go variable has an interface type, it can be assigned only an instance of any type that implements all the methods of that interface. Often, this is more flexible but less disciplined than Java's polymorphism.

Go Scopes

Both Java and Go are *block-scoped* languages. Identifiers are visible in the block they are declared in, in any lexically nested blocks, and potentially other blocks based on their visibility. Often, especially in Go, the enclosing block is implied and not explicitly coded. Nested blocks can redeclare (and thus hide) declarations from containing blocks.

Note that scopes are a compile-time concept; lifetimes (discussed later) are a runtime concept.

Blocks can act as *namespaces*, which are sometimes named collections of identifiers (generally unique in a namespace but not necessarily unique across different namespaces). While blocks are nested, namespaces can often be overlapping. In Go, like in Java, namespaces are implied. In some other languages (such as C++), they can be explicitly declared.

Java supports several identifier scopes. In general, an identifier is declared in these scopes:

- Package – A namespace for types

- Type (class, interface, enum) – A namespace for nested types, fields, or methods

- Method or block – A namespace for nested (aka local) variables (a method creates a block)

Go supports several scopes. In general, an identifier is declared in some scope:

- Package – A namespace for global variables, constants, functions, or type declarations; aka top level

- Struct – A namespace for nested fields or methods (functions associated with a struct)

- Interface – A namespace for method prototypes (aka signatures)

- Function or block – A namespace for nested variables (a function creates a block)

A key difference is Go allows global (not included in some type as Java requires) variable declarations. Java `static` fields are an approximation for global variables. Also, in Go, but not in Java, a function, type, or constant can be declared globally.

To be more complete, Go has these conceptual block scopes:

- A *universal* block that encompasses all Go source files compiled together.

- Each package creates a *package* block containing all Go source files for that package; this is where top-level declarations live.

- Each Go source file acts as a *file* block containing all Go source text in that file.

- Each Go struct or interface creates its own block.

- Each if, else, for, switch, or select statement is its own implicit block.

- Each switch or select case or default clause is its own implicit block.

Built-in (or predeclared) identifiers are in the universal block which consists of multiple file blocks. The package specification (not a declaration) is at the file block level (each file block has its own set of imports). Package blocks do not span across different directories. Top-level declarations are in the package block. Any local variable (including function receiver, parameter, and return names) is in its containing block (which can be a function body). Local declarations start at the point of declaration, not the containing block start. The same identifier can be declared only once in the same block.

The predeclared (and thus considered reserved, especially by IDEs – some can be redeclared, but this is ill advised) identifiers in the universal block are

- Types – `bool byte complex64 complex128 error float32 float64 int int8 int16 int32 int64 rune string uint uint8 uint16 uint32 uint64 uintptr`

- Constants or zero values – `false iota nil true`

- Functions – `append cap close complex copy delete imag len make new panic print println real recover`

Go supports statement labels in their own namespace in a block. They are used by the `break`, `continue`, and `goto` statements. Labels are at function block (but not nested function) scope. They must be both unique and used in that block. Cross-function control flow transfers are not allowed.

Like with Java, a Go package is a namespace for declarations. Like Java, a Go package maps to a directory in some file system. Unlike Java, the package name must always be used to qualify an imported declaration. There is nothing equivalent to

```
import java.util.*;
```

In Go, one must do the equivalent of the following (conceptual, not allowed in Java):

```
import java.util;
:
util.List l = new util.ArrayList();
```

or:

```
import java.util as u;
:
u.List l = new u.ArrayList();
```

Go has a feature like Java `static` field imports, where the imported names are merged into the importing namespace. For example:

```
import . "math"
```

would include all public names in the math package in the current package, so they could be used unqualified. The use of this feature is discouraged (it is sort of a deprecated language feature). For example, imported name conflicts can occur. See the *Go Language Specification* for more details.

In Java, the package directory holds type (class, interface, enum) source code, typically, but not required to be, one top-level type per source (`.java`) file. Any number of types can be in the package. Any such type has special privileged visibility (called *default* visibility) into the other types in the same package. In Java, all methods of a type must be inside the type's definition (and thus in the same source file).

Go's private visibility is nearly identical to Java's default visibility. Go has no means to make a member of a type (say a struct) private to that type alone.

Java supports nested type declarations (e.g., an enum defined as a member of a class and thus qualified (made distinct) by that class). These nested types can be named (has a developer-assigned name) or, if a class or interface, anonymous (has a compiler-generated name).

Public nested named types can be used by other types. These nested types get compiled into separate class files (with compiler-constructed names) and to the JVM are distinct (as if from different source files). Go does not allow this nesting, but a single Go source file can define any number of types.

Go Scopes vs. Go Source Files

In Go, the package directory holds one or more Go source files (`.go`). The text of each file is logically concatenated (in source file name lexical order) to form the content of the package. There are a few restrictions on how the declarations in the package are arranged across the source files. This means Go source is less organized but more flexible than Java source is.

Also, like with Java, the generated binary code (`.class` in Java) is often placed in a different directory than the source is. In Java, the binary files are persisted and can be managed (say placed into a JAR). In Go, the generated binary files are often temporary (possibly in memory only) and generally deleted once the target EXE is built.

One requirement is each source file in a Go package includes a `package` statement as the first statement. In Go, there is no default package. This statement declares the name of the package. Files in the same package should be in the same directory. Often, the directory name matches the package name; for example, the `main` package is typically in a directory named "main." Go allows the main package to be in a directory of a different name, possibly with code from different packages if the program is started in the directory containing the main package, but this is not recommended.

In general, each Go program's source is rooted in a directory (called GOPATH) that forms the start of any package paths. Library packages can also be located by the GOROOT path. GOROOT can be a list of directories (much like the Java CLASSPATH). A package can reside in some path from this root. When importing a local package, the path from this root is used.

If we look at Figure 4-13, on the upper left, we see this set of directories. The *LifeServer* project uses the GOROOT (Go SDK directory in the following) to access the Go compiler and runtime and the standard libraries. Under this directory are all the Go standard packages (in source form, which helps when debugging code). It uses the GOPATH to access any additional libraries (accessed via "go get ...") used by the project.

We also see how several of the Go command options are easily accessed. Some, such as Go compilation, are automatically launched and thus are not listed.

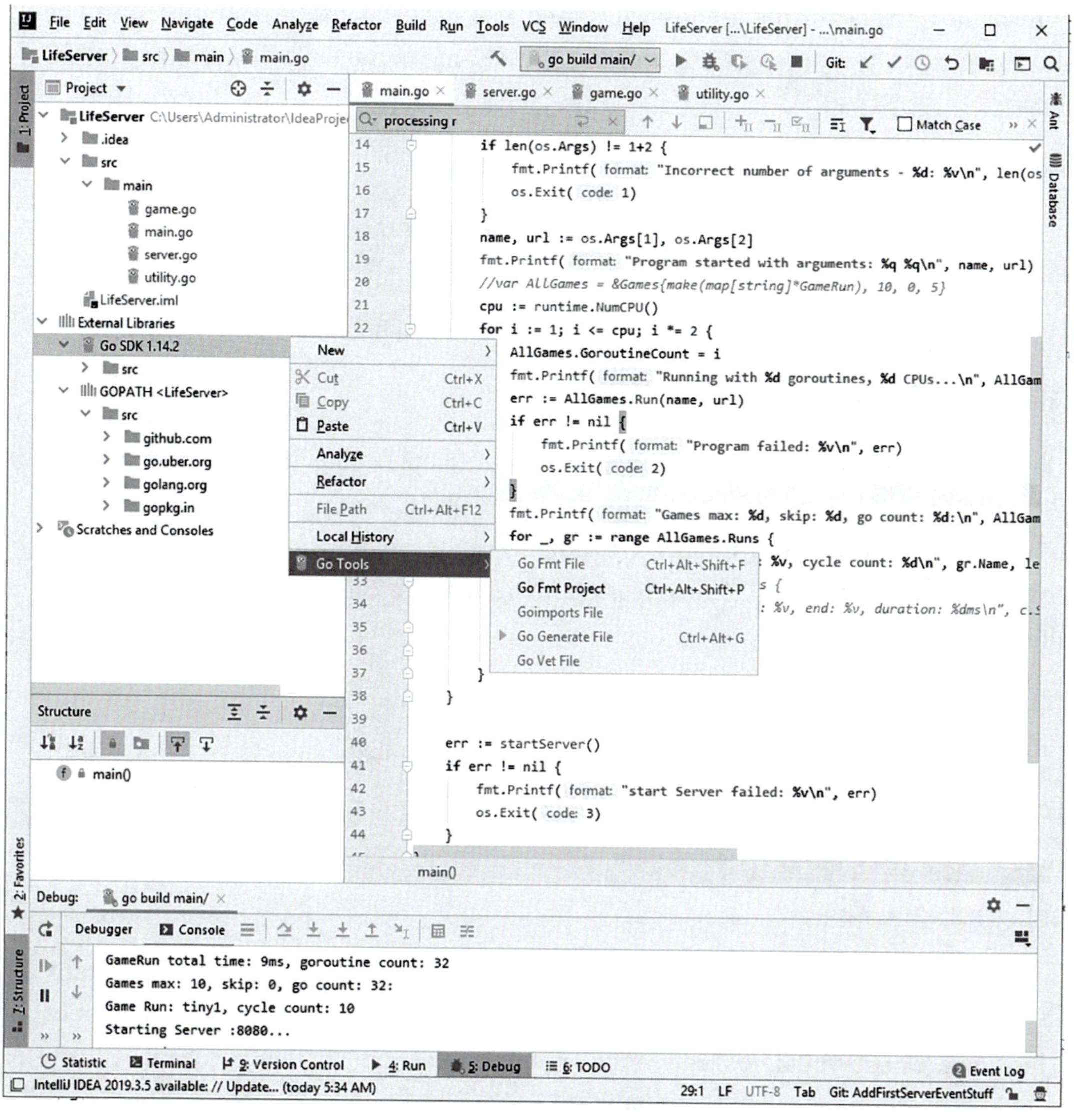

Figure 4-13. *Goland with select Build tools shown*

It is possible to import a package in a remote repository (say GitHub) directly (via doing the equivalent "go get" first; IDEA helps automate this). In this case, the URL of the repository (minus the protocol prefix) is used. For example:

```
import "github.com/google/uuid"
```

imports the *uuid* package, with the local package reference (or alias) uuid, into the current file namespace.

By default, the last name in the path is used as the local package reference. It can be overridden (say if two different imports end in the same name or just by preference) as follows:

```
import guid "github.com/google/uuid"
```

Often, one uses a local, say Git, repository plus one or more remote repositories to provide a complete set of importable code.

Initializing Go Variables

In Java, a variable is initialized when it is declared. Except for block locals, all variables have a default value, per type, used if no initial value is explicitly supplied. Local variables must be explicitly initialized or assigned to before first being read (or a compiler error is generated). The following string (say as a class field) has the default value of `null`:

```
String name;
```

Most variables are initialized by an expression value provided as part of the declarations. For example:

```
String name = "John Smith";
String name2 = name;
```

Here, the variable `name` is set to reference a literal string value (stored in a constant pool). Then `name2` is set to reference the same string. Remember in Java all variables of `Object` type (or subtypes) hold references, not values.

In Java, fields of types can be initialized in a separate "initializer" block. There can be any number of these initializer blocks in a type. These blocks can be `static` for static variables (set when the class loads) or nonstatic for instance variables (set when the instance is created via `new`). Instance initializer blocks are an alternative to defining a constructor. For example:

```
String name;
{
  name = "John Smith";
}
```

These blocks are typically used when one cannot initialize the variable via a simple expression. In Java, a variable or field can only be initialized once.

Go has similar behavior except all variables (locals too) are always initialized. If a value is omitted, the "zero" value is used, much like the default value of Java. For example:

```
var name string
```

Here, the name string has the empty (not nil) string value, which is the zero value for a string. In some ways, this type of initialization makes Go a bit safer than Java.

Top-level values can also be initialized by a function (vs. a block in Java). The special parameter-less void function init() is used for this purpose. There can be any number of these initialization functions inside and between packages.

These functions are only used for top-level variables. These functions should be placed close to and after the declarations of the variables they initialize. These functions are typically used when one cannot initialize the variable via a simple expression. These functions are called by the Go runtime at program startup (before the main function is called), not by developer code. Each init() function is only called once. For example:

```
var name string

func init() {
        name = "John Smith"
}
```

In Go, the init function can reset a variable initialized at declaration time or in other init functions. The last one called wins. This can cause some surprises. Go has a mechanism to sort the order that the init functions in a program are called based on dependencies of the code.

Sorting of init() processing across source files is based on the packages that are imported. Source files with no imports are initialized first, then the files that directly import the packages in those source files, and so on until the main package is reached. The files (and thus the init() function) are sorted by these dependencies. This ordering within a package can be partially controlled by the alphabetical sort order of the Go source file names in a package to order the processing of the source file.

This is one of the reasons there can be no loops in package importing (i.e., A imports B and B imports A (directly or indirectly)). Java has no such restrictions. It can sometimes be a challenge to prevent (or remove) import loops. It is possible code segments or defined data types need to be moved between packages (i.e., repackaged) to change the needed import list to resolve any loops. Often, the Go compiler will provide information to help locate the loop import pattern.

In Go, instance initialization, if the zero values are insufficient, requires the creation of a constructor function (i.e., NewXxx).

Some Gophers do not like to use init() functions because they cannot take parameters and the time when (or if) the function is run cannot be explicitly controlled. You can choose to make your own initialization functions for this purpose and call them explicitly when needed.

Note a package must be imported by some code for its init() functions to be run. Therefore, the *blank* identifier is allowed in an import. For example, the following import statement does not import any symbols; it only runs any init() functions that may be in the package (and packages included by the package transitively):

```
import _ "github.com/google/uuid"
```

Like any function, the code in an init() function can cause panics. This is like throwing an exception in an initializer block in Java. Due to the point init functions run in the program's flow, these panics may need to be addressed a bit differently from panics elsewhere. There are two major ways to handle them:

1. Ignore them and allow the program to fail before main() is launched.

2. Capture them in a defer'ed function inside the init() function and recover to allow the program to continue to the main function.

Lifetimes of Go Identifiers

A *lifetime* is the runtime duration in which the value a variable holds is alive. The variable itself exists if it is in scope.

Java variables have these basic lifetimes:

Static – These values exist if the type (class, interface, or enum) they are associated with (i.e., are static fields of) is loaded in the JVM. These values exist on the heap (inside some type; remember runtime types in Java are objects).

Most developers think of them as lasting for the lifetime of the JVM, but this is not always true. Types get loaded lazily (on first reference) and can be unloaded at any time they have no remaining instances, and the heap becomes constrained. Java programmers also tend to think `static` values are unique, but this is not always so. The same class, loaded by a different class loader, would have distinct sets of static values.

Instance – These values last while the object they are associated with (i.e., are instance fields of) exists. These values exist on the heap (inside instances). As objects in Java are garbage collected, this is at least while one reference to the instance exists.

Method/block – Local values last as long as the block they were declared in is on the call stack.

Go variables have similar lifetimes:

Top level or package – These values are allocated as part of the Go executable and thus exist for the lifetime of the executable.

Instance – These values last while the object they are associated with (i.e., are instance fields of) exists. These values exist (inside structs) on the heap or call stack. As heap objects in Go are garbage collected, this is at least while one reference to the instance exists.

Method/block – Local values last as long as the block they were declared in is on the call stack.

Closure – Block local values last while there is at least one reference to them existing in some closure (function literal), even if the allocating block has ended. These values typically exist on the heap. Java has no equivalent of this, but it has a similar behavior for read-only (`final`) local variables; it achieves this by creating a copy of the variable.

Go Module Summary

Go packages can be grouped into *modules*. Modules are important structures to use when providing code to other developers to consume. They are typically less critical for an individual application.

From the Go site:[18] "A *module* is a collection of packages that are released, versioned, and distributed together." A Go module is a collection of packages in a source tree. Nothing new here. But to become a module, there is an additional file in the root of the source tree called `go.mod`. This file sets the *module path*, which identifies the import root location of source files, and optionally the module's version.

---

[18] `https://golang.org/ref/mod`

Note future Go versions may enable modules even when go.mod does not exist.

Typically, the module path is a URL (minus the protocol header, address, and a port) to the server (say GitHub) that is hosting the published module; for example, xyz. com/libraries/library/v2. This is the path other code would import the module by. The go.mod file also indicates any dependent packages with their module's paths and their required versions. It also indicates the Go version the module was built with (or minimum required; this is not always enforced by the Go builder).

Note that for standard libraries, the hostname part of the import URL is missing. Only the library package path is used. The packages are typically resolved from the GOROOT or GOPATH.

Note that in Go version 1.16 (and beyond), modules are used by default. A go.mod file is no longer required to enable module behavior. The older version behavior can be activated if desired.

In general, Go modules are imported in source form (the code is copied/ downloaded to your local machine from whatever hosting location is used, often automatically when first referenced). They are then compiled with any of your own code much as if you had written them yourself. So, there is generally no formal building of library code. Module definitions can also reside on a local (or remote) file system. This is typical during module development and testing before it is published.

In Java, this is often different. It is rare that a Java dependency is provided in source form. Instead, JARs of compiled Java classes are provided. The JARs are generally prebuild by the library authors and hosted on some repository (say *Maven Central*[19]). The JARs are sometimes downloaded on demand. Java code can thus be distributed in binary form only and thus with more privacy. Go code is generally more open.

With modules, this is expanded, allowing the developer source to be in another directory, called the *module path*. So, each module can and often is placed in a different source tree, some of which can be remote.

Go modules can have *semantic versions*, which fields have meaning, as follows:

```
<major>.<minor>.<fix>
```

where the fields mean

- Major – Any increase indicates a breaking (non-backward compatible) change from the past.

---

[19] https://search.maven.org/

- Minor – Any increase indicates a nonbreaking change (often an addition) from the past.

- Fix (aka patch) – Any change indicates some minor change (such as a bug fix).

The Go builder can upgrade dependent modules when a newer version is found. This helps you keep your dependencies current, but it can cause unexpected/undesired changes. Since Go 1.16, this is no longer automated by default; changes to versions of dependent modules need to be explicitly done via updates to the go.mod file and explicit go get (or equivalent) commands. This provides more explicit control of the versions of dependencies used and when/if they are updated.

With more use of the go.mod file, the need to explicitly specify a version in dependency import paths (as shown in the following) has lessened, but some packages may still use this approach. When using modules, only the module path (without version information) is imported; the version used comes from the go.mod file. This makes the Go behavior more closely match the behavior seen using Maven or Gradle to do Java builds. The go.mod file acts somewhat like the Maven POM file's *dependencies* section.

To get the prior behavior when using Go 1.16+, you need to build code with the following environment option:

```
GO111MODULE=auto
```

Introduced in Go 1.11, the default for this option was changed from auto to on in Go 1.16. Some of the samples in this text require this value to be set to auto to build correctly. This represents a small (but reasonable) breaking change in Go 1.16.

These versions are used on imports to control the used version as follows:

```
import {<alias>} "<path>{.v<version>}"
```

where

<alias> is an optional alias for the import.

<path> is the local or remote name of the package.

<version> is the package version to use. By default, it means the first. The general form is

```
<major>{.<minor>{.<fix>}}
```

For example:

```
import xxx "gitworld.com/xxx/somecoolpackage/v2"
```

causes the second version to be used. The "v" prefix on the version is conventional to recognize it as a version specification. Often, when a new version (say v2) is provided, any (or at least a few revisions) older versions are also maintained to allow one to choose which version to use. This allows incremental upgrades across major versions, especially if some breaking change was made. Often, v1 or the first release is selected if no version indicator is provided.

It is also possible, via go get, to fetch any version of a package and then use it locally without a version qualifier. In this way, the developer has complete control of which version is used and when, if ever, an upgrade is done. Again, this is done less frequently if a go.mod file exists to explicitly state the desired dependency version.

Each go.mod file starts with a module statement as follows:

```
module <module path>
```

where the path is the name of the module's code, which does not have to be, but often is, the directory tree rooted by the directory containing the go.mod file.

This file is generally created by using the go mod command as follows:

```
go mod init <module path>
```

This command is used once per module, no matter how many packages are in that module. A module path usually consists of

```
<source>/<name>
```

where <source> is typically a repository (or directory) locator. And <name> is the module name. For example:

```
mycompany.com/example
```

Also included in the go.mod file is the Go version the file was built with or requires.

When you import packages (e.g., mycompany.com/example) from an external (say remote) repository, the Go builder can resolve the import and add it as a dependency to the go.mod file. In Go 1.16 and beyond, this is no longer automated by default; explicit updates via (say) go get are needed. Any available version of the import library may be selected. The Go builder may (and typically does) cache the content of this remote module locally for faster build performance. If needed, transitive dependencies may be added.

Adding a dependency can also be done manually, which allows one to select a different version of the dependency. For example, once the code is rebuilt with the added dependency, the go.mod file might look like

```
module mycompany.com/example
go 1.16
require xyz.com/utils v1.1.3
```

Often, more than one dependency will be listed. The require keyword can be factored out, as follows:

```
require (
  xyz.com/utils v1.1.3
  abc.com/common v2.2.3
   :
)
```

The version on the "go" command indicates to the Go compiler what language version the code is targeted to. It may cause the compiler to reject code that uses features defined after that version. It may also cause subtle differences in how the code is compiled. It may not cause errors if any dependent libraries require different versions. See the Go site for more details.

The go mod command provides options to manage (often upgrade) the downloaded dependencies over time.

You may notice a file called go.sum in your module root. This file contains the dependency checksums and is managed by the go tools. Do not change or delete it.

This book will not go deeper into using modules. See the Go documentation for more details. Go also provides a dependency resolution approach called "vendoring" (the act of making copies of the third-party packages your project depends on placing each in a vendor directory within your project). See the Go documentation for more details.

In Java, a similar module description, in the file `module-info.java`, would look like

```
module com.mycompany.example {
  requires com.xyz.utils;
  requires com.abc.common;
}
```

Java modules also allow a developer to restrict the packages exposed by a Java module via the `exports` statement. Go modules have no similar feature, but the Go builder has a convention that any packages under an `/internal` directory at the module root will not be importable by code using the library. This makes the code effectively private to the module. When modules are used, often and by convention, the public program source is placed in the `/pkg` directory (sort of a parallel to `/internal`) instead of `/src`. In this case, the meaning of pkg is a bit different from its use before modules as described in the following.

Go does not require the preceding structure. For example, some of the programs listed in this text are defined in a directory structure as is shown in Figure 4-14.

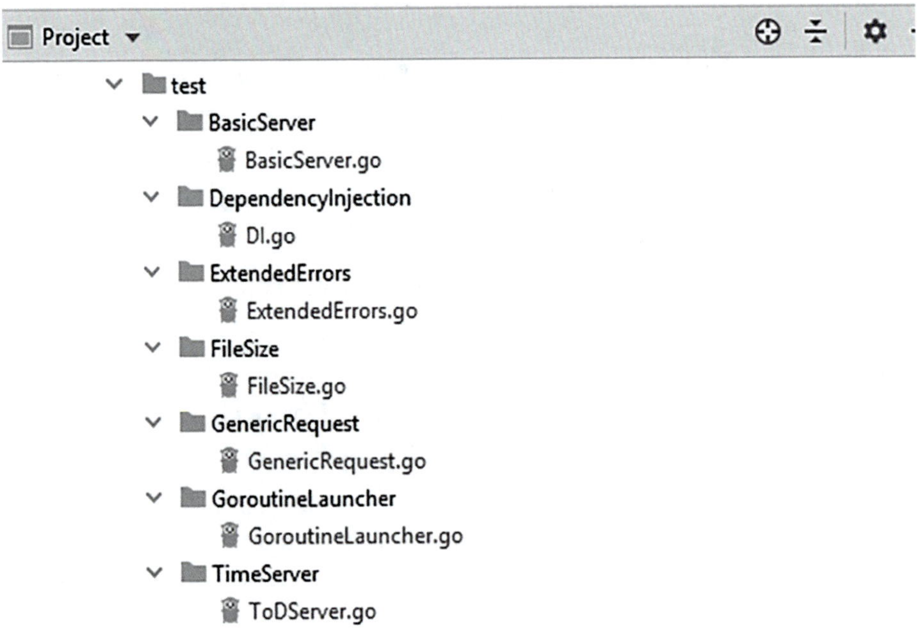

Figure 4-14. *Programs defined in a directory structure*

Each of the .go files includes a package main statement, any needed imports, any program-specific code, and a main() function. Thus, each .go file is an executable program.

Before modules, most developer-written code was in a directory listed in the GOPATH often under the /src directory. Third-party binary code (typically with the .a extension) is often installed under a /pkg directory. Some locally built packages will also go here. Code delivered with Go or other third parties is often placed in a directory in the GOROOT set. The typical structure is like this:

```
<GOPATH>
    /src
        /main - your application and associated packages
        /xxx - some third-party packages (in source form)
        /yyy - some third-party packages (in source form)
        /zzz - some third-party packages (in source form)
    /pkg
        /ggg - some third-party packages (perhaps binary only)
    /bin - executable results
```

The directories under the <GOPATH> can be looked at as a *workspace* for a Go program. You can change <GOPATH> (say by a CHDIR and/or EXPORT command) to access different workspaces.

This premodule structure is used most frequently in this book. Often, the code is shown without reference to the directories it is in.

Go Assignments and Expressions

The most basic function of a computer is to calculate (i.e., a computer is a form of programmed calculator). In Java and Go, calculation is done by using *expressions*. In many cases, the results of the expression are stored in some variables (so they can be accessed later) by an *assignment* to a variable. Assignments (in both Go and Java, the "=" operator) remember some value in a variable. This is the essence of imperative programming.

Expressions can be simple, such as a single literal[20] value:

```
x = 1
```

---

[20] In formal language theory, a literal is also a term.

or a single variable value (a term):

```
x = y
```

or a swap of values:

```
x, y = y, x
```

or they can be complex by mixing literals, terms, operators, and function calls:

```
c = 1 / (math.Sqrt(a * a + b * b) + base )
```

Note the preceding expression is legal in Go only if a, b, c, and base are all `float64` types, say declared as

```
var a, b, c, base float64
```

In Go, like in Java, expressions have types and can only be stored in a variable of a compatible type. Go is stricter on this than Java is; the types must match exactly (except for interface types, where the value can be any type that conforms to the interface).

This includes when using numeric values. In Go, an, say, `int16` will not be converted automatically into an `int32`, and an `int32` will not be made into an `int64` or `float64`. Any such conversion must be explicitly done by a "cast" function. This can be inconvenient, but since types can be derived from built-in types, it is necessary. For example:

```
var x int16
var y int32
var z float64
z = float64(x) + float64(y)
```

As a convenience, Go will automatically adjust the type of a literal numeric value (say 1) to match the target (say a `float64` (1.0) or `complex128` (1.0+0.0i)). Go can do this because literal values are "type-less." Any type is assigned by the context in which the literal is used. Numeric literals have essentially unlimited size and can be at least as large as the largest formal numeric type.

Note that Go compilers typically use the `Int` and `Float` types from the `math` package to implement numeric literals.

Like with identifiers, Go's numeric, string, and character literals closely follow Java syntax. So, use your Java experience here (any issues will be reported by the compiler). See the *Go Language Specification* for the specific rules.

Go has an extended syntax for string literals. If the backtick (`) is used instead of the quote (") character as the delimiter, the string can span lines. These strings are called "raw strings." Any character in the string is taken as a literal value, so escaping is not needed (or recognized). Any carriage return character is removed from a raw literal. Quoted strings are called "interpreted strings." Both strings are encoded into UTF-8 characters.

Note Java 15 offers multiline strings with escapes allowed when delimited by triple quotes ("""..."""`).

Like in Java, Go interpreted strings support escaped values:

> Octal (\###) – Converts to a byte (# is an octal digit – 01234567)

> Hexadecimal (\x##) – Converts to a byte (# is a hexadecimal digit – 0123456789abcdef|ABCDEF)

> Unicode (\u#### or \U########) – Converts to a 16- or 32-bit value (# is a hexadecimal digit)

> ASCII (\a, \b, \f, \n, \r, \t, \v, \\, \', \") – Like Java escapes

Care must be taken when using numeric escapes such that they must represent a UTF-8 encoded character.

Go has a character type, called rune, that is 32 bits long (vs. Java's 16-bit char type). Rune literals are like string literals but only allow one character. Like in Java, rune literals are surrounded by an apostrophe ('). Rune literals are encoded in 32-bit Unicode.

Text Formatting in Go

Being able to compute values is not interesting unless the results can be presented to users. Often, this means displayed to the user or formatted to be printed or written to some persistent storage. Most operating systems have two paths to display plain text to the user (via the console):

- Standard out (STDOUT) – Normal output

- Standard error (STDERR) – Error output

In Java, these are provided as *PrintStreams*:

- System.out

- System.err

Java allows values to be written to these streams with default formatting using the print() or println() methods or with developer-specified formatting using the printf() method. One can also format to a string by using the String.format() method (which printf uses under the covers).

Go does something similar. Go supports printing to STDOUT by default, to any Writer (including STDOUT, STDERR, files, etc.), and to strings via functions provided in the format ("fmt") package. See the "Go Library Survey" part for more details.

Here are some illustrating samples:

```go
fmt.Print(1, 2, 3)          // like System.out.print(1 + " " + 2 + " " + 3)
fmt.Fprintf(os.Stdout, 1, 2, 3)    // like above explicitly to standard out
fmt.Print(1)                // like above, but just 1 value
fmt.Fprintf(os.Stderr, 1)    // like above but to standard error
fmt.Println(1)              // same as fmt.Print(1); fmt.Print("\n")
fmt.Printf("%v\n", 1)       // similar to above
```

which output (assume standard out and error are both to the console)

```
1 2 31 2 3111
1
```

The formatted forms (names end in "f") accept a format string and zero or more values (one per "%" in the format string) to format. The file forms (names start with "F") take an io.Writer as the first argument. The result is written to that writer, which could be an open file. The string forms (names start with "S") return a string with the formatted text. The fmt.Sprintf() function is very frequently used to format values.

As Go allows a developer to make custom types, it is desirable to provide a custom string formatter (like the Java toString() method) for these types. This is done by the fmt.Stringer interface. Many Go library types do this.

Given a custom type, it can be done this way:

```go
type MyIntType int

func (mt MyIntType) String() string {  // conforms to Stringer interface
    return fmt.Sprintf("MyType %d", mt)
}
```

which can be used as follows:

```
var mt MyIntType = 1
formatted := fmt.Sprintf("%s", mt)  // could use "%v" too
fmt.Println(formatted)
```

which outputs: `MyType 1`

Note the use of "%s" (vs. "%v") to ensure the use of the Stringer interface.

The formatting provided by the generic (%v) specifier varies based on the actual data type being formatted. The other specifiers should match the actual type of the value. The effective formats for scalar data types are listed in Table 4-1.

Table 4-1. *Format Options for Primitive Types*

Type	Effective Format
Bool	%t
int types	%d
uint types	%d, %#x when formatted via %#v
float and complex types	%g
String	%s
Chan	%p
&above (pointer)	%p

And for compound data types, the elements are formatted, possibly recursively, using the rules listed in Table 4-2.

Table 4-2. *Default Format Options for Complex Types*

Type	Effective Presentation
struct types	{field0 field1 ...}
array, slice types	[elem0 elem1 ...]
map types	map[key0:value0 key1:value1 ...]
&above (pointer)	&{}, &[], &map[]

Note in Java, commas (",") and not spaces (" ") are generally used to separate elements. Also, Java formatting often prefixes nonprimitive data with the type name of the data.

As shown earlier, the Go `fmt` (format) package has great utility. It is the main means to format Go values into strings, often to print them out, and to convert text input from the user, a file, or strings into values.

Basic formatting is done via the `Print` family of functions. Printing can be done to the user, files, or strings. The general form is

```
func Printf(format string, args ...interface{}) (n int, err error)
```

which causes the arguments to be matched, one-for-one, to the format specifiers (%x) embedded in the format string with the formatted count or some error returned. Often, the returned count and error values are not checked by callers. This is one place where the "always check for errors" rule is often violated. So, it's possible such output can get lost. This likely has implications only when output is directed to files or over networks. See the Capstone Project `utility.go` file for a function that can be used to overcome this.

Multiple values can be output, each with different format specifications:

```
fmt.Printf("Value 1: %d, value 2: %s, value 3: %q\n", 1, "2", "3")
```

To accept input, one of the `Scan` family of functions is used. The general form is

```
func Scanf(format string, args ...interface{}) (n int, err error)
```

which, like with Printf, causes text from an input source to be matched against the format string and placed, one-for-one, into the `args` values with the scanned count or some error is returned. The `args` values must be pointers to variables of the correct type to set.

Multiple values can be input, each with different format specifications:

```
var one int
var two, three float64
fmt.Scanf("%d %e %v\n", &one, &two, &three)
```

The format string is any string with format specifications embedded in it. When scanning, text other than format controls in the specification must match exactly. On printing, such text is output as is. Like with Java, any such string is interpreted at runtime and not compiled. This means failures can happen at runtime. Go is often more forgiving (no panics raised) of these types of errors than Java. These specifications are rich and are summarized here. Like in Java, the specifications are introduced with a percent ("%") and end in a case-sensitive format code letter. Modifiers and widths may proceed the format code. The general format is

`%{[<index>]}{<modifier>}{<width>}{.<precession>}<code>`

The codes are listed in Table 4-3.

Table 4-3. *fmt Package Formatting Codes*

Code	Usage	Applicable Types
%	% character	
v	General value	Any (like %s in Java)
b, t	Boolean	Boolean or if integer base 2
s	String	String
d	Decimal	Integer base 10
f	Float decimal	Number
g, G	Float general	Number
e, E	Float scientific	Number
o, O	Octal	Integer base 8
x, X	Hexadecimal	Integer base 16
u, U	Unicode escaped	Rune or string
q	Quoted and escaped string	String
c	Character	Rune
p	Pointer	Any pointer type
T	Type of value	Any

The modifiers listed in Table 4-4 are allowed (vary per code).

93

Table 4-4. *fmt Package Formatting Code Modifiers*

Modifier	Usage	Note
+	Always add a sign	
-	Pad width on the right (vs. left) side	
#	Use a more detailed format	Add a base indicator on integers; field names on structs
<space>	Add leading space on positive values	
0	Pad width on the left with zeros	

The `<width>` value sets the minimum value width. The `<precision>` value sets the number of digits to show to the right of any decimal point or a minimum number of characters to show.

If present, the `<index>` is the argument position starting at one. This allows the format to reuse arguments or reorder arguments.

Goroutines

One of Java's most important features is the support for relatively (vs. C and C++) easy multithreading built into the languages and via types, such as *Threads*, supplied in the standard library, and language features such as *synchronized* methods/blocks. Go offers similar features based on the use of *Goroutines* which are a lightweight Thread-like means to run code combined with channels (discussed later in this text).

Issues with Concurrency

Before we discuss the mechanism to do concurrent programming in Go, let us look at a problem concurrent programming can cause. Both Java and Go use a shared memory model (all threads can access the same memory locations), so *critical sections* (CS), regions of code when access to variables can be impacted by parallel access, are common. The Java language has `synchronized` blocks to help control access to CS. Java allows any object to be a gate (aka *condition*) on such a CS.

Consider an example:

```java
public class Main {
  public static void main(String[] args) {
    int N = 10;

    var sum = new int[1];
    var rand = new Random();
    var threads = new ArrayList<Thread>();
    for (var i = 0; i < N; i++) {
      var t = new Thread(() -> {
        try {
          Thread.sleep(rand.nextInt(10));
        } catch (InterruptedException e) {
          // ...
        }
        sum[0] += 100;
      });
      threads.add(t);
      t.start();
    }
    try {
      for (var t : threads) {
        t.join();
      }
      System.out.printf("Sum result: %d%n", sum[0]);
    } catch (InterruptedException e) {
      // ...
    }
  }
}
```

Note sum is an array of one int so it is writable in the thread body. This is needed as Java does not have closures.

Here, the expected result is sum equals N * 100. Sometimes (maybe most times) it will be this value, but it can also be smaller. For example, with N = 10:

```
Sum result: 900
```

This is because the statement

```
sum[0] += 100; // same as sum[0] = sum[0] + 100
```

is a (hidden) critical section because the += operation is not an atomic operation between threads, and thus a thread switch can happen between the fetch of sum and the addition of 100 to it and the setting of the new sum value. Any such read-modify-write sequence not done atomically creates a CS.

This can be fixed by changing the assignment as follows:

```
synchronized (threads) {
    sum[0] += 100;
}
```

which ensures only one of the threads executes this statement at a time. Other values besides threads can be used in this case, possibly also this. A simpler approach is to use an atomic value:

```
var sum = new AtomicInteger(0);
:
sum.addAndGet(100); // replaces synchronized block
```

Like Java, Go has memory access order peculiarities. Java explains this with the (somewhat complex) *happens-before* (HB) relationship.[21] Go also has an HB relationship[22] for memory access. Care must be taken, especially when multiple goroutines are involved, to ensure code honors all HB relationships. Go channels, atomic access, and locking function can be used to make this happen.

---

[21] https://golang.org/ref/mem
[22] https://golang.org/doc/go1compat

Go Concurrency

Go has support for concurrent programming via a feature, called *Goroutines*, that enables relatively (to Java) ease asynchronous or parallel processing. The most similar concept in Java is a *Thread* as shown earlier. Goroutines can introduce the same critical section issues. We will discuss handling critical section in Go later.

Note that *parallelism* and *concurrency* are not the same thing. Being concurrent means being capable of running in parallel. It does not mean the code is always run in parallel. Being concurrent generally means the code behaves predictably independent of whether it is run in parallel or not. Often, this is a function of code design.

On multi-processor (or core) systems, code can truly run in parallel (at the same time) but only if its design supports concurrency. Sometimes, parallel behavior can be simulated by multiplexing different code execution threads on a single processor (often called multitasking or timesharing).

Note most modern computers contain at least two cores, so parallel processing is a likely possibility. Server-class machines often contain dozens (maybe 100s) of cores.

A goroutine is just a normal Go function. A goroutine is created and started with the go statement. The go statement returns immediately, and the goroutine function runs asynchronously to and possibly in parallel with the caller.

Goroutines, combined with channels (discussed later), provide an implementation of *Communicating Sequential Processes*[23] (CSP). The basic CSP concept is independent paths of execution (call them threads in Java or goroutines in Go) can interact by passing data between themselves in a controlled (often first-in, first-out as with channels) fashion. This is often easier and safe than managing CS and is an alternative to Java's synchronization approach.

With CSP, each thread does not share the data concurrently (note nothing in Go prevents this, but it is generally not needed), but instead they use a form of message passing; data is "sent" (transferred) by a source goroutine and "received" by a target/processor goroutine. This prevents the possibility of critical sections. By buffering such messages, the sender and receiver can work asynchronously.

CSPs are like *Actor*[24] systems. Actor systems also send messages between actors. Actors generally are objects that have a special method that runs on an assigned thread and receives any messages; actors are not generally threads in themselves but

---

[23] https://en.wikipedia.org/wiki/Communicating_sequential_processes
[24] https://en.wikipedia.org/wiki/Actor_model

share threads managed by some actor runtime. This gives actor systems some of the better instance scale seen by goroutines. The actor runtime is responsible for routing/delivering messages to actors. In Go, channels take this role.

The Java community provides several good actor libraries/frameworks, for example, *Akka*.[25] Again, Go provides this capability by default; in Java, it is an add-on.

Both CSP and Actors simplify programming by making the processing of a message sequential (uninterrupted). The processors do not get a new message until they are ready to receive one. They also allow only one thread at a time to access any data.

A goroutine is lightweight (uses less resources) compared to a Java Thread. Goroutines are like what are often called *Green*[26] *Threads* (which are thread-like functions created by a runtime, not the operating system, and are typically both lighter weight and offer faster context switching than native operating system threads) in Java.

Often, there can be many green threads per operating system thread. The same is true for goroutines. The maximum number of Java threads that can practically[27] be used is generally around a few thousand, while many tens of thousands (in large systems, into the millions) of goroutines can often be used.

The details of how goroutines are implemented can change across Go versions and are thus not deeply explained in detail in this text. One aspect worth noting is each goroutine has its own call stack (which accounts for most of the resources a goroutine consumes).

Unlike with Java Threads, which often have stacks that only grow and are often of several megabytes, the goroutine stack can grow and shrink over time as needed. So, the stack a goroutine consumes is just what it requires and little more. This is one of the reasons goroutines are lightweight, especially relative to Java threads.

Another aspect is that in Go operating system threads are created and ended on demand and kept in pools for reuse, and thus there are typically only as many as needed to support the active goroutines.

---

[25] https://en.wikipedia.org/wiki/Akka_(toolkit)

[26] Used in early Java implementations when operating system threads were not available. Early versions of Java were named Oak and then Green. So green was selected. See https://en.wikipedia.org/wiki/Green_threads.

[27] A Java thread often takes several megabytes of memory to support its state. In contrast, a goroutine often needs only a few kilobytes of memory. This is a three order of magnitude difference.

Consider that if all goroutines were CPU bound (i.e., they do not do much I/O), there would need to be only as many threads as processor cores (others, without employing multitasking, would be necessarily idle). Since code being completely CPU bound, at least over long spans of time, is rare, additional threads are needed to support both concurrent CPU- and I/O-intensive goroutines.

In Go, the goroutine scheduler typically maintains a thread pool, as shown in Figure 4-15. It assigns goroutines to inactive threads in the pool. This association is not static but can vary over time. It adds new I/O threads as needed but often limits CPU threads based on the actual number of processors (cores) in the machine. In general, the ratio of goroutines to threads can be large (say >> 100).

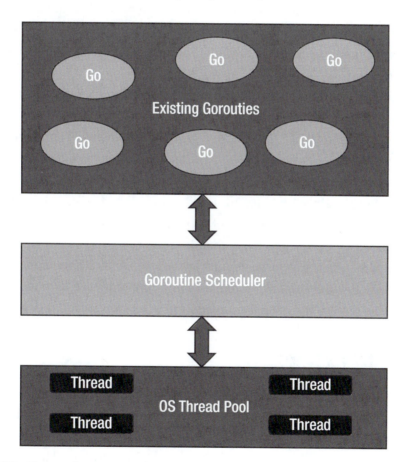

Figure 4-15. *Goroutine processing overview*

If the goroutine does something to block its continued execution (or voluntarily gives up its thread), its thread is detached and given to another goroutine. If the goroutine issues blocking operating system calls (such as doing a file or socket I/O operation), the Go scheduler can also detach the thread. So, schedulers may have two thread pools: one for CPU-bound goroutines and one for I/O-bound goroutines.

Go offers limited means to control the operating system threads Go uses to execute goroutines. One can set the maximum CPUs (or cores) for running goroutines available with the GOMAXPROCS environment value and the equivalent `runtime.GOMAXPROCS(n int)` function.

Go offers the ability to programmatically cancel or time out long-running asynchronous processes, such as loops in goroutines and network or database requests, by use of *Contexts*.[28] A context also provides a channel to notify listeners that such a long-running process has completed (normally or via a timeout). Contexts are discussed more later in this text.

The `runtime.Goexit()` function kills the calling goroutine after running all deferred functions. Note that the `main` function runs on a goroutine. The EXE ends when the goroutine for `main` exits (returns). This is like a JVM ending when all non-daemon threads end.

The `runtime.Gosched()` function causes the current goroutine to voluntarily give up (yield) its thread but remain runnable. This is like using `Thread.yield()` in Java. Yielding is good to do inside long-running sections of code such as loops.

Since goroutines are more lightweight than Java threads, there is less support to pool and reuse them as Java supports; new goroutines are generally created as needed. Goroutines do not offer identities like threads do and similar means to manage them. Channels generally replace the need for thread local as used in Java.

Goroutines by Example

Like with Java, there is no language means to test for the completion of a goroutine, but standard library functions do exist for this purpose. Java uses the `Thread.join()` method to do this. In Go, a common way to do this is via *WaitGroups* (WG). A WG is effectively an up/down counter where a client can wait for it to count down to zero. The common way this is done is as follows:

---

[28] `https://golang.org/pkg/context/`

```go
var wg sync.WaitGroup
    :
wg.Add(1)
go func() {
        defer wg.Done() // idiomatic. Done() is equivalent to Add(-1)
        :
}()
    :
wg.Add(1)
go func() {
        defer wg.Done()
        :
}()
    :
wg.Wait()
```

Before each goroutine is launched, the WG is incremented. This increment must be outside the goroutine body to work correctly. In each goroutine, the WG is decremented (by Done) when the goroutine ends. The launching goroutine then waits (is suspended) for all (there can be any number of goroutines) the launched goroutines to end.

Here is a similar solution in Java:

```java
var threads = new ArrayList<Thread>();
var t1 = new Thread(() -> {
    :
});
t1.start();
threads.add(t1);
:
var t2 = new Thread(() -> {
    :
});
t2.start();
threads.add(t2);
:
```

```
for (var t : threads)
  try {
    t.join();
  } catch (InterruptedException e) {
    // ...
  }
}
```

Something similar can be done with Go channels:

```
var count int
// support up to 100 completed before any blocked
var done = make(chan bool, 100)
  :
count++
go func() {
      defer sayDone(done)  // must be a function call
      :
}()
  :
count++
go func() {
      defer sayDone(done)  // must be a function call
      :
}()
  :
waitUntilAllDone(done, count)

func sayDone(done chan bool) {
      done <- true
}
func waitUntilAllDone(done chan bool, count int) {
      for count > 0 {
            if <- done {
                  count--
            }
      }
}
```

A slightly different expression of the preceding approach as a fully runnable example is shown in Listing 4-2.

Listing 4-2. Complete Example of the Use of Channels

```go
package main

import (
        "fmt"
)

var count int
var done = make(chan bool, 100)

func sayDone(index int) {
        done <- true
        fmt.Printf("go %d done\n", index)
}

func waitUntilAllDone(done chan bool, count int) {
        for count > 0 {
                if <-done {
                        count--
                }
        }
}

func main() {
        fmt.Println("Started")
        for i := 0; i < 5; i++ {
                count++
                go func(index int) {
                        defer sayDone(index)
                        fmt.Printf("go %d running\n", index)
                }(i)
        }

        waitUntilAllDone(done, count)
        fmt.Println("Done")
}
```

It produces this output:

```
Started
go 4 running
go 1 running
go 1 done
go 0 running
go 0 done
go 4 done
go 3 running
go 3 done
go 2 running
go 2 done
Done
```

If you reduce the done channel size to 1, you get something like this output:

```
Started
go 4 running
go 4 done
go 3 running
go 3 done
go 1 running
go 1 done
go 0 running
go 0 done
go 2 running
go 2 done
Done
```

Note there is less interleaving of work. A channel's capacity can strongly affect the parallelism of the goroutines using it. Also note the output pattern can be different if instead the "fmt.Printf(...)" is placed before the "done <- true" in sayDone(...).

Go has an equivalent to the atomic values in Java discussed earlier in package `sync/atomic`:

```
var sum int32
:
atomic.AddInt32(&sum, 100)
```

Go routines can behave unpredictably, especially when multiple goroutines are running concurrently. Consider the simple example shown in Listing 4-3.

Listing 4-3. Complete Serial Printing Example

```
package main

import (
        "fmt"
        "time"
)

func printNum(id string, count int) {
        for i := 0; i < count; i++ {
                fmt.Printf("%s: %d\n", id, i)
                delay := time.Duration(rand.Intn(10)) * time.Millisecond
                time.Sleep(delay)  // delay a bit
        }
}

func main() {
        printNum("one", 5)
        printNum("two", 5)
        printNum("main", 5)
}
```

What can come out? Exactly the following:

```
one: 0
:
one: 4
two: 0
:
```

```
two: 4
main: 0
:
main: 4
```

But with this small change:

```go
func main() {
        go printNum("one", 5) // now a goroutine
        go printNum("two", 5) // now a goroutine
        printNum("main", 5)
}
```

What can come out? Possibly the same lines as before but in any possible order (where the preceding order is unlikely). But it is possible only some of the one and/or two lines come out. This is because the Go scheduler can run only ready goroutines (and Sleep makes them not ready) but in any order and can switch between them at any time. Also, the main function, also run inside a goroutine, can end, causing the program to end, before the other goroutines get to finish. Thus, goroutines generally act like *Daemon* threads do in Java.

Here is one sample output:

```
main: 0
one: 0
two: 0
main: 1
two: 1
one: 1
two: 2
main: 2
main: 3
two: 3
two: 4
one: 2
main: 4
one: 3
```

As a final example of using goroutines, let's provide a program that can compress all the files named as command-line arguments in parallel. It uses the CompressFileToNewGZIPFile function defined in the "Go Library Survey" part. It has this signature:

```
func CompressFileToNewGZIPFile(path string) (err error)
```

Our main is defined this way (with a dummy version of CompressFileToNewGZIPFile just to demonstrate concurrency).

Listing 4-4. Parallel File Compression Example

```
package main

import (
        "fmt"
        "log"
        "math/rand"
        "os"
        "sync"
        "time"
)

func CompressFileToNewGZIPFile(path string) (err error) {
        // dummy compression code
        fmt.Printf("Starting compression of %s...\n", path)
        start := time.Now()
        time.Sleep(time.Duration(rand.Intn(5) + 1) * time.Second)
        end := time.Now()
        fmt.Printf("Compression of %s complete in %d seconds\n", path,
        end.Sub(start) / time.Second)
        return
}

func main() {
        var wg sync.WaitGroup
        for _, arg := range os.Args[1:] { // Args[0] is program name
                wg.Add(1)
                go func(path string) {
                        defer wg.Done()
```

```
            err := CompressFileToNewGZIPFile(path)
            if err != nil {
                    log.Printf("File %s received error: %v\n", path, err)
                    os.Exit(1)
            }
        }(arg)  // prevents duplication of arg in all goroutines
    }
    wg.Wait()
}
```

This produces the following output with a command line consisting of

```
file1.txt file2.txt file3.txt file4.txt file5.txt

Starting compression of file5.txt...
Starting compression of file1.txt...
Starting compression of file3.txt...
Starting compression of file2.txt...
Starting compression of file4.txt...
Compression of file4.txt complete in 2 seconds
Compression of file5.txt complete in 2 seconds
Compression of file1.txt complete in 3 seconds
Compression of file3.txt complete in 3 seconds
Compression of file2.txt complete in 5 seconds
```

Note that the goroutines start in an unpredictable order.

It is important to note that a goroutine cannot return a result to its caller, so results (or errors) that occur in a goroutine must be reported in some other way. In this example, they are logged (and the program is terminated), but it is common to have a channel on which such errors (or results) are reported to a channel listener.

Back to critical sections. Unlike in Java, in Go there is no *synchronized* statement or block. The *Locker* interface is often used instead. It is essentially

```
type Locker interface {
        Lock()    // better named: WaitUntilAvailableAndLock()
        Unlock()  // better named: UnlockAndThusMakeAvailable()
}
```

The sync.Mutex type implements this interface. It can be used to control access to a critical section. It is used basically as follows:

```
var mx sync.Mutex
:
func SomeAction() {
    mx.Lock()
    defer mx.Unlock()
    : do something that is a critical section

}
```

Note Locks do not allow reentry by the same goroutine like synchronized does with Java threads. So, use them carefully to prevent self-deadlocks.

Channels can do something similar:

```
var ch = make(chan bool, 1)  // allow only one received message at a time
:
func SomeAction() {
    ch <- true
    defer func() {
        <- ch    // discards the value
    }()
    : do something that is a critical section
}
```

The send at the top blocks if there is no room to accept the value. Since the channel has room for exactly one value, only one user can be allowed. The receive at the bottom removes the value. By increasing the channel size, we can permit a limited number of goroutines to enter the action concurrently.

Go has an additional option to avoid locking around critical sections. By using *Channels* in alternate ways, as discussed more later in this text, locks can often be eliminated. Instead, data is transferred between consumers via the channel, so the critical section simply does not exist. This is often preferred.

CHAPTER 5

Go Basic Features

In this chapter, we will drill down some of the important characteristics that make Go what it is. When we are done with this chapter, you should be able to characterize the finer Go language similarities and differences from Java.

Language Keywords

The Go reserved (cannot be used for any other purpose) words are

```
break, case, chan, const, continue, default, defer, else, fallthrough, for,
func, go, goto, if, import, interface, map, package, range, return, select,
struct, switch, type, var
```

Table 10 Go reserved words

Both Java and Go have keywords, some of which are reserved words. They are listed in Table 5-1. They are listed in the same row if they have the same/similar purpose. Some of the keywords are reserved words (can only be used as defined in the language and never as a variable name).

© Barry Feigenbaum 2022

B. Feigenbaum, *Go for Java Programmers*, https://doi.org/10.1007/978-1-4842-7199-5_5

Table 5-1. *Reserved Word and Keyword Comparison*

Java	Go	Purpose
	_	Discardable value; not in Java
abstract		Go has no equivalent
assert		Go has no direct equivalent; using panics is similar
boolean	bool	Same
break	break	Same
byte	byte	Unsigned in Go; signed in Java
case	case	Same; Go has some extensions
catch		Go has a built-in recover() function in a deferred function instead of try/catch
	chan	Java has no equivalent
char		Go has a rune (32-bit) type instead
class		Go has no OOP; a struct type is the closest approximation
const	const	Unused in Java
continue	continue	Same
default	default	Same in switch; no similar visibility in Go. In Go, no use on functions
	defer	Like Java try/finally
do		Go has no direct equivalent
double		Go has a float64 type
enum		Go uses int (iota) constants instead (like C)
else	else	Same
extends		Go has no inheritance
	fallthrough	Creates Java switch fall through behavior
final		Go has a const declaration instead
finally		Go uses a deferred function instead of try/finally
float		Go has a float32 type

(continued)

Table 5-1. (*continued*)

Java	Go	Purpose
`for`	`for`	Similar
	`func`	Java has Lambdas
	`go`	Java has threads
`goto`	`goto`	Unused in Java; in Go, similar in purpose to `break` but can be used outside a loop
`if`	`if`	Same
`implements`		Go does this implicitly
`import`	`import`	Similar
`int`	`int`	Go also has an `int32` type
`instanceof (type)x`	`x.(type)`	Go has a type assertion test instead; casting part of assertion
`interface`	`interface`	Similar role
`long`		Go has an `int64` type
	`map`	Java has a *HashMap* (and others) library type
`native`	Function definition without a body	Go has no direct equivalent; but CGo does a similar thing
`new`	`new`	Creates an object; Go has a built-in new function that does similar; Go has no notion of constructors associated with a type
`package`	`package`	Similar role
`private`		Go uses a lowercase name (more package protected)
`protected`		Not needed; Go has no inheritance
`public`		Go uses an uppercase name
	`range`	Java has a `for` statement
`return`	`return`	Same; Go can return multiple values
	`select`	Java has no equivalent

(*continued*)

Table 5-1. (*continued*)

Java	Go	Purpose
short		Go has an `int16` type
static		Go has global (vs. class) variables
strictfp		Go has no equivalent
	struct	Java `class` can be used in a similar way
super		Go has no equivalent
switch	switch	Similar; Go has extensions
synchronized		Go has no direct equivalent; libraries can provide similar behavior
this		Go can use any name for this role
throw		Go has a built-in panic function instead
throws		Not needed; Go has no exceptions to declare
transient		No equivalent in Go
try		Go has no direct equivalent but supports a `try/catch` and `try/finally` like behavior
	type	Java has no equivalent
var	var	Java uses a type name (except optionally for block locals)
void		Omitted return type serves the same purpose in Go
volatile		Go has no equivalent
while		Go has `for`

Operators and Punctuation

Both Java and Go have operators and punctuation. Many have the same or similar purpose, but each language has some unique ones. Some operators work a bit differently due to the signed vs. unsigned integer types Go supports (Java does not support unsigned integers in the language). Also, Go does not automatically convert smaller-sized numbers into larger-sized numbers (e.g., byte -> short -> int -> double); such conversion must be explicit in Go. Table 5-2 summarizes the Go and Java operators and how they compare to each other.

Table 5-2. *Java and Go Operator Comparison*

Java	Go	Purpose
+	+	Same; (binary) addition and (unary) positive or string concatenation
-	-	Same; (binary) subtraction and (unary) negative
*	*	Same (binary) multiplication; in Go, also pointer declaration and (unary) dereference
/	/	Same; division
%	%	Same; modulo
&	&	Same; bit-wise and; in Go, also (unary) take address of
|	|	Same; bit-wise or
^	^	Same; bit-wise exclusive-or; (unary) not on Booleans in Go
<<	<<	Same; bit-wise shift left
>>	>>	Same; bit-wise shift right
>>>		Unsigned bit-wise shift right; in Go, use >> with unsigned int types
	&^	Bit clear (and not); not in Java
=	=	Assignment; in Go, a statement, not an operator
+=	+=	Plus assignment; in Go, a statement, not an operator
-=	-=	Minus assignment; in Go, a statement, not an operator
*=	*=	Multiply assignment; in Go, a statement, not an operator
/=	/=	Divide assignment; in Go, a statement, not an operator
%=	%=	Modulo assignment; in Go, a statement, not an operator
&=	&=	And assignment; in Go, a statement, not an operator
|=	|=	Or assignment; in Go, a statement, not an operator
^=	^=	Exclusive-or assignment; in Go, a statement, not an operator
<<=	<<=	Shift-left assignment; in Go, a statement, not an operator
>>=	>>=	Shift-right assignment; in Go, a statement, not an operator

(continued)

115

Table 5-2. (*continued*)

Java	Go	Purpose
>>>=		Unsigned shift-right assignment; not in Go
	&^=	Bit clear assignment; not in Java
&&	&&	Same; logical and; short circuit
||	||	Same; logical or; short circuit
++	++	Auto-increment; in Go, only postfix; in Go, a statement, not an operator
--	--	Auto-decrement; in Go, only postfix; in Go, a statement, not an operator
==	==	Same; equals test
!=	!=	Same; not equals test
<	<	Same; less than test
<=	<=	Same; less or equals test
>	>	Same; greater than test
>=	>=	Same; greater or equals test
	:=	Simple (aka short) declaration; not in Java
...	...	Similar; varargs declaration; in Go, list expansion on function arguments
(	(	Same; open parameter list or open sub-expression
)	)	Same; close parameter list or close sub-expression
[	[	Same; open index
]	]	Same; close index
{	{	Same; open block or initialization list
}	}	Same; close block or initialization list
;	;	Same; in Go, can often be omitted if placed at the end of the line
:	:	Same; separator
@		Annotation indicator; not in Go

(*continued*)

Table 5-2. (*continued*)

Java	Go	Purpose
::		Method reference; not in Go
.	.	Same; field reference
,	,	Same; list or argument separator; not an operator in Go
~		No bit-wise; not in Go
?:		Ternary choice; not in Go
!	!	Same; logical not
->		Lambda expression declaration; not in Go
	<-	Send to or receive from (based on position) a channel; not in Java
instanceof (type)value	x. (y)	Test type; not in Go; Go has an assertion expression that casts a type and returns a Boolean if the cast is possible; can if test the Boolean
new	New make	Allocate and construct an object; Go has functions new and make instead. Also, Go structs can be declared and the address taken, which results in the same action. In Go, new does not run any constructor; that is the role of make

Both Java and Go have the relational operators (==, !=, <, <=, >, >=), but they do not always work the same. For example, to compare two strings s1 and s2 (or any other reference type) for equality in Java, one must use

if(s1.equals(s2)) { ... }

While in Go, one would use

if s1 == s2 { ... }

This comparison only works if the type is comparable. Most built-in types are. See the Go Language Specification for details. Slice, map, and function values are not comparable except to the nil value. Pointer, channel, and interface values can also be compared to nil.

The following has a different meaning in Java where the references are being compared (i.e., a sameness test):

```
if(s1 == s2) { ... }
```

This is a test to see if the s1 and s2 references are to the same object (i.e., are *aliases* of each other). To get the equivalent test in Go, a test like this is needed that compares the address (not values) of the strings:

```
if &s1 == &s2 { ... }
```

Java does not implicitly support relational tests of reference types; the type itself must provide some means to do that. For strings, the test could be

```
if(s1.compareTo(s2) < 0) { ... }
```

In Go, this would be

```
if s1 < s2 { ... }
```

This comparison only works if the type is ordered by some means. In Go, many types are. See the Go Language Specification for details. For example, strings are ordered as a byte array with shorter strings having implied additional zero cells.

Like in Java, the && and || operators are short circuit and may only evaluate the left argument.

The Go *take address* (&, aka *address of*) unary operator returns the address of its operand, which must be addressable (have a storage location; e.g., a constant and many expressions do not). Java has no equivalent to this action. For any value of type T, the & operator returns a value of type *T. One cannot take the address of a nil value.

Addressable values are

- A declared variable

- A pointer dereference (*p) – Returns p

- An array or slice index expression

- A struct field selector expression

- A composite (array, slice, map, struct) literal

Note for any expression exp that causes a panic, the expression &exp will also.

Go Operator Precedence

Java operator precedence is complex and will not be restated here (see the Java Language Specification for more details). Go precedence is generally simpler. Unary operators have precedence over binary operators.

Unary from high to low:

- Wrapping (...)
- Prefix + - * &
- Suffix [...] (...)

Note in Go ++ and -- are statements, not operators.

Binary from high to low:

- / % << >> & &^
- + - | ^
- == != < <= > >=
- &&
- ||

It is best practice that when in doubt use parentheses (...) to clarify precedence, especially for unary operators.

Note Go has the bit clear (&^) operator that Java does not.

The expression x &^ y is effectively x AND (NOT y).

Note Go does not have the binary not (~) operator Java does. Use the exclusive-or operator instead. For example:

```
func not32(x uint32) uint32 {
        return x ^ 0XFF_FF_FF_FF
}
func not64(x uint64) uint64 {
        return x ^ 0XFF_FF_FF_FF_FF_FF_FF_FF
}
```

or:

```
func not32(x uint32) uint32 {
        y := int32(-1)
        return x ^ uint32(y)
}
func not64(x uint64) uint64 {
        y := int64(-1)
        return x ^ uint64(y)
}
```

when run by

```
fmt.Printf("%X\n", not32(10))
fmt.Printf("%x\n", not64(10))
```

produces (note case difference)

```
FFFFFFF5
fffffffffffffff5
```

Go Built-in Functions

Go has several built-in functions, summarized in Table 5-3, for access to common behaviors. These functions in general are generic (or overloaded) in that they work on different data types. Java generally has type-specific methods that perform similar behavior.

Note that the Go built-in function names are not reserved keywords; the names may be used for other purposes (possibly hiding the built-in function).

Table 5-3. *Java and Go Common Function Comparison*

Java	Go	Purpose
.length, .length(), .size(), ...	len(...)	Get the length of a string, array, slice, map, channel
Varies per collection type	cap(...)	Get the capacity of a slice, map, channel; for some collections, the cap and len are the same
new ... or factory method	make(...) or new(...) or &<structureType>{}	Create (and for make initialize) a collection or structure; new returns a pointer to the allocated memory; for new no constructor call done in Go
System.arraycopy	copy(...)	Copies/moves array elements between same/ different arrays
Varies per collection type	delete(...)	Remove element from a map; generally used as a statement
Not in Java; some types have methods to do this	close(...)	Close a channel; generally used as a statement
(<type>)...	<type>(...)	Covert the parameter to the specified type (i.e., a cast)
throw <throwable>	panic(...)	Raise a panic; can send any type as the panic value, but sending an error instance is preferred; generally used as a statement; avoid using panic(nil)
try/catch	v := recover()	Catch a panic. Typically used in a deferred function
Varies per collection type; often add()	append(...)	Appends values to a slice; reallocate the slice if needed; should assign result to input slice
Not in Java	complex(...)	Make a complex value
Not in Java	real(...)	Get the real part of a complex value
Not in Java	imag(...)	Get the imaginary part of a complex value

CHAPTER 6

Go Types

In this chapter, we will drill down on Go's type system and how it differs from Java's type system. When done with this chapter, you should be able to clearly identify the similarities and differences between the Go and Java type systems.

Primitive/Built-in Types

Java and Go have similar primitive types. In Java, primitive types cannot be placed in collections (except arrays). This makes for a big difference from reference types. Also, primitive types cannot have methods. The notion of a primitive type has less meaning in Go as any type can be an element of a collection and any derived type can have methods.

The Go Boolean type, like in Java, is the simplest type. It has only `true` and `false` as values.

Both languages have character, signed integer, and floating-point types as numeric types. Go adds unsigned integers and `complex` numbers.

Go also has a pointer (somewhat like Java reference) type. Both languages have a `null` (called `nil` in Go) value. In Go, pointers can be converted into unsigned integers and vice versa. The use cases for this are not common and thus not discussed in this text. Mostly, this is done to interface with code written in C (aka CGo).

Numbers

Built-in numeric types:

- Signed integer types – `int8`, `int16`, `int32` (aka `rune`), `int64`, `int`
- Unsigned integer types – `uint8` (aka `byte`), `uint16`, `uint32`, `uint64`, `uint`

© Barry Feigenbaum 2022
B. Feigenbaum, *Go for Java Programmers*, https://doi.org/10.1007/978-1-4842-7199-5_6

- Floating types – `float32`, `float64`

- Complex types (as `real` and `imag` pairs) – `complex64`, `complex128`

The suffix number, if present, is the number of bits in the value.

Nonbuilt-in numeric types:

- Big integers – `Int`

- Big floats – `Float`

- Rational – `Rat` (of two `int64` values)

Note that Java has a set of library functions to emulate unsigned integers using its signed integers; the Go approach is better. Go has no big decimal type.

Like in Java, numeric literal values may have a base prefix:

- 0b, 0B – Binary, digits: 0, 1

- 0o, 0O – Octal, digits: 0, 1, 2, 3, 4, 5, 6, 7

- 0x, 0X – Hexadecimal, digits: 0, 1, 2, 3, 4, 5, 6, 7, 8, 9, A, B, C, D, E, F (or a, b, c, d, e, f)

Like in Java, numeric values may include an underscore ("_") between digits. Like Java, if a number starts with a "0" digit and no base indicator, it is in octal.

Floating-point numbers add an optional fraction ("." introducer) and/or an optional signed decimal exponent ("E" or "e" introducer for decimal numbers or "P" or "p" introducer for hexadecimal numbers – P exponents are rarely used).

Unlike in Java, there is no size indicator or limit on the value of a numeric literal.

Like in C, Go adds architecture-sensitive types (integers and pointers of 32- or 64-bit word sizes based on the architecture). Java explicitly hides architecture-dependent numeric characteristics.

Go adds complex floating-point types with imaginary literals, which are any numeric literal suffixed with "i". Go does not support polar notation for complex numbers.

Go uses untyped numeric literals of indefinite precision. These literals are automatically cast to the types needed for an expression or initialization. Java numeric literals have a specific type (`short`, `int`, etc.) suffix.

Characters and Strings

Go's built-in characters, called Rune, are signed 32-bit (int32) Unicode integers. Java uses unsigned 16-bit Unicode integers called char where larger characters need char pairs (awkward at best). Both are treated as integer numeric values.

Go has a built-in string type that is essentially an array of byte values (byte is an uint8 synonym) expected to represent a string of 0+ characters in UTF-8 form. Java has a *String* (JRE library) type that is essentially an array of Java char. Both Java and Go strings are immutable.

The length of a Go string is the number of bytes (not characters) in the string, while in Java, the length of a string is the number of char values. Note if ASCII encoding is used, a character and a byte are synonymous. Strings can be indexed up to their length to extract characters. Care must be taken when indexing them as bytes as they may contain UTF-8 (multibyte) characters. See the scanner package for help in processing runes.

For example:

```
s := "Hello World"
firstByte, hello, world, copy, lenS :=
    s[0], s[:5], s[6:], s[:], len(s)
```

Much like Java's charAt() method, single index expressions are [index].

Strings are immutable, so an expression like the following is illegal:

```
s[0] = 'a'
```

Much like Java's substring method, range index expressions are [{start}:{end+1}]; missing start == 0; missing end == length.

Go also has a byte *slice* type that is like a string, but not necessarily expected to be in UTF-8. It can be considered as a string if all bytes are ASCII.

All the numeric and string types can be compared (==, !=, >, >=, <, <=). Strings are compared as if they were byte arrays.

Note strings cannot be nil (but a pointer to a string can be). It is not legal to assign a nil value to any string variable. Use the len(s) function (vs. s == "") to test for empty strings.

Note most of the functions one sees in Java as static or instance methods of the String (or StringBuilder/Buffer) class are defined as functions in the Go fmt, strings, or strconv packages.

Reference vs. Pointer Types

Java has basically two classes of variable data:

1. Primitive value – Numbers and Booleans

2. Reference (or Object) – A value that is a locator for an object
    instance or `null`

    Objects are always allocated in the heap.

Go has a similar classification:

1. Value – Of any (non-pointer) type

2. Pointer – A value that is an address of another value, including
    another pointer, or `nil`

    Often, data values located by a pointer are generally allocated in
    the heap.

Note variables of an interface type can behave like either a value or a pointer.

A Java reference selects some object (or none if `null`). How references are
implemented is JVM dependent but could be implemented as shown in Figure 6-1,
where each reference is an index into an array of pointers to objects. Variables (A,
B, and C) are on the left. The reference index table is in the middle. The referenced
objects are on the right. This approach makes garbage collection easy as when unused
objects are removed and the remaining objects compacted in memory, only the index
table needs to be updated. Note that more than one reference can be to the same
index; this creates aliases.

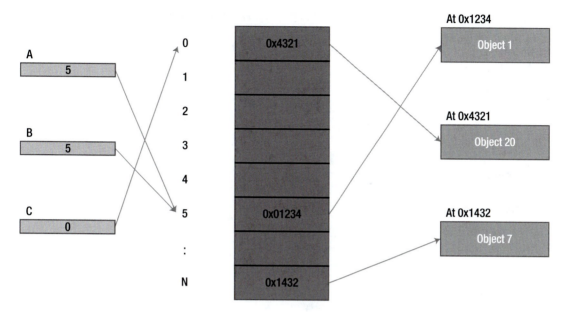

Figure 6-1. *Possible Java reference implementation*

In Go, as shown in Figure 6-2, a pointer is a direct reference to the data (an object or a value of any type). Variables (A, B, and C) are on the left. The referenced objects are on the right. Note that more than one variable can be to the same address; this creates aliases. This approach makes compaction during garbage collection hard and thus not often done.

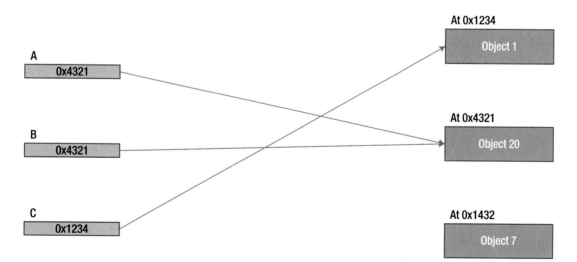

Figure 6-2. *Possible Go pointer implementation*

A Java reference is like a pointer, but it is generally implicitly dereferenced (as shown earlier). For example:

```
public class Xxx {
  public int x, y, z;
}
    :
Xxx xxx = new Xxx();
int v = xxx.z;
```

Here, the reference xxx refers to an *Xxx* instance on the heap, and it is dereferenced by the "." operator.

Similarly, in Go, using a struct instead of a class:

```
type Xxx struct{
      X, Y, Z int
}
    :
var xxx *Xxx  // creates a "zero" valued (or nil) pointer variable
xxx = &Xxx{} // assign instance address (a new is implied)
v := xxx.Z
```

or

```
var xxx = &Xxx{}  // alternate declaration
```

Here, the pointer xxx points to an *Xxx* instance, and it is implicitly dereferenced by the "." operator. This is logically equivalent to

```
v := (*xxx).Z
```

where the dereference is explicit.

Note it is legal in Go (but nonsensical in Java as xxx would have a `null` value) to do this:

```
var xxx Xxx // creates a "zero" valued variable
v := xxx.Z
```

In Go, it is possible to take the address of this instance:

```
pToXxx := &xxx
```

Java has no equivalent to this. In Go, it then becomes possible to update the xxx instance this way:

```
pToXxx.Z += 10
```

It is also possible to take the address of a field:

```
pToXxxZ := &(xxx.Z)
```

where it then becomes possible to update the xxx instance this way:

```
*pToXxxZ += 10
```

This ability to get the address of an object means Go must provide true *Closures*. A closure is a capturing of some values in a function call history, such that the function can get or set them for the lifetime of the function. Java has a limited form of closure where all the variables in the closure must be final so they cannot be changed. Go allows them to also be changed. Go programs often take advantage of this capability.

Drill Down on Basic Data Types

Like in Java, the Boolean, integer, and floating-point types combined with the character and string types are the commonly used types.

Boolean Type

Java and Go support several a Boolean type. See Table 6-1.

Table 6-1. *Boolean Types*

Java Type	Size (Bits)	Go Type	Go Examples
boolean	Not defined[1]	bool	true

Integer Types

Java and Go support several Integer types. See Table 6-2.

---

[1] Usually takes a byte of memory. See https://stackoverflow.com/a/383597/13103095

Table 6-2. *Integer Types*

Java Type	Size (Bits)	Go Type	Go Examples
byte	8	int8	10, −1
short	16	int16	10, −1
int	32	int32 or int[2]	10, −1
long	64	int64 or int[3]	10, −1
char	16	uint16	"A" or 10 (ASCII value)
	8	uint8 or byte	"A" or 10 (ASCII value)
	16	uint16	"A" or 10 (ASCII value)
	32	uint32	"A" or 10 (Rune value)
	64	uint64	10
	32	rune[4] (an int32 alias)	"A" and Unicode escapes

Note   Java has a library that provides unsigned operations on signed values.

Java has Object wrappers for all the integer types. Go has no such equivalents as they are not needed.

Floating-Point Types

Java and Go support several floating-point types. See Table 6-3.

---

[2] Based on 32-bit architecture.

[3] Based on 64-bit architecture.

[4] Go's version of char.

Table 6-3. *Float Types*

Java Type	Size (Bits)	Go Type	Go Examples
float	32	float32	10.0, 1e10
double	64	Float64	10.0, 1e10
	64	complex64	10.1+3.2i
	128	complex128	−4.0i

Java has Object wrappers for all the float types. Go has no such equivalents as they are not needed.

Note Go allows floating-point literals using nondecimal mantissa (exponents are still in decimal).

When nil Can Go Wrong

Java programmers often experience the dreaded *NullPointerException* (NPE – which should have been named *NullReferenceException* as Java does not have pointers). Go does not fix this; most dereferencing of a `nil` pointer results in a similar runtime panic. But Go's style of function calling tends to reduce the occurrence rate of NPE. Also, in Go, a `nil` can sometimes be used like a value; for example, a `nil` slice can be appended to, while in Java a `null` collection cannot be appended/added to. Again, this reduces the occurrences of panics in Go vs. NPEs in Java.

Often, functions in Java can return `null`. Frequently, programmers do not test the result first to see if it's `null` and thus get an NPE. In Go, testing the result of a function for failure is idiomatic and thus generally always done. For example, consider this typical Java pattern which can get NPE:

```
:
var xs = getXxx().toString();
:
```

131

One should, but often does not, code this:

```
var x = getXxx();
if(x != null) {
  var xs = x.toString()
  :
}
```

which in Go would be

```
if x, err := GetXxx(); err == nil {
    xs := x.String()
    :
}
```

where the chance that x is nil is low (0 in well-written Go) when err is nil (the opposite is also likely – x will be nil if err is not nil). Go does not have the equivalent of the Java Optional type that can help reduce NPEs in Java coding. Also, in Go one cannot declare a pointer type to be non-nil (i.e., always point to something).

Note in Go all variables have a "zero" value if they are not specifically initialized when created. With pointers, that is a nil value. With non-pointer types, it is generally a usable value.

Programmer-Defined Types

Both Go and Java allow programmers to create new data types. Java uses the class, interface, or enum constructs to do this. Go uses the type statement, which creates a named type based on preexisting or immediate (literal) base types. Java has no equivalent of this.

The base type can be a primitive type, an array type, a struct type, a map type, an interface type, a channel type, or pointers to any type (including other pointers). It can also be a declared type.

Each such declared type is distinct, even if the base type is the same. For example:

```
type weight      float64
type temperature float64
type age         float64
```

are all different types (cannot be directly assigned to each other or compared) even though they share the same base type (float64). The preceding example could also be written as

```
type (
      weight      float64
      temperature float64
      age         float64
)
```

Given:

```
var w weight = 10
var a age = 10
```

The following will not compile as the types are not the same (even though all are both based on float64); this is one way Go adds more type safety:

```
var sum = w + a
```

But this will compile (even if nonsensical) as the types are now the same:

```
var sum = age(w) + age(a)   // second age(...) not required
```

Of course, one should not do something like this unless it makes sense in the circumstance.

Go supports creating aliases to existing types like this:

```
type weight = float64
type temperature = float64
type age = float64
```

Here, these new types are all the same type (vs. different if the "=" is missing). This is like how byte is a built-in alias for uint8. This feature should be used with caution.

Consider this example (adapted from the Go Language Specification example):

```
type TimeZone int
const (
      EST TimeZone = -(iota + 5)
      CST
      MST
```

```
        PST
        AKST
        _    // blank value
        _    // blank value
        HST
)
func (tz TimeZone) String() string {
        return fmt.Sprintf("GMT%+dh", tz)
}
func (tz1 TimeZone) Difference(tz2 TimeZone) int {
        return int(tz1) - int(tz2)
}
func Gap(tz1, tz2 TimeZone) int {
        return tz1.Difference(tz2)
}
```

Here, a new type *TimeZone*, based on the int type (really should be a float type as some time zones are offset from the hour by 30 minutes (or 0.5 hours)), has associated constants (two as placeholders), methods, and an independent utility function. It also implements the fmt.Stringer interface.

This concept of creating distinct types from preexisting types can help make Go code much safer and arguably clearer (as the type names help make the code more self-explanatory). It is impossible to accidentally (no explicit conversion) assign a value of one type to another type, for example, assigning a weight value to a temperature variable.

This can prevent scale and loss of precision errors that Java is more vulnerable to. In Java, variable naming schemes can partially provide more safety, but Go does this one better.

To make a Go aggregate type as an approximation of a Java class type, one would do something like this:

```
type Person struct {
        Age          float64
        Name         string
        PlaceOfBirth string
        privateValue int32
}
```

134

vs. for Java:

```java
public class Person {
  public double age;
  public String name;
  public String placeOfBirth;
  private int    privateValue;
}
```

Note Go uses the capitalization of the field (and type) names to determine private vs. public visibility.

Like in Java, declarations differ for aggregate members vs. local variables.

In Go, local and global variables are declared with the "var," "const," or "func" statements. Struct fields do not use the "var" introducer. Interface functions do not use the "func" introducer.

In a struct, fields of structs are declared like this:

```go
type S struct {
    s string
    x, y, z int
    f func(int, int) int
}
```

where there is no permitted initial (beyond the zero value) field value. The initial value must come from a struct literal:

```go
var s = S{"abc", 0, 1, 2, nil}
```

or a constructor function:

```go
var s = NewS("abc", 0, 1, 2, func(x, y int) int {
    return x * y
})
```

where the second s is of pointer (*S) type. The NewS function must be coded by a person; the Go compiler will not generate one. All constructor (aka factory) functions of concrete (e.g., struct) type, like the new function, should return pointers. In Go, by convention, factory methods (methods that create instances as their primary function) start with New, such as New<typename>. If the package defines only one type, then the name is, again by convention, just New.

135

For example:

```go
func NewS(name string, a, b, c int, f func(int, int) int) (s *S) {
        s = &S{}  // or s = new(S)
        s.s = name
        s.x = a
        s.y = b
        s.z = c
        s.f = f
        return
}
```

or more briefly:

```go
func NewS(name string, a, b, c int, fx func(int, int) int) (s *S) {
        s = &S{name, a, b, c, fx}
        return
}
```

Note the variable name differences (a vs. x, ...).

Note no code body was provided for function fx in the S struct definition. Here, fx is a variable holding a function (like a reference), not the function itself. Any function definition is done outside the structure.

In an interface, methods are declared like this:

```go
type Openable interface {  // or Opener (especially if 1 function)
        Open([]byte) (int, error)
        Close() error
}
```

Unlike in Java, only function signatures can be defined in Go interfaces.

Note no code body was provided for any function. Like in Java, interface methods are always purely abstract. Go has no equivalent of (static final) fields in an interface nor concrete (default) methods in an interface.

Like in Java, it is better if factory (and similar) functions return interfaces, not concrete types. This allows the factory to return any type that meets the interface. In Java, this means

```java
public <I extends Integer> List<I> makeIntegerList() { ... }
```

is a better choice than this definition:

```
public <I extends Integer> ArrayList<I> makeIntegerList() { ... }
```

Similarly, it is better in Go to do something like this:

```
type IntegerList interface {
    Len() int
    GetAt(index int) int
    SetAt(index int, v int)
}
func makeIntegerList() IntegerList { ... }
```

Such factory methods, like the new function, should return pointers. Alternate factory names, like Make<typename> (after the various make functions), are allowed, and they can return an instance (vs. a pointer to an instance) if that is best. Consider:

```
func NewIntegerList() *IntegerList { ... }
```

which can return any type that implements IntegerList. Or:

```
func MakeIntegerList() IntegerList {
    return *NewIntegerList()
}
```

Remember to take care when not passing and returning pointers, as the value is copied into and out of the function. This can increase overhead and in some cases cause behavior issues.

Factory methods rarely have a receiver argument. An exception can be a copy or prototype-based method, perhaps named Copy or Clone:

```
func (il *IntegerList) Clone() *IntegerList { ... }
```

Arrays

Both Go and Java support dense arrays (one-dimensional fixed-length packed lists) of any single (homogeneous) type. Both use zero-based indexing. Both are set to a fixed length at creation time that cannot change. Both support multidimensional arrays in similar ways. Like in Java, arrays give $O(N)$ search and $O(1)$ access.

All Java arrays live on the heap; Go may allow arrays to also live on the call stack.

Arrays are declared using the [<length>]type syntax. For example:

```
var x [10]int              // array of 10 ints, each set to 0
var x [10]string           // array of 10 strings, each set to ""
var x [10][10]int          // array of 10x10 ints, each set to 0
var x = [3]int{1,2,3}      // array of 3 ints, each set to provided values
```

The Java equivalent is

```
var x = new int[10];
var x = new String[10]; // need a loop to create the 10 empty strings
var = new int[10][];     // need a loop to create the 10 nested arrays
var x = new int[]{1,2,3};
```

In Go, the array length is part of its type, so [10]int and [20]int are of different types. This is not true in Java.

Arrays of the same type can be compared (==, !=, >, >=, <, <=).

Array elements are accessed by zero-origin index expressions as follows:

```
a := [...]int{1,2,3}  // has implied length of 3
a[0] = a[1]
```

Here, len(a) and cap(a) are, by the definition of an array, both 3. Like in Java, an index access outside the bounds of the array causes a panic.

Like in Java, arrays can have literal values. Often, the literals imply the length of the array. Some examples:

```
var x [...]int{1,2,3}      // array of 3 ints; each set to provided values
var x [10]int{1:1,5:5,6}   // array of 10 ints; select values set, others 0
```

Note that array literals can have explicit indexes (constant expressions of int type). All or some entries can have indexes. If all indexes are present, the index order can be arbitrary. Any missing indexes are the next value in sequence. Any supplied indexes must be unique. So, the preceding example is the equivalent of

```
var x = [10]int{0,1,0,0,0,5,6,0,0,0}
```

which could also be written as

```
var x = [10]int{0,1,0,0,0,5,6}
```

where the last values are implied.

An important difference from Java is in Go assigning an array makes a copy. For example:

```
var a1 = [...]int{1,2,3}
var a2 = a1
a2[0] = 10
```

In Go, a1[0] is still one. In Java, a1[0] is also now ten. This is because in Java a2 is an alias of a1. This happens because in Java all arrays are heap objects.

The copy function (like Java's System.arraycopy method) makes it easy to copy the elements of one array into another array. The source and target arrays can be the same, which allows elements to be moved to different indexes in the array:

```
array1 := [...]int{1,2,3,4}
copy(array1[N:], array1[N+1:])    // shift (overwrite) elements down
array1[len(array1)-1] = 0         // set zero value (optional)
```

An array can be converted into a slice (next section) on the array by taking a range across all elements:

```
var a1slice = a1[:]
```

Note when you pass arrays as function arguments or return values, the array is copied, just like with assignment. Pass a pointer to the array (or preferably a slice on the array) to allow access to the original array.

Note that the direct use of arrays in Go is less common than in Java; slices are used much more frequently.

Slices

Like Java *Vectors* or *ArrayLists*, Go allows a variable-sized Array-like construct called a *slice*. A slice is a built-in (vs. library) type. Slices resemble arrays but without a predeclared size. Slices are generic (in that different instances can hold different types, but just one type per slice instance). A special case is []interface{} which can hold any type (similar to List<Object> in Java). Unlike in Java, in Go there are no alternative *List* interface implementations; only one implementation is available. Like in Java, slices give *O(N)* search and *O(1)* access.

Slices are declared using the [ ]type syntax. For example:

```
var x []int          // slice of ints
var x []string       // slice of strings
var x [][]int        // slice of slice of ints
var x []int{1,2,3}   // slice of 3 ints, each set to provided values
```

Note that slice declarations look like array declarations, but with the length value missing.

In most cases, one uses slices in Go, not arrays. The slices implicitly wrap an array.

Empty slices are generally explicitly created with the make function. For example:

```
var x = make([]int, 0, 10)      // slice of up to 10 ints
var x = make([]string, 0, 10)   // slice of up to 10 strings
var x = make([][]int, 0, 10)    // a loop to create the 10 nested slices
```

Each example slice has an initial length of zero and a capacity of ten. If only the length (first number) is provided, the capacity is set to the length. Note the slice is fully allocated with the zero value:

```
var x = make([]int, 10)         // slice of 10 ints, each 0
```

As an alternative to using make, but less typically done, a slice can be created like this:

```
var x = []int{} // or []int{1, 2, 3 } to initialize
```

Note that make and new are interrelated. The following examples are equivalent:

```
var x = make([]int, 5, 10)
var x = new([10]int)[0:5]
```

This shows how a slice is a wrapper on an array.

The preceding example also shows how it is possible to select subelements (here the first five) from an array using indexes. Java cannot do this in the language, but most collection types have methods that can do this. This works in Go because a slice is a built-in type.

Under the covers, it is like (not actually done) a slice is defined as follows:

```
type Slice[T any] struct { // slices behave as if generic
  data *[cap]T  // data "held" by the slice (an array)
```

```
  len int        // current length; always <= cap
  cap int        // max capacity; can append until exceeded
}
```

If you need the slice to hold more than its current capacity of items, it needs to be expanded with the append(...) built-in function. Java *List* implementations do not need to be explicitly expanded. For example:

```
x = append(x, 100)      // add 100 to x increasing its length by 1
```

If x's capacity is exhausted, it will be recreated with more capacity; thus, the assignment back to x is necessary. Append can return either the input slice or a new slice if the slice's capacity (not length) needs to be extended. Therefore, slices have both a length (actual count of elements) and capacity (maximum count of elements), so an extension is not necessarily needed on each addition of an item. This is an optimization.

From the preceding structure, it is easy to see how different slice instances can access (share) the same data. The data pointer just points to some shared array. Also, each slice can possibly point to a different index in the shared array. For example:

```
slice1 := make([]int, 5, 10)  // len: 5, cap: 10
slice2 := slice1[2:5]         // len: 3 (5-2), cap: 8 (10-2)
```

Here, slice1 and slice2 share a common array of data (of length 10), but slice1 points to the first element of the array, and slice2 points at the third element. Each slice has different length and capacity values. The slice2 length and capacity values must be within the limits of slice1.

A slice is a wrapper on either an array or another slice (a slice of a slice…). As described earlier, a slice is a view into a subrange of the backing array or slice. Changing elements via any slice can be seen by the other slices. Expanding a slice can replace the backing array for that slice.

The Java equivalent is

```
List<Integer> x = new ArrayList<>(10);
List<String> x = new ArrayList<>(10); // need a loop to add the 10 empty
                                                     strings
List<List<Integer>> x = new ArrayList<>(10); // need a loop to add the 10
                                                     nested lists
List<Integer> x = new ArrayList<>(10); // need a loop to add the values
```

Note in Java if the list can be immutable, a more literal form (with values) is possible:

```
List<Integer> x = List.of(1,2,3);
```

Slice elements are accessed by zero-origin index expressions as follows:

```
a := []int{1,2,3}  // a slice literal
a[0] = a[1]
```

Here, `len(a)` and `cap(a)` are both 3. Like in Java, an index access outside the length of the slice causes a panic.

Consider this definition:

```
var x = []int{1:1,5:5,6} // slice of ints
```

Note that slice literals can have explicit indexes (constant expressions of int type). All or some entries can have indexes. If all indexes are present, the index order can be arbitrary. Any missing indexes are the next value in sequence. Any supplied indexes must be unique. So, the preceding example is the equivalent of

```
var x = []int{0,1,0,0,0,5,6}
```

The indexed form of initialization can be useful when the slice is sparsely filled.

The copy function makes it easy to copy the elements of one slice into another slice. The source and target slices can be the same, which allows elements to be moved in the slice. For example, to remove the Nth element from a slice, you can do this:

```
slice1 := []int{1,2,3,4}            // slice to remove from
copy(slice1[N:], slice1[N+1:])      // shift (overwrite) elements down
slice1 = slice1[: len(slice1) - 1]  // remove (now dup) last element
```

In Go, like with Java arrays, multidimensional slices are implemented as slices containing slices. This can be less efficient in storage usage. To make such slices both regular and as dense as possible, use a single dimensional slice and partition it into rows by code. Given:

```
type PackedIntSlice struct {
    width, height int
    data []int
}
```

```go
func NewPackedIntSlice(width, height int) (pas *PackedIntSlice) {
    if width <= 0 || height <= 0 {
        panic(errors.New("size must be positive"))
    }
    pas = &PackedIntSlice{width, height, make([]int, width * height)}
    return
}
func(pas *PackedIntSlice) Get(x, y int) int {
    pas.check(x, y)
    return pas.data[x * pas.width + y]
}
func(pas *PackedIntSlice) Set(x, y int, v int) {
    pas.check(x, y)
    pas.data[x * pas.width + y] = v
}
func(pas *PackedIntSlice) check(x, y int) {
    if x < 0 || x >= pas.width || y < 0 || y >= pas.height {
        panic(ErrIndexOutOfRange)
    }
}
var ErrIndexOutOfRange = errors.New("index out of range")
```

To make a dense 100x200 slice of integers, you can do this:

```go
var packed = NewPackedIntSlice(100, 200)
topLeft, topRight, bottomLeft, bottomRight :=
    packed.Get(0, 0), packed.Get(0, 199),
    packed.Get(99, 0), packed.Get(99, 199)
```

This concept can be extended to higher dimensions, as often used by mathematicians and scientists. Other types, like Booleans, floats, complex, or even strings, can be used. Several Go libraries do just this.

Maps

Like Java, Go supports *Hashtable-* or *HashMap-*like associative arrays. Go has a built-in (vs. library) *map* type for this purpose. Maps are *Generic* (in that they can have keys and hold values of any type, but just one type per map instance). Like in Java, maps give *O(1)* lookup.

Maps are declared using the `map[keyType]valueType` syntax. For example:

```
var x map[string]int          // map of ints with string keys
var x map[int]string          // map of strings with int keys
var x map[string]interface{}  // map of any type with string keys
```

A map only has one entry per distinct key. Like with Java, keys must be hash-able and comparable (thus generally primitive) types. Unlike in Java, in Go there are no alternative *Map* interface implementations; only one implementation is available. The enumeration order of a Go map is undefined and possibly random. This prevents the programmer from depending on any predetermined order. In Java, the order is fixed for a map of a certain type and key set (and sometimes key insertion order); this can be deliberate.

Note Go does have an approximation of the `map` type in the `sync.Map` type. It is used for safe concurrent access, but it is not exactly equivalent (substitutable for) to the built-in `map` type.

Maps are generally explicitly created with the `make` function. For example:

```
var x = make(map[string]int, 10)          // empty map with capacity 10
```

The capacity of a map is automatically expanded; the initial value is an optimization and can generally be omitted but should be set to a value >= the maximum expected item count.

The Java equivalent is

```
Map<String,Integer> x = new HashMap<>(10);
```

Unlike Java, Go can create literal maps by supplying key/value pairs in any order, each separated by a colon (":"). Such maps are mutable. For example:

```
var m = map[string]int{"key1":1, "key2":2, "key3":3}
```

or

```
var m = map[int]string{1:"key1", 2:"key2", 3:"key3"}
```

All values in such a literal must have a key. Both the key and value are expressions. Unless single terms, they should be enclosed in parentheses. If constant expressions, the keys must be unique:

```
var m = map[int]string{(1 + 5):"key6", 2:"key2", (3*6):("key3"+"key6")}
```

Map elements are accessed by a key value, which must support the == and != operators, as follows:

```
a := map[int]int{1:3,2:2,3:1} // a map literal
a[0] = a[1]
```

Here, len(a) is 3 (cap() on a map is not allowed). Unlike with Java, an undefined key returns the zero (vs. nil) value of the value type. To determine if a key is contained in the map, a modified get expression is needed:

```
valueAt99, ok := a[99]
```

Here, the ok value will be false if the key is not defined, else it will be true, and the value variable is set. This is like the Java Map.contains() method. Compare with this Java example:

```
var a = new HashMap<Integer,Integer>();
:
if(a.contains(99)) {
  var valueAt99 = a.get(99);
  :
}
```

vs.

```
var valueAt99 = a.get(99);
if(valueAt99 != null) {
  :
}
```

In Go, map keys can be removed by using the built-in delete(<map>,<key>) function.

Unlike Java, Go does not support a Set type. But one can be simulated, such as a set of integers, with a map type as follows:

```
s := map[int]bool{1:true, 20:true, 50:true}
```

where the key can be any comparable type, but the value is always (by convention for ease of testing) Boolean. Membership can be tested this way:

```
if s[5] { // is 5 in set }
```

While not specified explicitly in Go, a map type is conceptually (not legal Go) described by the following type:

```
type map[K builtin, V any] struct {  // maps are generic
  data      *[hashLimit][]mapEntry[K builtin, V any]
  cap       int
  hashLimit int   // often a prime number
}

func (m *map) hash(k *K) (h int) { ... } // 0 <= h < hashLimit

type mapEntry[K builtin, V any] struct {
  key   K
  value *T  (or just T for a primitive type (say int, string))
}
```

The cap field is a hint on how big to make the first dimension of data. The data array+slice can be replaced (recomputed) as the number of keys grows or shrinks. The array of data is indexed by the hash of the key value. Its size is based on the number of possible hash values. The key types are limited to data types the Go compiler understands (can hash) and are immutable (such as numbers or strings). The MapEntry slice holds key/value pairs where the key hashes to the same value.

When a map is copied, the internals are copied but not the data contents. Therefore, a map acts much like a pointer type.

Functions

In Java, functions (called *methods*) are a source time–only construct. They are not runtime values. Java has a concept of a *Lambda*, which looks like a function literal, but under the covers it is syntactic sugar that is effectively an instance of a compiler-written class with a single method conforming to the lambda signature (defined by a @FunctionalInterface annotation). In Go, a function is a value just like any integer or a string (i.e., its first class).

Go functions can have 0+ arguments and can have 0+ return values. A function with no return values is like a void method in Java. Functions are defined using the following pattern:

```
func <name>({<arg>{,<arg>}...}) {(<return>{,<return>}...)} {
    :
}
```

where <arg> and <return> are of the form <name>{, <name>} <type>.

If there is only one unnamed return value, this can be reduced to

```
func <name>({<arg>{,<arg>}...}) <type> {
    :
}
```

If there is no return value, this can be reduced to

```
func <name>({<arg>{,<arg>}...}) {
    :
}
```

The author recommends that all return values be named as a matter of habit. This creates local variables that can be assigned inside the function and allows all returns to be expressed without any values.

For example:

```
func xxx(x, y, z int) (result int, err error) {
    :
    if err != nil {
        return
    }
```

```
      :
   result = x * y * z
      :
   return
}
```

where the `return` is the same everywhere, and the last assignment to the returned variables is used. Often, this is the zero value the return variables were created with.

Some Gophers recommend against this pattern, especially for longer functions where the explicit return with values provides more local context. If functions are kept short, this is less of an issue. Even if the named variables are not used (i.e., the `return` has values), they create better *self-documentation* for the code.

The preceding example is equivalent to

```
func xxx(x, y, z int) (int, error) {
      :
   err := ...
   if err != nil {
         return nil, err
   }
      :
   var result = x * y * z
      :
   return result, nil
}
```

The last (or only) <arg> of a function can look like this:

```
name... type
```

which means the argument can be repeated zero or more time. This is referred to as a *variadic argument* (or a *vararg*). Java has a similar feature, for example:

```
void xxx(String... strings) { ... }
```

Like in Java, any vararg parameter must be the last parameter.

Under the covers, the implementation is slightly different.

In Java, the vararg is passed as a possibly empty (if no arguments were provided) array of the declared type. This means the following form is effectively the same from the method's point of view:

```
void xxx(String[] strings) { ... }
```

In Go, the vararg is passed as a non-empty slice of the declared type or `nil` if no arguments were provided.

At times, it is desired to send the contents of a slice to a vararg parameter as individual values. To do this, use this form:

```
aStringSlice := []string{"123", "456", "789"}
xxx(aStringSlice...)
```

An alternate form of a function (but not method) declaration is

```
var <name> := func({<arg>{,<arg>}...}) {(<return>{,<return>}...)} {
    :
}
```

This creates a function literal (often also a closure; we will talk about closures more later in this text). Here, the function has no name; the `<name>` is just a variable set to an instance of the function literal. Used this way, these function literals (but not declared/named function) can create closures on all local variables in the calling context used in the body of the function. This is often seen in functions passed to the `defer` or `go` statements.

It is not legal to declare a named function inside another function, but a function literal is allowed as follows:

```
func xxx() {
    func yyy() {          // illegal
    }
    yyy := func() {       // legal
    }
}
```

This way of defining functions through assignment partially explains[5] a limit Go has relative to Java. Go, like C, does not permit *overloaded* functions. An overloaded function is one of a set of distinct functions, in the same scope, that has the same name but different arguments than another function.

For a Java (or C++) programmer, this can be a big loss. Instead of using overloading, one must use (author's term) *multiloading* (sometimes called *name mangling*) where the function name is adjusted (often via suffixes) to make it unique. For example, in Java, one might make these functions (ignoring a Java Generics–based approach):

```
int max(int... values) { ... }
long max(long... values) { ... }
double max(double... values) { ... }
while in Go it would be (say):
func maxInt(values ...int32) int32 { ... }        // or maxInt32
func maxLong(values ...int64) int64 { ... }        // or maxInt64
func maxDouble(values ...float64) float64 { ... } // or maxFloat64
```

Like in Java, Go has function parameters and return values that are passed by value which means they are copied into and out of the function. Changes made to the copy of parameters in the function are not seen by the caller.

For larger (say arrays) or complex (say structs) data types, this copying can be expensive. Often, a pointer to these types is passed instead. Note when a slice is passed, the slice itself (which is small) is copied, not the backing data array (which can be shared between slices), so slices are most often passed by value unless they are optional values. Similar for map types except it is rare to pass them by pointer unless they are created as a function output.

To pass mutable data in Java, one must pass in an object (say an array, a collection, or a wrapper object) that the function can modify. In Go, it is similar except a pointer (vs. reference) to some mutable object is passed in.

Note that the Go map type is effectively always passed this way; any change made to a map passed into a function can be seen by the function's caller.

---

[5] Also, the Go compiler can be faster if it does not need to sort out overloaded functions.

It is even possible, in certain contexts, to set the named variable to a different function that has the same signature. This kind of variable is often called a *function adapter*. This is common to some languages, such as *JavaScript*. In Java, this is most often seen by use of variables of a *@FunctionalInterface* type and assigning lambdas to them.

In Go, often function signatures are defined as types to enable this. For example:

```go
type MultFunction func(x... int) int
```

and used like this:

```go
func DoFunction(f MultFunction) int {
    return f(1)
}
```

where a function (note not a pointer to the function) is passed as the argument.

Most importantly, in Go a function instance can be passed into and/or returned by a different function. This means functions are "first class" in Go (vs. in Java where they are not). This gives Go a Java *Lambda*-like feature. It also enables a rich, functional programming-like ability to compose functions.

Functions that take functions as a parameter or return functions are called "second-order functions." This can be expanded (rarely) to "third-order functions" and beyond. If neither a parameter nor a return is a function, then the function is "first-order."

Go functions can exit in these ways:

1) Return a result – When a failure is not possible by design.

2) Return either a success or a failure value – A special value(s) indicates a failure.

3) Return a value and a success/failure Boolean – A Boolean value is often named ok.

4) Return a value and a possibly nil error – Generally the preferred error reporting mechanism; an error value is often named err.

5) Raise a panic – Only if the issue is rare or because of bad programming (e.g., divide by zero); panics are considered abnormal exits like Java *Error* exceptions.

Note that the preceding *result* may be multiple values itself. Idiomatically, any special Boolean or error return value, if declared, should be the last one.

Methods As Functions

In Go, a function associated with a type is called a *Method*. A method is declared like a function with a special additional argument using this pattern:

```
func (<receiver>) <name>({<arg>{,<arg>}...}) {(<return>{,<return>}...)}  {
       :
}
```

where `<receiver>` is of the form `<name> <type>`. There can be only one receiver. Note this is not the same as

```
func <name>(<receiver>, {<arg>{,<arg>}...}) {(<return>{,<return>}...)}  {
       :
}
```

which, while legal, is not considered a method of the receiver type. This form is more like a static method in Java.

The receiver type is the associated type that the function is a method of. This method can see any fields, even private ones, of that type (assuming the type is a struct type). Note that these methods are not declared inside the containing type but are separate (possibly even in a different source file of the same package; quite different from Java). For example:

```
type SomeStruct struct {
       x,y,z int
}

func (ss *SomeStruct) X() int {
       return ss.x
}
func (ss *SomeStruct) SetX(v int) {
       ss.x = v
}
```

```
func (ss *SomeStruct) Z() int {
    return ss.z
}
func (ss *SomeStruct) SetZ(v int) {
    ss.z = v
}
```

could give public access to private values, like with Java access methods. Go makes less use of access methods; often all fields are made public. Unlike Java, Go has no consistent naming convention for such access methods. Java follows the (isXxx|getXxx)/setXxx naming pattern. Some Gophers use the Xxx/SetXxx pattern.

The <receiver> can be of the direct receiver named type or a pointer to the receiver named type (as used earlier). It cannot be directly a pointer or interface type. If the receiver needs to be changed in the method, a pointer must be passed; else a value can be passed.

If a type has multiple methods, it is recommended that all methods take either a receiver or a pointer to a receiver and not some mixture. The author recommends always passing a pointer for struct types.

Note in Go there is no equivalent to the Java this and super references to the receiver. There is no implicit use of this. An explicit name must always be used (like in *Python*). In Go, the receiver name can be anything. It is not restricted to be this as in Java. Some Gophers use the name self (or me) for this purpose (like in Python), but more often some abbreviation of the receiver type name is used.

Any Declared Type Can Have Custom Functions

Types based on primitive types can also have methods. This is a big difference from Java and is a powerful feature. For example, consider some well-known temperature ranges (which can be converted to each other):

```
type Celsius float64
func (c Celsius) ToFahrenheit() Fahrenheit {
    return Fahrenheit(c * RatioFahrenheitCelsius + 32)
}
func (c Celsius) String() string {
    return fmt.Sprintf("%GC", float64(c))
}
```

```go
type Fahrenheit float64
func (f Fahrenheit) ToCelsius() Celsius {
      return Celsius((f - 32) / RatioFahrenheitCelsius )
}
func (f Fahrenheit) String() string {
      return fmt.Sprintf("%GF", float64(f))
}
```

Often with a new type, one would provide some constants, such as

```go
const (
      FreezingPointFahrenheit Fahrenheit = 32.0
      BoilingPointFahrenheit Fahrenheit = 212.0
      FreezingPointCelsius Celsius = 0.0
      BoilingPointCelsius Celsius = 100.0
      RatioFahrenheitCelsius = 9.0/5.0
)
```

There is a standard interface in the fmt package called *Stringer* defined as follows:

```go
type Stringer interface {
      String() string
}
```

This interface is Go's alternative to all Java Object subtypes implementing toString(). In Java, a toString() method (inherited from *Object* by default) is always provided; this is not true in Go. The various formatters (such as Sprintf) provided by the fmt package can format most types, even if no String() method is provided. The "%#v" formatter will show labeled struct fields.

Both the *Celsius* and *Fahrenheit* types implicitly implement this interface and are thus *Stringer* types and can be used wherever a Stringer type is allowed. A common example would be

```go
fmt.Printf("Celsius: %s\n", Celsius(100.1))
```

which would print:

```
Celsius: 100.1C
```

Functions As Values

In Go, functions are values, just like numbers and strings, and thus can be assigned and used in similar ways. Each function has a built-in action that invokes the function. This happens when the function value is followed by a call operator (parenthesis), such as

```go
var identity = func(x int) int {
    return x
}
:
var fx = identity
var result = fx(1)  // fx followed by the call operator
```

Here, the function literal is called indirectly. It is the same as calling `identity(1)`. Declared function types can have additional actions. For example:

```go
type MyFunction func(int) int
func (f MyFunction) Twice(x int) int {
    return f(x) + f(x)
}
:
var xf = MyFunction(identity)
var aCharm = xf.Twice(1) + xf(1)
```

It is possible, but rare, to have a function pointer, such as

```go
var fp *MyFunction
```

```go
var result = (*fp)(1)
```

Note that calling a function variable with a `nil` value causes a panic.

Unlike in Java, Go has functions that can return multiple values, such as

```go
type Returns3 func(int) (int, int, int)
type Takes3 func(x, y, z int) int
:
var f Takes3 = ...
var g Returns3 = ...
```

155

These could be used like this:

```
a, b, c := g(1)
result := f(a, b, c)
```

Go has a convenient shortcut for this composition of functions with matching return and argument counts and types:

```
result := f(g(1))
```

Go functions provide a feature not fully available in Java. A Go function literal can act as a *closure* (a block of code that captures variables defined outside it to make them live for as long as the block is alive). In Java, only read-only variables can be captured this way, while in Go read-write variables can be captured.

This is a powerful feature, but it has an issue that often trips up developers. Consider this example:

```
for _, v := range []int{1,2, ..., N} {
    go func() {
        fmt.Printf("v=%v\n", v)
    }()
}
```

Here, the func() captures the v variable. What N values will be printed?

Many people would expect the values 1 to N to be printed in some apparently random order. While possible, this is not likely.

The v variable inside the goroutine is the same v as in the for loop (in Java, if supported, which it is not, it would be a copy of the outer v), and it is captured by the goroutine and eventually printed.

The most likely (depending on how fast the goroutine instances start relative to the execution of the for loop) situation is there are N occurrences of the value N printed. This can happen because some of the goroutines do not start until after the for loop ends, which is likely.

There are two common fixes to this issue:

1) Send the v value as a goroutine parameter:

```go
for v := range []int{1,2,..., N} {
        go func(v int) {
                fmt.Printf("v=%v\n", v)
        }(v)
}
```

Here, the v value is copied to the parameter when the goroutine is called (not when it runs), and thus it is the current iteration's value. Note that the name of the goroutine parameter can be (and should be for clarity) different.

2) Send the v value as a distinct variable:

```go
for v := range []int{1,2,..., N} {
        vx := v
        go func() {
                fmt.Printf("v=%v\n", xv)
        }()
}
```

Here, the v value is copied to the vx local variable before the goroutine is called, and thus xv is the variable captured by the goroutine. Since xv is created on each iteration of the for loop, it is a different storage location inside each goroutine instance's capture.

Note that this subtle variant also works:

```go
for v := range []int{1,2,..., N} {
        v := v // only change from original loop
        go func() {
                fmt.Printf("v=%v\n", v)
        }()
}
```

Here, the new local variable inside the block happens to have the same name as the variable outside the block. It hides the for loop's value. This is a commonly used idiom in Go.

A function declaration may omit a body. This indicates the function is defined as a *foreign* function (in a different language (often C)). For example, a binary search written in C could be accessed with this declaration:

```
// Search for float64 value v in float64 slice values.
// Values must be sorted.
// Returns the index or < 0 if not found.
func BinarySearchDouble(values []float64, v float64) int
```

The techniques for writing such foreign functions are beyond the scope of this text. See the *CGo* facility at the Go online documentation site. Foreign functions are often used to access some existing function written in C, such as a database system. CGo functions must be specially coded to consume or return Go data types and run in the Go runtime environment.

Note that single-line functions can be entered in a more concise way. For example:

```
func square(x float64) float64 { return x * x }
```

This is generally not the recommended form, except perhaps for anonymous functions passed to other functions. For example:

```
type Floater func(x, y float64) float64
func DoFloater(f Floater, x, y float64) float64 {
        return f(x, y)
}
```

used as

```
var v = DoFloater(func(x, y float64) float64 { return x * y }, 2.5, 3)
```

which is much like the Java implementation:

```
@FunctionalInterface public interface Floater {
    double op(double x, double y);
}
```

```
public double doFloater(Floater f, double x, double y) {
  return f.op(x, y);
}
```

used as

```
var v = doFloater((x, y) -> x * y , 2.5, 3);
```

Or the more verbose, but equivalent, full representation that is much like the Go version:

```
var v = doFloater((double x, double y) -> { return x * y; }, 2.5, 3);
```

To encourage their use, Java has very concise options for writing lambda calls, including method references. Go is often not as concise.

Structs

Both Go and Java support aggregates of multiple (heterogeneous) types. In Java, these aggregates are *Classes* (and to a lesser extent, Enums). In Go, these aggregates are *Structs*. Classes are conceptually an extension to a struct that supports full Object-Oriented Programming (OOP) tenants. Go has no concept of an OOP class.

Structs, like classes, consist of 0+ fields for data/state and 0+ methods for behavior. Structs do not support inheritance, but a struct can contain another struct, so direct (vs. referential as is supported by Java) *composition* is supported. Struct fields can be of any type, including other struct types.

The lack of OOP is perhaps the biggest difference between Go and Java as languages. It has profound impacts on how one codes Java vs. Go programs. Go is not an OOP language, even though many pundits claim it is.

This is not to say Go is lacking vs. Java. It is different from Java. Go's alternatives to Java's OOP are either positive or negative based on your point of view. For example, Go's interface concept differences (e.g., Duck Typing) can offer more flexibility than Java's interfaces provide.

Go has features that allow a programmer to emulate many OOP language features, but OOP is not built-in to the language itself. The Go designers considered several OOP features to be too complex (and perhaps runtime inefficient), and thus they were deliberately not included.

An example struct definition (defined as a type, which is typical – literal structs are also allowed wherever a custom type name is allowed):

```go
type Person struct {
        Name string
        Address string
        Age float32
        Sex int
}
const(
        UndeclaredSex int = iota
        MaleSex
        FemaleSex
        TransgenderSex
)
```

The constants defined earlier provide specific values for the Sex field. The use of constants like this is common. The preceding enum (aka iota constants) set is not type specific. Type-specific enums can be created, as shown in Listing 6-1.

Listing 6-1. Format Enum Values

```go
package main

import "fmt"

type FileSize uint64
const (
        B FileSize = 1 << (10 * iota)
        KiB
        MiB
        GiB
        TiB
        PiB
        EiB
)
```

```
var fsNames = [...]string{"EiB","PiB","TiB","GiB","MiB","KiB",""}
func (fs FileSize) scaleFs(scale FileSize, index int) string {
      return fmt.Sprintf("%d%v", FileSize(fs + scale / 2) / scale,
fsNames[index])
}
func (fs FileSize) String() (r string) {
      switch {
      case fs >= EiB:
            r = fs.scaleFs(EiB, 0)
      case fs >= PiB:
            r = fs.scaleFs(PiB, 1)
      case fs >= TiB:
            r = fs.scaleFs(TiB, 2)
      case fs >= GiB:
            r = fs.scaleFs(GiB, 3)
      case fs >= MiB:
            r = fs.scaleFs(MiB, 4)
      case fs >= KiB:
            r = fs.scaleFs(KiB, 5)
      default:
            r = fs.scaleFs(1, 6)
      }
      return
}

func main() {
      var v1, v2 FileSize = 1_000_000, 2 * 1e9
      fmt.Printf("FS1: %v; FS2: %v\n", v1, v2)
}
```

Note the Go community has libraries to generate these kinds of enum to string functions. This can be quite convenient.

When run, it reports (rounded to an integer size): FS1: 977KiB; FS2: 2GiB

Structure Fields

In Java, it is common to make class fields `private` and provide access methods to access their values. For example:

```java
public class Data {
  private int value1, value2;
  public int getValue1() { return value1; }
  public void setValue1(int value1) { this.value1 = value1; }
  public int getValue2() { return value2; }
  public void setValue2(int value2) { this.value2 = value2; }
}
```

Go has no such strong naming conventions, but often this pattern (omit get on getter, prefix setter with set) is used:

```go
type Data struct {
      value1, value2 int
}
func (d *Data) Value1() int {
      return d.value1;
}
func (d *Data) SetValue1(value1 int) {
      d.value1 = value1
}
func (d *Data) Value2() int {
      return d.value2;
}
func (d *Data) SetValue2(value2 int) {
      d.value2 = value2
}
```

It is more common in Go to make struct fields public than to make them private and provide access methods as is typical in Java. Only if some added behavior (say value validation in setters) is needed is a method generally used. There is consideration among some Gophers to always make fields private and use access methods more like Java does.

Sometimes, even the types containing these fields are private. See this documented use case[6] (a returned anonymous type) for private structs with public methods as an example. Of course, in an interface type, access methods are required as there can be no data fields.

This reflects the strong C (where all struct fields are always public) influence on Go. Structs are not classes in the Java sense. Thus, they do not offer the same degree of *encapsulation* (or data hiding) that classes typically do.

Given the definitions:

```go
type X struct {
      : some fields
}
func (x X) value(arg int) int {
      return arg
}
func (px *X) pointer(arg int) int {
      return arg
}
:
var x  X
var p *X
```

The function expression X.value yields a result with the type func(x X, arg int) int.

Such a function can be called in several ways:

- x.value(1)   // like a Java instance method

- X.value(x, 1)   // like a Java static method

- var f = X.value; f(x, 1)   // as a function value

- var f = x.value; f(1)   // similar to above

In the last case, the f variable is a function bound to an instance. This is called a *method value*. Such a value is first class. This is somewhat like a curried[7] function.

---

[6] https://stackoverflow.com/a/37952786/13103095
[7] https://en.wikipedia.org/wiki/Currying

Similarly, the function expression `(*X).pointer` yields a function with the type `func(px *X, arg int) int`.

Such a function can be called in several ways:

- `(*p).pointer(1) // like a Java instance method`
- `X.pointer(p, 1) // like a Java static method`

Any struct field can have *tags*. Tags are a string attached to the field that often (but not required to) represents a set of key and string values. Such formatted tags are metadata to code that looks at the struct reflexively (at runtime). Tags are a simple form of annotations as Java provides. The meaning of the tags is completely up to the code doing the field introspection. The general form of a tag is

```
<name>:"<CSL>"...
```

or

```
<name>:"<string>",...
```

A more complete example:

```
StructField string `json:"aField" gorm:"varchar,maxLength:100"`
```

or

```
StructField string `json:"aField" gorm:"varchar","maxLength:100"`
```

Note the Go reflection libraries have helper functions to access and parse tags.

Here are two tag sets, one for a JSON processor and one for a GORM processor. It is up to the processors to have unique keys (unfortunately, collisions are possible, especially with short keys). Note that using raw strings makes the entry of tags, with nested quoted text, easier.

Structs of identical structure can be compared (==, !=, >, >=, <, <=) if the elements by position are comparable. If you do this, the order of the fields becomes significant.

Structure Literals

Structure literals are possible. Consider these examples:

```
p := Person{Name:"Barry", Address: "123 Fourth St.", Sex: MaleSex,
Age:25.5}
```

or

```
p := Person{"Barry", "123 Fourth St.", 20.5, MaleSex}
```

Note that while named values can be supplied to structure literal elements, the same cannot be said for function arguments.

When the field names are present, all must have names, but they can be entered in any order. When no names are present, the values are assigned in the order defined in the struct. Any omitted fields have their zero values. Note that adding, removing, or reordering the fields in a struct can break any such positional struct literals, and adding or removing fields can break named struct literals.

If the Person class has an appropriate constructor, something similar can be done in Java. There is no equivalent to field name–driven initialization:

```
var p = new Person("Barry", "123 Fourth St.", 25.5, MaleSex);
```

The Go equivalent of the preceding example is

```
p := &Person{"Barry", "123 Fourth St.", 25.5, MaleSex}
```

Nested Structures

Java supports nested type definitions inside of other type definitions, such as classes inside of other classes. Go does not allow this. Java allows class fields to reference classes, including the class itself. Go allows this using a pointer to the struct type. For example:

```
type Node struct {
    Value interface{}
    Next, Previous *Node
    Parent *Node
    Children []*Node  // maybe *[]*Node to make Children optional
}
var head *Node
```

A struct may embed another struct (as a defined type or struct literal). This can be with or without a field name. This is like any other scalar type; the fields of the struct are embedded (possibly recursively) into the embedding struct. A struct may not embed itself directly or transitively.

If no field name is provided, it is as if the embedded struct fields are copied into the embedding struct. This can cause issues if the multiple embedded structs contain fields with the same name. This is solved by using the embedded type name as a qualifier. Thus, the same type cannot be embedded more than once without a label.

In Java, the standard *Object* methods are implemented by the runtime. Go has no such automatic implementations, but depending on the field types, the == (and !=) operator may be allowed.

Java 16 recently introduced a `record` type that is like a Go struct except instances are immutable. A record acts like the classical *tuple*[8] type (an often immutable heterogeneous fixed size collection of values). An example is

```
public record Point(int x, int y) { }
    :
var r = new Point(0, 0);
int x = r.x(), y = r.y();
System.out.printf("Point r: " + r + " " + x + " " + y);
```

which produces

```
Point r: Point[x=0, y=0] 0 0
```

Consider the Go equivalent:

```
type Point struct {
    X, Y int
}

func (p *Point) String() string {
    return fmt.Sprintf("Point(%d %d)", p.X, p.Y)
}
```

which is used this way:

```
var r = Point{0, 0}  // or &Point{0, 0}
x, y := r.X, r.Y
fmt.Println("Point r:", r, x, y)
```

---

[8] https://en.wikipedia.org/wiki/Tuple

which produces

Point r: {0 0} 0 0

Note in Java the appropriate `toString` method is generated by the compiler. In Go, it must be explicitly created. Also note that the fields are public and thus need no access methods.

Structure Field Alignment

In Java, one cannot know the order class fields are laid out in memory (the JIT can choose any order). Go structs are generally laid out in memory in the order the fields are declared. Each type has its own alignment needs; generally based on the number of bytes, the type takes up to a 16-byte boundary. Because of this, it is best to place the larger fields first; otherwise, there can be internal gaps in the structure to reestablish alignment. You can force alignment using *blank* (name is "_") fields of specific size. For example:

```
type Xxx struct {
        i1 int64
        b int8
        _ [3]byte  // add 3 bytes
        i2 int16
        _ [2]byte  // add 2 bytes
        i3 int32
}
```

These alignments are defined in Table 6-4.

Table 6-4. *Alignment of Struct Fields*

Type	Size (in Bytes)
byte, uint8, int8, bool	1
uint16, int16	2
uint32, int32, float32, rune	4
uint64, int64, float64, complex64	8
complex128	16
int, uint	4 or 8 based on machine architecture
*<any type>	4 or 8 based on machine architecture

Note most modern computers use 64-bit (8-byte) words, so int, uint, and pointers are 8 bytes in length.

You can also sort fields such that the bigger ones (in terms of bytes used to represent them) come first.

Interfaces

Both Go and Java support interfaces, but they do it in different ways. This is a key difference between Go and Java.

In Java, an interface is a (some Java 8+ extensions ignored) collection of abstract method signatures any concrete class must implement if the class implements (conforms to) the interface. This is also true in Go except any type (not just structs) can implement (conform to) the interface methods.

The big difference is in Go there is no need to formally say the type implements the interface; any type that has all the methods of the interface (by signature) implicitly implements (or often referred to by Gophers as *satisfies*; this text will use implements as that is the Java term) the interface. In fact, the interface can be (and often is) created after the type was, and still the type can conform to the interface.

This is often referred to as "duck" (if it walks like a duck and it quacks like a duck, it is a duck) typing. In other words, it is the behavior, not the state, of the object that determines the type. If an object implements the behavior of some type, it can be considered an instance of that type. In general, the Go approach is far more flexible than the Java approach to interfaces.

In Java, any class type can be declared to implement any number of interfaces. If a Java class does not implement all its declared interface methods, it must be declared `abstract`. Any interface can be extended by another interface, which adds to the extended interface's methods.

In Java, all interfaces are `abstract`. The same is true in Go. The rules are different in Go. In Go, if all methods of an interface are not implemented by some type, then the type simply does not implement the interface. Period! The opposite is also true; if all methods of an interface are implemented, the type does implement the interface. Period!

Java interface calls are implemented by the *InvokeInterface*[9] JVM instruction. This instruction determines which concrete method implements the interface signature on the actual receiver object and calls it. In Go, a similar process is used. Any variable of an interface type is conceptually (not actually; not legal Go) represented by a struct like the following at runtime:

```go
type InterfaceValue struct {
    Type  *type   // nil or current runtime concrete type
    Value *value  // nil or current runtime value (of type *type)
}
```

So, in effect all interface types are forms of pointer types (and thus can be set to pointer values or to non-pointer values the compiler automatically takes the address of). Any reference is indirect through the `Value` pointer. Any type assertion tests the `Type` value. These fields are set on each assignment to an interface variable. Only types that conform to the interface type can be assigned to the variable.

Because of the preceding design, one should rarely, if ever, declare a variable or type as a pointer to an interface type. The interface type acts much like a pointer implicitly.

Effectively, under the covers, on each assignment to a variable of interface type, a dispatch table is created that is indexed by the methods of the interface type. Pointers to the matching functions in the assigned type are set into this dispatch table, so they can be called by their index, not name (this is much faster).

Note the assigned type may have many other functions beyond the ones of the assigned to interface.

---

[9] https://docs.oracle.com/javase/specs/jvms/se15/html/jvms-6.html#jvms-6.5.
invokeinterface

Often, this dispatch table is created lazily, so, if no interface method is ever called on the value, no dispatch table is made. It may also be cached for better performance. This process can make any initial method invocations a bit slower.

The preceding structure allows an interface value to have two forms of nil value, each with subtly different behavior:

1. Both the Type and Value fields are nil (or not set) – the typical case.

2. If the Type is some pointer type, only the Value field is nil.

If you make a declaration like this:

```go
var xxx interface{}  // zero value is nil
```

you get the first case. But if you make an assignment like

```go
var data *int   // zero value is nil
xxx = data      // dynamic type is now *int; dynamic value is nil
```

you get the second case.

Consider these definitions:

```go
type Xxx interface {
    DoIt()
}

type XxxImpl struct {
}
func (xi *XxxImpl) DoIt() {
    :
}
:
func DoXxx(xxx Xxx) {
    if xxx != nil {
        xxx.DoIt()
    }
}
```

In the preceding example, the DoXxx function can receive an instance of Xxx that is
nil or an instance that has a Type but a nil Value. The if test will only detect the first
case, but in the second case, using the value to call a method of the interface can fail with
a runtime panic.

Application of Interfaces

In Go, it is common for interfaces to have only a few (very often just one) methods. This
is like the @FunctionalInterface annotation in Java but by convention. When there is
just one method and its name is (say) Xxx, then the interface is conventionally named
Xxxer. For example:

```
type Stringer interface {
    String() string
}
```

and

```
type Reader interface {
    Read(n int) []byte
}
```

It is possible to have multiple interfaces with the same function signatures.
For example:

```
type ToString interface {
    String() string
}
```

Any type that provides the String() method implements all such interfaces.

The Go runtime libraries define and use such interfaces extensively. Many Go
types implement multiple such interfaces. Instances of these types can be sent to any
functions accepting such an interface as a parameter or returning the interface.

For example, the Go File type implements the *Reader* and *Writer* interfaces
(among others), and so a file instance itself can be directly used to access the file's
contents. In Java, separate access classes (that implement the Java *Reader* or *Writer*
interfaces) must be used on the file instance.

An example interface (defined as a type, which is typical – literal interfaces are also allowed):

```
type Worker interface {
    RecordHoursWorked(hours float32) (err error)
    GetPay() (pay Payment, err error)
}

type Payment float32
```

Note that in Go an interface can only contain method prototypes (signatures of abstract methods). There can be no fields, methods with bodies, or nested types. That is why the prototypes are not prefixed with "func".

Also note that the parameter and return names are optional, as shown in the following. This definition means the same, but is less self-explanatory, and is thus not preferred:

```
type Worker interface {
    RecordHoursWorked(float32) error
    GetPay() (Payment, error)
}
```

In Go, any type that has all the methods defined in an interface implicitly implements the interface. Unlike in Java, no `implements` clause is needed. For example:

```
type HourlyWorker struct {
    HoursWorked    float32
    Overtime       float32
    Rate           float32
}
func (hw * HourlyWorker) RecordHoursWorked(worked float32) (err error) {
    hw.HoursWorked += worked
    return
}
func (hw * HourlyWorker) GetPay() (pay Payment, err error) {
    reg := hw.HoursWorked * hw.Rate
    ot := hw.Overtime * 1.5 * hw.Rate
```

```
      if hw.Overtime > 20 {
             ot = 20 * 1.5 * hw.Rate + (hw.Overtime - 20) * 2 * hw.Rate
      }
      pay = Payment(reg + ot)
      return
}
:
var worker Worker = &HourlyWorker{40.0, 10.5, 15.50}
var pay, err := worker.GetPay()
:
```

A special case of an interface type is the empty interface (i.e., it has no methods). It looks like this:

```
interface{}
```

This says to conform to the interface, you need to implement no method at all. This is something all types can do. So, an empty interface acts like a universal type (much like *Object* acts as a universal reference type in Java). Any type, including primitive types, can be assigned to an empty interface.

For example:

```
var x interface{}
x = 10                     // value 10 (no boxing needed as Java does)
x = "hello"                // value "hello"
x = make([]string, 0, 10)  // an empty slice
```

Often, the empty interface type is used for variadic parameters where different types can be passed for each argument as shown in the following signature:

```
func Printf(format string, args... interface{})
```

Note that empty interfaces can be distinct types. Types any and all in the following are different types:

```
type any interface{}
type all interface{}
```

Composite Interfaces

In Go, like in Java, one can build interfaces out of other interfaces. In Java, this is done by extends. In Go, it is done by embedding the interfaces. For example, in Java

```java
public interface A {
  void a();
}
public interface B {
  void b();
}
public interface C {
  void c();
}
public interface All extends A, B, C {
  void all();
}
```

would be this in Go:

```go
type A interface {
     A()
}
type B interface {
     B()
}
type C interface {
     C()
}
type All interface {
     A
     B
     C
     All()
}
```

Interface All has these methods: A(), B(), C(), All(). An interface may not embed itself directly or indirectly. Like in Java, in Go if multiple embedded interfaces have the same method (by name, arguments, and returns), the embedding interface has only one method. If the embedded methods have the same name but different signatures, a compile-time error occurs.

Instances of interfaces of identical dynamic type can be compared (==, !=, >, >=, <, <=) if the dynamic type is comparable.

One powerful aspect of Go's duck typing is this example. Given:

```
type XBytes []byte

func (x *XBytes) Write(bs []byte) (n int, err error) {
    n = len(bs)
    *x = XBytes(append([]byte(*x), bs...))
    return
}
```

then

```
var b = make(XBytes, 0, 100)
xb := &b
xb.Write([]byte("hello - "))
fmt.Fprintf(xb, "this is a %s", "test")
fmt.Printf("%q\n", *xb)
```

works on the custom XBytes type because it implements the io.Writer interface. It produces "hello - this is a test".

Channels

Go has a *Channel* type for which Java has no standard equivalent. Channels, combined with *Goroutines*, are one of Go's most distinguishing and powerful features.

A channel is basically an ordered pipe or first-in, first-out (FIFO) queue through which values can be sent or received. The sender and receiver are often running in different goroutines and are thus asynchronous to each other. A channel can hold only one type of data (but as it can be a struct, the data can be complex, or as it can be an interface, the data can be polymorphic). A channel may be used as one way or bidirectional. A channel is declared as follows:

```
chan <type>           // bidirectional (receive and send)
chan <type> <-  // receive only
chan <- <type>  // send only
```

where <type> is any Go type (but channels of channels are rare).

Channels are constructed using make as follows:

```
<chanVar> = make(<chan declaration>{, <cap>})
```

where <cap> is the capacity of the channel. The default is zero. The capacity determines how many sent items can be buffered awaiting reception. A capacity of zero means there is no buffering; a sender and receiver operate in lock step. For a channel, the cap() function returns this capacity, and the len() function returns the currently buffered count.

Some example channel definitions:

```
var ichan = make(chan int)
var schan = make(chan string)
var roichan = make(chan <- int)
var woichan = make(<- chan int)
type Celsius float64
var cchan = make(chan Celsius)
```

A channel can be open or closed. While open, more values can be sent to the channel. When closed, they cannot. The receive (<-) operator can test if a channel is open or not. The close() function is used to close a channel.

It is common to read channels until they are closed. This is most easily done as follows:

```
for <value> := range <channel> {
    : process next value from the channel
}
```

The preceding logic is often placed inside some goroutine. The loop blocks if the channel is currently empty. The loop continues until some sender closes the channel.

176

Channels can be used to help support generic request processors. For example, see the program shown in Listing 6-2.

Listing 6-2. Request Handler and Summation Action

```go
package main

import (
	"fmt"
	"time"
)

type RequestFunc func(arg interface{}) interface{}

type GenericRequest struct {
	Handler		RequestFunc
	Args		interface{}
	Result		chan interface{}
}

func NewGenericRequest(h RequestFunc, a interface{},
	r chan interface{}) (gr * GenericRequest) {
	gr = &GenericRequest{h, a, r}
	if gr.Result == nil {
		gr.Result = make(chan interface{})
	}
	return
}

func HandleGenericRequests(requests chan *GenericRequest) {
	for req := range requests {
		req := req
		go func() {
			req.Result <- req.Handler(req.Args)
		}()
	}
}
```

```
var Requests = make(chan *GenericRequest, 100)

func sumFloat(arg interface{}) interface{} {
        var res float64
        values, ok := arg.([]float64)
        if ok {
                for _, v := range values {
                        res += v
                }
        }
        return res
}

func main() {
        reqs := make([]*GenericRequest, 0, 10)
        reqs = append(reqs, NewGenericRequest(sumFloat, []float64{1, 2, 3}, nil))
        reqs = append(reqs, NewGenericRequest(sumFloat, []float64{5, 6, 7}, nil))
        reqs = append(reqs, NewGenericRequest(sumFloat, []float64{7, 8, 9}, nil))
        for _, r := range reqs {
                // accepts < 100  requests without blocking
                Requests <- r
        }
        go HandleGenericRequests(Requests)

        time.Sleep(5 * time.Second)  // simulate doing other work

        for i, r := range reqs {
                fmt.Printf("sum %d: %v\n", i+1, <-r.Result) // wait for each to
                finish
        }
        close(Requests)
}
```

This when run produces

```
sum 1: 6
sum 2: 18
sum 3: 24
```

178

By changing the input values and matching functions, any calculation can be done, all concurrently.

Variable Declarations

Like Java, Go allows a programmer to declare variables of different types. Java places the type (int, String, List, etc.) of the variable first as the statement introducer. Go has special statements for declarations. In Go, variable declarations use the *var* statement, much like recent Java 10+ versions can for local variables. In Go, the type follows the variable name. Here are some examples:

```
var x int                  // x is int, value 0
var x, y, z int            // x, y, z are int, values all 0
var x, y, z int = 1, 2, 3  // x, y, z are int, corresponding value 1, 2, 3
var x, y, z = 1, 2, 3      // x, y, z are int (implied by values),
                           //     corresponding value 1, 2, 3
var z *int = &x            // z is address of x (or var x = &x)
```

The "var" can be factored out. For example:

```
var (
    x int                  // x is int, value 0
    z *int = &x            // z is address of x
)
```

In Go, the type is optional if it can be inferred by any supplied values. In Go, if the value assignment is omitted, the "zero" value is used. The zero value is false for Booleans, 0 for numbers, the empty string for strings, and the nil pointer for pointers. For slices, maps, and channels, the zero value is like nil, but it does not behave exactly like nil. While they have zero values, the author recommends to not depend on the zero values for slices, maps, or channels; instead, always make them explicitly.

Java has a similar form for method or block locals, such as

```
var x = 10;
var s = "string";
for (var i = 0; i < 10; i++)  {...}
```

Like in Java, Go has variable names (i.e., identifiers) that are case sensitive and conventionally (but are not required to) use camel case (each word has an initial capitalized letter). In Go, the use of underscore ("_") in names, even constants, is discouraged. Also, the use of only uppercase letters is discouraged (e.g., XXX_YYY). An underscore (_) by itself is used to name a special `blank` variable that can be ignored.

In Go, declarations have no visibility modifier. Instead, the identifier's case determines the visibility. If the identifier starts with a capital letter, it's public (can be seen by code in any package); else the identifier is package private (can be seen only by code in the same package). This distinction is not important for block local declarations; private style names are preferred.

For example:

- `T - public`
- `t – private`
- `Bird - public`
- `aFriendOfAFriend - private`

Unlike in Java, embedded acronyms are conventionally all capitals (vs. mixed case). For example:

`MyURLPath (vs. MyUrlPath)`

Thus, the naming conventions shown in Table 6-5 are used.

Table 6-5. *Situational Name Case Examples*

Role	Rule	Example
Private type names	camelCase	myType
Public type names	CamelCase	MyType
Private field names	camelCase	myField
Public field names	CamelCase	MyField
Private Top-level names (var, const, func)	camelCase	packagePrivateValue
Public top-level names (var, const, func)	CamelCase	PackagePublicValue
Function/block/argument/return local names of any role	camelCase	aLocalValue
Package name	One short word (or "/" separated words)	fmt net/http

While not a language standard, there are recommended soft rules about creating names. Names need to be informative and self-explanatory, especially for type, field, and function names. They are a primary form of description about the code, and as such one should concentrate on making definitive, often multiword, names vs. the use of equivalent commentary.

Global names need more rigor (and thus often length) than local names. Avoid the use of abbreviations (e.g., len for length), but well-known acronyms are appropriate. Local names can (long local names can make reading the code more difficult) be briefer. Here, abbreviations can be more appropriate – for example, a variable named len, fmt, ctx, or err.

Names of limited context, such as loop indexes, can often be short, say a single letter, or (all lowercase) acronyms. For loop indexes, for historical reasons,[10] often use single letters starting at "i" with nested loops using the next letter, say "j".

---

[10] Early FORTRAN compilers treated names starting with I, J, ...N as integers and other names as floating-point types.

Constant Declarations

Like Java, Go allows a programmer to declare constants of different types. In Go, a constant is a compile-time construct (like a literal in Java), while in Java it is most closely approximated by a `static final` value that exists at runtime (in some class). Constant declarations are like variable declarations except the `const` keyword is used and a value is required. For example:

```
const x, y, z int = 1, 2, 3    // x, y, z are int, corresponding value
                                   1, 2, 3
const x, y, z = 1, 2, 3        // x, y, z are int (implied by values),
                                   corresponding value 1, 2, 3
```

The "const" can be factored out. For example:

```
const (
      x, y, z = 1, 2, 3        // x, y, z are int (implied by values),
                                   corresponding value 1, 2, 3
)
```

The value expression must be a constant (i.e., the compiler can evaluate it) expression. Each value can be of a different type.

A special case is to define identifiers for enumeration sets (enums). Unlike in Java, Go enums types are not special types and should be integers. The "iota" value is used, which is assigned incremental values (starting from 0) from a prior value:

```
const (
      v1 = iota     // 0
      v2 = iota     // 1
      v3 = iota     // 2
)
```

or briefer:

```
const (
      v1 = iota     // 0
      v2            // 1
      v3            // 2
)
```

where the value is implied as a repeat of the previous value. The value can be an expression, such as to create bit masks:

```
const (
    bit0mask = 1 << iota      // 1
    bit1mask                  // 2
    bit2mask                  // 4
)
```

The preceding form (with implied values) is a more concise and idiomatic form of

```
const (
    bit0mask = 1 << iota      // 1
    bit1mask = 1 << iota      // 2
    bit2mask = 1 << iota      // 4
)
```

The iota value is reset for each const group.

Another example:

```
const (
    Sunday = iota
    Monday
    Tuesday
    Wednesday
    Thursday
    Friday
    Saturday
)
const (
    FirstDay  = Sunday
    HumpDay   = Wednesday
    FunDay    = Saturday
    LastDay   = Saturday
)
```

These values can be displayed with

```
fmt.Fprintf(os.Stdout, "%v %v %v %v %v %v %v %v %v\n",
Sunday, FirstDay, Monday, Wednesday, HumpDay, Friday, Saturday, FunDay, LastDay)
```

which produces

---

0 0 1 3 3 5 6 6 6

Type Casting

In Java, most operations, such as assignments and comparisons, cannot be done across different types. Only compatible types can be allowed. Java allows select types to be automatically promoted to make them compatible for arithmetic, comparison, and/or assignment as follows:

- byte -> short -> int -> long
- byte -> char -> int -> long
- float-> double
- long -> double
- int -> double
- subclass -> superclass
- sub interface -> super interface
- class -> implemented interface

Other conversions require explicit casting. Except for numeric type casting, casting does not change the actual type of a value, just how it is looked at. Numeric casts may change the data representation as follows:

double d = (**double**)anInt;

but the following cast makes no change in the data:

Object o = (Object)aString;

CHAPTER 6   GO TYPES

In fact, these casts (called *up-casts*) need never be explicitly coded as the Java compiler can imply it. But the reverse (called *down-casts*) must be done explicitly as the compiler considers it unsafe and will not automatically do it:

```
String s = (String)anObject;
```

This is like casting from double back to int where data (e.g., the fractional part) can be lost:

```
int i = (int)aDouble;
```

Go has a similar casting (called conversion) policy, except all different types must be explicitly cast; there is little automatic casting. So, for numeric values, one would do

```
i := int64(aDouble)
d := float64(anInt)   // this is automatic in Java
```

Note converting a constant gives it a type. For example:

```
var i = int32(1)   // i is of type int32 while 1 has no type
```

Some interesting special cases:

```
var s1 = string(123)                   // s is string "123"
var s2 = string([]byte{48, 49, 50})    // s is string "123"
var s3 = []byte("123")                 // s is []byte{48, 49, 50}
```

Type Testing

Like in Java, for any cast source type other than an interface type, Go can determine at compile time if the cast (aka conversion) is legal or not. To cast an interface (abstract) type into a non-interface (concrete) type, a cast expression is needed. In Java, this takes the following form:

```
var x = (<concreteType>)<value>;
```

In Go, it takes the following form, called a *type assertion*:

```
x := <value>.(<concreteType>)
```

where `<value>` is some expression of an interface type and `<concreteType>` is the desired type. For example:

```
aString := couldBeAString.(string)
```

If this works, `aString` is a value of type `string`. But if `couldBeAString` was not a string value, a panic (like Java's *ClassCastException*) is raised. To overcome this, one does the following in Java:

```
if(couldBeAString instanceof String) {
     var aString = (String)couldBeAString;
     // use aString
}
```

while in Go, one does

```
aString, ok := couldBeAString.(string)
if ok {
     // use aString
}
```

or more concisely and idiomatically done:

```
if aString, ok := couldBeAString.(string); ok {
     // use aString
}
```

Like in Java's `instanceof` tests, a type assertion on a `nil` value is always `false`.

The Go Switch statement can also do this logic and is more concise than using the if statements for multiple type tests:

```
switch <expr>.(type) {  // here type is a keyword, not a variable
  case <type> {, <type>}...:
    <statements>
  default:
    <statements>
}
```

where `<type>` is the target type. It can also be the value `nil`.

There is a helpful extension:

```
switch <v> := <expr>.(type) {
  case <type> {, <type>}...:
    <statements>
  default:
    <statements>
}
```

where `<v>` is the casted value, and in each case, it will be a value of the matching case type. If multiple types are listed per case, the casted type is `interface{}`; otherwise, it is the case type. For example:

```
func DoSomething(v interface{}) (err error) {
    switch xv := v.(type) {
    case string:
        : process string value xv
        return
    case int:
        : process int value xv
        return
        :
    case nil:
        return errors.New("nil not supported")
    default:
        return errors.New(fmt.Sprintf("type %T not supported", v))
    }
}
```

Note Java's new `switch` expression provides like conversion without the use of `instanceof` as shown earlier.

When testing types, it is important to note that a pointer type (*T) and non-pointer type (T) are considered different types and must have their own `case` tests.

Derived Type Declarations

Go supports a feature not available in Java. The closest Java feature is using inheritance to declare subtypes. In Go, new types can be derived from other (called *base*) types. These new types are not aliasing the base type; each derived type is a different type, even when derived from the same base type (so assignment cannot be done without cast conversions). One can even derive from derived types. For example, we can define some temperature types:

```go
type Temperature float64
type Celsius Temperature
type Fahrenheit Temperature
type Kelvin Temperature
```

We can also define derived types like

```go
type anything interface {}
```

or

```go
type Person struct {
    :
}
```

Note in Java, types are generally given initial capital names. This is not always true in Go; like for all identifiers, only if the defined type is to be public are initial capitals used.

Go does not support inheritance (extends or implements in Java). The closest equivalent is composition. For example, given

```go
type Address struct {
    city  string
    state string
    zip   string
}
func (a *Address) Format() string {
    return fmt.Sprintf("%s\n%s, %s", a.city, a.state, a.zip)
}
```

then one can use this type as follows:

```
type Person struct {
    :
    Address
    :
}
```

This means that an Address instance (and all its state) is embedded directly in a Person instance (much like the fields of a Java superclass exist in any Java subclass). Also, any methods an Address has are implicitly added to any Person (if not already defined for Person). These methods in Person delegate the work to the methods of the Address type. Thus, this works:

```
p := Person{...}
x := p.city
f := p.Format()
```

This also works, where the embedded type is used as a qualifier:

```
p := Person{...}
x := p.Address.city
f := p.Address.Format()
```

which is the actual form; the previous one is a convenient simplification.
Consider this option:

```
type Person struct {
    :
    address Address
    :
}
```

This means that an address instance (and all its state) is embedded as the field
address. Thus, this works (address is required here):

```
p := Person{...}
x := p.address.city
f := p.address.Format()
```

but consider this:

```
type Person struct {
    :
    address *Address
    :
}
```

where an address instance is pointed to by field address. A Person does not have any
data of an Address instance embedded in it, just the instance's address. Still this works:

```
p := Person{...}
x := p.address.city
f := p.address.Format()
```

because here p.address is implicitly treated like the expression *(p.address).

In general, the author recommends the use of pointers to structs over embedding of
structs to construct composite types. This mimics how it is done in Java by composition
(vs. inheritance). Only if the embedding type cannot exist without the embedded type
should physical embedding be used.

Unlike in Java, Go has no inheritance of methods for an embedded named type. But
if the type is embedded anonymously (without a name), as noted earlier, the embedded
type's methods are copied into the embedding type if the embedding type does not have
such a method already. This is referred to as *delegation* to the embedded methods.

It is important to note that when the methods of the embedded struct are called,
even via delegation from the embedding struct, it is the embedded struct that is the
receiver, not the embedding struct as it would be if the embedding struct had inherited
the embedded struct (i.e., there would only be a single object, not two objects with one
inside the other) as there would be with Java inheritance.

It is also important to note that the embedded struct has no knowledge that the embedding struct exists. Also, when a field name is given, the address of the embedded struct can be taken and used to manipulate the embedded struct independently from the embedder.

When multiple structs are embedded anonymously, there is the chance that they both have fields of the same name (this is always true if the same struct type is embedded anonymously multiple times, so this is not allowed). If so, this must be dealt with. A field must be declared in the embedding struct of the same name to resolve (and hide the embedded names) the name. Or the field's reference must be qualified by the embedded type name. The same is true for methods. This is only an issue if the field or method is used by some code.

CHAPTER 7

Errors and Panics

In this chapter, we will drill down on Go's error detection and recovery features and how they differ from Java's approach. When you have completed this chapter, you should be able to clearly identify the similarities and differences between the Go and Java error approaches.

Code, especially code in functions, can exit in several ways:

1. Success – The function was accomplished as expected.

2. Failure – The function was not accomplished as expected due to some predictable situation.

3. Gross failure (aka panics) – The function was not accomplished due to some unexpected or unusual situation or bad code.

In languages like Java that have only one return value per function, cases 1 and 2 are often combined, and the returned value itself makes the determination. Consider the `String.indexOf` function which returns either the index of the target or a value < 0 to indicate the target was not found. For functions that return objects, often `null` is returned to indicate a failure (this is problematic if `null` is a legitimate value). This is often the cause for many NullPointerExceptions.

Go Errors

Go functions can return zero or more results. Many Go functions return (at least) an error value. This is a common example:

```go
func DoSomething() (err error) { ... }
```

© Barry Feigenbaum 2022
B. Feigenbaum, *Go for Java Programmers*, https://doi.org/10.1007/978-1-4842-7199-5_7

This says the *DoSomething* function can return an `error` (a built-in Go interface type), in this case (conventionally and idiomatically) named `err`. The `err` value can be `nil` or some `error` instance. A more complete example:

```go
func DoSomething() (err error) {
    :
    err = DoSomePart()
    if err != nil {
        return
    }
    :
    return
}
```

Go has a frequently used and less verbose way to code this pattern that combines the assignment and the if test:

```go
if err = DoSomePart(); err != nil {
    return
}
```

Each function that can fail follows this pattern. While far more verbose than in typical Java code that exploits exceptions to report failures, this follows the more transparent/obvious style Go uses.

Note that the return does not have an explicit value. This works because the return value is named `err` and `err` was assigned a value. An alternate (less preferred by the author) is

```go
func DoSomething() error {
    :
    xxx := DoSomePart()  // unconventional name
    if xxx != nil {
        return xxx            // explicitly returned
    }
    :
    return xxx
}
```

In most cases, Go prefers one to return an error value from a function. This pattern is often considered bad practice in Java as it forces the caller to test for the returned error. In Go, this pattern is considered best practice; the programmer must remember to test for returned errors. This is a major difference between Go and Java programming styles, and many Java programmers newly coding in Go have some trouble getting used to it.

For some simple functions where just a success/failed indicator is enough, the returned error value is replaced by a Boolean. This is often the case for Go built-in operations such as map lookup and type assertions.

Go Panics

In Java, more serious failures are indicated by throwing some *Exception*. There is often confusion about when an exception should be thrown vs. an error returned (e.g., say when reading past the end of a file), and Java (and many community) library code makes this type of choice inconsistently.

Go makes this behavior more consistent by using multivalued functions that always return an error value as the last (or only) return value. The error value is tested against nil to determine if an error occurred. In general, any other return values only have meaningful values if there was no error. Only if the function failed catastrophically (out of memory, divide by zero, index out of bounds, invalid arguments, etc.) is a panic raised.

Java supports the notion of Exceptions (technically *Throwables*, which are a superclass of Exceptions). An exception is an object that can be *thrown* when an unexpected/unusual condition arises. An example is the *DivideByZeroException* that is thrown by the JVM when zero is used as a divisor. Another, more serious, example is the *OutOfMemoryError* that is thrown when the JVM cannot satisfy a new operation. Java processes throwables in catch blocks of try statements. Throwable instances are thrown and caught pervasively in Java code.

Go has a similar, but less used, notion called a *panic*. A panic is much like a throwable that can be raised by code (yours or some library) by using the Go built-in panic(<value>) function. The value can be any type (but often it is a string or (preferred) an error instance); a nil value should not be used.

It should be rare that Go code raises a panic. In most cases, the code should return an error instead. A panic should be used only in cases so unexpected that reporting them by errors would be onerous, such as a Go equivalent of Java's OutOfMemoryError.

Go does not have Exception types like Java does. Instead, it has panic arguments (which are more like Java *Errors* mixed with some *RuntimeExceptions*). Go has no notion of the Java distinction between RuntimeException and non-RuntimeException throwables. All are mapped to a single panic value. One never declares the panic arguments a function can raise.

Java has `try/finally` and `try/catch/finally` statement sets. Go does not. It uses *deferred* functions to achieve the effect of `finally`. Go uses a different but similar mechanism to catch panics.

Much like in Java, if not caught, panics generally cause a program exit after printing a traceback. To catch a panic in Go, one uses the built-in `recover()` function which returns the value sent with the most recent panic (in a particular goroutine). To do this, `recover()` must be called inside an already deferred function.

Much like a Java `catch` clause can examine the thrown exception, the deferred function can examine the value, do some correction, and return or raise the panic again. Like in Java, the deferred function can be anywhere on the current call stack. Here is a simple example:

```go
func DoIt() (err error) {
    defer func() {
        p := recover()
        if p != nil {  // a panic occurred
            // process the panic by (say) testing p value
            err = nil  // make containing function not return an error
        }
    }()
    :
     // any code that can panic
    if err != nil {
        panic(errors.New(fmt.Sprintf("panic: %v", err)))
          // or equivalently
        panic(fmt.Errorf("panic: %v", err))
    }
    :
    return
}
```

In general, the Go libraries and the Go runtime avoid raising panics. Your code should also. One common situation does utilize panics. If a function gets an illegal argument value, it is often reported via a panic instead of an error return. This situation is considered a programming error, not a situation the code should recover from. Note not all Gophers follow this approach and thus do not validate arguments and generate panics; some other issue generally occurs later. The code depends on being provided with valid inputs.

Note one should generally avoid causing a new panic in a panic recovery deferred function. This is like in Java avoiding throwing an exception in a catch or finally clause.

One area where it is critical to capture panics is in goroutines. An unhandled panic in a goroutine can crash a Go program. So, it is best to not allow them to occur. This requires systematic discipline. To achieve this, the author suggests all goroutines be created by a helper function, something like Listing 7-1.

Listing 7-1. Capture Panics in a Goroutine Launcher Function

```go
package main

import (
    "errors"
    "fmt"
    "time"
)
var NoError = errors.New("no error")  // special error

func GoroutineLauncher(gr func(), c *(chan error)) {
    go func(){
        defer func(){
            if p := recover(); p != nil {
                if c != nil {
                    // ensure we send an error
                    if err, ok := p.(error); ok {
                        *c <- err
                        return
                    }
                    *c <- errors.New(fmt.Sprintf("%v", p))
                }
```

```
                    return
             }
             if c != nil {
                  *c <- NoError  // could also send nil and test for it
             }
        }()
        gr()
    }()
}

var N = 5

func main() {
    var errchan = make(chan error, N)  // N >= 1 based on max active
    goroutines
    // :
    GoroutineLauncher (func(){
         time.Sleep(2 * time.Second)  // simulate complex work
         panic("panic happened!")
    }, &errchan)
    // :
    time.Sleep(5 * time.Second)           // simulate other work
    // :
    err := <- errchan  // wait for result
    if err != NoError {
         fmt.Printf("got %q" , err.Error())
    }
}
```

Note that the error channel can be omitted if no error report is needed by the client. This when run produces

```
got "panic happened!"
```

Errors and Panics Illustrated

The built-in error type is simple. Many third-party packages have extended it, for example, *JuJu Errors*.[1] Listings 7-2, 7-3 and 7-4 are some possible examples of how it can be extended. For example, to collect multiple occurance of errors (say when processing elements of a slice).

Listing 7-2. Multiple Cause Errors

```go
type MultError []error

func (me MultError) Error() (res string) {
    res = "MultError"
    sep := " "
    for _, e := range me {
        res = fmt.Sprintf("%s%s%s", res, sep, e.Error())
        sep = "; "
    }
    return
}
func (me MultError) String() string {
    return me.Error()
}
```

This when used by

```go
me   := MultError(make([]error,0, 10))
for _, v := range []string{"one", "two", "three"} {
    me = append(me, errors.New(v))
}
fmt.Printf("MultipleError error: %s\n", me.Error())
fmt.Printf("MultipleError value: %v\n\n", me)
```

produces

```
MultipleError error: MultError one; two; three
MultipleError value: MultError one; two; three
```

---

[1]https://github.com/juju/errors

Or when an error is caused by another error (much like in Java where all *Throwables* can have a cause).

Listing 7-3. Error with a Cause

```go
type ErrorWithCause struct {
    Err   error
    Cause error
}

func NewError(err error) *ErrorWithCause {
    return NewErrorWithCause(err, nil)
}
func NewErrorWithCause(err error, cause error) *ErrorWithCause {
    if err == nil {
        err = errors.New("no error supplied")
    }
    return &ErrorWithCause{err, cause}
}
func (wc ErrorWithCause) Error() string {
    xerr := wc.Err
    xcause := wc.Cause
    if xcause == nil {
        xcause = errors.New("no root cause supplied")
    }
    return fmt.Sprintf("ErrorWithCause{%v %v}", xerr, xcause)
}
func (wc ErrorWithCause) String() string {
    return wc.Error()
}
```

This when used by

```go
fmt.Printf("ErrorWithCause error: %s\n", ewc.Error())
fmt.Printf("ErrorWithCause value: %v\n\n", ewc)
```

produces

```
ErrorWithCause error: ErrorWithCause{error cause}
ErrorWithCause value: ErrorWithCause{error cause}
```

Note that the presence of a method like the following makes any data type act as an error:

```
func (x <sometype>) Error() string
```

This is because the error type is effectively defined as

```
type error interface {
    Error() string
}
```

The Go errors[2] package has several useful utility functions:

> `errors.Is(<error>, <type>)` – Unwraps the error until it matches the supplied type and returns true if found.

> `errors.As(<error>, <*type>)` – Unwraps the error until it matches the supplied variable's type, casts the error to that type, sets the variable, and returns true if found.

> `errors.Unwrap(<error>)` – Returns any wrapped error (like any cause for a Java exception); the actual error type must have an Unwrap(<error>) method.

It is possible to emulate Java exception behavior in Go. For example, to introduce a Try/Catch/Finally-like behavior, one can implement a small library like the following. Here, Go functions take the place of the Java Try/Catch, Try/Finally, and Try/Catch/Finally statements.

Each function clause is provided as a (typically) function literal. There is no catch per exception type like in Java as Go only has a single panic for all issues. The overall function returns the error of the try clause. Since the try and catch clause can have errors, an error pair type, TryCatchError, is sometimes returned.

---

[2] https://golang.org/pkg/errors/

Note it is important to issue the `recover()` function directly in the deferred function and not in the `triageRecover(...)` function.

Listing 7-4. Try/Catch Emulation Example (Part 1)

```go
type TryFunc func() error
type CatchFunc func(error) (rerr error, cerr error)
type FinallyFunc func()

type TryCatchError struct {
    tryError   error
    catchError error
}

func (tce *TryCatchError) Error() string {
    return tce.String()
}
func (tce *TryCatchError) String() string {
    return fmt.Sprintf("TryCatchError[%v %v]", tce.tryError,
    tce.catchError)
}
func (tce *TryCatchError) Cause() error {
    return tce.tryError
}
func (tce *TryCatchError) Catch() error {
    return tce.catchError
}

func TryFinally(t TryFunc, f FinallyFunc) (err error) {
    defer func() {
        f()
    }()
    err = t()
    if err != nil {
        err = &TryCatchError{err, nil}
    }
    return
}
```

```go
func triageRecover(p interface{}, c CatchFunc) (err error) {
    if p != nil {
        var terr, cerr error
        if v, ok := p.(error); ok {
            terr = v
        }
        if xrerr, xcerr := c(terr); xrerr != nil {
            cerr = xcerr
            err = xrerr
        }
        if terr != nil || cerr != nil {
            err = &TryCatchError{terr, cerr}
        }
    }
    return err
}

func TryCatch(t TryFunc, c CatchFunc) (err error) {
    defer func() {
        if xerr := triageRecover(recover(), c); xerr != nil {
            err = xerr
        }
    }()
    err = t()
    return
}
func TryCatchFinally(t TryFunc, c CatchFunc, f FinallyFunc) (err error) {
    defer func() {
        f()
    }()
    defer func() {
        if xerr := triageRecover(recover(), c); xerr != nil {
            err = xerr
        }
    }()
```

```
    err = t()
    return
}
```

This can be used as shown in Listing 7-5.

Listing 7-5. Try/Catch Emulation Example (Part 2)

```
err := TryCatchFinally(func() error {
    fmt.Printf("in try\n")
    panic(errors.New("forced panic"))
}, func(e error) (re, ce error) {
    fmt.Printf("in catch %v: %v %v\n", e, re, ce)
    return
}, func() {
    fmt.Printf("in finally\n")
})
fmt.Printf("TCF returned: %v\n", err)

err = TryFinally(func() error {
    fmt.Printf("in try\n")
    return errors.New("try error")
}, func() {
    fmt.Printf("in finally\n")
})
fmt.Printf("TCF returned: %v\n", err)

err = TryCatch(func() error {
    fmt.Printf("in try\n")
    panic(errors.New("forced panic"))
}, func(e error) (re, ce error) {
    fmt.Printf("in catch %v: %v %v\n", e, re, ce)
    return
})
fmt.Printf("TCF returned: %v\n", err)
```

```
err = TryCatch(func() error {
    fmt.Printf("in try\n")
    return nil
}, func(e error) (re, ce error) {
    fmt.Printf("in catch %v: %v %v\n", e, re, ce)
    return
})
fmt.Printf("TCF returned: %v\n", err)
```

This outputs the following:

```
in try
in catch forced panic: <nil> <nil>
in finally
TCF returned: TryCatchError[forced panic <nil>]
in try
in finally
TCF returned: TryCatchError[try error <nil>]
in try
in catch forced panic: <nil> <nil>
TCF returned: TryCatchError[forced panic <nil>]
in try
TCF returned: <nil>
```

CHAPTER 8

Go Statements

In this chapter, we will describe Go's various language statements in greater detail. When we are done with this chapter, you should be able to clearly identify the similarities and differences between the Go and Java language statements and their function.

Much like with Java, in Go, computation is based on an imperative model. Computations are performed in a sequence and are saved in variables. Go has little of the functional programming style of computation that Java also supports. Control flow is based on only conditional and looping statements and not embedded inside function calls as Java can support with (say) its stream libraries. Some discussion on attempting functional methods in Go can be found at `https://github.com/robpike/filter`.

Go has several conditional statements:

- One- or two-way conditional (can also be used to form multiway conditionals) – if/else

- Multiway value conditional – switch

- Multiway channel conditional – select

Go has one looping statement (for) with several subforms:

- Infinite loop

- Loop with adjusting index

- Loop while a condition is true

- Loop over a collection

Go can exit/iterate loops in different ways:

- Loop condition test fails

- Abrupt exit – Break or return

- Advance to next iterations – Continue

© Barry Feigenbaum 2022
B. Feigenbaum, *Go for Java Programmers*, https://doi.org/10.1007/978-1-4842-7199-5_8

Like in Java, all Go code must be grouped into reusable units called *functions*. In Go, it is best practice to keep functions short (say a few dozen, at most, lines long) and make more functions as needed. Go can call functions by name or indirectly via a function value. Java can call methods only by name. Some function Java does by statements, Go does by built-in function calls.

Go can return zero or more results per function. Java supports only zero or one. Like in Java, returns can occur anywhere in a function.

Package and Import Statements

Like Java, each Go source file needs a Package statement as the first statement that declares the package the source belongs to, such as

package main

There can be any number of source files in a package. The Go source file names do not need to match the package name (often they do not if there are multiple source files for a package), but it is recommended that they do, especially for the directory that contains the main entry point, for better code organization. For example, it is recommended that you use a main.go file to hold the main package source that has the main() function in it. Note the main function in a main package convention is needed so the Go builder can recognize that an executable must be built.

If the source file uses any public declarations in another package, that package must be imported, such as

import "math"
import "net/http"

or grouped like this:

import (
  "math"
  "net/http"
)

There can be more than one group of imports in a source file. All import statements must come after the package statement and before any other statements. The imports can come in any order but are often sorted by the last name in the import path, especially in the same import group. If no public item from a package is referenced in a source file, the package cannot be imported (the compiler will report an error).

Imports are done at the file, not package, level and thus must, like in Java, be repeated in each source file that uses the import. Different source files in the same package can and often do have different import lists.

All references to public names in an imported package must be prefixed with the package name like this:

```
r := new(http.Request)
```

The last name in any imported package path is used by default as the imported prefix name. Sometimes, you would desire to use a different (say shorter) name for a package. You can give the package an alias during imports like this:

```
import net "net/http"
```

Go packages can have several init() functions. Sometimes, you need these functions to run even if you do not use the symbols in the package. To do this, add the *blank* alias (an underscore) in the import, like this:

```
import _ "net/http"
```

The init() functions of a package are run only once, no matter how many source files import the package.

Assignment Statements

Perhaps the most basic action one can take in Go is the assignment of a value to a variable. In Go, like in Java, this is done explicitly by *assignment* statements. It is also done by passing arguments into or returning values from a function. The assigned values can be constants, other variables, or expressions involving these items.

The most fundamental assignment is

```
<variable> = <expression>
```

While a declaration, rather than an assignment, there is also a convenient way to both declare and assign values that resembles an assignment statement:

```
<variable> := <expression>
```

There are also augmented (aka compound) assignments in this form:

```
<variable> <binaryOperation>= <expression>
```

which are interpreted as

```
<variable> = <variable> <binaryOperation> <expression>
```

Like in Java, not all supported binary operators can be combined with the assignment operator. For example, the logical operators (&& and ||) cannot be used as they have short-circuited behavior.

Note the statement:

`<variable>++` is equivalent to `<variable> += 1`

`<variable>--` is equivalent to `<variable> -= 1`

Go allows parallel (aka tuple) assignments of the form:

```
<variable1>,<variable2>,...,<variableN> = <expression1>,<expression2>,...,
<expressionN>
```

where N must be the same on each side. Any (but typically not all) `<variableX>` can be replaced with an underscore ("_") to ignore that expression position which is often done on function call results.

All right-side values must be compatible with (able to be assigned to) the corresponding variables on the left side without any implied conversion (except for some numeric literal values). In general, this means the left-side variable and right-side value in the corresponding positions must be of the same type.

The declaration form is allowed if at least one of the variables on the left side is being newly declared:

```
<variable1>,<variable2>,...,<variableN> := <expression1>,<expression2>,...,
<expressionN>
```

In all the preceding examples, `<variableX>` is any expression that defines an assignable target (aka left value). Often, these are simple identifiers (variable names), but could also be indexed arrays, slices, maps, or pointer variable dereferences.

Declaring Variables

Java allows variables to be declared one at a time and in groups. Go does as well. In both Java and Go, any initial values are optional. Note in Java, block/method locals can be created with no initial value. The same is not possible in Go; all declared values have an initial (called *zero*) value if none is specified.

Java's declaration:

```
{<vis>} {<mod>}... <type> <id> {= <value>} {, <id> {= <value>}}...;
```

The type is any built-in or declared type (class, interface, enum, etc.). The values must be convertible into the type. If omitted, the default value (except for block/method locals) is used. The value may be an expression.

The `<vis>` modifier is allowed only on field declarations. It is one of `public`, `private`, `protected`, or omitted (which implies default or package protected). The Java `<mod>` modifiers, like `abstract` and `final`, are generally allowed only on field declarations and have no Go equivalents.

Go's equivalent to a declaration statement:

var `<id> {, <id>}... <type>`

or

var `<id> {, <id>}... <type> = <value> {, <value>}...`

or

var `<id> {, <id>}... = <value> {, <value>}...`

The type is any built-in or declared type. Each value must be of the same type. If the value is a literal, it must be convertible into the type. If omitted, the zero value is used. A type is only required if all values are omitted; if a value is present, its type will be used to infer any missing type. The inferred type may be different for each position. Any value may be an expression. There must be the same number of ids and values.

As mentioned earlier, Go does not have a visibility modifier. If the id starts with an uppercase letter, it is public; else, it is package private (can be seen only by code in the same package).

Go allows a more concise form of declaration:

var (`{<xxx> {, <xxx>...})`

where xxx is a declaration as before without the "var" prefix. The closing ")" is usually on a line by itself. This is the conventional way to declare variables.

For example:

```
var (
        p = 1
        q = "hello"
        l int
        f float64 = 0
)
```

In top-level declarations, any comment on var is shared by all members of the group. Go has an alternate declaration form for block local (not field) declarations:

`<id> {, <id>}... := <value> {, <value>}...`

where the count of ids and values must match. Also, at least one id must not already be declared in the same block. The types of the ids can be different and are implied by the values.

Tuple assignment (or declarations) has many uses, but some common ones are

- Swap values without using temporary variables

  For example:

  ```
  var x, y = 1, 2
  x, y = y, x // after x==2, y == 1
  ```

- Split the results of the range operations

  For example:

  ```
  for index, next := range collection { ... }
  - or -
  for _, next := range collection { ... }
  ```

- Split the results returned from a function or operator

For example:

```
file, err := os.Open(...)
- or -
if v, ok := map[key]; ok { ... }
```

Declaring Named Constants

Java allows constant-like[1] (`static final`) values to be declared. Go has true constants. Go supports constants defined one at a time and in groups. In both Java and Go, an initial value is required.

Java's declaration (inside some type):

```
{<vis>} static final <type> <id> {= <value>} {, <id> {= <value>}}...;
```

The values must be convertible into the type. The value must be a constant expression.

The `<vis>` is allowed only on field declarations. It is one of `public`, `private`, `protected`, or omitted (which implies default or package protected).

Go's equivalent to a declaration statement:

```
const <id> {, <id>}... <type> = <value> {, <value>}...
```

or

```
const <id> {, <id>}... = <value> {, <value>}...
```

The type is any built-in or declared type that has a literal initializer. The value must be of the same type. If the value is a literal, it must be convertible into the type. The value must be an expression that can be evaluated at compile time (i.e., all referenced identifiers are to other constants with no circular references). There must be the same number of ids and values.

Go does not have a visibility modifier. If the id starts with an uppercase letter, it is public; else, it is package private (can be seen only by code in the same package).

---

[1] These are not true constants (exist at compile time only), but instead are immutable values.

Go allows a more concise form of declaration:

const ({<xxx> {**,** <xxx>...})

where xxx is a declaration as before without the "const" prefix. The closing ")" is usually on a line by itself. This is the conventional way to declare constants.

For example:

```
const (
        p = 1
        q = "hello"
        f float64 = 0
)
```

If/Else Statements

If/Else is the most basic condition testing mechanism. It allows alternate flows in a sequence of code.

Java's if statements:

if(<cond>**)** <block>

or

if(<cond>**)** <block> **else** <block>

Java allows arbitrary executable statements in addition to blocks as if/else targets.

Go's if statement:

if {<simpleStmt>;} <cond> <block>

or

if {<simpleStmt>;} <cond> <block>
else (<ifStmt>|<block>)

If/else targets are statement blocks (which is also best practice in Java). The Else statement also allows another if statement as a target; this allows a multiple condition test. In Go, a multiple condition test is best done by using a Switch statement instead.

214

The optional simple statement is one of

- Empty (omitted – no semicolon) statement

- Expression statement

- Send (channel <-) statement

- Inc/dec statement

- Assignment

- Short variable declaration (most common option)

The if statement creates an implied block, so any declarations hide such names from containing scopes. For example:

```
var x, y = 0, 0
if t := x; t < 0 {  // t in new scope
    var x = 1 // a new x variable; hides x above
    y = t + x
} else {
    y = -1
}
```

Note the `else` clause, if present, must start on the same line as the close of the `if` block.

In idiomatic Go, the use of `else` is minimized. So, it is common to return from conditional (say If) blocks. When one does this, it is unconventional to use the `else` clause (which is superfluous). For example:

```
if t < 0 {
    return true
} else {
    return false
}
```

is more conventionally written as

```
if t < 0 {
    return true
}
return false
```

It can also be expressed even more concisely as

```
return t < 0
```

In this way, idiomatic Go code tends to stay aligned on the left edge of the containing function and not get deeply nested. If your code is nested more than (say) two levels, consider rewriting it to reduce the levels using the return, break, or continue statements or by extracting deeply nested code as a new function.

Go has strong source style rules. One is how to test Boolean values. Consider the (common) example:

```
if v, ok := aMap[someKey]; !ok {
        return
}
```

vs.

```
if v, ok := aMap[someKey];  ok == false {
        return
}
```

The first form (direct use of Boolean) is idiomatic and generally used over the second (comparison of Booleans) form.

Java has a *ternary* expression (?:) that allows (often convenient) conditional testing. For example:

```
int x = input < 0 ? -input : input;   // a simple abs(input)
```

This is a short form of

```
if(input < 0) x = -input; else x = input;
```

but as an expression (vs. a statement).

Go has no equivalent to this expression. One must do this:

```
var x int
if input < 0 {
        x = -input
} else {
        x = input
}
```

216

or

```
var x int = input // (or x := input)
if input < 0 {
     x = -input
}
```

Or, for simple bodies (say variables or constants), more concisely:

```
var x int; if input < 0 { x = -input } else { x = input }
```

or

```
x := input; if input < 0 { x = -input }
```

Note even if entered as shown earlier, most Go source formatters will split these lines at the semicolons.

Switch Statement

Like Java, Go has a Switch statement. In general, Go's Switch statement is more flexible. The Java Switch statement follows this general form:

```
switch (<expr>) {
  case <value1>:
    :
  case <value2>:
    <statements>
    break;
  :
  default:
    <statements>
}
```

Each group of statements can be proceeded by one or more case introducers. The expr value is matched (tested for equality) against each case value (which must be unique), and any code after the match is executed. If not provided in the code, the flow continues through following cases until a break is found. The expr can be of any integer type, a String type, or any enum type. If no match occurs and the `default` introducer is present, that code is run.

The Go equivalent of the preceding example is

```
switch <expr> {
  case <value> {, <value>}...:
    <statements>
  default:
    <statements>
}
```

The switch statement and each case create an implied block, so any declarations hide such names from containing scopes.

In the Go case, multiple match values are used per case instead of multiple case introducers. Also, in the Go case, each group of statements has an implicit break at the end. Like in Java, the values must be distinct. Also, in Go, each case is its own block, as if it had been entered as (which would be needed in Java)

```
case <value>: {
    <statements>
}
```

This means variables may be declared as local in that set of statements.

To get Java-like no-break fall through, end the set of statements with the Fall Through statement as follows:

```
switch <expr> {
  case <value1>:
    <statements>
    fallthrough
  case <value2>
    <statements>
  default:
    <statements>
}
```

Java supports cascaded if statements as follows:

```
if(<expr1>) {
  :
} else if(<expr2>) {
  :
} ... else if(<exprN>) {
:
} else {
  :
}
```

The approach is also supported in Go, but the idiomatic way to do this is with a different form of switch:

```
switch {
  case <expr1>:
    <statements>
  case <expr2>
    <statements>
  :
  case <exprN>
    <statements>
  default:
    <statements>
}
```

The expressions can be arbitrary except they must be of Boolean type. The cases (except the default case) are tested in the order entered.

So, this switch statement:

```
var c, ditto rune = 'c', '\0'
switch c {
case 'a', 'b', 'c':
      ditto = c
default:
      ditto = 'x'
}
```

and this switch statement are equivalent:

```
var c, ditto rune = 'c', '\0'
switch {
case c == 'a', c == 'b', c == 'c':
        ditto = c
default:
        ditto = 'x'
}
```

Java recently added an expression (has a resulting value) form of the Switch statement (sort of an enhanced ternary expression). A switch can be a term in any expression. Go has nothing like this. These switch expressions add the no fall through case style Go has. Also, the cases create their own blocks like in Go. Associated with this new switch is the new yield statement that returns the switch's value.

While Statement

While is a basic looping mechanism. It allows conditionally (pretest) repeated flows in a sequence of code.

Java's while statement:

```
while (<cond>) <block>
```

Java allows arbitrary executable statements as while targets.

Go's equivalent to a while statement:

```
for <cond> <block>
```

The statement's target is a block (which is best practice in Java).

For example:

```
var x, y = 10, 0
for x > 0 {
  y++
  x--
}
```

Do-While Statement

Do-While is a basic looping mechanism. It allows conditionally (posttest) repeated flow in a sequence of code.

Java's do-while statement:

do <block> **while (**<cond>**);**

Go has no direct equivalent to a Do-While statement. One can be made from a for statement with a test included in the block as follows:

```
var x, y = 10, 0
for {
     y++
     x--
     if x < 0 {
          break
     }
}
```

For with Index Statement

For is the primary indexed looping mechanism. It allows an index to span a range and be acted on by repeated flow in a sequence of code. Go's For statement provides a similar function as Java's For statements.

Java's for statement:

for({<init>}**;**{<cond>}**;**{<inc>}**)** <block>

Java allows arbitrary executable statements as for targets.

Go's equivalent to a for statement:

for {<init>}**;**{<cond>}**;**{<inc>} <block>

Unlike in Java, Go does not support comma (",") separated expressions in the <init> and <inc> clauses.

221

The statement's target is a block (which is best practice in Java). The `<cond>` clause is optional and is `true` if omitted. The optional `<init>` and `<inc>` groups can be one of

- Empty (omitted – no semicolon) statement
- Expression statement
- Send (channel <-) statement
- Inc/dec statement
- Assignment
- Short variable declaration

The statement creates an implied block, so any declarations hide such names from containing scopes.

For example:

```
var x, y = 10, 0
for i := 0; i < 10; i++ {
      y++
}
```

For over a Collection Statement

For is the primary looping mechanism for iterating over a (possibly empty) collection (or other stream of values). It allows the elements of a collection to be processed one at a time by repeated flow in a sequence of code. The processing order is determined by the collection.

Java's for statement:

```
for(<varDecl>: <iterable>) <block>
```

Or (more verbosely) one can do

```
Collection<SomeType> c = <some collection>;
Iterator<SomeType> it = c.iterator();
for(; it.hasNext();) {  // could use while here instead
  <varDecl> = it.next();

  :
}
```

Or (more verbosely) one can do (over an indexable collection)

```
Collection<SomeType> c = <some collection>;
for(int i = 0, count = c.size(); i < count; i++) {
  <varDecl> = c.get(i);
  :
}
```

Go's equivalent to a for statement over a collection:

```
for <indexVar>,<valueVar> := range <collection> <block>
```

The statement's target is a block (which is best practice in Java). The optional (at least one is needed) <indexVar> and <valueVar> receive the index (or key) of the next item and the next item's value. The <collection> must be some collection or stream type, like an array, a slice, a map, or a channel.

Go requires all declared variables (left of :=) to be used in the block body. To avoid this requirement, some can be replaced with an underscore ("_") if they are not referenced.

For example:

```
for _, v := range []string{"x", "y", "z"} {
     fmt.Println(v)
}
```

or

```
aMap := make(map[string]string)
:
for k, v := range aMap {
     fmt.Printf("%s = %s", k, v)
}
```

A Java equivalent could be

```
Map<String,String> m = <some map>;
for(Iterator<String> it = m.keySet().iterator(); it.hasNext();) {
  var k = it.next();
  var v = m.get(k);
  System.out.printf("%s = %s", k, v);
}
```

The order that range presents keys for maps is unspecified and can be different for each map instance. This is on purpose. To process the keys in some order, they must first be explicitly ordered, say sorted. For example:

```
aMap := make(map[string]string)
:
keys := make([]string, 0, len(aMap)) // note created empty
for k, _ := range aMap {
    keys = append(keys, k)
}
sort.Strings(keys)
for _, k := range keys {
    fmt.Printf("%s = %s", k, aMap[k])
}
```

Note Java's TreeMap type makes this much simpler.

The keys slice can also be made like this:

```
keys := make([]string, len(aMap))   // note created full size
index := 0
for k, _ := range aMap {
    keys[index] = k  // "keys[index++] = k" not supported
    index++
}
```

The preceding approach can be more time efficient.

Forever Statement

For is the primary infinite looping mechanism. It allows an indefinite repeated flow in a sequence of code.

Java's for statement:

```
for(;;) <block>  // while (true) also works
```

Go's equivalent to a for statement:

```
for <block>
```

The target is a block (which is best practice in Java).

For example:

```
var x, y = 10, 0
for {
        y++
        x--
        if x < 0 {
                break
        }
}
```

Break and Continue Statements

Go, like Java, has break and continue statements that work in basically the same way. Break exits a loop, while continue moves to the next iteration of the loop. Often, these statements are in the bodies of some conditional statement like if or for. The syntax is

```
break {<label>}
continue {<label>}
```

If a label is present, it must be a label attached to some containing loop. This allows an exit from multiple levels of nested loops. If omitted, the most nested loop is assumed. Any loop can be labeled as follows (but the label must be referenced by some break or continue):

```
{<label> :}... <forStatement>
```

Note the Java use of a break statement in the switch statement to exit a case is automatic in Go, so break is not needed in Go's switch (or select) statements to avoid fall through. A break or continue may be used (say as an if body) to exit a case before the end.

Goto Statement

Go supports a Go-To (unconditional jump) statement; Java does not (although it is a reserved word). It allows jumps within the same block (but not out of a block or into a nested block). Declarations cannot be skipped by using Go-To. Any labeled statement in the same block can be a target. The format is

goto `<label>`

Go-To can be used instead of more structured forms. For example, a loop of this conceptual form:

```
for cur:=0; cur < 10; cur++ {
    : body of loop
}
```

can be created this way:

```
cur := 0
L1: if cur >= 10 {
        goto L2
}
: body of loop
cur++
goto L1
L2:
```

Note in the author's opinion, the goto statement should never be used; if, switch, and for provide enough local control flow. Your code should follow the principles of structured programming[2] with its Goto[3]-less approach.

---

[2] https://en.wikipedia.org/wiki/Structured_programming; https://en.wikipedia.org/wiki/Structured_program_theorem

[3] https://en.wikipedia.org/wiki/Goto

Return Statement

In Java, every method exits (possibly implicitly on void methods as running off the end of a void function implicitly returns) with a return statement. The return statement provides the value to return and looks like this:

return {<value>} // <value> present only on non-void methods

In Go, Return is nearly identical except that multiple values can be returned like this:

return {<value>{,<value>...}} // <value>... only on non-void methods

The number of returned values must match the number of declared return values on the function prototype. If the returned values are named, the return statement can omit them.

For example:

```
func threeInts() (int, int, int) {
    :
    return 1, 2, 3 // required explicit return values
}
```

or:

```
func threeInts() (x, y, z int) {
    :
    return 1, 2, 3 // explicit return values (ignore names)
}
```

or:

```
func threeInts() (x, y, z int) {
    x, y, z = 1, 2, 3   // set return values before returning
    :
    return // implicit return values
}
```

This last form is generally recommended by this author. Others may take a different position.

Defer Statement

Java has two popular resource cleanup mechanisms:

1. Try/Finally (or Try/Catch/Finally)

2. Try with resources

Try/Finally, in general, looks like this:

```
try <block>
finally <block>
```

where the `finally` clause is executed no matter how the `try` clause ends (normally, via return or via some exception).

Try with resources typically looks like this:

```
try (<declaration> = <new Resource>{;<declaration> = <new Resource>}...) {
    // use the resource(s)
}
```

where any resource allocated in the `try` clause is automatically released (in a compiler-written `finally` clause) when the `try` ends (normally, via return or via some exception).

Go has a feature like try/finally but nothing like try with resources. Go uses the Defer statement that acts much like a `finally` clause. This statement looks like

```
defer <function call>
```

Each time the defer statement is executed (even in a loop), a call of the provided function is placed on the call stack. When the function that contains the defer statement exits, the deferred function calls are executed in reverse order. There can be many deferred functions. This happens even if the containing function ends in a `return` or a panic (Go's equivalent of a thrown exception).

The typical approach is shown in this example:

```
func someFunction() {
    // acquire some resource
    defer func() {
        // release the resource
    }() // note the function is called
    : use the resource
}
```

In this pattern, immediately after any resource is acquired, a deferred function to release the resource is registered. The deferring function continues and eventually returns or panics which results in the deferred function being called.

Note that the deferred function has access to the local variables (must be declared before the defer is coded) of the deferring function (it is a closure) and is called before the deferring function returns to its caller, which allows it to change the deferring function's return values. This can be useful, especially in panic (such as on a divide by zero) or other error recovery. For example:

```
func someFunction() (result int, err error) {
    defer func() {
        if result == 0 {   // default value
            result = -1
            err = errors.New("bad value")
        }
    }()
    :
    result = 1
    :
    return
}
```

Go Statement

The Go statement launches a goroutine. A goroutine is just a normal Go function that typically does not return any values (if it does, they are discarded). A goroutine is created and started with the Go statement as follows:

```
go <func>({arg, {arg}....})
```

The Go statement returns immediately, and the function runs asynchronously to (possibly in parallel with) the caller. The function is called with any supplied arguments in a different goroutine from the caller.

Note that all code in Go runs in some goroutine, including the `main()` function. Often, a function literal, instead of a predeclared function, is used, such as

```
go func(x int) {
    :
}(1)  // note the function is called
```

Note the author recommends naming functions that are expected to be run with Go with a suffix of "Go" (or similar) to make this use case explicit.

Select Statement

Go has a Select statement which has no counterpart in Java. The Select statement is used to process items received over channels or to send items to channels. Make sure you understand channels before using Select. Select statements look much like Switch statements:

```
select {
  case <receiver>{, <receiver>}... = <- <channel>:
    <statements>
  case <identifier>, <var> := <- <channel>:
    <statements>
  case <channel> <- <expression>:
    <statements>
  default:
    <statements>
}
```

The `<receiver>` is an expression (often just an identifier) that specifies a variable to receive the channel's value. The Select statement and each case create an implied block, so any declarations hide such names from containing scopes.

The first two cases trigger when an item is available to receive from a channel. The third case triggers (if the receiving channel has room) when it is possible to send an item to the channel. All cases are evaluated/tested. If any cases are triggered, one of them is selected randomly and is executed, and any associated assignments and/or statements are done.

The second case has a <var> (often named "ok") which is set to indicate if the source channel is closed or not. It will be `false` when the channel is closed.

The `default` case is triggered if no other cases are triggered. It is often omitted. Select statements with no default clause can block waiting to receive or send an item.

Select statements are frequently done inside an infinite loop as follows:

```
for {
  select {
    :
  }
}
```

This allows for items to be received from a channel and processed for as long as they are sent (i.e., the channel is open).

An example that can receive a value for two different channels:

```
var cchan chan int
var ichan chan int
var schan chan string
var scount, icount int
select {
case <- schan:                    // receive
      scount++                    // count receive
case <- ichan:                    // receive
      icount++                    // count receive
case cchan <- scount + icount:    // send current total
default:
      fmt.Println("no match")
}
```

CHAPTER 9

Applications for Interfaces

In this chapter, we will discuss some interesting applications of interfaces in Java and how they relate to Go coding.

An Interface Is the Key

Just like in Java, using interfaces (over concrete types) as parameter and return types is important in Go. It enables many options, such as substituting mock objects[1] for normal objects, which is critical for testing. So, especially when you pass a struct type into or out of a function, see if you can replace the struct with an interface type. This is generally possible if your function uses only methods of the struct and not its fields.

If no existing interface exists that matches the methods you use, create one and publish it for others to use. For example, given this type:

```go
type Xxx struct {
    :
}
func (x *Xxx) DoSomethingGood() {
    :
}
func (x *Xxx) DoSomethingBad() (err error) {
    :
}
```

---

[1]https://en.wikipedia.org/wiki/Mock_object

© Barry Feigenbaum 2022
B. Feigenbaum, *Go for Java Programmers*, https://doi.org/10.1007/978-1-4842-7199-5_9

You can create the interfaces:

```
type DoGooder interface {
    DoSomethingGood()
}
type DoBader interface {
    DoSomethingBad() error
}
```

Then in some client that uses Xxx, say like this:

```
func DoWork(xxx *Xxx) {
    xxx.DoSomethingGood()
}
```

You can convert this to

```
func DoWork(dg DoGooder) {
    dg.DoSomethingGood()
}
```

But now the DoWork caller can send an instance of Xxx or any other type that has a DoSomethingGood() method. Sometimes, you need to call multiple methods of the struct type. There are two main options:

1. Give the function multiple parameters, one for each different interface type needed, and the caller passes in the same object for all parameters.

2. Create combining interfaces and pass in that type.

Option two is generally preferred over option one.

For option one, this can be used as

```
func DoWork(dg DoGooder, db DoBader) {
    dg.DoSomethingGood()
    db.DoSomethingBad()
}
```

It can be called like this:

```
var xxx *Xxx
:
DoWork(xxx, xxx)
```

For option two, the combined interface could be

```
type DoGoodAndBad interface {
    DoGooder
    DoBader
}
```

It can be used like this:

```
func DoWork(dgb DoGoodAndBad) {
    dgb.DoSomethingGood()
    dgb.DoSomethingBad()
}
```

It can be called like this:

```
var xxx *Xxx
:
DoWork(xxx)
```

Somewhat surprisingly, this can also be called like this (with an object, and not a pointer to the object):

```
var xxx Xxx
:
DoWork(xxx)
```

The Go compiler detects the use of pointers to an object vs. an object and does the right thing. This happens only with parameters of an interface type.

Similarly, for functions that currently return struct types, one can change them to either return multiple interfaces or return a combined interface.

There is an issue with interfaces that can be quite problematic. As Go does not allow overloaded (same name, different signatures) functions for the same type, you easily create multiple interfaces with the same method names, often with different parameter and/or return types. But you cannot combine them into a new interface. This also means that a type cannot simultaneously implement these different interfaces.

There is no easy fix for this. So be careful in choosing the method names in an interface, as you can end up reserving that name for the behavior. For example, the io. Writer interface pretty much claims the Write method (with its particular parameters) to mean only what it thinks it means. Other interfaces cannot create a method called Write for another purpose without conflicting with this interface.

For example, you can create an interface as such:

```
type MyWriter interface {
    // vs. io.Writer: Write([]byte) (int,error)
    Write([]byte, int) error
}
```

It is not possible to create a type that implements both the MyWriter and io.Writer interfaces.

One way to avoid this issue is to create methods with longer, often multiword, names and leave short names for the Go runtime developers to use.

On Dependency Injection

Taking the use of interfaces even further, one should utilize *Dependency Injection*[2] (DI) wherever possible. DI is a design approach where code is provided with its dependencies instead of acquiring them for itself (in other words, let someone else provide you with all your dependencies). DI separates the responsibility for creating the dependency from the code that is dependent on it. DI implementations often require that the injected type conforms to some interface type.

This approach offers far greater flexibility, especially when (1) testing code (one can inject mock objects) or (2) when configuring complex relationships between objects. This second situation is so pervasive in Java development that a major framework,

---

[2] https://en.wikipedia.org/wiki/Dependency_injection

Spring,[3] along with *Spring Boot*,[4] was created just to provide it. Other options also exist, such as Google's *Guice*.[5]

Wikipedia defines DI as follows:

"Dependency injection separates the creation of a client's dependencies from the client's behavior, which allows program designs to be loosely coupled and to follow the dependency inversion[6] and single responsibility[7] principles."

Wikipedia describes Spring DI:

Central to the Spring Framework is its inversion of control[8] (IoC) container, which provides a consistent means of configuring and managing Java objects using reflection. The container is responsible for managing object lifecycles of specific objects: creating these objects, calling their initialization methods, and configuring these objects by wiring them together. Objects created by the container are also called managed objects or beans. Objects can be obtained by means of either dependency lookup or dependency injection.

So, what is a dependency? It is an object that (at least)

1. Has a state and/or behavior.

2. The state should be encapsulated (hidden from any users) so the implementation can change. Thus, the behavior is best represented as an interface.

3. Is used by some (the dependent) code.

In the Spring case, there is a DI *Container* that manages what are called *Beans* (POJOs[9] that can be linked together). Containers often act like a map, providing named objects that can be resolved at runtime. In most cases, the container creates the bean instances based on either an annotation (say @Bean) on factory methods or external (say in XML) definitions. DI is often directed via annotations (such as @Inject or @Wired) to tell the container to link (inject) a source POJO to a target POJO.

---

[3] https://en.wikipedia.org/wiki/Spring_Framework; https://spring.io/
[4] https://spring.io/projects/spring-boot
[5] https://en.wikipedia.org/wiki/Google_Guice
[6] https://en.wikipedia.org/wiki/Single-responsibility_principle
[7] https://en.wikipedia.org/wiki/Dependency_inversion_principle
[8] https://en.wikipedia.org/wiki/Inversion_of_control
[9] https://en.wikipedia.org/wiki/Plain_old_Java_object

The container owns ordering prerequisite bean creation and injection. Often, the beans are singleton objects (one instance shared across the application). Containers are generally not sources of objects that come and go during program execution. Often, the container takes the role of the main program, creating beans and then "wiring" them together while the program is being launched.

Java DI frameworks often use reflection to create the object to be injected. They often take a POJO as defined by the application developer and wrap it in a *Proxy*[10] that adds extra function, such as logging or database transaction management. Key to the notion of a proxy is that the proxy's client cannot, by the proxied interface alone, tell it from the object it is the proxy of; it fully implements the proxied object's behavioral contract, and it is thus a drop-in replacement for the object. In most cases, the POJO class must implement one or more interfaces that can have a concrete implementation defined dynamically at runtime.

Go currently does not support this dynamic creation of a proxy as it seems impossible to define types at runtime, by using reflection, that can be used to implement interface conforming objects. This is partially why the code generation approach is often used. Perhaps this will change in the future. Go does support creating proxy-like façade objects that the client may be aware of.

Let us define the term POGO as the Go equivalent of POJO. POGOs are generally implemented as Go structs.

Go has no standard DI container implementation. The Go community has provided some, such as Uber's *Dig*[11] (or *Fx*[12]) and Google's *Wire*.[13]

Dig is described as follows:

A reflection-based dependency injection toolkit for Go that is good for:

- *Powering an application framework*
- *Resolving the object graph during process startup*

Wire is described as follows:

a code generation tool that automates connecting components using dependency injection. Dependencies between components are represented

---

[10] https://en.wikipedia.org/wiki/Proxy_pattern, https://docs.oracle.com/javase/8/docs/api/java/lang/reflect/Proxy.html

[11] https://github.com/uber-go/dig

[12] https://pkg.go.dev/go.uber.org/fx

[13] https://github.com/google/wire

in Wire as function parameters, encouraging explicit initialization instead of global variables. Because Wire operates without runtime state or reflection, code written to be used with Wire is useful even for hand-written initialization.

These two example containers exemplify the major approaches to implementing Go containers:

1. Use reflection (like Spring does) to set fields in POGOs to wire them together.

2. Use code generation to create logic (much like if manually done in main) to wire POGOs together.

DI containers are especially good for providing dependencies such as loggers, database connection pools, data caches, HTTP clients, and similar pseudo-global values. In fact, if done to the maximum, the container itself is the only public top-level object in the application; all others are managed by the container.

In Go, there are several options for injection:

1. Instance initialization – Here, the dependency is injected by being set when the instance literal is declared.

2. Constructor/factory – Here, the dependency is injected by being passed to a constructor (New...) function or some other factory method. Generally, this is the preferred option.

3. Direct field assignment – Here, the dependency is injected by assigning the field directly. Generally, the field must be public (as the dependent type is often in a different package) to enable this. This option should be avoided.

4. Setter method – Here, the dependency is injected by it being passed to a "setter" method. This is rarely done as structs do not generally offer a get/set method for all private fields, especially as part of the dependency's public interface.

The first two forms are limited in that it is not possible to set up POGOs that circularly depend on each other. In general, it is best to avoid such dependency graphs; dependencies should form a hierarchy. For the last two, the dependency is set after the instance is created, so there is a window when the dependency is not set.

239

As an example of manual DI, consider these three dependency types (Cache, HTTPClient, and Logger) shown in Listing 9-1. An example of the base function (no DI) shown via a browser in Figure 9-1.

Listing 9-1. Dependency Injection in a Go Example

```go
package main
import (
    "fmt"
    "time"
)
type Cache interface {
    Get(name string) (interface{}, bool)
    Set(name string, value interface{}) error
    ClearName(name string)
    ClearAll()
}
type MapCache map[string]interface{}
func (c MapCache) Get(name string) (res interface{}, ok bool) {
    res, ok = c[name]
    return
}
func (c MapCache) Set(name string, value interface{}) (err error) {
    c[name] = value
    return
}
func (c MapCache) ClearName(name string) {
    delete(c, name)
    return
}
func (c MapCache) ClearAll() {
    for k, _ := range c {
        delete(c, k)
    }
    return
}
```

```go
type HTTPClient interface {
    SendReceive(url, method string, in interface{}) (out interface{},
        err error)
}

type EchoHTTPClient struct {
}

func (c *EchoHTTPClient) SendReceive(url, method string, in interface{})
(out interface{},
    err error) {
    out = fmt.Sprintf("SENT %s %s with %v", method, url, in)
    return
}

type Logger interface {
    Log(format string, args ...interface{})
}

type StdoutLogger struct {
}

func (l *StdoutLogger) Log(format string, args ...interface{}) {
    fmt.Printf("%s - %s\n", time.Now().Format(time.StampMilli), fmt.
    Sprintf(format, args...))
}

type HTTPService struct { // also a HTTPClient
    log     Logger
    client HTTPClient
    cache   Cache
    // :  other fields not using dependencies
}

func NewService(client HTTPClient, log Logger,
    cache Cache) (s *HTTPService) {
    s = &HTTPService{}
    s.log = log
    s.client = client
```

```go
        s.cache = cache
        // : set other fields
        return
}

func (s *HTTPService) SendReceive(url, method string,
        in interface{}) (out interface{}, err error) {
        key := fmt.Sprintf("%s:%s", method, url)
        if xout, ok := s.cache.Get(key); ok {
                out = xout
                return
        }
        out, err = s.client.SendReceive(url, method, in)
        s.log.Log("SendReceive(%s, %s, %v)=%v", method, url, in, err)
        if err != nil {
                return
        }
        err = s.cache.Set(key, out)
        return
}

func main() {
        log := StdoutLogger{}      // concrete type
        client := EchoHTTPClient{} // concrete type
        cache := MapCache{}        // concrete type
        // create a service with all dependencies injected
        s := NewService(&client, &log, cache)
        // :
        for i:= 0; i < 5; i++ {
                if i % 3 == 0 {
                        cache.ClearAll()
                }
                data, err := s.SendReceive("some URL", "GET",
                        fmt.Sprintf("index=%d", i))
                if err != nil {
                        fmt.Printf("Failed: %v\n", err)
```

```
        continue
      }
      fmt.Printf("Received: %v\n", data)
   }
   // :
}
```

The preceding example shows how three injectable interfaces are defined, and a simple sample (perhaps called a mock) implementation is provided for each interface, and then each implementation is injected. Here, the main() function sends five transactions and clears the cache part way through the sequence. Note the following output shows the impact of the caching (only two of the five transactions were executed):

```
Jul 20 09:10:40.348 - SendReceive(GET, some URL, index=0)=<nil>
Received: SENT GET some URL with index=0
Received: SENT GET some URL with index=0
Received: SENT GET some URL with index=0
Jul 20 09:10:40.349 - SendReceive(GET, some URL, index=3)=<nil>
Received: SENT GET some URL with index=3
Received: SENT GET some URL with index=3
```

Some in the Go community argue that using DI, especially when managed by containers, is not idiomatic for Go. DI via containers can hide the relationships between objects, while manually creating them in code (as shown earlier) is more obvious. There is merit to this argument. But as the complexity of applications grows and the piece parts (POGOs) involved increase, the manual code can get out of hand, and an automated DI solution may be appropriate (or even necessary).

Regardless of how you end up on this argument, in the author's opinion, making your code capable of supporting DI is the better approach. Also, if both Google and Facebook offer libraries to do DI, it must be useful.

On Aspect-Oriented Programming

Java supports a style of programming called *Aspect-Oriented Programming*[14] (AOP). AOP allows one to augment (with what is called *advice*) code (often called base or original code) with new behavior (also code). Wikipedia describes it as follows:

> *a programming paradigm that aims to increase modularity by allowing the separation of cross-cutting concerns*[15] (XCC). *It does so by adding additional behavior to existing code (an advice) without modifying the code itself, instead separately specifying which code is modified via a "pointcut" specification, such as "log all function calls when the function's name begins with 'set'". This allows behaviors that are not central to the business logic to be added to a program without cluttering the code, core to the functionality.*

There are three key concepts in AOP:

1. Pointcut – Specifies where to apply advice; often, some predicate (often a pattern such as a regular expression) that selects code or data to advise. Pointcuts are often limited to matching one or more methods in one or more types, but some AOP systems also allow matching of data fields. Many joint points can match a pointcut.

2. Advice – What to do when the pointcut is triggered. There are many kinds of advice, but the most common are Before, After, and Around.

3. Join point – The actual location in the code where the advice is applied.

The pointcuts and advising code are often defined by a class-like construct called an *Aspect*, which is a means to describe the pointcuts and/or advice desired. With Java, there are several approaches to applying advice at joint points:

1. Statically rewrite source code – Some preprocessor (before compilation) edits the base source code.

---

[14] https://en.wikipedia.org/wiki/Aspect-oriented_programming
[15] https://en.wikipedia.org/wiki/Cross-cutting_concern

2. Statically rewrite object code – Some postprocessor (after compilation) edits the base object code (this would be difficult to do in Go; easier if done during the code generation phase which requires compiler changes).

3. Dynamically rewrite object code – Some runtime processor edits the object code, generally when it is first loaded (this would be difficult to do in Go).

4. Use dynamic proxies – Some runtime processor wraps the code, generally when it is first loaded (this would be difficult to do in Go).

Java has several AOP implementations. The most popular are *AspectJ*[16] and *Spring AOP.*[17] AspectJ is more comprehensive and principally uses augmentation options two and three. Spring AOP principally uses augmentation option four.

AOP is often used to add behavior to code. Common examples are to add logging, authorization checks, and transaction support to web API handlers. These are examples of XCC which typically are not part of the mainline purpose or core concerns of the code but support contextual needs. It is better if the main code is not cluttered with code to provide them.

Go AOP options are limited. There is no direct support in the standard library. Some community-provided options exist, but they may not be mature. They are not as comprehensive as the Java offerings. Currently, no Go AOP offering seems to support noninvasively (neither the client nor service code is changed) adding advice to base types like Java AOP does.

AOP style programming can appear to be "magical" (code has new behavior, and the source of the behavior is not always obvious). Like with DI containers, AOP style programming is not idiomatic in Go. But like with DI, it can be a powerful means to add support.

In Go, AOP-like behavior can be achieved by applying code, often called *middleware*[18] (aka software glue). This is a function added between a client and a service (thus the term middle) by wrapping the service in processors that conform to the prototype of the service. Since Go supports first-class functions, middleware can be relatively easy to implement.

---

[16] www.eclipse.org/aspectj/

[17] https://howtodoinjava.com/spring-aop-tutorial/

[18] https://en.wikipedia.org/wiki/Middleware

Note any HTTP handler must conform to this interface defined in net/http:

```
type HandlerFunc func(http.ResponseWriter, *http.Request)
```

Given these helper functions, shown in Listings 9-2 and 9-3 (aka middleware or around advice):

Listing 9-2. Advice/Middleware for HTTP Requests (Part 1)

```
package main

import (
    "fmt"
    "log"
    "net/http"
    "time"
)

func LogWrapper(f http.HandlerFunc) http.HandlerFunc {
    return func(w http.ResponseWriter, req *http.Request) {
        method, path := req.Method, req.URL
        fmt.Printf("entered handler for %s %s\n", method, path)
        f(w, req)
        fmt.Printf("exited handler for %s %s\n", method, path)
    }
}

func ElapsedTimeWrapper(f http.HandlerFunc) http.HandlerFunc {
    return func(w http.ResponseWriter, req *http.Request) {
        method, path := req.Method, req.URL
        start := time.Now().UnixNano()
        f(w, req)
        fmt.Printf("elapsed time for %s %s: %dns\n",
            method, path, time.Now().UnixNano() - start)
    }
}
```

Note that these wrapper functions return other functions that are applied when the target service is invoked, not when the wrapper is called. Both methods are examples of an Around advice (the most common kind) as they take actions both before the target service is called and after the service has returned.

If you need the around behavior to cover possible panics, rewrite the wrappers like so:

```
:
defer func(){
    if p := recover(); p != nil {
        fmt.Printf("elapsed time for %s %s failed: %v\n",
            method, path, p)
        panic(p)
    }
}()
f(w, req)
:
```

For example, let us look at adding logging and timing to HTTP request handlers.

Listing 9-3. Advice/Middleware for HTTP Requests (Part 2)

```go
var spec = ":8086"  // localhost

func main() {
    // regular HTTP request handler
    handler := func(w http.ResponseWriter, req *http.Request) {
        fmt.Printf("in handler %v %v\n", req.Method, req.URL)
        time.Sleep(1 * time.Second)
        w.Write([]byte(fmt.Sprintf("In handler for %s %s", req.Method,
        req.URL)))
    }
    // advised handler
    http.HandleFunc("/test", LogWrapper(ElapsedTimeWrapper(handler)))
    if err := http.ListenAndServe(spec, nil); err != nil {
        log.Fatalf("Failed to start server on %s: %v", spec, err)
    }
}
```

run by:

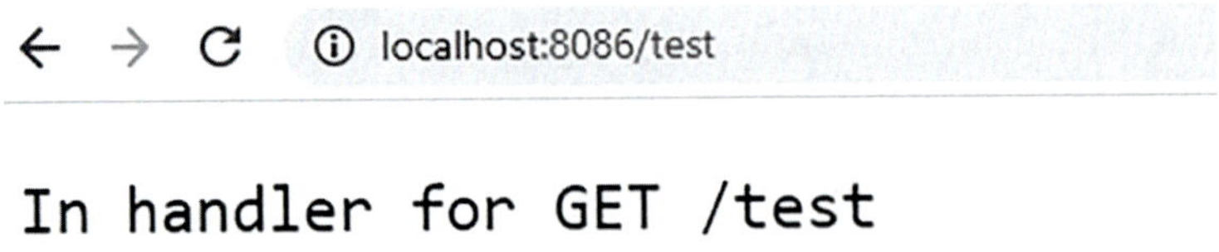

```
In handler for GET /test
```

Figure 9-1. *Invoking a request with advice*

It produces this log output:

```
entered handler for GET /test
in handler GET /test
elapsed time for GET /test: 1000141900ns
exited handler for GET /test
```

Here, the separate concerns of logging and timing are added by distinct pieces of middleware; the original handler is not impacted in any way. Nor is the HTTP engine. Any number of wrappers can be applied (at the cost of some increased execution time). A full-fledged AOP system would likely automate the application of such middleware, but it can also be applied manually as shown earlier.

CHAPTER 10

Go Unit Tests and Benchmarks

Doing frequent and comprehensive unit testing of your code is best practice. Having repeatable (and automated) tests to use for regression test after changes is also best practice. Often, these practices are combined. Similarly, running frequent benchmarks of the performance of your code is best practice. Often, one should create a test suite that achieves as close to 100% code coverage as practical.[1] While not covered deeply in this text, the Go standard runtime supports code coverage tests. A style of development, called *Test-Driven Development*[2] (TDD), emphasizes creating all test cases before any *code under test* (CUT) (i.e., the code to test) is created.

The Go standard runtime provides means to run basic unit test cases and benchmarks of Go code. It also supports advanced profiling of Go programs, but this will not be discussed deeply in this text. See the Go documentation for more information. For Java, similar support requires community-provided libraries and frameworks. The Go test framework resembles the Java *JUnit*[3] framework, especially its earlier (before Java Annotations existed) versions.

A Go test suite often provides multiple unit tests (a unit is a small amount of related code, often a single function or maybe a type with associated methods, or perhaps a package with several types and functions). One can also create functional tests (that test a complex group of types and functions to see if they work, as a set, as expected). Other tests, such as performance, system, security, load, etc., are possible but stretch the

---

[1] 100% coverage generally requires many test cases, often exceeding the volume of CUT. So, some lower target (say ~80%) is often made.

[2] https://en.wikipedia.org/wiki/Test-driven_development

[3] https://en.wikipedia.org/wiki/JUnit. Recent JUnit versions depend on Java Annotations, which Go does not support.

B. Feigenbaum, *Go for Java Programmers*, https://doi.org/10.1007/978-1-4842-7199-5_10

standard testing feature. Like with Java, the Go community provides enhanced testing and benchmarking support for these more advanced tests.

Examples of creating and running test cases in both Go and Java are provided in the following. Both language examples do not cover the full capabilities of the libraries. See the Go testing documentation at `https://golang.org/pkg/testing/`.

Test Cases and Benchmarks in Go

The test concept is best explained by examples. First the sample CUT is shown in Listing 10-1.

Listing 10-1. Code Under Test

```go
package main

import (
    "errors"
    "math/big"
    "math/rand"
    "time"
)

// a set of functions to be tested

// Echo my input

func EchoInt(in int) (out int) {
    randomSleep(50 * time.Millisecond)
    out = in
    return
}

func EchoFloat(in float64) (out float64) {
    randomSleep(50 * time.Millisecond)
    out = in
    return
}
```

```go
func EchoString(in string) (out string) {
    randomSleep(50 * time.Millisecond)
    out = in
    return
}

// Sum my inputs

func SumInt(in1, in2 int) (out int) {
    randomSleep(50 * time.Millisecond)
    out = in1 + in2
    return
}

func SumFloat(in1, in2 float64) (out float64) {
    randomSleep(5)
    out = in1 + in2
    return
}

func SumString(in1, in2 string) (out string) {
    randomSleep(50 * time.Millisecond)
    out = in1 + in2
    return
}

// Factorial computation: factorial(n):
// n < 0 - undefined
// n == 0 - 1
// n > 0 - n * factorial(n-1)

var ErrInvalidInput = errors.New("invalid input")

// Factorial via iteration
func FactorialIterate(n int64) (res *big.Int, err error) {
    if n < 0 {
        err = ErrInvalidInput
        return
    }
```

```go
    res = big.NewInt(1)
    if n == 0 {
        return
    }
    for  i := int64(1); i <= n; i++ {
        res.Mul(res, big.NewInt(i))
    }
    return
}

// Factorial via recursion
func FactorialRecurse(n int64) (res *big.Int, err error) {
    if n < 0 {
        err = ErrInvalidInput
        return
    }
    res = big.NewInt(1)
    if n == 0 {
        return
    }
    term := big.NewInt(n)
    facm1, err := FactorialRecurse(n - 1)
    if err != nil {
        return
    }
    res = term.Mul(term, facm1)
    return
}

// a helper

func randomSleep(dur time.Duration ) {
    time.Sleep(time.Duration((1 + rand.Intn(int(dur)))))
}
```

Note the factorial functions use the big Int type so that the (rather large) results of factorial can be represented.

And now the test cases.

Each test case is a function of this form:

```
func TestXxx(t *testing.T) {
    expect := <expected vale>
    got := <actual value from CUT>
    if got != expect {
        reportNoMatch(t, got, expect)
    }
}
```

Note that often the word "want" is used instead of "expect."

All test cases start with the required "Test" prefix followed and the specific test case name. Each function has a type T argument to link to the testing library.

Each benchmark is a function of this form:

```
func BenchmarkXxx(b *testing.B) {
    for i := 0; i < b.N; i++ {
        <do something to be timed>
    }
}
```

All benchmarks start with the required "Benchmark" prefix followed and the specific test case name. Each function has a type B argument to link to the testing library.

Test cases and benchmarks are generally placed in a file of the form XXX_test.go where XXX is the test suite name. The "_test" suffix is required, so the test case runner knows not to look for a main function to call. This can be convenient as one does not need to create a main package and main function to run test cases for code as would be needed without a test case runner.

Often, the CUT and the test suite are in the same package/directory, such as shown in Figure 10-1.

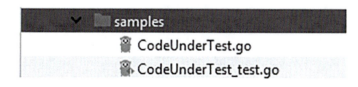

Figure 10-1. *Code under test and corresponding test case*

Listing 10-2 are some sample test cases.

Note the big result from factorial, even for a relatively small input value like 100. Factorial grows rapidly (in digits) as the input gets bigger. No normal integer (say uint64) can begin to hold such results.

Listing 10-2. Test Cases and Benchmarks

```
package main

import (
     "fmt"
     "math/big"
     "os"
     "testing"
     "time"
)
const factorialnput = 100
const factorialExpect = "933262154439441526816992388562667004907159682643816
21468592963895217599993229915608941463976156518286253697920827223758251185
2109168640000000000000000000000000"

// test the functions; happy case only

func TestEchoInt(t *testing.T) {
     //fmt.Println("in TestEchoInt")
     expect := 10
     got := EchoInt(expect)
     if got != expect {
          reportNoMatch(t, got, expect)
     }
}

func TestSumInt(t *testing.T) {
     //fmt.Println("in TestSumInt")
     expect := 10
     got := SumInt(expect, expect)
```

```go
    if got != expect+expect {
        reportNoMatch(t, got, expect+expect)
    }
}

func TestEchoFloat(t *testing.T) {
    //fmt.Println("in TestEchoFloat")
    expect := 10.0
    got := EchoFloat(expect)
    if got != expect {
        reportNoMatch(t, got, expect)
    }
}

func TestSumFloat(t *testing.T) {
    //fmt.Println("in TestSumFloat")
    expect := 10.0
    got := SumFloat(expect, expect)
    if got != expect+expect {
        reportNoMatch(t, got, expect+expect)
    }
}

func TestEchoString(t *testing.T) {
    fmt.Println("in TestEchoString")
    expect := "hello"
    got := EchoString(expect)
    if got != expect {
        reportNoMatch(t, got, expect)
    }
}

func TestSumString(t *testing.T) {
    //fmt.Println("in TestSumString")
    expect := "hello"
    got := SumString(expect, expect)
```

```go
        if got != expect+expect {
            reportNoMatch(t, got, expect+expect)
        }
}

func TestFactorialIterate(t *testing.T) {
        //fmt.Println("in TestFactorialIterate")
        expect := big.NewInt(0)
        expect.SetString(factorialExpect, 10)
        got, err := FactorialIterate(factorialnput)
        if err != nil {
            reportFail(t, err)
        }
        if expect.Cmp(got) != 0 {
            reportNoMatch(t, got, expect)
        }
}

func TestFactorialRecurse(t *testing.T) {
        //fmt.Println("in TestFactorialRecurse")
        expect := big.NewInt(0)
        expect.SetString(factorialExpect, 10)
        got, err := FactorialRecurse(factorialnput)
        if err != nil {
            reportFail(t, err)
        }
        if expect.Cmp(got) != 0 {
            reportNoMatch(t, got, expect)
        }
}

// benchmarks

func BenchmarkFacInt(b *testing.B) {
        for i := 0; i < b.N; i++ {
            FactorialIterate(factorialnput)
        }
}
```

```go
func BenchmarkFacRec(b *testing.B) {
    for i := 0; i < b.N; i++ {
        FactorialRecurse(factorialnput)
    }
}

// helpers

func reportNoMatch(t *testing.T, got interface{}, expect interface{}) {
    t.Error(fmt.Sprintf("got(%v) != expect(%v)", got, expect))
}

func reportFail(t *testing.T, err error) {
    t.Error(fmt.Sprintf("failure: %v", err))
}

var start time.Time

// do any test setup
func setup() {
    // do any setup here
    fmt.Printf("starting tests...\n")
    start = time.Now()
}

// do any test cleanup
func teardown() {
    end := time.Now()
    // do any cleanup here
    fmt.Printf("tests complete in %dms\n", end.Sub(start)/time.Millisecond)
}

// runs test with setup and cleanup
func TestMain(m *testing.M) {
    setup()
    rc := m.Run()
    teardown()
    os.Exit(rc)
}
```

The tests and/or benchmarks are run using the go `test {<option>...}` command. A key option is -bench=<re> which specifies a regular expression (<re>), often "." for all, to match benchmarks with. If not specified, then any benchmarks are not run. Note that benchmarks can make the test suite take significant time to run, and thus you may not want to run them each time.

Here is the result of the preceding suite run inside an IDE:

```
GOROOT=C:\Users\Administrator\sdk\go1.14.2 #gosetup
GOPATH=C:\Users\Administrator\IdeaProjects;C:\Users\Administrator\
IdeaProjects\LifeServer;C:\Users\Administrator\go #gosetup
C:\Users\Administrator\sdk\go1.14.2\bin\go.exe test -c -o C:\Users\
Administrator\AppData\Local\Temp\1\___CodeUnderTest_test_go.exe samples
#gosetup
C:\Users\Administrator\sdk\go1.14.2\bin\go.exe tool test2json -t C:\Users\
Administrator\AppData\Local\Temp\1\___CodeUnderTest_test_go.exe -test.v
-test.run "^TestEchoInt|TestSumInt|TestEchoFloat|TestSumFloat|TestEchoString|
TestSumString|TestFactorialIterate|TestFactorialRecurse$" -test.bench=.
#gosetup
starting tests...
=== RUN    TestEchoInt
--- PASS: TestEchoInt (0.05s)
=== RUN    TestSumInt
--- PASS: TestSumInt (0.02s)
=== RUN    TestEchoFloat
--- PASS: TestEchoFloat (0.03s)
=== RUN    TestSumFloat
--- PASS: TestSumFloat (0.00s)
=== RUN    TestEchoString
in TestEchoString
--- PASS: TestEchoString (0.01s)
=== RUN    TestSumString
--- PASS: TestSumString (0.03s)
=== RUN    TestFactorialIterate
--- PASS: TestFactorialIterate (0.00s)
=== RUN    TestFactorialRecurse
--- PASS: TestFactorialRecurse (0.00s)
```

```
goos: windows
goarch: amd64
pkg: samples
BenchmarkFacInt
BenchmarkFacInt-48              76730               15441 ns/op
BenchmarkFacRec
BenchmarkFacRec-48             52176               23093 ns/op
PASS
tests complete in 2924ms

Process finished with exit code 0
```

In this example, all the tests pass. The two benchmarks show the significantly different elapsed time the iterative (faster, ~15μs) and recursive (slower, ~23μs) factorial implementations take. This is expected as the recursive implementation adds significant extra call/return overhead based on the input value.

Note the messages added by the setup and teardown code. Also note the benchmark runner selected different iteration counts (N in the for loop) to test based on the time each iteration takes. It does this by first doing a few preliminary runs before calling the full run.

Just to demonstrate the code coverage, the test suite was run with coverage. Figure 10-2 shows the coverage summary report.

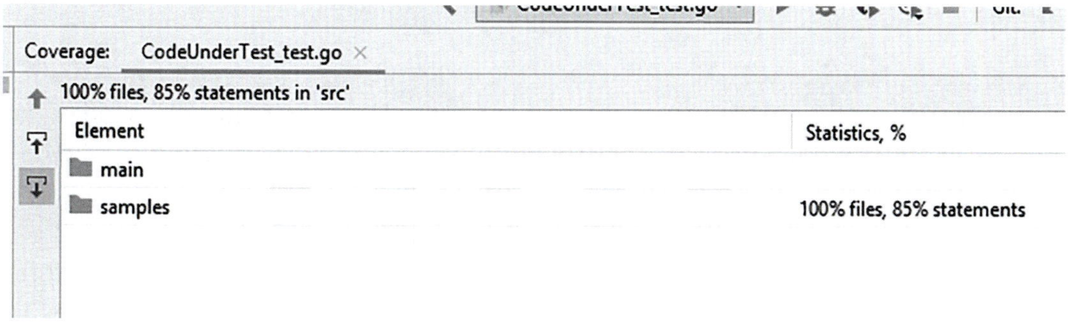

Figure 10-2. *Test case coverage report summary*

Figure 10-3 shows a snippet of the CUT with coverage coloring applied.

```
53    // Factorial computation: factorial(n):
54    // n < 0 - undefined
55    // n == 0 - 1
56    // n > 0 - n * factorial(n-1)
57
58    var ErrInvalidInput = errors.New( text: "invalid input")
59
60    // Factorial via iteration
61    func FactorialIterate(n int64) (res *big.Int, err error) {
62        if n < 0 {
63            err = ErrInvalidInput
64            return
65        }
66        res = big.NewInt( x: 1)
67        if n == 0 {
68            return
69        }
70        for  i := int64(1); i <= n; i++ {
71            res.Mul(res, big.NewInt(i))
72        }
73        return
74    }
```

Figure 10-3. *Test case coverage indicators against source tested*

The green parts (lines 61, 66, 70–73) show the code run; the yellow parts (lines 62, 67) show code with only partial paths covered (often `if` or `switch` statements). The red parts (lines 63–65, 68, 69) show the code not run at all. This report can suggest additional test cases to make to increase the coverage.

Some IDEs can run Go profiling and produce reports and/or graphs or the results. Here is a sample of running profiles against the test suite. The details are difficult to see in these examples (and are not critical to our discussion), but this ability to profile code using just standard Go libraries and tools is powerful. In Java, community support is required.

Figure 10-4 shows CPU usage profile results.

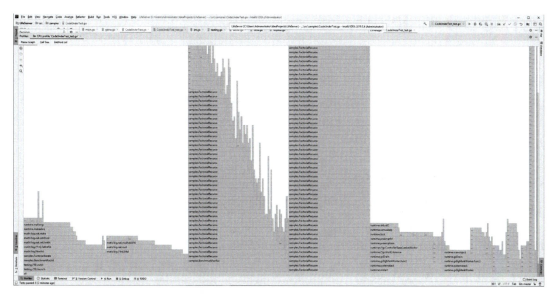

Figure 10-4. *CPU profile results graphed by the IDE*

Memory usage profile results are displayed in Figure 10-5.

Figure 10-5. *Memory profile results graphed by the IDE*

Test Cases in Java

For a comparison with Java, Listing 10-2 combines similar CUT and test case examples. JUnit has no simple benchmark feature, so the benchmarks are constructed[4] by hand as test cases. The following Java examples use JUnit 5. Note that the JUnit test cases use Java annotations (such as @Test, vs. method naming conventions) to identify test cases; the "test" prefix is not required.

Listing 10-3. Java JUnit Test Cases

```java
package org.baf.test;

import static org.junit.jupiter.api.Assertions.fail;

import java.math.BigInteger;

import org.baf.CodeUnderTest;
import org.junit.jupiter.api.AfterAll;
import org.junit.jupiter.api.BeforeAll;
import org.junit.jupiter.api.Test;

public class CodeUnderTestTester {
  private static final String factorial100Expect = "9332621544394415268169
923885626670049071596826438162146859296389521759999322991560894146397615651
182862536979208272237582511852109168640000000000000000000000000";

  static long start;
  static int limit = 10_000;

  @Test
  void testEchoInt() {
    int expect = 10;
    int got = CodeUnderTest.echoInt(expect);
    if (got != expect) {
      reportNoMatch(got, expect);
    }
  }
}
```

---

[4] As written, they do not discount the time the for loop adds. Production benchmarks must do this.

```java
@Test
void testEchoFloat() {
  double expect = 10;
  double got = CodeUnderTest.echoFloat(expect);
  if (got != expect) {
    reportNoMatch(got, expect);
  }
}

@Test
void testEchoString() {
  String expect = "hello";
  String got = CodeUnderTest.echoString(expect);
  if (!got.equals(expect)) {
    reportNoMatch(got, expect);
  }
}

@Test
void testFactorialIterate() {
  BigInteger expect = new BigInteger(factorial100Expect);
  BigInteger got = CodeUnderTest.factorialIterative(100);
  if (!got.equals(expect)) {
    reportNoMatch(got, expect);
  }
}

@Test
void testFactorialRecurse() {
  BigInteger expect = new BigInteger(factorial100Expect);
  BigInteger got = CodeUnderTest.factorialRecursive(100);
  if (!got.equals(expect)) {
    reportNoMatch(got, expect);
  }
}
```

```java
@Test
void benchmarkFactorialInt() {
  long start = System.currentTimeMillis();
  for (int i = 0; i < limit; i++) {
    CodeUnderTest.factorialIterative(1000);
  }
  long end = System.currentTimeMillis(), delta = end - start;
  System.out.printf("factorialIterativeve : iterations=%d,
  totalTime=%.2fs, per call=%.3fms%n", limit,
      (double) delta / 1000, (double) delta / limit);

}

@Test
void benchmarkFactorialRec() {
  long start = System.currentTimeMillis();
  for (int i = 0; i < limit; i++) {
    CodeUnderTest.factorialRecursive(1000);
  }
  long end = System.currentTimeMillis(), delta = end - start;
  System.out.printf("factorialRecursive : iterations=%d, totalTime=%.2fs,
  per call=%.3fms%n", limit,
      (double) delta / 1000, (double) delta / limit);

}

@BeforeAll
static void setUp() throws Exception {
  System.out.printf("starting tests...%n");
  start = System.currentTimeMillis();
}

@AfterAll
static void tearDown() throws Exception {
  long end = System.currentTimeMillis();
  System.out.printf("tests complete in %dms%n", end - start);
}
```

```java
    private void reportNoMatch(Object got, Object expect) {
        fail(String.format("got(%s) != expect(%s)", got.toString(), expect.
        toString()));
    }

    private void reportFail(String message) {
        fail(String.format("failure: %s", message));
    }
}
```

Using the Eclipse IDE, the test cases are run against the CUT. As with the Go example, they all pass, as shown in Figure 10-6.

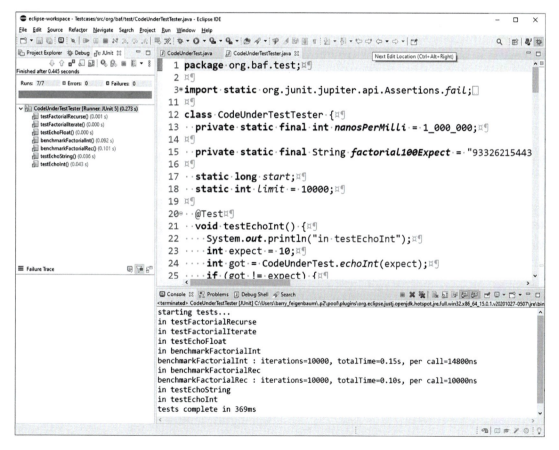

Figure 10-6. *JUnit run report in the IDE*

The summary report (expanded) is shown in Figure 10-7.

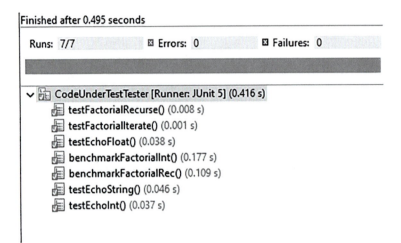

Finished after 0.495 seconds

Runs: 7/7   ⊠ Errors: 0   ⊠ Failures: 0

∨ 🔳 CodeUnderTestTester [Runner: JUnit 5] (0.416 s)
  📄 testFactorialRecurse() (0.008 s)
  📄 testFactorialIterate() (0.001 s)
  📄 testEchoFloat() (0.038 s)
  📄 benchmarkFactorialInt() (0.177 s)
  📄 benchmarkFactorialRec() (0.109 s)
  📄 testEchoString() (0.046 s)
  📄 testEchoInt() (0.037 s)

Figure 10-7. JUnit run summary in the IDE

The tests output this summary:

```
benchmarkFactorialInt : iterations=10000, totalTime=0.17s, per call=17400ns
benchmarkFactorialRec : iterations=10000, totalTime=0.11s, per call=10700ns
```

Note that the elapsed time difference between the iterative and recursive factorial implementations is small. This means the call/return overhead is small compared to calculating the factorial; most of the time is in the factorial method.

Contrast the preceding Java results with the following Go results. While not the same, they are similar:

```
BenchmarkFacInt-48          76730          15441 ns/op
BenchmarkFacRec-48          52176          23093 ns/op
```

CHAPTER 11

Going into the Future

Before we close our journey learning Go, we will take a brief look at some possible future enhancements. We will then bring much that we have learned together in the form of a capstone program, a sizable example web server implementation, that hopefully should also be entertaining.

The Go library introduction and survey parts in the next part provide some background on and examples of using the individual Go libraries that you should review as part of studying the capstone example.

Before we look to the future, let us consider the past. Like with Java, Go did not start out as it is today. The Go implementation has evolved and matured over time. It has a history[1] of continual improvement that will certainly continue.

Go will continue to improve over time. There are many proposed enhancements to the language and the runtime libraries. Some may make it into Go. Some proposals are not backward compatible. Whether any of these proposed changes come in a version of Go 1.x or wait until a Go 2.x, if ever, to come at all is to be determined.

Among many potential enhancements, two key potential enhancements are being discussed.

Improved Error Handling

Go's idiomatic way to deal with errors can be tedious. There is a proposal to improve this situation that is discussed more at https://go.googlesource.com/proposal/+/master/design/go2draft-error-handling-overview.md.

Today, a typical section of Go code would deal with errors like this:

```
func FileCopy(fromPath, toPath string) (count int64, err error) {
    reader, err := os.Open(fromPath)
```

---

[1] https://golang.org/doc/devel/release.html.

B. Feigenbaum, *Go for Java Programmers*, https://doi.org/10.1007/978-1-4842-7199-5_11

```go
    if err != nil {
          return
    }
    defer reader.Close()
    writer, err := os.Create(toPath)
    if err != nil {
          return
    }
    defer writer.Close()
    count, err = io.Copy(writer, reader)
    return
}
```

which is repetitive. Also, a significant fraction of the code is error handling.

Even with all this checking, the output file can remain even if the copy function fails; in production it should be removed. Also, the reported errors may not provide enough contextual information to recover from the cause. Things should be better. The proposed design is to allow something like this:

```go
func FileCopy(fromPath, toPath string) (count int64, err error) {
    handle err {
          return fmt.Errorf("copy(%q,%q) failed: %v",
          fromPath, toPath, err)
    }
    reader := check os.Open(fromPath)
    defer reader.Close()
    writer := check os.Create(toPath)
    handle err {
          writer.Close()
          os.Remove(toPath) // clean up
    }
    count = check io.Copy(writer, reader)
    return
}
```

Another brief example:

```
func main() {
    handle err {
        log.Fatalf("main failed due to %v", err)
    }
    text := check ioutil.ReadAll(os.Stdin)
    check os.Stdout.Write(text)
}
```

Here, the handle statement works somewhat like the defer statement, processing errors and passing them to previous handle blocks until a return is done. The check prefix on an action statement looks for (and consumes) a returned error value and if present triggers the handle chain passing the error to it. Note that the verbose if/return idiom is replaced by using check. This makes error processing more like panic processing.

Go Generics

Another key area that seems missing in the current Go definition is the ability to create *Generic* types. This is being defined[2] and is now an accepted[3] enhancement. As a preview, here is an introduction of what Generics in Go will be like. This introduction is not intended to cover all aspects of Generics.

The concept is summarized in the proposal:[4]

> *We suggest **extending the Go language to add optional type parameters to type and function declarations**. Type parameters are constrained by interface types. Interface types, when used as type constraints, permit listing the set of types that may be assigned to them. Type inference via a unification algorithm permits omitting type arguments from function calls in many cases. The **design is fully backward compatible with Go 1**.*
>
> *... the term **generic** is ... a shorthand to mean a function or type that takes type parameters.*

---

[2] https://blog.golang.org/generics-next-step

[3] https://github.com/golang/proposal#accepted

[4] https://go.googlesource.com/proposal/+/refs/heads/master/design/43651-type-parameters.md

In Go, these type parameters are enclosed in square brackets (**[...]**). In Java, angled brackets (**<...>**) serve a similar purpose. For example, consider this generic function:

```
func DoIt[T any](s []T) {
    :
}
```

where [T any] defines a type parameter that can take on any type. Note that here any is a synonym for interface{}.

The Java equivalent is

```
public <T> void doIt(List<T> s) {
    :
}
```

The proposal is further detailed[5] with a summary of the proposed changes:

- *Functions can have an additional type parameter list that uses square brackets but otherwise looks like an ordinary parameter list:* func F[T any](p T) { ... }.

- *These type parameters can be used by the regular parameters and in the function body.*

- *Types can also have a type parameter list:* type MySlice[T any] []T.

- *Each type parameter has a type constraint, just as each ordinary parameter has a type:* func F[T Constraint](p T) { ... }.

- *Type constraints are interface types.*

- *The new predeclared name* any *is a type constraint that permits any type.*

- *Interface types used as type constraints can have a list of predeclared types; only type arguments that match one of those types satisfy the constraint.*

- *Generic functions may only use operations permitted by their type constraints.*

---

[5] https://github.com/golang/go/issues/43651

- *Using a generic function or type requires passing type arguments.*
- *Type inference permits omitting the type arguments of a function call in common cases.*

In Java, Generics can only be on reference (Object and its subclasses) types, not primitive types. Go has no such restriction.

This Go function can be used by supplying a real type for the T type parameter. For example:

```
DoIt[int]([]int{1, 2, 3, 4, 5})
```

where the generic type is set to int. Often, this type can be inferred by the compiler, letting this be written as

```
DoIt([]int{1, 2, 3, 4, 5})
```

which resembles a nongeneric call.

Often, one needs to restrict (constrain) the actual (aka real/reified) type a generic type can take on. Often, this means an interface that restricts the type so its methods can be called.

Let us say we want to restrict the type parameter to be something that conforms to the fmt.Stringer interface. To do this, one writes

```
func DoIt[T fmt.Stringer](s []T) {
      :
}
```

The Java (near) equivalent is

```
public <T extends Stringer> void doIt(List<T> s) {
    :
}
```

Like in Java, a function can have multiple type parameters, such as

```
func DoIt[S fmt.Stringer, R io.Reader](r R, s []S) {
      :
}
```

Here, these type parameters are distinct (even if based on the same real type).
The following examples are adapted from content at the Go proposal site.

Types can also be generic. Consider this generic slice type:

```
type Slice[T any] []T
```

To realize (or instantiate) such a type parameter, one provides a type to use like this:

```
var s Slice[int]
```

Generic types, like nongeneric types, can have methods:

```
func (v *Slice[T]) AddToEnd(x T) {
    *v = append(*v, x)
}
```

The implementation has some restrictions to keep it simple. A method is limited to the same type parameters as the type it is a method of; it cannot add any more. There are no plans to allow reflection on generic type parameters or composite literals.

To perform operations on generic types, one must map the type to a real type that has the operation. In Go, operations are generally restricted to the predefined types. So, one needs to constrain the generic type to be limited to one or more predefined types. One does this by declaring an interface type that enumerates the allowed predefined types. For example:

```
type SignedInt interface {
  type int, int8, int16, int32, int64
}
```

which represents any signed integer type or any types derived from them. This is not a normal interface and cannot be used as a base type, only as a constraint. Commonly used grouping interfaces will likely be provided by the standard Go runtime.

Like the any predefined constraint, the comparable constraint allows any type that supports an equality comparison.

Examples of generic functions using slices:[6]

```
func SliceMap[T1, T2 any](s []T1, mapper func(T1) T2) (res []T2) {
    res := make([]T2, len(s))
    for i, v := range s {
```

---

[6] Based on the samples in https://go.googlesource.com/proposal/+/refs/heads/master/design/go2draft-type-parameters.md

```go
            res[i] = mapper(v)
    }
    return
}
func SliceReduce[T1, T2 any](s []T1, first T2,
    reducer func(T2, T1) T2) (acc T2) {
    acc := first
    for _, v := range s {
            acc = reducer(acc, v)
    }
    return
}
func SliceFilter[T any](s []T, pred func(T) bool) (match []T) {
    match = make([]T, 0, len(s))
    for _, v := range s {
            if pred(v) {
                    match = append(match, v)
            }
    }
    return
}
```

Note that Go's generic types do not have the contra/covariant issues[7] that Java generics can have. This is because Go does not support type inheritance. In Go, each type is distinct and cannot be mixed in a generic type, such as a collection.

For an early look at generics in action, one can use the extended Go Playground.[8] In Figure 11-1, we see a generic version of the min (minimum) function on integer and floating numeric values.

---

[7] https://dzone.com/articles/covariance-and-contravariance
[8] https://go2goplay.golang.org/

```
1 package main
2
3 import (
4         "fmt"
5 )
6
7 type numeric interface {
8         type int, int8, int16, int32, int64, uint, uint8, uint16, uint32, uint64, float32, float64
9 }
10
11 func min[T numeric](a, b T) T {
12         if a < b {
13                 return a
14         }
15         return b
16 }
17
18 func main() {

42
2.7182

Program exited.
```

Figure 11-1. *Playground with Generics support example*

Other samples are available, such as the one shown in Figure 11-2.

Figure 11-2. *Available Generic examples*

Capstone *Game of Life* Example

This final section on Go provides a significant coding example, aka *capstone*, written in both the Java and Go languages. The Go capstone implementation demonstrates many basic Go functions, the use of goroutines, and HTTP server implementations. The Java capstone implementation demonstrates how a similar program could be coded in Java for a comparison.

The capstone program plays the *Game of Life*[9] (GoL) defined by John Conway. This game is a zero-player game that simulates multiple generations (aka turns or cycles) of "microbial life" inside a pseudo–Petri dish[10] like constrained context. In this case, the Petri dish is represented by a rectangular grid of cells that contains either alive (filled) or dead (empty) cells. Iterations (discrete time steps) of the game cause the cells to stay in stasis, reproduce, or die, according to Conway's rules.

Depending on the grid size, the initial placement of the "alive" cells, and the number of generations played, many possible, often interesting, patterns can emerge. Often, the patterns end up cycling or becoming fixed. Some patterns eventually result in an empty (all dead) grid.

The general rules of the game are, across a generation

- Any dead cell with three living adjacent cells becomes alive.

- Any living cell with just two or three adjacent living cells remains alive; other living cells die.

- All other dead cells remain dead.

Figure 11-3 offers a sample snapshot of a different GoL implementation in progress. Notice the live cells in black and the dead cells in gray. As the game progresses (aka cycles), the cells move from being alive to dead or dead to alive and thus can appear to move around the grid and/or change the group shape.

---

[9] https://en.wikipedia.org/wiki/Conway%27s_Game_of_Life
[10] https://en.wikipedia.org/wiki/Petri_dish

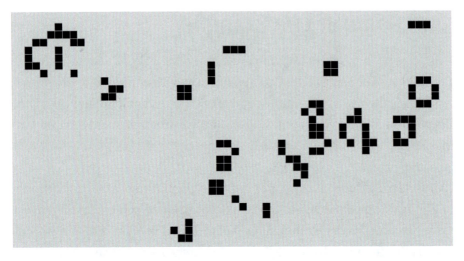

Figure 11-3. *Sample Game of Life grid*

Figure 11-3 was taken obtained from `http://pi.math.cornell.edu/~lipa/mec/lesson6.html`.

The capstone GoL grid is initialized by loading a PNG[11] image. This can be a real image, such as a photograph or a cartoon, or some (typically) smaller grid with specific cells set, often created in a program such as Microsoft *Paint* as shown in Figure 11-4.

---

[11] PNG is a lossless format, and thus all details are retained.

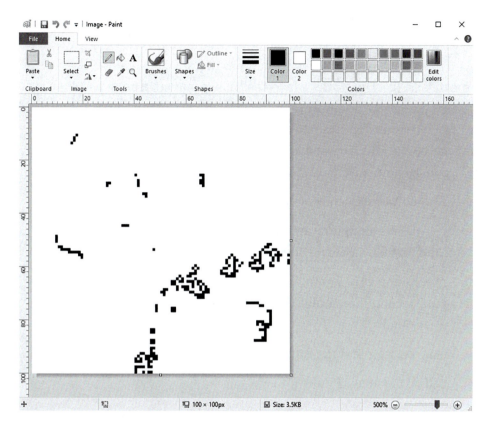

Figure 11-4. *Creating a GoL grid in Microsoft Paint*

This can be saved in PNG format as shown in Figure 11-5.

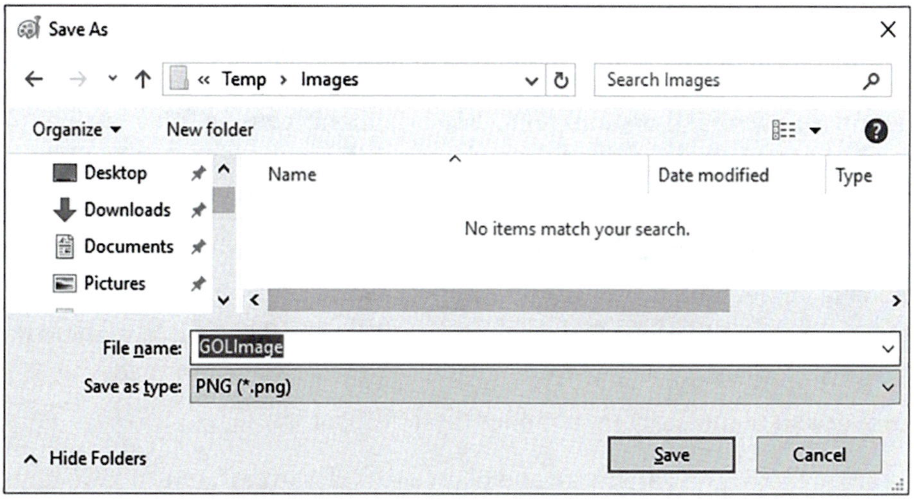

Figure 11-5. *Saving a GoL grid in Microsoft Paint*

The image width and height set the grid width and height (100 x 100 in this example). If the image is in color, it is mapped to black and white (BW). Colors that have an RGB sum above a threshold are considered white, else they are considered black. See the GoL code for the details. Black indicates a living cell. Once loaded, a predetermined set of cycles are run and saved in memory (a production version of the GoL program would probably use a file system or database to hold previously generated cycles).

There is a web API (REST-like) that allows one to see the generated results in a browser. Two image formats are provided:

1. GIF – Allows a sequence of cycles (animated) to be presented

2. PNG – Allows a single cycle to be presented, generally with better resolution than a GIF provides

See the image samples below the code listings.

The program accepts these optional command-line flag arguments (see the Go flag package for more details):

- A name to reference the game by

- A URL to the image (file or HTTP)

- A magnification factor (1–20)

- A flag to start the HTTP server (default true)

- A flag to enable a game timing loop (default false)

- A flag to enable a report rendering statistics (default false)

- A flag to enable saving the generated images into files (default false)

If present, the *name* and *url* command-line arguments cause a "play" action to occur before the server starts. This can preload a GoL result.

Note the presence of the various flags is primarily to demonstrate command-line argument processing, not to make the GoL program very sophisticated; the flags may not be robustly implemented as flag processing is not the key point of this capstone. A production game would probably take more care with the flags and have more flags (such as a server port value).

The server part of the program provides these API paths:

- GET /play – Load an image and play GoL cycles over it; return JSON statistics on the play process.

- Query parameters:

- name – A name to reference the game by

- url – A URL to the image (file or HTTP)

- GET /show – Return a previously run game as an image.

  - Query parameters:

  - name – A name to reference the game by.

  - form – Image format: GIF or PNG; if GIF, it may be animated (contain several cycles).

  - maxCount – Maximum number of cycles to return (up to the saved cycle count).

  - mag – A magnification factor (1–20).

- GET /history – Return the history of played games. This history is not persistent across GoL runs.

- DELETE /history – Empty the history of played games.

Note the GoL code is generally intended to be used with local (file: protocol) initial board images vs. web (http: protocol) images. All examples use local images.

The preceding APIs do not meet the standard REST definition well. They exist only to demonstrate basic HTTP request handling. Often, production REST APIs, with embedded path parameters and other options, can be more complex to match and parse. The Go standard library parsing support can be challenging to use in this situation. The Go community has several libraries that extend the standard support, for example, *Gorilla Mux*,[12] to make this easier. These libraries can make API matching comparable to that offered by Java's JAX-RS and Spring MVC.

The server starts and listens on port 8080.

The GoL can be computationally heavy, especially with large grids, as the time complexity is $O(n^2)$. Since the work is easily partitioned (each cell's new cycle state only depends on its immediate neighbors of the prior cycle), it is a good example to demonstrate how goroutines can be used to improve program performance with low coding effort.

---

[12] See https://github.com/gorilla/mux

Game of Life Go Source

Two forms of the GoL implementation will be presented, one in Java and one in Go. This allows for a detailed apples-to-apples implementation comparison of a substantial program written in Go and Java.

Most of the core code is essentially the same in both versions. In general, the same variable, type, and function names (but with case difference to match the language style) are used to help in matching the implementation parts. This comparison also shows how Go is generally capable of implementing most programs that Java SE can implement with comparable effort.

To make the comparison as direct as possible, the Go form was written and tested first and then the Java implementation was created based on it. That means the Java code typically follows Go idioms and does not exploit the Java language to its fullest (e.g., uses Lambdas and streams). The Java version differs from the Go version in these key areas:

- Use of Exceptions (vs. Go-style error returns)

- HTTP server library differences

- Image library differences

- Command-line parsing differences (Java has no standard library to parse command lines)

- Wrapping of all functions in some class

In the Java code, in general, only public and default visibility is used. This is to match the Go visibilities. Most Java developers would choose to use private instead of default visibility. Visibility is explicit (vs. implied by identifier case).

The Java code, like the Go code, is generally limited to using standard (vs. community) libraries. Go supports standard JSON and XML creation from structures. Java does not. JSE does not have a standard JSON renderer, so a basic one was implemented instead of requiring a community implementation. An equivalent custom XML renderer is more complex and not critical to the purpose of the capstone, so it was not implemented. The Go version uses standard library JSON and XML renderers.

The Java version uses a semi-standard HTTP server, `com.sun.net.httpserver.HttpServer`. It is shipped with the Java SDK but does not use the standard Java package names. The alternative of requiring community support for, say, JAX-RS or Spring MVC violates the use only standard libraries constraint of this capstone. Writing an HTTP server using only the Java HTTP packages would be an excessively large effort. The Go version uses standard library HTTP servers.

The Java version will be presented first, followed by the Go version. Once you understand the Java implementation, the Go version should be straightforward pickup. You should note the high similarity in the implementations, which is deliberate. It may be helpful to jump between the Java and Go sources as you inspect the code. Or you may start with the Go implementation and refer to the Java implementation. Do whatever feels most comfortable.

Note the Java code for the capstone programs was developed using the Eclipse IDE and the Go code using the IntelliJ IDEA IDE. This has some effect on the formatting of the code.

Capstone Project in Java

The Java form of the GoL program consists of a single `org.baf.gol` package that has these source files:

- Main.java – The main command processor

- Server.java – The HTTP server and request handlers

- Game.java – The GoL playing logic

- Utility.java – Helper functions

- AnnimatedGifWriter.java – A helper to combine multiple images into a GIF

- Logger.java – A simple equivalent of the Go logger

- ParameterProvider.java – A helper interface for passing command-line arguments between classes (public global values used in the Go version)

- Formatter.java – A helper interface for formatting maps

- JsonFormatter.java – A Formatter that formats maps into JSON

- XmlFormatter.java – A Formatter that formats maps into XML (not implemented)

Note the first four sources also exist in the Go version. They are nearly identical function wise in both versions. The other sources are needed to deal with differences in Java vs. Go runtimes.

Note this example uses Java 14[13] features and must be compiled and run on at least that version. Some used Java features are previewed in that release.

Main.java

Main.java contains the main function which detects any command-line arguments and processes them. It uses custom, but simple, code to process any command-line flags. It also optionally starts the HTTP server.

Listing 11-1 (Main.java) contains this code.

Listing 11-1. Source File 1 Main.java

```java
package org.baf.gol;

import  org.baf.gol.Logger;

import java.util.ArrayList;
import java.util.Arrays;

/**
 * Main GoL engine.
 */
public class Main implements ParameterProvider {
  // command line values
  String urlString, nameString;
  int magFactorInt = 1, gameCycles = 10;
  boolean startServerFlag, runTimingsFlag, reportFlag, saveImageFlag;
  public static String saveImageRoot = "/temp"; // change per OS type

  @Override
  public String getUrlParameter() {
    return urlString;
  }
```

---

[13] https://en.wikipedia.org/wiki/Java_version_history

```java
@Override
public String getNameParameter() {
  return nameString;
}

@Override
public int getMagFactorParameter() {
  return magFactorInt;
}

@Override
public boolean startServerFlag() {
  return startServerFlag;
}

@Override
public boolean runTimingsFlag() {
  return runTimingsFlag;
}

@Override
public boolean reportFlag() {
  return reportFlag;
}

@Override
public boolean saveImageFlag() {
  return saveImageFlag;
}

@Override
public int getGameCyclesParameter() {
  return gameCycles;
}
```

```java
/**
 * Main entry point.
 *
 * Sample: -n tiny1 -u file:/.../tiny1.png
 */
public static void main(String[] args) {
  if (args.length == 0) {
    printHelp();
    return;
  }
  try {
    var main = new Main();
    if (!main.parseArgs(args)) {
      Logger.log.tracef("Command arguments: %s", Arrays.toString(args));
      printHelp();
      System.exit(1);
    }
    main.launch();
  } catch (Exception e) {
    Logger.log.exceptionf(e, "launched failed");
    System.exit(3);
  }
}

private void launch() throws Exception {
  Game.coreGame = new Game(this);
  Game.coreGame.saveImageRoot = saveImageRoot;
  Game.coreGame.maxCycles = gameCycles;

  // need timings
  if (!urlString.isEmpty()) {
    if (nameString.isEmpty()) {
      System.err.printf("a name is required when a URL is provided%n");
      System.exit(1);
    }
  }
```

```
    if (runTimingsFlag) {
      runCycleTimings();
    }
  }

  // need server
  if (startServerFlag) {
    // launch HTTP server
    var server = new Server(this);
    server.saveImageRoot = saveImageRoot;
    server.startHttpServer();
  }
}

// approximation of flag package in Go
private boolean parseArgs(String[] args) {
  boolean ok = true;
  try {
    for (int i = 0; i < args.length; i++) {
      switch (args[i].toLowerCase()) {
        case "-url":
        case "-u":
          urlString = args[++i];
          break;
        case "-name":
        case "-n":
          nameString = args[++i];
          break;
        case "-magfactor":
        case "-mf":
        case "-mag":
          magFactorInt = Integer.parseInt(args[++i]);
          if (magFactorInt < 1 || magFactorInt > 20) {
            throw new IllegalArgumentException("bad magFactor: " +
            magFactorInt);
          }
```

```java
        break;
      case "-gamecycles":
      case "-gc":
        gameCycles = Integer.parseInt(args[++i]);
        if (gameCycles < 1 || gameCycles > 1000) {
          throw new IllegalArgumentException("bad gameCycles: " +
          gameCycles);
        }
        break;
      case "-start":
        startServerFlag = true;
        break;
      case "-time":
        runTimingsFlag = true;
        break;
      case "-report":
        reportFlag = true;
        break;
      case "-saveimage":
      case "-si":
        saveImageFlag = true;
        break;
      default:
        throw new IllegalArgumentException("unknown parameter key: " +
        args[i]);
    }
  }
} catch (Exception e) {
  System.err.printf("parse failed: %s%n", e.getMessage());
  ok = false;
}
return ok;
}
```

```java
// get execution timings
private void runCycleTimings() throws Exception {
  var cpuCount = Runtime.getRuntime().availableProcessors();
  for (var i = 1; i <= 64; i *= 2) {
    Logger.log.tracef("Running with %d threads, %d CPUs...", i,
    cpuCount);
    Game coreGame = Game.coreGame;
    coreGame.threadCount = i;
    coreGame.run(getNameParameter(), getUrlParameter());

    if (reportFlag()) {
      Logger.log.tracef("Game max: %d, go count: %d:", i, coreGame.
      maxCycles, coreGame.threadCount);
      for (var grk : coreGame.runs.keySet()) {
        var gr = coreGame.runs.get(grk);
        Logger.log.tracef("Game Run: %s, cycle count: %d", gr.name,
        gr.cycles.size());
        for (var c : gr.cycles) {
          long start = c.startedAt.getTime(), end = c.endedAt.getTime();
          Logger.log.tracef("Cycle: start epoch: %dms, end epoch: %dms,
          elapsed: %dms", start, end, end - start);
        }
      }
    }
  }
}

private static void printHelp() {
  System.err.printf("%s%n%n%n%s%n", trimWhitespace(golDescription),
  trimWhitespace((golArgs)));
}

private static Object trimWhitespace(String lines) {
  var xlines = lines.split("\n");
  var result = new ArrayList<String>();
  for (int i = 0, c = xlines.length; i < c; i++) {
    String tline = xlines[i].trim();
```

```java
      if (!tline.isEmpty()) {
        result.add(tline.replace("%n", "\n"));
      }
    }
    return String.join("\n", result);
  }

  static String golDescription = """
        Play the game of Life.
        Game boards are initialized from PNG images.
        Games play over several cycles.%n
        Optionally acts as a server to retrieve images of game boards during
        play.%n
        No supported positional arguments.
        """;

  static String golArgs = """
        Arguments (all start with '-'):
        url|u <url>               URL of the PNG image to load
        name|n <name>             name to refer to the game initialized by the
        URL
        magFactor|mf|mag <int>    magnify the grid by this factor when
        formatted into an image   (default 1; 1 to 20)
        gameCycles|gc <int>       sets number of cycles to run (default 10)
        start <boolean>           start the HTTP server (default false)
        time <boolean>            run game cycle timings with different thread
        counts (default false)
        report <boolean>          output run statistics (default false)
        saveImage|si <boolean>    save generated images into a file (default
        false)
        """;
}
```

Server.java

Server.java launches an HTTP server with several path handlers. The handlers access any query parameters and then generate and/or access GoL data. `Game.coreGame` represents the root of a history of past played games. Images or JSON/XML statistics stored in it are returned.

Currently, JSON is not supported in the standard JRE; a third-party implementation must be used. Like is often the case, the Java versions are generally more complex to use but are often more powerful.

Some example Java JSON processors:

- Jackson[14] – Popular; often the default implementation in JEE editions
- Gson[15] – From Google, need we say more
- Json-io[16]
- Genson[17]

This example uses standard library support as much as possible so JSON is processed by custom code.

Server.java (Listing 11-2) contains this code.

Listing 11-2. Source File 2 Server.java

```
package org.baf.gol;

import static org.baf.gol.Logger.log;
import static org.baf.gol.Utility.NANOS_PER_MS;
import static org.baf.gol.Utility.isNullOrEmpty;

import java.io.IOException;
import java.net.InetSocketAddress;
import java.nio.file.Files;
import java.nio.file.Paths;
```

---

[14] https://en.wikipedia.org/wiki/Jackson_(API); https://github.com/FasterXML/jackson
[15] https://en.wikipedia.org/wiki/Gson; https://github.com/google/gson/
[16] https://github.com/jdereg/json-io
[17] http://genson.io/

```java
import java.util.ArrayList;
import java.util.LinkedHashMap;
import java.util.List;
import java.util.Map;
import java.util.Objects;
import java.util.stream.Collectors;

import com.sun.net.httpserver.HttpExchange;
import com.sun.net.httpserver.HttpHandler;
import com.sun.net.httpserver.HttpServer;

/**
 * Provides a HTTP server for the GoL.<br>
 * Uses com.sun.net.httpserver.HttpServer for basic function.<br>
 * Can be opened only one time.
 **/
public class Server implements AutoCloseable {
  private static final String GIF_IMAGE_FILE_PATTERN = "/Image_%s.gif";

  String address;
  int port;
  Map<String, HttpHandler> handlers = new LinkedHashMap<>();
  HttpServer server;
  ParameterProvider pp;
  public String saveImageRoot = "/temp"; // change per OS type

  public Server(ParameterProvider pp) {
    this(pp, "localhost", 8080);
  }

  public Server(ParameterProvider pp, String address, int port) {
    this.pp = pp;
    this.address = address;
    this.port = port;
  }
```

```java
@Override
public String toString() {
  return "Server[address=" + address + ", port=" + port + ", open=" +
  isOpen() + ", handlers=" + handlers.keySet() + "]";
}

String getRequestPath(HttpExchange ex) {
  return ex.getRequestURI().toString().split("\\?")[0];
}

// assumes only one value; redo if more than one possible
String getQueryParamValue(HttpExchange ex, String name) {
  String result = null;
  var parts = ex.getRequestURI().toString().split("\\?");
  if (parts.length > 1) {
    parts = parts[1].split("&");
    for (var part : parts) {
      var xparts = part.split("=");
      if (xparts[0].equals(name)) {
        result = xparts[1];
        break;
      }
    }
  }
  return result;
}

/**
 * Used to allow clients outside this class to send data.
 */
public interface ResponseDataSender {
  void sendResponseData(byte[] data) throws IOException;
}
```

```java
public class DefaultResponseDataSender implements ResponseDataSender {
  HttpExchange ex;

  public DefaultResponseDataSender(HttpExchange ex) {
    this.ex = ex;
  }

  @Override
  public void sendResponseData(byte[] data) throws IOException {
    Server.this.sendResponseData(ex, data);
  }

}


void sendResponseData(HttpExchange ex, byte[] data) throws IOException {
  ex.sendResponseHeaders(200, data.length);
  var os = ex.getResponseBody();
  os.write(data);
  os.flush();
  os.close();
  log.tracef("Sent %d bytes", data.length);
}

void sendResponseJson(HttpExchange ex, Object data) throws IOException {
  ex.getResponseHeaders().add("Content-Type", "text/json");
  var jf = new JsonFormatter();
  sendResponseData(ex, jf.valueToText(data).getBytes());
}

void sendResponseXml(HttpExchange ex, Object data) throws IOException {
  ex.getResponseHeaders().add("Content-Type", "text/xml");
  var xf = new XmlFormatter();
  sendResponseData(ex, xf.valueToText(data).getBytes());
}

void sendStatus(HttpExchange ex, int status) throws IOException {
  ex.sendResponseHeaders(status, 0);
}
```

```java
// Show request handler.
  HttpHandler showHandler = new HttpHandler() {

    @Override
    public void handle(HttpExchange exchange) throws IOException {
      try {
        switch (exchange.getRequestMethod()) {
          case "GET": {
            if (!Objects.equals(getRequestPath(exchange), "/show")) {
              sendStatus(exchange, 404);
              return;
            }
            // process query parameters
            var name = getQueryParamValue(exchange, "name");
            if (isNullOrEmpty(name)) {
              name = "default";
            }
            var form = getQueryParamValue(exchange, "form");
            if (isNullOrEmpty(form)) {
              form = "gif";
            }
            var xmaxCount = getQueryParamValue(exchange, "maxCount");
            if (isNullOrEmpty(xmaxCount)) {
              xmaxCount = "50";
            }
            var maxCount = Integer.parseInt(xmaxCount);
            if (maxCount < 1 || maxCount > 100) {
              sendStatus(exchange, 400);
              return;
            }
            var xmag = getQueryParamValue(exchange, "mag");
            if (isNullOrEmpty(xmag)) {
              xmag = "1";
            }
            var mag = Integer.parseInt(xmag);
            var xindex = getQueryParamValue(exchange, "index");
```

```java
    if (isNullOrEmpty(xindex)) {
      xindex = "0";
    }
    var index = Integer.parseInt(xindex);
    if (index < 0) {
      sendStatus(exchange, 400);
      return;
    }

    // get a game
    var gr = Game.coreGame.runs.get(name);
    if (gr == null) {
      sendStatus(exchange, 404);
      return;
    }

    // return requested image type
    switch (form) {
      case "GIF":
      case "gif": {
        var b = gr.makeGifs(maxCount, mag);
        sendResponseData(exchange, b);

        if (pp.saveImageFlag()) {
          var imageFormat = saveImageRoot + GIF_IMAGE_FILE_PATTERN;
          var saveFile = String.format(imageFormat, name);
          Files.write(Paths.get(saveFile), b);
          log.tracef("Save %s", saveFile);
        }
      }
        break;
      case "PNG":
      case "png": {
        if (index <= maxCount) {
          var rs = new DefaultResponseDataSender(exchange);
          gr.sendPng(rs, index, mag);
        } else {
```

```
            sendStatus(exchange, 400);
          }
        }
          break;
        default:
          sendStatus(exchange, 405);
      }
    }
  }
} catch (Exception e) {
  log.exceptionf(e, "show failed");
  sendStatus(exchange, 500);
}
    }
  };

// Play request handler.
  HttpHandler playHandler = new HttpHandler() {

    @Override
    public void handle(HttpExchange exchange) throws IOException {
      try {
        switch (exchange.getRequestMethod()) {
          case "GET": {
            if (!Objects.equals(getRequestPath(exchange), "/play")) {
              sendStatus(exchange, 404);
              return;
            }
            // process query parameters
            var name = getQueryParamValue(exchange, "name");
            var url = getQueryParamValue(exchange, "url");
            if (Utility.isNullOrEmpty(name) || Utility.isNullOrEmpty(url)) {
              sendStatus(exchange, 400);
              return;
            }
```

```
var ct = getQueryParamValue(exchange, "ct");
if (Utility.isNullOrEmpty(ct)) {
  ct = exchange.getRequestHeaders().getFirst("Content-Type");
}
if (Utility.isNullOrEmpty(ct)) {
  ct = "";
}
ct = ct.toLowerCase();
switch (ct) {
  case "":
    ct = "application/json";
    break;
  case "application/json":
  case "text/json":
    break;
  case "application/xml":
  case "text/xml":
    break;
  default:
    sendStatus(exchange, 400);
}

// run a game
Game.coreGame.run(name, url);
var run = makeReturnedRun(name, url);

// return statistics as requested
switch (ct) {
  case "application/json":
  case "text/json": {
    sendResponseJson(exchange, run);
  }
    break;
  case "application/xml":
```

```
        case "text/xml": {
          sendResponseXml(exchange, run);
        }
          break;
      }
    }
      break;
    default:
      sendStatus(exchange, 405);
    }
  } catch (Exception e) {
    log.exceptionf(e, "play failed");
    sendStatus(exchange, 500);
  }
 }
};

// History request handler.
 HttpHandler historyHandler = new HttpHandler() {

  @Override
  public void handle(HttpExchange exchange) throws IOException {
    try {
      switch (exchange.getRequestMethod()) {
        case "GET": {
          if (!Objects.equals(getRequestPath(exchange), "/history")) {
            sendStatus(exchange, 404);
            return;
          }
          // format history
          Map<String, Object> game = new LinkedHashMap<>();
          var runs = new LinkedHashMap<>();
          game.put("Runs", runs);
```

```java
          var xruns = Game.coreGame.runs;
          for (var k : xruns.keySet()) {
            runs.put(k, makeReturnedRun(k, xruns.get(k).imageUrl));
          }
          sendResponseJson(exchange, game);
        }
          break;
        case "DELETE":
          if (!Objects.equals(getRequestPath(exchange), "/history")) { //
          more is bad
            sendStatus(exchange, 404);
            return;
          }
          // erase history
          Game.coreGame.clear();
          sendStatus(exchange, 204);
          break;
        default:
          sendStatus(exchange, 405);
      }
    } catch (Exception e) {
      log.exceptionf(e, "history failed");
      sendStatus(exchange, 500);
    }
  }
};

Map<String, Object> makeReturnedRun(String name, String imageUrl) {
  var xrun = new LinkedHashMap<String, Object>();
  var run = Game.coreGame.runs.get(name);
  if (run != null) {
    xrun.put("Name", run.name);
    xrun.put("ImageURL", run.imageUrl);
    xrun.put("PlayIndex", run.playIndex);
    xrun.put("DelayIn10ms", run.delayIn10ms);
    xrun.put("Height", run.height);
```

```
    xrun.put("Width", run.width);
    xrun.put("StartedAMst", run.startedAt);
    xrun.put("EndedAMst", run.endedAt);
    xrun.put("DurationMs", run.endedAt.getTime() - run.startedAt.
    getTime());
    var cycles = new ArrayList<Map<String, Object>>();
    xrun.put("Cycles", cycles);
    for (var r : run.cycles) {
      var xc = new LinkedHashMap<String, Object>();
      xc.put("StartedAtNs", r.startedAt.getTime() * NANOS_PER_MS);
      xc.put("EndedAtNs", r.endedAt.getTime() * NANOS_PER_MS);
      var duration = (r.endedAt.getTime() - r.startedAt.getTime()) *
      NANOS_PER_MS;
      xc.put("DurationNs", duration);
      xc.put("Cycle", r.cycleCount);
      xc.put("ThreadCount", Game.coreGame.threadCount);
      xc.put("MaxCount", Game.coreGame.maxCycles);
      cycles.add(xc);
    }

  }
  return xrun;
}

public void startHttpServer() throws IOException {
  registerContext("/play", playHandler);
  registerContext("/show", showHandler);
  registerContext("/history", historyHandler);
  open();
  log.tracef("Server %s:%d started", address, port);
}

public void open() throws IOException {
  if (isOpen()) {
    throw new IllegalStateException("already open");
  }
```

```java
    server = HttpServer.create(new InetSocketAddress("localhost", 8080), 0);
    for (var path : handlers.keySet()) {
      server.createContext(path, handlers.get(path));
    }
    server.start();
    Runtime.getRuntime().addShutdownHook(new Thread(() -> {
      try {
        close();
      } catch (Exception e) {
        log.exceptionf(e, "shutdown failed");
      }
    }));
  }

  public boolean isOpen() {
    return server != null;
  }

  @Override
  public void close() throws Exception {
    if (isOpen()) {
      server.stop(60);
      server = null;
    }
  }

  public void registerContext(String path, HttpHandler handler) {
    if (handlers.containsKey(path)) {
      throw new IllegalArgumentException("path already exists: " + path);
    }
    handlers.put(path, handler);
  }

  public void removeContext(String path) {
    if (!handlers.containsKey(path)) {
      throw new IllegalArgumentException("unknown path: " + path);
    }
```

```
    handlers.remove(path);
  }

  public List<String> getContextPaths() {
    return handlers.keySet().stream().collect(Collectors.toUnmodifiableLi
st());
  }
}
```

Game.java

Game.java contains the logic to play a GoL. Each *Game* consists of a set of named *GameRun* instances. Each GameRun consists of a set of *GameCycle* instances and some statistics. Each GameCycle consists of a before and after *Grid* snapshot and some statistics. Each Grid has the cell data (as a byte[ ]) and the grid dimensions. The REST show API returns the after-grid instance made into images.

The processRows function is called in a thread inside the NextCycle method. This allows a variable number of threads to be used. Using more threads can significantly speed up GoL cycle processing, especially for larger grids, as shown later in this section. The Java example uses a new thread for each place the Go version uses a goroutine. This is atypical in Java code; a thread pool is typically used.

The Java version of Game supports a Swing GUI to present cycles. The Go version has no equivalent. The GUI implementation is included but is not critical to the comparison with Go.

Game.java (Listing 11-3) contains this code.

Listing 11-3. Source File 3 Game.java

```
package org.baf.gol;

import  org.baf.gol.Logger;

import java.awt.GridLayout;
import java.awt.Rectangle;
import java.awt.image.BufferedImage;
import java.io.BufferedOutputStream;
import java.io.ByteArrayOutputStream;
```

```java
import java.io.IOException;
import java.nio.file.Files;
import java.nio.file.Paths;
import java.util.ArrayList;
import java.util.Date;
import java.util.LinkedHashMap;
import java.util.List;
import java.util.Map;

import javax.imageio.ImageIO;
import javax.imageio.stream.MemoryCacheImageOutputStream;
import javax.swing.ImageIcon;
import javax.swing.JFrame;
import javax.swing.JLabel;
import javax.swing.JPanel;
import javax.swing.JScrollPane;
import javax.swing.border.TitledBorder;

import org.baf.gol.Server.ResponseDataSender;

/**
 * Represents a GoL Game with a set of Game runs.
 */
public class Game {
  public static Game coreGame; // global instance

  static int threadId;

  private int nextThreadId() {
    return ++threadId;
  }

  // play history
  public Map<String, GameRun> runs = new LinkedHashMap<>();

  public int maxCycles = 25; // max that can be played
  public int threadCount; // thread to use in timings
  ParameterProvider pp; // source of command line parameters
```

```java
public String saveImageRoot = "/temp"; // change per OS type

public Game(ParameterProvider pp) {
  this.pp = pp;
}

/**
 * Represents a single run of a GoL Game.
 */
public class GameRun {
  static final int offIndex = 255, onIndex = 0;
  static final int midvalue = 256 / 2; // separates black vs. white

  public Game parent;
  public String name;
  public String imageUrl;
  public Date startedAt, endedAt;
  public int width, height;
  public Grid initialGrid, currentGrid, finalGrid;
  public List<GameCycle> cycles = new ArrayList<>();
  public int delayIn10ms, playIndex;
  public int threadCount;

  private String author = "Unknown";

  public String getAuthor() {
    return author;
  }

  public void setAuthor(String author) {
    this.author = author;
  }

  public GameRun(Game game, String name, String url) throws Exception {
    this.parent = game;
    this.name = name;
    this.imageUrl = url;
    this.delayIn10ms = 5 * 100;
```

```java
    // make the game grid and load initial state
    String[] kind = new String[1];
    BufferedImage img = Utility.loadImage(url, kind);
    Logger.log.tracef("Image kind: %s", kind[0]);
    if (!"png".equals(kind[0].toLowerCase())) {
      throw new IllegalArgumentException(
          String.format("named image %s is not a PNG", url));
    }
    var bounds = new Rectangle(img.getMinX(), img.getMinY(),
        img.getWidth(), img.getHeight());
    var size = bounds.getSize();
    initialGrid = new Grid(size.width, size.height);
    width = initialGrid.width;
    height = initialGrid.height;
    initGridFromImage(bounds.x, bounds.y, bounds.width, bounds.height, img);
    currentGrid = initialGrid.deepClone();
  }

  @Override
  public String toString() {
    return "GameRun[name=" + name + ", imageUrl=" + imageUrl +
        ", startedSt=" + startedAt + ", endedAt=" + endedAt
        + ", width=" + width + ", height=" + height +
        ", cycles=" + cycles + ", delayIn10ms=" + delayIn10ms
        + ", playIndex=" + playIndex + ", threadCount=" + threadCount + "]";
  }

  private void initGridFromImage(int minX, int minY, int maxX, int maxY,
      BufferedImage img) {
    for (int y = minY; y < maxY; y++) {
      for (int x = minX; x < maxX; x++) {
        var pixel = img.getRGB(x, y);
        int r = (pixel >> 16) & 0xFF,
            g = (pixel >> 8) & 0xFF,
            b = (pixel >> 0) & 0xFF;
```

```java
      var cv = 0; // assume all dead
      if (r + g + b < midvalue * 3) {
        cv = 1; // make cell alive
      }
      initialGrid.setCell(x, y, cv);
    }
  }
}

public void sendPng(ResponseDataSender rs, int index, int mag)
    throws IOException {
  Grid grid = null;
  switch (index) {
    case 0:
      grid = initialGrid;
      break;
    default:
      index--;
      if (index < 0 || index >= cycles.size()) {
        throw new ArrayIndexOutOfBoundsException("bad index");
      }
      grid = cycles.get(index).afterGrid;
  }

  var img = new BufferedImage(width * mag + 1, height * mag + 1,
      BufferedImage.TYPE_BYTE_BINARY);
  fillImage(grid, mag, img);
  var b = encodePngImage(img);
  rs.sendResponseData(b);
  showImageInGui(img); // show in GUI

  if (parent.pp.saveImageFlag()) {
    var saveFile = String.format(saveImageRoot + "/Image_%s.gif", name);
    Files.write(Paths.get(saveFile), b);
    Logger.log.tracef("Save %s", saveFile);
  }
}
```

```java
  private byte[] encodePngImage(BufferedImage img) throws IOException {
    var baos = new ByteArrayOutputStream();
    var bos = new BufferedOutputStream(baos);
    var ios = new MemoryCacheImageOutputStream(bos);
    ImageIO.write(img, "png", ios);
    ios.flush();
    return baos.toByteArray();
  }

  private void fillImage(Grid grid, int mag, BufferedImage img) {
    for (var row = 0; row < grid.height; row++) {
      for (var col = 0; col < grid.width; col++) {
        var index = grid.getCell(col, row) != 0 ? onIndex : offIndex;
        // apply magnification
        for (var i = 0; i < mag; i++) {
          for (var j = 0; j < mag; j++) {
            img.setRGB(mag * col + i, mag * row + j,
                index == onIndex ? 0 : 0x00FFFFFF);
          }
        }
      }
    }
  }

  /**
   * Run a game.
   */
  public void run() {
    this.threadCount = coreGame.threadCount;
    startedAt = new Date();
    int maxCycles = parent.maxCycles;
    for (int count = 0; count < maxCycles; count++) {
      nextCycle();
    }
    endedAt = new Date();
```

```
    Logger.log.tracef("GameRun total time: %dms, cycles: %d, thread
    count: %d", endedAt.getTime() - startedAt.getTime(),
        maxCycles, threadCount);
    finalGrid = currentGrid.deepClone();
}

// Advance and play next game cycle.
// Updating of cycle grid rows can be done in parallel;
// which can reduce execution time.
private void nextCycle() {
    var gc = new GameCycle(this);
    gc.beforeGrid = currentGrid.deepClone();
    var p = gc.parent;
    var threadCount = Math.max(p.parent.threadCount, 1);
    gc.afterGrid = new Grid(gc.beforeGrid.width, gc.beforeGrid.height);
    gc.startedAt = new Date();
    var threads = new ArrayList<Thread>();
    var rowCount = (height + threadCount / 2) / threadCount;
    for (var i = 0; i < threadCount; i++) {
        var xi = i;
        var t = new Thread(() -> {
            procesRows(gc, rowCount, xi * rowCount, gc.beforeGrid,
            gc.afterGrid);
        }, "thread_" + nextThreadId());
        threads.add(t);
        t.setDaemon(true);
        t.start();
    }
    for (var t : threads) {
        try {
            t.join();
        } catch (InterruptedException e) {
            // ignore
        }
    }
```

```
    gc.endedAt = new Date();
    currentGrid = gc.afterGrid.deepClone();
    cycles.add(gc);
    gc.cycleCount = cycles.size();
  }

  // process all cells in a set of rows
  private void procesRows(GameCycle gc, int rowCount, int startRow,
      Grid inGrid, Grid outGrid) {
    for (var index = 0; index < rowCount; index++) {
      var rowIndex = index + startRow;
      for (var colIndex = 0; colIndex < width; colIndex++) {
        // count any neighbors
        var neighbors = 0;
        if (inGrid.getCell(colIndex - 1, rowIndex - 1) != 0) {
          neighbors++;
        }
        if (inGrid.getCell(colIndex, rowIndex - 1) != 0) {
          neighbors++;
        }
        if (inGrid.getCell(colIndex + 1, rowIndex - 1) != 0) {
          neighbors++;
        }
        if (inGrid.getCell(colIndex - 1, rowIndex) != 0) {
          neighbors++;
        }
        if (inGrid.getCell(colIndex + 1, rowIndex) != 0) {
          neighbors++;
        }
        if (inGrid.getCell(colIndex - 1, rowIndex + 1) != 0) {
          neighbors++;
        }
        if (inGrid.getCell(colIndex, rowIndex + 1) != 0) {
          neighbors++;
        }
```

```
    if (inGrid.getCell(colIndex + 1, rowIndex + 1) != 0) {
      neighbors++;
    }
    // determine next generation cell state based on neighbor count
    var pv = inGrid.getCell(colIndex, rowIndex);
    var nv = 0;
    switch (neighbors) {
      case 2:
        nv = pv;
        break;
      case 3:
        if (pv == 0) {
          nv = 1;
        }
        break;
    }
    outGrid.setCell(colIndex, rowIndex, nv);
    }
  }
}

/**
 * Make images from 1+ cycles into GIF form.
 */
public byte[] makeGifs(int count, int mag) throws IOException {
  var cycleCount = cycles.size();
  var xcycles = Math.min(count, cycleCount + 1);
  List<BufferedImage> bia = new ArrayList<>();
  var added = addGridSafe(initialGrid, 0, xcycles, mag, bia);
  for (int i = 0; i < cycleCount; i++) {
    added = addGridSafe(cycles.get(i).afterGrid, added, xcycles, mag, bia);
  }
  return packGifs(added, mag, delayIn10ms,
      bia.toArray(new BufferedImage[bia.size()]));
}
```

```
int addGridSafe(Grid grid, int added, int max, int mag,
List<BufferedImage> bia) {
  var img = new BufferedImage(mag * width + 1, mag * height + 1,
      BufferedImage.TYPE_BYTE_BINARY);
  if (added < max) {
    fillImage(grid, mag, img);
    bia.add(img);
    added++;
  }
  return added;
}

byte[] packGifs(int count, int mag, int delay, BufferedImage[] bia)
    throws IOException {
  showImagesInGui(bia);

  var baos = new ByteArrayOutputStream();
  var bos = new BufferedOutputStream(baos);
  var ios = new MemoryCacheImageOutputStream(bos);
  AnnimatedGifWriter.createGifs(ios, delay, author, bia);
  ios.flush();
  return baos.toByteArray();
}

// not in Go version.
void showImagesInGui(BufferedImage[] bia) {
  // create a Swing Frame to show a row of images
  var frame = new JFrame("Show Images rendered at " + new Date());
  frame.setDefaultCloseOperation(JFrame.DISPOSE_ON_CLOSE);
  JPanel imagePanel = new JPanel(new GridLayout());
  var sp = new JScrollPane(imagePanel);
  frame.setContentPane(sp);
  frame.setSize(1000, 800);

  var index = 1;
  for (var bi : bia) {
    var icon = new ImageIcon(bi);
```

```
      JLabel labelledIcon = new JLabel(icon);
      labelledIcon.setBorder(new TitledBorder(String.format("Image: %d
      (%dx%d)", index++, icon.getIconWidth(), icon.getIconHeight())));
      imagePanel.add(labelledIcon);
    }
    frame.setVisible(true);
  }

  // not in Go version.
  void showImageInGui(BufferedImage bi) {
    var frame = new JFrame("Show Image rendered at " + new Date());
    JPanel imagePanel = new JPanel(new GridLayout());
    var sp = new JScrollPane(imagePanel);
    frame.setContentPane(sp);
    frame.setDefaultCloseOperation(JFrame.DISPOSE_ON_CLOSE);
    frame.setSize(1000, 800);
    var icon = new ImageIcon(bi);
    JLabel labelledIcon = new JLabel(icon);
    labelledIcon .setBorder(new TitledBorder(String.format("Image: (%dx%d)",
            icon.getIconWidth(), icon.getIconHeight())));
    imagePanel.add(labelledIcon);
    frame.setVisible(true);
  }
}

/**
 * Clear all runs.
 */
public void clear() {
  runs.clear();
}

/**
 * Run a game.
 */
```

```java
  public void run(String name, String url) throws Exception {
    var gr = new GameRun(this, name, url);
    runs.put(gr.name, gr);
    gr.run();
  }

  /**
   * Represents a GoL Game grid.
   */
  public static class Grid {
    public byte[] data;
    public int width, height;

    public Grid(int width, int height) {
      this.width = width;
      this.height = height;
      data = new byte[width * height];
    }

    @Override
    public String toString() {
      return "Grid[width=" + width + ", height=" + height + "]";
    }

    public int getCell(int x, int y) {
      if (x < 0 || x >= width || y < 0 || y >= height) {
        return 0;
      }
      return data[x + y * width];
    }

    public void setCell(int x, int y, int cv) {
      if (x < 0 || x >= width || y < 0 || y >= height) {
        return;
      }
      data[x + y * width] = (byte) cv;
    }
```

```java
  public Grid deepClone() {
    var ng = new Grid(width, height);
    for (int i = 0; i < data.length; i++) {
      ng.data[i] = data[i];
    }
    ng.width = width;
    ng.height = height;
    return ng;
  }
}

/**
 * Represents a GoL Game cycle.
 */
public static class GameCycle {
  public GameRun parent;
  public int cycleCount;
  public Date startedAt, endedAt;
  public Grid beforeGrid, afterGrid;

  public GameCycle(GameRun parent) {
    this.parent = parent;
  }

  @Override
  public String toString() {
    return "GameCycle[cycle=" + cycleCount + ", "
        + "startedAt=" + startedAt + ", endedAt=" + endedAt + "]";
  }
}
}
```

Utility.java

Utility.java (Listing 11-4) provides some helper functions and shared values.
Utility.java contains this code.

Listing 11-4. Source File 4 Utility.java

```java
package org.baf.gol;

import static org.baf.gol.Logger.log;

import java.awt.image.BufferedImage;
import java.io.File;
import java.io.IOException;
import java.net.URL;

import javax.imageio.ImageIO;

public class Utility {
  public static final int NANOS_PER_MS = 1_000_000;
  public static final String FILE_PREFIX = "file:";

  public static boolean isNullOrEmpty(CharSequence cs) {
    return cs == null || cs.length() == 0;
  }

  public static boolean isNullOrEmptyTrim(String cs) {
    return cs == null || cs.trim().length() == 0;
  }

  public static BufferedImage loadImage(String url, String[] kind) throws
  IOException {
    BufferedImage bi = null;
    if (url.startsWith(FILE_PREFIX)) {
      String name = url.substring(FILE_PREFIX.length());
      log.tracef("loadImage %s; %s", url, name);
      bi = ImageIO.read(new File(name));
    } else {
      var xurl = new URL(url);
```

```
        bi = ImageIO.read(xurl);
    }
    var posn = url.lastIndexOf(".");
    kind[0] = posn >= 0 ? url.substring(posn + 1) : "gif";
    return bi;
  }

}
```

Formatter.java

{Json|Xml}Formatter.java provides some helper functions for response formatting. JsonFormatter does all formatting directly. XmlFormatter is not implemented.

Formatter.java (Listing 11-5) contains this code.

Listing 11-5. Formatter.java

```
package org.baf.gol;

/**
 * Define a formatter (object to text).
 */
@FunctionalInterface
public interface Formatter {

  String valueToText(Object v);

}
```

JsonFormatter.java (Listing 11-6) contains this code.

Listing 11-6. JsonFormatter.java

```
package org.baf.gol;

import java.util.Date;
import java.util.List;
import java.util.Map;
```

```java
/**
 * A simple (but restricted) JSON object formatter.
 */
public class JsonFormatter implements Formatter {
  boolean pretty;
  String eol;

  public JsonFormatter(boolean pretty) {
    this.pretty = pretty;
    this.eol = pretty ? "\n" : "";
  }

  public JsonFormatter() {
    this(true);
  }

  @Override
  public String toString() {
    return "JsonFormatter[pretty=" + pretty + "]";
  }

  @Override
  public String valueToText(Object v) {
    StringBuilder sb = new StringBuilder();
    var size = 0;
    if (v instanceof List) {
      size = ((List) v).size();
    } else if (v instanceof Map) {
      size = ((Map) v).size();
    }
    valueToText(v, 0, "  ", "", size, ",  ", sb);
    return sb.toString();
  }

  // Format worker.
  void valueToText(Object v, int depth, String indent, String label, int
  len, String join, StringBuilder out) {
```

```java
if (join == null) {
  join = ", ";
}
var xindent = indent.repeat(depth);
out.append(xindent);
if (!label.isEmpty()) {
  out.append(label);
  out.append(": ");
}
if (v == null) {
  out.append("null");
  return;
}
// treat all implementations the same
var c = v.getClass();
var cname = c.getName();
if (v instanceof List) {
  cname = List.class.getName();
} else if (v instanceof Map) {
  cname = Map.class.getName();
}
// process all supported embedded types
switch (cname) {
  case "java.util.Date":
    out.append(((Date) v).getTime());
    break;
  case "java.lang.String":
    v = '"' + v.toString().replace("\"", "\\\"") + '"';
  case "java.lang.Byte":
  case "java.lang.Short":
  case "java.lang.Integer":
  case "java.lang.Long":
  case "java.lang.Double":
  case "java.lang.Float":
  case "java.lang.Boolean":
```

```java
        out.append(v.toString());
        break;
    case "java.util.List":
        out.append("[\n");
        List list = (List) v;
        for (int i = 0, xc = list.size(); i < xc; i++) {
            valueToText(list.get(i), depth + 1, indent, "", xc, join, out);
            out.append(i < len - 1 ? join : "");
            out.append(eol);
        }
        out.append(xindent + "]");
        break;
    case "java.util.Map":
        out.append("{\n");
        Map map = (Map) v;
        int i = 0, xc = map.size();
        for (var k : map.keySet()) {
            valueToText(map.get(k), depth + 1, indent, "\"" + k + "\"", xc,
            join, out);
            out.append(i < len - 1 ? join : "");
            i++;
            out.append(eol);
        }
        out.append(xindent + "}");
        break;
    default:
        throw new IllegalArgumentException("unknown type: " + cname);
    }
  }
 }
}
```

XmlFormatter.java (Listing 11-7) contains this code.

Listing 11-7. XmlFormatter.java

```java
package org.baf.gol;

public class XmlFormatter implements Formatter {

  @Override
  public String valueToText(Object v) {
    throw new IllegalThreadStateException("not implemented");
  }
}
```

ParameterProvider.java

ParameterProvider.java provides access to command parameters.

ParameterProvider.java (Listing 11-8) contains this code.

Listing 11-8. ParameterProvider.java

```java
package org.baf.gol;

/**
 * Provides a selected set of parameter values.
 */
public interface ParameterProvider {
  String getUrlParameter();

  String getNameParameter();

  int getMagFactorParameter();

  int getGameCyclesParameter();

  boolean startServerFlag();

  boolean runTimingsFlag();

  boolean reportFlag();

  boolean saveImageFlag();
}
```

AnnimatedGifWriter.java

AnnimatedGifWriter.java provides support to combine images.

AnnimatedGifWriter.java (Listing 11-9) contains this code.

Listing 11-9. AnimatedGifWriter.java

```java
package org.baf.gol;

import java.awt.image.BufferedImage;
import java.awt.image.RenderedImage;
import java.io.IOException;

import javax.imageio.IIOImage;
import javax.imageio.ImageIO;
import javax.imageio.ImageTypeSpecifier;
import javax.imageio.ImageWriteParam;
import javax.imageio.ImageWriter;
import javax.imageio.metadata.IIOMetadata;
import javax.imageio.metadata.IIOMetadataNode;
import javax.imageio.stream.ImageOutputStream;

/**
 * Supports combining multiple images into a single animated GIF.
 *
 */
public class AnnimatedGifWriter implements java.io.Closeable {
    private static final String CODE = "2.0";
    private static final String ID = "NETSCAPE";
    private static final String ZERO_INDEX = "0";
    private static final String NONE = "none";
    private static final String FALSE = "FALSE";

    protected IIOMetadata metadata;
    protected ImageWriter writer;
    protected ImageWriteParam params;

    public AnnimatedGifWriter(ImageOutputStream ios, int imageType, boolean
    showAsLoop, int delayMs, String author)
```

```
    throws IOException {
  var imageTypeSpecifier = ImageTypeSpecifier.createFromBufferedImageType
  (imageType);
  writer = ImageIO.getImageWritersBySuffix("gif").next();
  params = writer.getDefaultWriteParam();
  metadata = writer.getDefaultImageMetadata(imageTypeSpecifier, params);
  configMetadata(delayMs, showAsLoop, "Author: " + author);

  writer.setOutput(ios);
  writer.prepareWriteSequence(null);
}

@Override
public void close() throws IOException {
  writer.endWriteSequence();
}

/**
 * Creates an animated GIF from 1+ images.
 */
public static void createGifs(ImageOutputStream ios, int delay, String
author, BufferedImage... images)
    throws IOException {
  if (delay < 0) {
    delay = 5 * 1000;
  }
  if (images.length < 1) {
    throw new IllegalArgumentException("at least one image is required");
  }
  try (var writer = new AnnimatedGifWriter(ios, images[0].getType(),
  true, delay, author)) {
    for (var image : images) {
      writer.addImage(image);
    }
  }
}
```

```java
// configure self
void configMetadata(int delay, boolean loop, String comment) throws
IOException {
  var name = metadata.getNativeMetadataFormatName();
  var root = (IIOMetadataNode) metadata.getAsTree(name);
  metadata.setFromTree(name, root);

  var cel = findOrAddMetadata(root, "CommentExtensions");
  cel.setAttribute("CommentExtension", comment);

  var gce = findOrAddMetadata(root, "GraphicControlExtension");
  gce.setAttribute("transparentColorIndex", ZERO_INDEX);
  gce.setAttribute("userInputFlag", FALSE);
  gce.setAttribute("transparentColorFlag", FALSE);
  gce.setAttribute("delayTime", Integer.toString(delay / 10));
  gce.setAttribute("disposalMethod", NONE);

  byte[] bytes = new byte[] { 1, (byte) (loop ? 0 : 1), 0 };
  var ael = findOrAddMetadata(root, "ApplicationExtensions");
  var ae = new IIOMetadataNode("ApplicationExtension");
  ae.setUserObject(bytes);
  ae.setAttribute("authenticationCode", CODE);
  ae.setAttribute("applicationID", ID);
  ael.appendChild(ae);
}

static IIOMetadataNode findOrAddMetadata(IIOMetadataNode root, String
metadataType) {
  for (int i = 0, c = root.getLength(); i < c; i++) {
    if (root.item(i).getNodeName().equalsIgnoreCase(metadataType)) {
      return (IIOMetadataNode) root.item(i);
    }
  }
  var node = new IIOMetadataNode(metadataType);
  root.appendChild(node);
  return (node);
}
```

```java
void addImage(RenderedImage img) throws IOException {
    writer.writeToSequence(new IIOImage(img, null, metadata), params);
  }
}
```

Logger.java

Logger.java provides support to emulate (not exactly) the standard Go logger.

Logger.java (Listing 11-10) contains this code.

Listing 11-10. Logger.java

```java
package org.baf.gol;

import java.io.PrintStream;
import java.text.SimpleDateFormat;
import java.util.Date;

/**
 * Approximates the default Go logger function.
 *
 */
public class Logger {
  static public Logger log = new Logger();

  public PrintStream ps = System.out;
  public String lineFormat = "%-25s %-20s %-8s %-30s %s%n";
  public String contextFormat = "%s#%s@%d";
  public String threadFormat = "%s:%s";
  public SimpleDateFormat df = new SimpleDateFormat("yyyy-MM-dd HH:mm:ss.SSS");

  public void fatalf(String format, Object... args) {
    output(2, "FATAL", format, args);
    System.exit(3);
  }
```

```
  public void exceptionf(Exception e, String format, Object... args) {
    output(2, "EXCPT", "%s; caused by %s", String.format(format, args),
    e.getMessage());
    e.printStackTrace(ps);
  }

  public void errorf(String format, Object... args) {
    output(2, "ERROR", format, args);
  }

  public void tracef(String format, Object... args) {
    output(2, "TRACE", format, args);
  }

  void output(int level, String severity, String format, Object... args) {
    var text = String.format(format, args);
    Thread ct = Thread.currentThread();
    var st = ct.getStackTrace();
    StackTraceElement ste = st[level + 1];
    var tn = String.format(threadFormat, ct.getThreadGroup().getName(),
    ct.getName());
    var ctx = String.format(contextFormat, reduce(ste.getClassName()),
    ste.getMethodName(), ste.getLineNumber());
    ps.printf(lineFormat, df.format(new Date()), tn, severity, ctx, text);
  }

  String reduce(String name) {
    var posn = name.lastIndexOf(".");
    return posn >= 0 ? name.substring(posn + 1) : name;
  }
}
```

While this text is not a tutorial on building and running Java programs, the Java GoL program can be built and run by commands such as those in the following. The command forms can vary by your setup and the tools used (in this text, the author used the Eclipse IDE and thus not command-line tools). Assuming the source root is the current directory:

```
javac -d . -sourcepath ./org/baf/gol *.java
java -cp . org.baf.gol.Main -start -url ''
```

If the GoL program is built into a runnable JAR, it can be launched like this:

```
$>java --enable-preview -jar gol.jar
```

Note the GoL program uses new Java features.

This command produces this output:

```
Play the game of Life.
Game boards are initialized from PNG images.
Games play over several cycles.
Optionally acts as a server to retrieve images of game boards during play.
No supported positional arguments.
Arguments (all start with '-'):
url|u <url>              URL of the PNG image to load
name|n <name>           name to refer to the game initialized by the URL
magFactor|mf|mag <int>  magnify the grid by this factor when formatted
into an image  (default 1; 1 to 20)
gameCycles|gc <int>     sets number of cycles to run (default 10)
start <boolean>         start the HTTP server (default false)
time <boolean>          run game cycle timings with different thread
counts (default false)
report <boolean>        output run statistics (default false)
saveImage|si <boolean>  save generated images into a file (default false)
```

This code produces tracing lines that look like these samples (varies some between the Go and Java versions, split at text column):

```
2021-01-16 09:49:17.686   main:main            TRACE
Server#startHttpServer@337
Server localhost:8080 started

2021-01-16 09:49:22.166   main:HTTP-Dispatcher TRACE
Utility#loadImage@28
loadImage file:/.../tiny1.png; /.../tiny1.png
```

```
2021-01-16 09:49:22.204    main:HTTP-Dispatcher TRACE
Game$GameRun#<init>@69
Image kind: png

2021-01-16 09:49:22.257    main:HTTP-Dispatcher TRACE
Game$GameRun#run@169
GameRun total time: 45ms, cycles: 10, thread count: 0

2021-01-16 09:49:22.259    main:HTTP-Dispatcher EXCPT    Server$2#handle@257
play failed; caused by not implemented
```

Capstone Project in Go

The Go form of the GoL program consists of a single main package that has these source files:

- main.go – The main command processor

- server.go – The HTTP server and request handlers

- game.go – The GoL playing logic

- utility.go – Helper functions

Note all the preceding Go sources are in the main package. In a more production-style implementation, each source would likely be in its own package. Using separate packages could require changing the case of some names to make them public.

Note this Go example was tested on Go 1.14. Use at least that version for tools and runtime.

Main.go

The main.go file contains the main function which detects any command-line arguments and processes them. It used the flag package to process any command-line flags (with names ending in ...Flag). It also optionally (but by default) starts the HTTP server. Note that the command-line name and url arguments are only used if run timing is requested.

Listing 11-11 (Main.go) contains this code.

Listing 11-11. Main.go

```go
import (
    "flag"
    "fmt"
    "os"
    "runtime"
    "strings"
)

// Command line flags.
var (
    urlFlag         string
    nameFlag        string
    gridFlag        string
    magFactorFlag   int
    startServerFlag bool
    runTimingsFlag  bool
    reportFlag      bool
    saveImageFlag   bool
)

// Command line help strings
const (
    urlHelp       = "URL of the PNG image to load"
    nameHelp      = "name to refer to the game initialized by the URL"
    magFactorHelp = "magnify the grid by this factor when formatted into
    an image"
    gridHelp      = "specify the layout grid (for PNG images); MxN,
    default 1x1"
    startHelp     = "start the HTTP server (default true)"
    timingHelp    = "run game cycle timings with different goroutine
    counts"
    reportHelp    = "output run statistics"
    saveImageHelp = "save generated images into a file"
)
```

```go
// Define command line flags.
// Some are aliases (short forms).
func init() {
    flag.StringVar(&urlFlag, "url", "", urlHelp)
    flag.StringVar(&urlFlag, "u", "", urlHelp)
    flag.StringVar(&nameFlag, "name", "", nameHelp)
    flag.StringVar(&nameFlag, "n", "", nameHelp)
    flag.StringVar(&gridFlag, "grid", "1x1", gridHelp)
    flag.IntVar(&magFactorFlag, "magFactor", 1, magFactorHelp)
    flag.IntVar(&magFactorFlag, "mf", 1, magFactorHelp)
    flag.IntVar(&magFactorFlag, "mag", 1, magFactorHelp)
    flag.BoolVar(&startServerFlag, "start", true, startHelp)
    flag.BoolVar(&runTimingsFlag, "time", false, timingHelp)
    flag.BoolVar(&reportFlag, "report", false, reportHelp)
    flag.BoolVar(&saveImageFlag, "saveImage", false, saveImageHelp)
    flag.BoolVar(&saveImageFlag, "si", false, saveImageHelp)
}

const golDescription = `
Play the game of Life.
Game boards are initialized from PNG images.
Games play over cycles.
Optionally acts as a server to retrieve images of game boards during play.
No supported positional arguments. Supported flags (some have short forms):
`

// Main entry point.
// Sample: -n bart -u file:/Users/Administrator/Downloads/bart.png
func main() {
    if len(os.Args) <= 1 {
        fmt.Fprintln(os.Stderr, strings.TrimSpace(golDescription))
        flag.PrintDefaults()
        os.Exit(0)
    }
    fmt.Printf("Command arguments: %v\n", os.Args[1:])
    fmt.Printf("Go version: %v\n", runtime.Version())
```

```go
        flag.Parse() // parse any flags
        if len(flag.Args()) > 0 {
                fatalIfError(fmt.Fprintf(os.Stderr,
                        "positional command arguments (%v) not accepted\n",
                        flag.Args()))
                os.Exit(1)
        }
        launch()
}

func launch() {
        if len(urlFlag) > 0 {
                if len(nameFlag) == 0 {
                        fatalIfError(fmt.Fprintln(os.Stderr,
                                "a name is required when a URL is provided"))
                }
                if runTimingsFlag {
                        runCycleTimings()
                }
        }

        if startServerFlag {
                startHTTPServer()
        }
}

// launch the HTTP server.
func startHTTPServer() {
        err := startServer()
        if err != nil {
                fmt.Printf("start Server failed: %v\n", err)
                os.Exit(3)
        }

}
```

```go
// Output information about recorded cycles.
func runCycleTimings() {
    cpuCount := runtime.NumCPU()
    for i := 1; i <= 64; i *= 2 {
        fmt.Printf("Running with %d goroutines, %d CPUs...\n", i,
        cpuCount)
        CoreGame.GoroutineCount = i
        err := CoreGame.Run(nameFlag, urlFlag)
        if err != nil {
            fmt.Printf("Program failed: %v\n", err)
            os.Exit(2)
        }
        if reportFlag {
            fmt.Printf("Game max: %d, go count: %d:\n",
                CoreGame.MaxCycles, CoreGame.GoroutineCount)
            for _, gr := range CoreGame.Runs {
                fmt.Printf("Game Run: %v, cycle count: %d\n",
                gr.Name, len(gr.Cycles))
                for _, c := range gr.Cycles {
                    start, end :=
                        c.StartedAt.UnixNano()/NanosPerMs,
                        c.EndedAt.UnixNano()/NanosPerMs
                    fmt.Printf(
                        "Cycle: start epoch: %dms, end epoch: "+
                        "%dms, elapsed: %dms\n",
                        start, end, end-start)
                }
            }
        }
    }
}
```

Server.go

The server.go file launches an HTTP server with several path handlers. The handlers access any query parameters and then generate and/or access GoL data. AllGames represents the root of a history of past played games. Images or JSON/XML statistics stored in it are returned.

The server returns statistics in either JSON or XML format. Note how little code is needed to do either format. Also note how similar the code is for each format. Most of the work is in defining the tags on any structs to be converted to/from text. In general, there is much less code here than is needed with any Java equivalent implementation.

The returned data structs have tags to control the formatting of this data. Note the returned data names are sometimes different from the field names.

Server.go (Listing 11-12) contains this code.

Listing 11-12. Server.go

```go
package main

import (
        "bytes"
        "encoding/json"
        "encoding/xml"
        "fmt"
        "image/gif"
        "io/ioutil"
        "log"
        "net/http"
        "os"
        "regexp"
        "strconv"
        "strings"
)

var spec = ":8080" // means localhost:8080

// launch HTTP server for th GoL.
func startServer() (err error) {
        http.HandleFunc("/play", playHandler)
```

```go
    http.HandleFunc("/show", showHandler)
    http.HandleFunc("/history", historyHandler)
    fmt.Printf("Starting Server %v...\n", spec)
    err = http.ListenAndServe(spec, nil)
    return
}

// XYyyy types are returned to clients as JSON or XML.
// They are subset of Yyyy types used by the game player.
// They have no reference loops (i.e., to parents) not allowed in JSON and
// omit large fields.
// The tags define how the data is named and formatted

// Represents a game.
type XGame struct {
    Runs map[string]*XGameRun
}

type XGameCycle struct {
    Cycle           int     `json:"cycle" xml:"Cycle"`
    StartedAt       int64 `json:"startedAtNS" xml:"StartedAtEpochNS"`
    EndedAt         int64 `json:"endedAtNS" xml:"EndedAtEpochNS"`
    Duration        int64 `json:"durationMS" xml:"DurationMS"`
    GorountineCount int   `json:"goroutineCount" xml:"GorountineCount"`
    MaxCycles       int     `json:"maximumCycles" xml:"MaximumCycles"`
}

type XGameRun struct {
    Name      string          `json:"name" xml:"Name"`
    ImageURL  string          `json:"imageURL" xml:"ImageURL"`
    StartedAt int64           `json:"startedAtNS" xml:"StartedAtEpochNS"`
    EndedAt   int64           `json:"endedAtNS" xml:"EndedAtEpochNS"`
    Duration  int64           `json:"durationMS" xml:"DurationMS"`
    Width     int             `json:"width" xml:"Width"`
    Height    int             `json:"height" xml:"Height"`
    Cycles    []*XGameCycle `json:"gameCycles" xml:"GameCycles>GameCycl
    e,omitempty"`
```

```
    DelayIn10MS int            `json:"delay10MS" xml:"Delay10MS"`
    PlayIndex   int            `json:"playIndex" xml:"PlayIndex"`
}

func getLead(s string) (res string) {
    res = s
    posn := strings.Index(s, "?")
    if posn >= 0 {
        res = s[0:posn]
    }
    return
}

// History request handler
func historyHandler(writer http.ResponseWriter, request *http.Request) {
    switch request.Method {
    case "GET":
        if getLead(request.RequestURI) != "/history" {
            writer.WriteHeader(405)
            return
        }
        game := &XGame{}
        game.Runs = make(map[string]*XGameRun)
        for k, g := range CoreGame.Runs {
            game.Runs[k] = makeReturnedRun(k, g.ImageURL)
        }
        ba, err := json.MarshalIndent(game, "", "  ")
        if err != nil {
            writer.WriteHeader(500)
            return
        }
        writer.Header().Add("Content-Type", "text/json")
        writer.WriteHeader(200)
        writer.Write(ba) // send response; error ignored
    case "DELETE":
```

```go
            if request.RequestURI != "/history" {
                writer.WriteHeader(405)
                return
            }
            for k, _ := range CoreGame.Runs {
                delete(CoreGame.Runs, k)
            }
            writer.WriteHeader(204)
    default:
            writer.WriteHeader(405)
    }
}

// Play request handler.
func playHandler(writer http.ResponseWriter, request *http.Request) {
    if request.Method != "GET" || getLead(request.RequestURI) != "/play"
{
            writer.WriteHeader(405)
            return
    }
    err := request.ParseForm() // get query parameters
    if err != nil {
            writer.WriteHeader(400)
            return
    }
    name := request.Form.Get("name")
    url := request.Form.Get("url")
    if len(url) == 0 || len(name) == 0 {
            writer.WriteHeader(400)
            return
    }
    ct := request.Form.Get("ct")
    if len(ct) == 0 {
            ct = request.Header.Get("content-type")
    }
    ct = strings.ToLower(ct)
```

```go
switch ct {
case "":
    ct = "application/json"
case "application/json", "text/json":
case "application/xml", "text/xml":
default:
    writer.WriteHeader(400)
    return
}

err = CoreGame.Run(name, url)
if err != nil {
    writer.WriteHeader(500)
    return
}
run := makeReturnedRun(name, url)

var ba []byte
switch ct {
case "application/json", "text/json":
    ba, err = json.MarshalIndent(run, "", "  ")
    if err != nil {
        writer.WriteHeader(500)
        return
    }
    writer.Header().Add("Content-Type", "text/json")
case "application/xml", "text/xml":
    ba, err = xml.MarshalIndent(run, "", "  ")
    if err != nil {
        writer.WriteHeader(500)
        return
    }
    writer.Header().Add("Content-Type", "text/xml")
}
```

```go
        writer.WriteHeader(200)
        writer.Write(ba) // send response; error ignored
}

// Build data for returned run.
func makeReturnedRun(name, url string) *XGameRun {
        run := CoreGame.Runs[name]
        xrun := &XGameRun{}
        xrun.Name = run.Name
        xrun.ImageURL = url
        xrun.PlayIndex = run.PlayIndex
        xrun.DelayIn10ms = run.DelayIn10ms
        xrun.Height = run.Height
        xrun.Width = run.Width
        xrun.StartedAt = run.StartedAt.UnixNano()
        xrun.EndedAt = run.EndedAt.UnixNano()
        xrun.Duration = (xrun.EndedAt - xrun.StartedAt + NanosPerMs/2) /
        NanosPerMs
        xrun.Cycles = make([]*XGameCycle, 0, 100)

        for _, r := range run.Cycles {
                xc := &XGameCycle{}
                xc.StartedAt = r.StartedAt.UnixNano()
                xc.EndedAt = r.EndedAt.UnixNano()
                xc.Duration = (xc.EndedAt - xc.StartedAt + NanosPerMs/2) /
                NanosPerMs
                xc.Cycle = r.Cycle
                xc.GorountineCount = CoreGame.GoroutineCount
                xc.MaxCycles = CoreGame.MaxCycles
                xrun.Cycles = append(xrun.Cycles, xc)
        }
        return xrun
}

var re = regexp.MustCompile(`^(\d+)x(\d+)$`)
```

```go
// Show request handler.
func showHandler(writer http.ResponseWriter, request *http.Request) {
    if request.Method != "GET" || getLead(request.RequestURI) != "/show" {
        writer.WriteHeader(405)
        return
    }
    err := request.ParseForm() // get query parameters
    if err != nil {
        writer.WriteHeader(400)
        return
    }
    name := request.Form.Get("name")
    if len(name) == 0 {
        name = "default"
    }
    form := request.Form.Get("form")
    if len(form) == 0 {
        form = "gif"
    }
    xmaxCount := request.Form.Get("maxCount")
    if len(xmaxCount) == 0 {
        xmaxCount = "20"
    }
    maxCount, err := strconv.Atoi(xmaxCount)
    if err != nil || maxCount < 1 || maxCount > 100 {
        writer.WriteHeader(400)
        return
    }
    xmag := request.Form.Get("mag")
    if len(xmag) > 0 {
        mag, err := strconv.Atoi(xmag)
        if err != nil || mag < 1 || mag > 20 {
            writer.WriteHeader(400)
            return
        }
```

```go
            magFactorFlag = mag
    }

    index := 0
    // verify parameters based on type
    switch form {
    case "gif", "GIF":
    case "png", "PNG":
            xindex := request.Form.Get("index")
            if len(xindex) == 0 {
                    xindex = "0"
            }
            index, err = strconv.Atoi(xindex)
            if err != nil {
                    writer.WriteHeader(400)
                    return
            }
            xgrid := request.Form.Get("grid")
            if len(xgrid) > 0 {
                    parts := re.FindStringSubmatch(xgrid)
                    if len(parts) != 2 {
                            writer.WriteHeader(400)
                            return
                    }
                    gridFlag = fmt.Sprintf("%sx%s", parts[0], parts[1])
            }
    default:
            writer.WriteHeader(400)
            return
    }

    gr, ok := CoreGame.Runs[name]
    if ! ok {
            writer.WriteHeader(404)
            return
    }
```

```go
// return requested image type
switch form {
case "gif", "GIF":
        gifs, err := gr.MakeGIFs(maxCount)
        if err != nil {
                writer.WriteHeader(500)
                return
        }
        var buf bytes.Buffer
        err = gif.EncodeAll(&buf, gifs)
        if err != nil {
                writer.WriteHeader(500)
                return
        }
        count, err := writer.Write(buf.Bytes()) // send response
        log.Printf("Returned GIF, size=%d\n", count)
        if saveImageFlag {
                saveFile := fmt.Sprintf("/temp/Image_%s.gif", name)
                xerr := ioutil.WriteFile(saveFile, buf.Bytes(),
                os.ModePerm)
                fmt.Printf("Save %s: %v\n", saveFile, xerr)
        }
case "png", "PNG":
        if gridFlag == "1x1" {
                if index <= maxCount {
                        var buf bytes.Buffer
                        err = gr.MakePNG(&buf, index)
                        if err != nil {
                                code := 500
                                if err == BadIndexError {
                                        code = 400
                                }
                                writer.WriteHeader(code)
                                return
                        }
```

```
                    writer.Write(buf.Bytes()) // send response; error
                    ignored
            } else {
                    writer.WriteHeader(400)
            }
        } else {
            // currently not implemented
            writer.WriteHeader(400)
        }
    }
}
```

Game.go

Game.go contains the logic to play a GoL. Each *Game* consists of a set of named *GameRun* instances. Each GameRun consists of a set of *GameCycle* instances and some statistics. Each GameCycle consists of a before and after *Grid* snapshot and some statistics. Each Grid has the cell data (as a [ ]byte) and the grid dimensions. The REST show API returns the after-grid instance made into images.

The processRows function is called in a goroutine inside the NextCycle method. This allows a variable number of goroutines to be used. Using more goroutines can significantly speed up GoL cycle processing, especially for larger grids, as shown later in this section.

Game.go (Listing 11-13) contains this code.

Listing 11-13. Game.go

```
package main

import (
        "bytes"
        "errors"
        "fmt"
        "image"
        "image/color"
        "image/gif"
        "image/png"
```

```go
    "io"
    "io/ioutil"
    "log"
    "os"
    "sync"
    "time"
)

// Default game history.
var CoreGame = &Game{
    make(map[string]*GameRun),
    10,
    0,
    1}

// Represents a game.
type Game struct {
    Runs            map[string]*GameRun
    MaxCycles       int
    SkipCycles      int // not currently used
    GoroutineCount  int
}

// Run a set of cycles from the grid defined by an image.
func (g *Game) Run(name, url string) (err error) {
    gr, err := NewGameRun(name, url, g)
    if err != nil {
        return
    }
    g.Runs[gr.Name] = gr
    err = gr.Run()
    return
}
```

```go
// Clear a game.
func (g *Game) Clear() {
    for k, _ := range g.Runs {
        delete(g.Runs, k)
    }
}

// Represents a single run of a game.
type GameRun struct {
    Parent          *Game
    Name            string
    ImageURL        string
    StartedAt       time.Time
    EndedAt         time.Time
    Width, Height   int
    InitialGrid     *Grid
    CurrentGrid     *Grid
    FinalGrid       *Grid
    Cycles          []*GameCycle
    DelayIn10ms     int
    PlayIndex       int
    GoroutineCount  int
}

// B & W color indexes
const (
    offIndex = 0
    onIndex  = 1
)

// B & W color palette
var paletteBW = []color.Color{color.White, color.Black}

// Generate a PNG result (single frame).
func (gr *GameRun) MakePNG(writer io.Writer, index int) (err error) {
    var grid *Grid
    switch index {
```

```go
        case 0:
                grid = gr.InitialGrid
        default:
                index--
                if index < 0 || index >= len(gr.Cycles) {
                        err = BadIndexError
                        return
                }
                grid = gr.Cycles[index].AfterGrid
        }
        mag := magFactorFlag
        rect := image.Rect(0, 0, mag*gr.Width+1, mag*gr.Height+1)
        img := image.NewPaletted(rect, paletteBW)
        gr.FillImage(grid, img)
        b, err := gr.encodePNGImage(img)
        if err != nil {
                return
        }
        count, err := writer.Write(b.Bytes())
        log.Printf("Returned PNG, size= %d\n", count)
        if saveImageFlag {
                saveFile := fmt.Sprintf("/temp/Image_%s_%d.png", gr.Name, index)
                xerr := ioutil.WriteFile(saveFile, b.Bytes(), os.ModePerm)
                fmt.Printf("Save %s: %v\n", saveFile, xerr)
        }
        return
}

// Make a PNG image.
func (gr *GameRun) encodePNGImage(img *image.Paletted) (b bytes.Buffer, err
error) {
        var e png.Encoder
        e.CompressionLevel = png.NoCompression
        err = e.Encode(&b, img)
        return
}
```

```go
// Generate a GIF result (>= 1 frame).
func (gr *GameRun) MakeGIFs(count int) (agif *gif.GIF, err error) {
      mag := magFactorFlag
      cycles := len(gr.Cycles)
      xcount := cycles + 1
      if xcount > count {
            xcount = count
      }
      added := 0
      agif = &gif.GIF{LoopCount: 5}

      rect := image.Rect(0, 0, mag*gr.Width+1, mag*gr.Height+1)
      img := image.NewPaletted(rect, paletteBW)
      if added < xcount {
            gr.AddGrid(gr.InitialGrid, img, agif)
            added++
      }
      for i := 0; i < cycles; i++ {
            if added < xcount {
                  img = image.NewPaletted(rect, paletteBW)
                  gc := gr.Cycles[i]
                  grid := gc.AfterGrid
                  gr.AddGrid(grid, img, agif)
                  added++
            }
      }
      return
}

// Fill in and record a cycle image in an animated GIF.
func (gr *GameRun) AddGrid(grid *Grid, img *image.Paletted, agif *gif.GIF)
{
      gr.FillImage(grid, img)
      agif.Image = append(agif.Image, img)
      agif.Delay = append(agif.Delay, gr.DelayIn10ms)
}
```

```go
// Fill in an image from a grid.
func (gr *GameRun) FillImage(grid *Grid, img *image.Paletted) {
    mag := magFactorFlag
    for row := 0; row < grid.Height; row++ {
        for col := 0; col < grid.Width; col++ {
            index := offIndex
            if grid.getCell(col, row) != 0 {
                index = onIndex
            }
            // apply magnification
            for i := 0; i < mag; i++ {
                for j := 0; j < mag; j++ {
                    img.SetColorIndex(mag*row+i, mag*col+j,
                        uint8(index))
                }
            }
        }
    }
}

const midValue = 256 / 2 // middle color value

// Error values.
var (
    NotPNGError   = errors.New("not a png")
    NotRGBAError  = errors.New("not RGBA color")
    BadIndexError = errors.New("bad index")
)

// Start a new game run.
func NewGameRun(name, url string, parent *Game) (gr *GameRun, err error) {
    gr = &GameRun{}
    gr.Parent = parent
    gr.Name = name
    gr.GoroutineCount = CoreGame.GoroutineCount
    gr.ImageURL = url
```

```
    gr.DelayIn10ms = 5 * 100
    var img image.Image
    var kind string
    img, kind, err = LoadImage(url)
    if err != nil {
        return
    }
    fmt.Printf("Image kind:  %v\n", kind)
    if kind != "png" {
        return nil, NotPNGError
    }
    bounds := img.Bounds()
    minX, minY, maxX, maxY := bounds.Min.X, bounds.Min.Y, bounds.Max.X,
    bounds.Max.Y
    size := bounds.Size()
    //xsize := size.X * size.Y
    gr.InitialGrid = NewEmptyGrid(size.X, size.Y)
    gr.Width = gr.InitialGrid.Width
    gr.Height = gr.InitialGrid.Height

    err = gr.InitGridFromImage(minX, maxX, minY, maxY, img)
    if err != nil {
        return
    }
    gr.CurrentGrid = gr.InitialGrid.DeepCloneGrid()
    return
}

// Fill in a grid from an image.
// Map color images to B&W.  Only RGBA images allowed.
func (gr *GameRun) InitGridFromImage(minX, maxX, minY, maxY int,
    img image.Image) (err error) {
    setCount, totalCount := 0, 0
    for y := minY; y < maxY; y++ {
        for x := minX; x < maxX; x++ {
```

```go
//                        r, g, b, a := img.At(x, y).RGBA()
            rgba := img.At(x, y)
            var r, g, b uint8
            switch v := rgba.(type) {
            case color.NRGBA:
                    r, g, b, _ = v.R, v.G, v.B, v.A
            case color.RGBA:
                    r, g, b, _ = v.R, v.G, v.B, v.A
            default:
                    err = NotRGBAError
                    return
            }
            cv := byte(0) // assume cell dead
            if int(r)+int(g)+int(b) < midValue*3 {
                    cv = byte(1) // make cell alive
                    setCount++
            }
            gr.InitialGrid.setCell(x, y, cv)
            totalCount++
        }
    }
    return
}

// Play a game.
// Run requested cycle count.
func (gr *GameRun) Run() (err error) {
    gr.StartedAt = time.Now()
    for count := 0; count < gr.Parent.MaxCycles; count++ {
        err = gr.NextCycle()
        if err != nil {
            return
        }
    }
    gr.EndedAt = time.Now()
    fmt.Printf("GameRun total time: %dms, goroutine count: %d\n",
```

```
                (gr.EndedAt.Sub(gr.StartedAt)+NanosPerMs)/NanosPerMs,
                gr.GoroutineCount)
        gr.FinalGrid = gr.CurrentGrid.DeepCloneGrid()
        return
}

// Represents a single cycle of a game.
type GameCycle struct {
        Parent      *GameRun
        Cycle       int
        StartedAt   time.Time
        EndedAt     time.Time
        BeforeGrid *Grid
        AfterGrid   *Grid
}

func NewGameCycle(parent *GameRun) (gc *GameCycle) {
        gc = &GameCycle{}
        gc.Parent = parent
        return
}

// Advance and play next game cycle.
// Updating of cycle grid rows can be done in parallel;
// which can reduce execution time.
func (gr *GameRun) NextCycle() (err error) {
        gc := NewGameCycle(gr)
        gc.BeforeGrid = gr.CurrentGrid.DeepCloneGrid()
        p := gc.Parent
        goroutineCount := p.Parent.GoroutineCount
        if goroutineCount <= 0 {
                goroutineCount = 1
        }
        gc.AfterGrid = NewEmptyGrid(gc.BeforeGrid.Width, gc.BeforeGrid.
        Height)
        gc.StartedAt = time.Now()
        // process rows across  allowed goroutines
```

```go
    rowCount := (gr.Height + goroutineCount/2) / goroutineCount
    var wg sync.WaitGroup
    for i := 0; i < goroutineCount; i++ {
        wg.Add(1)
        go processRows(&wg, gc, rowCount, i*rowCount, gc.BeforeGrid,
        gc.AfterGrid)
    }
    wg.Wait() // let all finish
    gc.EndedAt = time.Now()
    gr.CurrentGrid = gc.AfterGrid.DeepCloneGrid()
    gr.Cycles = append(gr.Cycles, gc)
    gc.Cycle = len(gr.Cycles)
    return
}

// Represents a 2-dimensional game grid (abstract, not as an image).
type Grid struct {
    Data          []byte
    Width, Height int
}

func NewEmptyGrid(w, h int) (g *Grid) {
    g = &Grid{}
    g.Data = make([]byte, w*h)
    g.Width = w
    g.Height = h
    return
}

func (g *Grid) DeepCloneGrid() (c *Grid) {
    c = &Grid{}
    lg := len(g.Data)
    c.Data = make([]byte, lg, lg)
    for i, b := range g.Data {
        c.Data[i] = b
    }
```

```go
        c.Width = g.Width
        c.Height = g.Height
        return
}

func (g *Grid) getCell(x, y int) (b byte) {
        if x < 0 || x >= g.Width || y < 0 || y >= g.Height {
                return
        }
        return g.Data[x+y*g.Width]
}
func (g *Grid) setCell(x, y int, b byte) {
        if x < 0 || x >= g.Width || y < 0 || y >= g.Height {
                return
        }
        g.Data[x+y*g.Width] = b
}

// Play game as subset of grid rows (so can be done in parallel).
func processRows(wg *sync.WaitGroup, gc *GameCycle, rowCount int,
        startRow int, inGrid, outGrid *Grid) {
        defer wg.Done()
        gr := gc.Parent
        for index := 0; index < rowCount; index++ {
                rowIndex := index + startRow
                for colIndex := 0; colIndex < gr.Width; colIndex++ {
                        // count any neighbors
                        neighbors := 0
                        if inGrid.getCell(colIndex-1, rowIndex-1) != 0 {
                                neighbors++
                        }
                        if inGrid.getCell(colIndex, rowIndex-1) != 0 {
                                neighbors++
                        }
                        if inGrid.getCell(colIndex+1, rowIndex-1) != 0 {
                                neighbors++
```

```
        }
        if inGrid.getCell(colIndex-1, rowIndex) != 0 {
            neighbors++
        }
        if inGrid.getCell(colIndex+1, rowIndex) != 0 {
            neighbors++
        }
        if inGrid.getCell(colIndex-1, rowIndex+1) != 0 {
            neighbors++
        }
        if inGrid.getCell(colIndex, rowIndex+1) != 0 {
            neighbors++
        }
        if inGrid.getCell(colIndex+1, rowIndex+1) != 0 {
            neighbors++
        }

        // determine next generation cell state based on neighbor
           count
        pv := inGrid.getCell(colIndex, rowIndex)
        nv := uint8(0) // assume dead
        switch neighbors {
        case 2:
            nv = pv // unchanged
        case 3:
            if pv == 0 {
                nv = 1 // make alive
            }
        }
        outGrid.setCell(colIndex, rowIndex, nv)
        }
    }
}
```

Utility.go

Utility.go provides some helper functions and shared values.

Utility.go (Listing 11-14) contains this code.

Listing 11-14. Utility.go

```go
package main

import (
        "bytes"
        "image"
        "io/ioutil"
        "log"
        "net/http"
        "strings"
)

const NanosPerMs = 1_000_000
const FilePrefix = "file:" // local (vs. HTTP) file

func LoadImage(url string) (img image.Image, kind string, err error) {
        switch {
        case strings.HasPrefix(url, FilePrefix):
                url = url[len(FilePrefix):]
                var b []byte
                b, err = ioutil.ReadFile(url) // read image from file
                if err != nil {
                        return
                }
                r := bytes.NewReader(b)
                img, kind, err = image.Decode(r)
                if err != nil {
                        return
                }
        default:
                var resp *http.Response
                resp, err = http.Get(url) // get image from network
```

```go
        if err != nil {
            return
        }
        img, kind, err = image.Decode(resp.Body)
        resp.Body.Close() // error ignored
        if err != nil {
            return
        }
    }
    return
}

// Fail if passed an error.
func fatalIfError(v ...interface{}) {
    if v != nil && len(v) > 0 {
        if err, ok := v[len(v)-1].(error); ok && err != nil {
            log.Fatalf("unexpected error: %v\n", err)
        }
    }
}
```

Go Doc Output

While not typically done for command-line programs, here is the output of running the command

```
go doc -cmd -u
```

on the GoL codebase:

```
package main // import "."
const offIndex = 0 ...
const urlHelp = "URL of the PNG image to load" ...
const FilePrefix = "file:"
const NanosPerMs = 1_000_000
const golDescription = ...
```

```
const midValue = 256 / 2
var NotPNGError = errors.New("not a png") ...
var urlFlag string ...
var AllGames = &Game{ ... }
var paletteBW = []color.Color{ ... }
var spec = ":8080"
func LoadImage(url string) (img image.Image, kind string, err error)
func fatalIfError(v ...interface{})
func init()
func main()
func playHandler(writer http.ResponseWriter, request *http.Request)
func processRows(wg *sync.WaitGroup, gc *GameCycle, rowCount int, startRow
int, ...)
func runCycleTimings()
func showHandler(writer http.ResponseWriter, request *http.Request)
func startHTTPServer()
func startServer() (err error)
type Game struct{ ... }
type GameCycle struct{ ... }
    func NewGameCycle(parent *GameRun) (gc *GameCycle)
type GameRun struct{ ... }
    func NewGameRun(name, url string, parent *Game) (gr *GameRun, err error)
type Grid struct{ ... }
    func NewEmptyGrid(w, h int) (g *Grid)
type XGameCycle struct{ ... }
type XGameRun struct{ ... }
    func makeReturnedRun(name, url string) *XGameRun
```

This output is elided (and thus incomplete) by the tool itself, but it outlines the key parts of the program well. It is possible to drill down into each reported struct to get more details. See the Go documentation for more details.

Unlike in Java with its JavaDoc tool (which pregenerates HTML output), the richer online HTML form of this documentation requires a *go doc* server to be running to be generated. See the Go online documentation on how to launch such a server.

API Outputs

The results shown in Figure 11-6, of a `play` action, show sample statistics returned. This JSON was created by Go functions in the `encoding/json` package.

```
1   {
2     "name": "tiny1",
3     "imageURL": "file:/Users/Administrator/Downloads/tiny1.png",
4     "startedAtNS": 1608671425935711300,
5     "endedAtNS": 1608671425943676400,
6     "durationMS": 8,
7     "width": 200,
8     "height": 200,
9     "gameCycles": [
10      {
11        "cycle": 1,
12        "startedAtNS": 1608671425936707000,
13        "endedAtNS": 1608671425936707000,
14        "durationMS": 0,
15        "goroutineCount": 64,
16        "maximumCycles": 10
17      },
18 >    { …
25      },
26 >    { …
33      },
34 >    { …
41      },
42 >    { …
49      },
50 >    { …
57      },
58 >    { …
65      },
66 >    { …
73      },
74 >    { …
81      },
82      {
83        "cycle": 10,
84        "startedAtNS": 1608671425942680700,
85        "endedAtNS": 1608671425943676400,
86        "durationMS": 1,
87        "goroutineCount": 64,
88        "maximumCycles": 10
89      }
90    ],
91    "delay10MS": 500,
92    "playIndex": 0
93  }
```

Figure 11-6. *Play output in JSON*

The XML equivalent of the preceding JSON was created by Go functions in the encoding/xml package (Figure 11-7).

```
1    <XGameRun>
2        <Name>tiny1</Name>
3        <ImageURL>file:/Users/Administrator/Downloads/tiny1.png</ImageURL>
4        <StartedAtEpochNS>1608671313767808300</StartedAtEpochNS>
5        <EndedAtEpochNS>1608671313774777600</EndedAtEpochNS>
6        <DurationMS>7</DurationMS>
7        <Width>200</Width>
8        <Height>200</Height>
9        <GameCycles>
10           <GameCycle>
11               <Cycle>1</Cycle>
12               <StartedAtEpochNS>1608671313767808300</StartedAtEpochNS>
13               <EndedAtEpochNS>1608671313767808300</EndedAtEpochNS>
14               <DurationMS>0</DurationMS>
15               <GorountineCount>64</GorountineCount>
16               <MaximumCycles>10</MaximumCycles>
17           </GameCycle>
18 >         <GameCycle> ...
25           </GameCycle>
26 >         <GameCycle> ...
33           </GameCycle>
34 >         <GameCycle> ...
41           </GameCycle>
42 >         <GameCycle> ...
49           </GameCycle>
50 >         <GameCycle> ...
57           </GameCycle>
58 >         <GameCycle> ...
65           </GameCycle>
66 >         <GameCycle> ...
73           </GameCycle>
74 >         <GameCycle> ...
81           </GameCycle>
82           <GameCycle>
83               <Cycle>10</Cycle>
84               <StartedAtEpochNS>1608671313774777600</StartedAtEpochNS>
85               <EndedAtEpochNS>1608671313774777600</EndedAtEpochNS>
86               <DurationMS>0</DurationMS>
87               <GorountineCount>64</GorountineCount>
88               <MaximumCycles>10</MaximumCycles>
89           </GameCycle>
90       </GameCycles>
91       <Delay10MS>500</Delay10MS>
92       <PlayIndex>0</PlayIndex>
93   </XGameRun>
```

Figure 11-7. *Play output in XML*

The results shown in Figure 11-8, of a history action, show the known played games.

```
1    {
2      "Runs": {
3        "tiny1": {
4          "name": "tiny1",
5          "imageURL": "file:/Users/Administrator/Downloads/tiny1.png",
6          "startedAtNS": 1608735086048043400,
7          "endedAtNS": 1608735086056007900,
8          "durationMS": 8,
9          "width": 200,
10         "height": 200,
11  >      "gameCycles": [ ...
92         ],
93         "delay10MS": 500,
94         "playIndex": 0
95       },
96       "tiny2": {
97         "name": "tiny2",
98         "imageURL": "file:/Users/Administrator/Downloads/tiny1.png",
99         "startedAtNS": 1608735135865397600,
.00        "endedAtNS": 1608735135873362800,
.01        "durationMS": 8,
.02        "width": 200,
.03        "height": 200,
.04  >     "gameCycles": [ ...
.85        ],
.86        "delay10MS": 500,
.87        "playIndex": 0
.88      }
.89    }
.90  }
```

Figure 11-8.   *History output in JSON*

At server start time or after DELETE /history, this looks like the one shown in Figure 11-9.

```
1   {
2        "Runs": {}
3   }
```

Figure 11-9. *Empty history output*

Game Outputs

In the following figures, the results of a show action are seen in a sample set of a few game cycles, starting with the original image. If allowed to have many cycles (not shown here), the cycles for this original eventually get into an alternating pattern that continues indefinitely.

Figure 11-10 offers an original sample image, a mix of a scribble and some simple shapes, used to play a GoL shown in a browser at small scale.

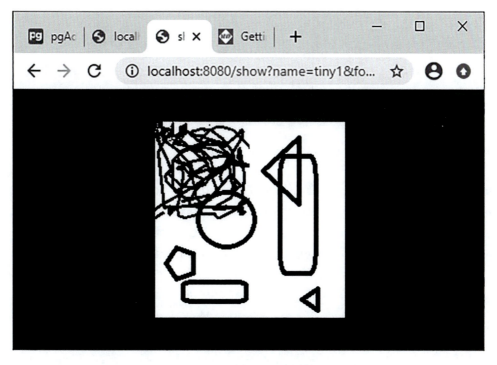

Figure 11-10. *Browser view of an initial game state*

Figure 11-11 shows a ten-cycle game of a similar PNG as presented by the Java implementation in a Swing GUI (there is no GUI equivalent in the Go version). The first image is the input image. The others are after a new game cycle. The wide output is split into the following two segments. Note that irregular patterns tend to die off quickly, while regular patterns remain longer.

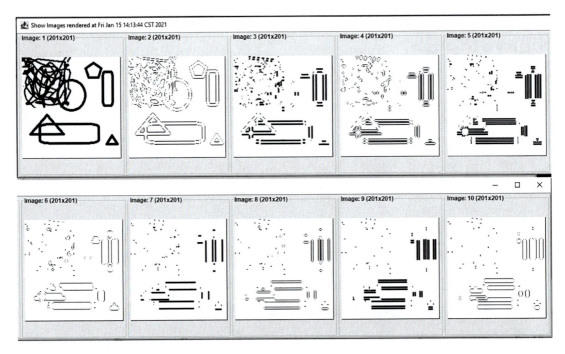

Figure 11-11. *Game cycle history (first nine cycles)*

Note images have 1-pixel padding (black) in width and height.

Due to the small grid size, the preceding GoL play takes little elapsed time to process a cycle. A similar Go run, as shown in Table 11-1, with a much larger (approx. 2000 x 2000) width and height sample image shows these cycle timing results.

Table 11-1. *Timings for Different Goroutine Counts*

```
GameRun total time: 2995ms, goroutine count:  1
GameRun total time: 1621ms, goroutine count:  2
GameRun total time:  922ms, goroutine count:  4
GameRun total time:  581ms, goroutine count:  8
GameRun total time:  487ms, goroutine count: 16
GameRun total time:  363ms, goroutine count: 32
```

Note these numbers are sensitive to the image's size and the processor capacity the server runs on. Your mileage may vary.

The graph in Figure 11-12 shows the performance numbers plotted in elapsed time (in milliseconds) vs. goroutine count. One can clearly see the advantage of having more goroutines in improving the execution time. The amount of improvement depends on the available number of cores, but even a few cores help a lot. Eventually, as shown, adding more goroutines will not improve the performance much.

The improvement is not linear[18] with the number of goroutines, but it is substantial. Here, the shortest observed time is only 16% of the maximum observed time. Given the minimal extra (approx. 10 lines) code needed to add the goroutines, this is a good return on investment.

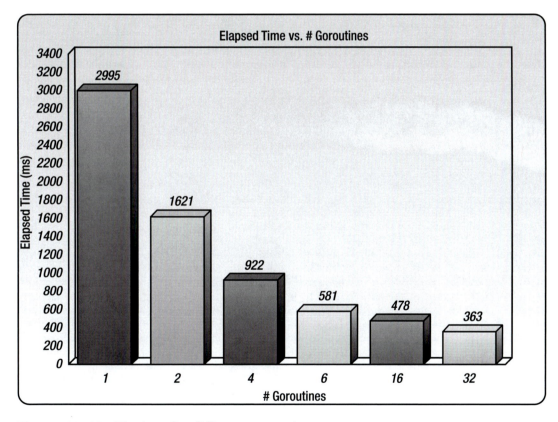

Figure 11-12. *Timings for different goroutine counts*

---

[18] All goroutines may not be allocated to different cores.

PART III

Go Library Survey

This part will look at the standard Go libraries in a summary fashion. It is intended to get you aware of and familiar with the libraries and what they can do, not to detail their use. Not all types and functions in each library will be mentioned, only some more generally useful (a somewhat opinionated selection) ones will be. Many functions are self-explanatory (their names essentially imply their function) and thus may not be further described. For other functions, only a brief description will be given. Some types and/or functions will include examples.

We will begin with a brief survey of the Go standard package libraries. It is intended to make the reader aware of and familiar with the Go runtime function. It is not intended to be a full tutorial or reference for each library function, but for many libraries, it provides enough details to begin to use them successfully. Additional information on each library is available on the online Go documentation (at `www.golang.org/pkg`). We will discuss only the standard Go libraries.

Go, like Java, has both standard (included in the Go install) libraries and third-party (aka community supplied) libraries. In the author's opinion, the Java standard libraries are generally more comprehensive in nature, but the Go libraries are rich enough to write many useful programs. Also, the Go versions are often easier to learn and use, at least initially.

Discussing all community-provided Go libraries, like for Java community libraries, would be a superhuman task resulting in many thousands of pages. It is also impossible to stay current with such libraries in a book. Thus, doing so is not attempted in this text.

In some cases, the Go standard libraries have capabilities the Java standard libraries do not. For example, Go has built-in support for creating production servers, especially HTTP servers. In Java, this typically requires additional libraries, such as from *Apache. org* or Spring.*org*. So standard Go resembles a reduced function *Java Extended Edition* (JEE – now known as *Jakarta Extended Edition*[1]) environment.

---

[1] `https://en.wikipedia.org/wiki/Jakarta_EE`

An area where Go is very weak when compared to Java is in native GUIs. Java has the *AWT*, *Swing*, and *JavaFX* GUI libraries, among others. Go has nothing comparable, but Go has libraries that help generate HTML (or CSS or JSON) for web GUIs which Java includes in JEE. Some Go community members offer native GUI support, but it seems not generally any that is fully cross-OS platform. Also, many are not pure Go and require CGo access to native OS libraries.

It would take many 100s (if not 1000s) of pages to compare these libraries on a function-by-function basis. Similarly, it would take many 100s of pages to provide just a programmer reference for all the functions in the Go libraries. This book will not attempt to do that. The online Go documentation is available for this purpose.

Note that the Go libraries are arranged into packages, so in this context, a package and a library are often synonymous terms (but some libraries may have multiple packages).

The library survey will be driven by what is available in Go. Thus, some Java libraries may not be covered at all. Some Go libraries will not be surveyed as they are less frequently used or intended for advanced or internal (say by the Go build system or runtime) use.

This book will compare some key libraries and provide examples for some of the functions they offer that most programmers will use. This is basically a comparison of some of the classes and functions in the `java.lang` and `java.util` (and their sub-packages) packages to their Go equivalents. A few classes and functions from other Java packages will be mentioned.

Some Go libraries are very low level (e.g., unsafe memory access or direct operating system access) that are generally wrapped by higher-level libraries; only the higher-level libraries will be discussed. Some Go libraries deal with the Go runtime and toolset implementation, and they will not be discussed. Some Go libraries deal will low-level debugging and tracing, and they will not be discussed.

Some Go libraries deal with *Remote Procedure Calls* (RPC) across processes and networks and will not be discussed. RPC is less frequently used today than HTTP access, which will be included. Similarly, Go's email support will not be discussed.

Not all the types and functions in a described package are listed here. See the Go online documentation described for the complete set. This site describes the standard packages and some supplemental packages (of which some are experimental) and provides some links to third-party packages. The site (`https://golang.org/pkg/`) is summarized in Figure P3-1 (standard libraries hidden).

≡GO

Packages

Standard library
Other packages
   Sub-repositories
   Community

Standard library ▷

Other packages

Sub-repositories

These packages are part of the Go Project but outside the main Go tree. They are developed under looser compatibility requirements than the Go core. Install them with "go get".

- benchmarks — benchmarks to measure Go as it is developed.
- blog — blog.golang.org's implementation.
- build — build.golang.org's implementation.
- crypto — additional cryptography packages.
- debug — an experimental debugger for Go.
- image — additional imaging packages.
- mobile — experimental support for Go on mobile platforms.
- net — additional networking packages.
- perf — packages and tools for performance measurement, storage, and analysis.
- pkgsite — home of the pkg.go.dev website.
- review — a tool for working with Gerrit code reviews.
- sync — additional concurrency primitives.
- sys — packages for making system calls.
- text — packages for working with text.
- time — additional time packages.
- tools — godoc, goimports, gorename, and other tools.
- tour — tour.golang.org's implementation.
- exp — experimental and deprecated packages (handle with care; may change without warning).

Community

These services can help you find Open Source packages provided by the community.

- Pkg.go.dev - the Go package discovery site.
- Projects at the Go Wiki - a curated list of Go projects.

Figure P3-1. *Summary of Go extension packages*

- Pkg.go.dev is mostly a search engine; you need to provide keywords.

- `https://github.com/golang/go/wiki/Projects` is a directory of Go search engines and a listing for projects across many domains. It is a good source to look for community library contributions.

The standard libraries contain many packages; some are summarized in the following. Many types and functions of the standard library have enhanced (often drop-in replacement) versions in community offerings. Some community offerings diverge from the standard library API patterns entirely and have different approaches to providing a feature. Before committing to using a standard library API, it is recommended that a survey (say web search) of community alternative libraries be conducted. Often, they are richer and more functional.

This phenomenon is less prevalent in Java, where most developers use the standard libraries for any function they provide. A notable exception is with the standard HTTP client, which can be hard to use and has limited function. Thus, many community enhancements of it exist. Note Java 11 offers a replacement HTTP client that is much improved and may obsolete some community offerings.

Not all types and functions/methods of the types are listed in the following, just the most used. Many packages come with constant and variable definitions. Only such values of common usage will be listed. If no constructor (NewXxx) method is defined for a type in the following, use the zero-value declaration.

It is common for the package variables to include standardized `error` types that can be used to compare against returned errors from the methods in the package. These values are used similarly to Java's standard Exception types (e.g., IllegalArgumentException or ArrayIndexOutOfBoundsException). For example, the zip package defines these errors:

```
var (
    ErrFormat    = errors.New("zip: not a valid zip file")
    ErrAlgorithm = errors.New("zip: unsupported compression algorithm")
    ErrChecksum  = errors.New("zip: checksum error")
)
```

Note that this sets a pattern for naming any similar errors in your code and a possible style for the text of error messages.

Many types, especially struct types, listed in the following implement the Stringer interface. That is not documented in the following method sets.

The Go standard packages are arranged in a shallow hierarchy. Some general functions are grouped under a parent package, and more specific functions are under a child package.

While the packages in the standard hierarchy can increase over time, here is a representative list of the packages with a brief description of their use:

- archive – Empty, see nested

- archive/tar – TAR read access

- archive/zip – ZIP read/write access

- bufio – Provides buffered I/O over lower-level unbuffered I/O functions

- builtin – Describes Go built-in types and identifiers

- bytes – Functions to process slices of bytes

- compress – Empty, see nested

- compress/bzip – BZIP 2 decompression

- compress/flate – Process DEFLATE format data

- compress/gzip – Process GZIP format data

- compress/lzw – Process Lempel-Ziv-Welch format data

- compress/zlob – Process zlib format data

- container – Empty, see nested

- container/heap – Process heaps (tree where each node is the minimum of any subtree with the minimum at the top)

- container/list – A doubly-linked list

- container/ring – A circular list

- context – Means to report timeouts and cancel operations

- crypto – Holds cryptographic constants

- crypto/aes – Provides AES encryption

- crypto/cipher – Supports block ciphers

- crypto/des – Provides DES and 3DES encryption

- cypto/dsa – Provides DSA support

- crypto/ecdsa – Provides Elliptic Curve DSA

- crypto/ed25519 – Provides Ed25519 signatures

- crypto/elliptic – Provides elliptic curve on prime fields

- crypto/hmac – Provides HMAC authentication

- crypto/md5 – Provides MD5 hashes

- crypto/rand – Provides cryptographically string random numbers

- crypto/rc4 – Provides RC4 encryption

- crypto/rsa – Provides RSA encryption

- crypto/sha1 – Provides SHA-1 hashes

- crypto/sha256 – Provides SHA-224 and SHA-256 hashes

- crypto/sha512 – Provides SHA-384 and several SHA-512 hashes

- crypto/subtle – Provides cryptographic helper functions

- crypto/tls – Provides TLS (used in HTTPS) support

- crypto/x509 – Provides X.509 certificate support

- crypto/pkix – Provides data for x509

- database – Empty, see nested

- database/sql – Support for JDBC-like access to databases

- database/driver – Support for database drivers (an SPI)

- debug – Empty, see nested

- debug/dwarf – Supports DWARF information

- debug/elf – Supports ELF object files

- debug/gosym – Access symbols/line numbers at runtime

- debug/macho – Supports Mach-O object files

- debug/pe – Supports Portable Executable files

- debug/plan9obj – Supports Plan9 object files

- encoding – Interfaces to support various format conversions
- encoding/ascii85 – Supports ASCII85 encoding
- encoding/asn1 – Supports ASN.1 encoding
- encoding/base32 – Supports base 32 encoding
- encoding/base64 – Supports base 64 encoding
- encoding/binary – Supports serializing base types
- encoding/csv – Supports reading/writing CSV format data
- encoding/gob – Supports serializing complex (struct) types
- encoding/hex – Binary to hex string conversions
- encoding/json – Binary to JSON string conversions
- encoding/pem – Provides PEM encoding
- encoding/xml – XML parser
- errors – Support for Go error type
- expvar – Support to export Go runtime state (like JMX)
- flag – Support to parse command-line flags (i.e., switches)
- fmt – Support to scan/format values
- go – Empty, see nested
- go/ast – Supports access to Go-based ASTs
- go build – Supports processing Go packages
- go/constant – Support for Go constants
- go/doc – Support for processing Go document comments in AST
- go/format – Supports formatting Go source code
- go/importer – Supports processing `import` statements
- go/parser – Parses Go source
- go/printer – Supports formatting an AST
- go/scanner – Lexical analysis (tokenization) for Go source

- go/tokens – Enums for various Go source tokens

- go/types – Support types and type checking in Go source

- hash – Defines various hashes

- hash/adler32 – Supports Adler 32 checksums

- hash/crc32 – Supports 32-bit CRC checksum

- hash/crc64 – Supports 64-bit CRC checksum

- hash/fnv – Supports FNV hashes

- hash/maphash – Hashes of byte sequences

- html – Support to escape HTML values

- html/template – HTML injection safe templates

- image – Functions to help make 2D images

- image/color – Provides a color library

- image/palette – Supports color palettes

- image/draw – Supports 2D drawing

- image/gif – Supports GIF format

- image/jpeg – Supports JPEG format

- image/png – Supports PNG format

- index – Empty, see nested

- index/suffixarray – Provides substring search using a suffix array

- io – Supports low-level I/O operations

- ioutil – Provides I/O helpers

- log – Provides basic logging

- log/syslog – Provides access to operating system logging

- math – Provides basic math functions

- math/big – Provides support for big integers, big floats, and rational numbers

- math/bits – Provides support for bit-level access in integers

- cmplx – Provides helpers/functions for complex numbers

- math/rand – Provides support for generating random numbers

- mime – Provides support for MIME types

- mime/multipart – Support for multipart data

- mime/quotedprintable – Support for quoted printable encoding

- net – Support for TCP/IP and UDP networking, DNS resolution, and sockets

- net/http – Support for HTTP clients and servers

- net/cgi – Support for CGI servers

- net/cookiejar – Support for HTTP cookies

- net/fgci – Support for "fast" CGI servers

- net/httptest – Supports mock testing of HTTP interactions

- net/httptrace – Support for HTTP request tracing

- net/httputil – Provides HTTP helper functions

- net/pprof – Supports HTTP server profiling

- net/mail – Supports email processing

- net/rpc – Supports basic RPC messaging and serialization

- net/rpc/jasonrpc – Supports RPC using JSON bodies

- net/smtp – Supports email send/receive

- net/textproto – Supports text header–based (e.g., HTTP) network protocols

- net/url – Supports parsing and processing URLs

- os – Provides access to operating system (OS) supplied function

- os/exec – Supports running external processes

- os/signal – Supports handling OS signals

- os/user – Supports OS users/groups and credentials

- os/path – Supports processing OS file system paths

- os/filepath – Path helper functions

- plugin – Provides (limited) support for dynamically loaded plugins

- reflect – Provides support to introspect and create types and instances at runtime

- regex – Provides support to evaluate regular expressions

- regex/syntax – Supports parsing regular expressions

- runtime – Support to manage a running Go application

- runtime/cgo – Support to access functions written in C

- runtime/debug – Provides support to runtime diagnostics

- runtime/pprof – Generates profiling data

- runtime/trace – Supports runtime tracing; more functional than logging

- sort – Supports sorting or slices and collections

- srtconv – Various converters to (formatter)/from (parser) strings

- strings – Various helpers for the `string` type

- sync – Provides synchronization primitives

- sync/atomic – Provides function to do atomic updates

- syscall – Provides various low-level operating system (OS) functions; may be OS specific and not available on all OS types

- testing – Provides JUnit-like testing and code timing

- testing/iotest – Helpers for testing I/O actions

- testing/quick – Provides helpers for use in test cases

- text – Empty, see nested

- text/scanner – Provides scanning/tokens on strings

- text/tabwriter – Provides column aligned text output

- text/template – Supports programmable insertion of text into a template

- text/parse – Supports parsing templates

- time – Provides support for dates, times, timestamps, durations, instants

- time/tzdata – Supports time zones without operating system assistance

- unicode – Empty, see nested

- unicode/utf16 – Provides support for 16-bit Unicode characters

- unicode/utf32 – Provides support for 32-bit Unicode characters (aka Runes)

- unicode/utf8 – Provides support for UTF-8 Unicode characters

- unsafe – Provides support for architecture-sensitive data and pointers

While substantial, this list is much shorter than a similar listing of all the packages that come in the Java Standard Edition. Still the function provided is generally enough to create rich web clients and servers that are the foundation of modern microservices which is a key Go use case.

As an example (based on a Go site example), the utf8 package allows one to extract runes from a (UTF-8) string:

```go
var text = "The 世界 is a crazy place!"  // world defined in UTF-8
var runes = make([]rune, 0, len(text))
for len(text) > 0 {
    rune, runeLen := utf8.DecodeRuneInString(text)
    fmt.Printf("%c(%d, %d)\n", rune, rune, runeLen)
    runes = append(runes, rune)
    text = text[runeLen:]
}
```

which outputs a slice with all the runes of the input; its length may (will be in this example) be shorter than the input length.

As another example, consider this simple way to measure the elapsed time of some code:

```go
func TimeIt(timeThis func() error) (dur time.Duration, err error) {
        start := time.Now()
        err = timeThis()
        dur = time.Now().Sub(start)
        return
}
```

with

```go
elapsed, _ := TimeIt(func() (err error) {
        time.Sleep(1 * time.Second)
        return
})
```

with the result of elapsed that is approximately 1e9.

This sample can be redone in an alternate way:

```go
func TimeIt(timeThis func() error) (dur time.Duration, err error) {
        start := time.Now()  // must declare before use
        defer func(){
                dur = time.Now().Sub(start)
        }()
        err = timeThis()
        return
}
```

The following chapters discuss several Go packages, each providing a more complete summary of the package. In many of these package descriptions, there are functions described with the name pattern:

Xxxx – Provides some behavior using a default parameter function

XxxxFunc – Provides the same behavior using a supplied parameter function to implement a custom behavior variant

The function provided is often a predicate.

CHAPTER 12

Key Package Comparison

Several key (frequently and widely used) Java packages are summarized in this chapter. When practical, any equivalent Go package or function is noted. As Go and Java are not one to one in their available libraries, a full match of every Java API (method) with a Go equivalent, if it exists at all in the standard Go libraries, is impractical.

Java Lang Packages

Java Standard Edition (JSE) has many bundled packages with types and methods. The available methods (aka APIs) number into the several thousands. Go also has a set of standard packages with types and functions that number into the many hundreds. There is a significant overlap in library behavior but not the organizational structure (in which package, type, or function a behavior is located) between these sets of packages and types.

It would take 100s of pages just to list (vs. describe) all the JSE packages and their contained types with methods. This book will not attempt to do this. Instead, it will list a select subset of the JSE packages and types. For some of these, it will compare the methods available for key Java types with any Go equivalents.

The JRE has some key types in the java.lang package. The following lists describe any Go environment equivalents.

Interface Summary

- Appendable – Can append to instances of this type; implicitly supported by a Go slice.

- AutoCloseable – Can be closed by try with resources; no direct Go equivalent.

© Barry Feigenbaum 2022
B. Feigenbaum, *Go for Java Programmers*, https://doi.org/10.1007/978-1-4842-7199-5_12

- CharSequence – A sequence of characters (such as a String or StringBuilder); no direct Go equivalent.

- Cloneable – Implements `Object.clone()`; no direct Go equivalent.

- Comparable<T> – Can support a `compareTo()` method; no direct Go equivalent; many types are implicitly comparable.

- Iterable<T> – Can be iterated; some Go types: array, slice, map, channel.

- Readable – Can read characters into a buffer; `io.Reader` for UTF-8.

- Runnable – Can be run as a thread body; in Go, any function can be run as a goroutine.

Class Summary

- Boolean – Boolean wrapper; not needed on Go collections.

- Byte – Byte wrapper; not needed on Go collections.

- Character – Char wrapper; not needed on Go collections.

- Class<T> – A runtime view of a class; a feature for reflection; Go has a reflection package.

- ClassLoader – Loads/manages classes at runtime; not needed in Go, no runtime classes.

- Double – Double wrapper; not needed on Go collections.

- Enum<E extends Enum<E>> – Base type of all enum types; not needed in Go (`int` is the base of most Go enums).

- Float – Float wrapper; not needed on Go collections.

- Integer – Int wrapper; not needed on Go collections.

- Long – Long wrapper; not needed on Go collections.

- Math – A class with a set of math utilities; Go has a similar `math` package.

- Module – A runtime view of a module; no direct Go equivalent.

- Number – A superclass of numeric wrapper types; no direct Go equivalent.

- Object – A superclass of all object types; no direct Go equivalent; `interface{}` is closest.

- Package – A runtime view of a package; no direct Go equivalent.

- Process – A runtime view of an external program; a Go `exec` package has similar.

- ProcessBuilder – A helper to run an external program; a Go `exec` package has similar.

- Record (new) – A structure like class; Go has the `struct` type.

- Runtime – Utilities to manage a running program; Go has a `runtime` package.

- RuntimePermission – Means to control access to a function in classes; Go has no equivalent.

- SecurityManager – Means to control access to a function in classes; Go has no equivalent.

- Short – Short wrapper; not needed on Go collections.

- StackTraceElement – Describes a call stack element; Go has a similar struct type.

- StackWalker – Crawls a stack; no direct Go equivalent; one can be written.

- StrictMath – Like a Math class with more rules on how the algorithms work; no direct Go equivalent.

- String – A string type; Go has a `string` type and `strings`, `strconv`, and `fmt` packages.

- StringBuffer, StringBuilder – A mutable string type; Go has a `strings.Builder` type.

- System – Utilities to manage a running program; Go has `runtime`, `time`, and `io` packages.

- Thread – An operating system thread; no direct Go equivalent; go has goroutines.

- ThreadGroup – A collection of related threads; no direct Go equivalent.

- ThreadLocal<T> – A variable with thread-dependent values; no direct Go equivalent; can be made.

- Throwable – A type that can be thrown; Go has panics.

- Void – No Go equivalent; Go functions can return nothing (vs. void).

- math.BigInteger – Indefinite precision integer; Go has a math.Int type.

- math.BigDecimal – Indefinite precision decimal float value; Go has math.Float (but it is binary, not decimal).

The *System* class:
Static Field Summary

- PrintStream err – STDERR – Go `os.Stderr`

- InputStream in – STDIN – Go `os.Stdin`

- PrintStream out – STDOUT – Go `os.Stdout`

Method Summary. No direct Go equivalent if not mentioned.

- arraycopy(…) – Copy an array; Go operator: array[:] and `copy(..)` function

- clearProperty(String key) – Empty system property

- console() – Get access to the OS console

- currentTimeMillis() – Get the current Epoch time; Go `time.Now()`

- exit(…) – See the Runtime class; Go `os.Exit(...)`

- gc() – See the Runtime class; Go `runtime.GC()`

- getenv() – Get all Environment values; Go `os.Environ()`

- getenv(…) – Get a single Environment value

- getLogger(...) – Get a named logger ; Go `log` package

- getProperties() – Get all properties

- getProperty(...) – Get a named property

- getSecurityManager() – Get a JVM security manager

- identityHashCode(Object x) – Get an object's identity; in Go, use the &x operator

- lineSeparator() – Get an OS line separator (e.g., NL, CR+NL)

- load(...), loadLibrary(...) – See the Runtime class

- nanoTime() – Get elapsed time in nanoseconds; Go `time` package

- runFinalization() – See the Runtime class

- setErr(...) – Change STDERR

- setIn(...) – Change STDIN

- setOut(...) – Change STDOUT

- setProperties(Properties props) – Set many system properties

- setProperty(String key, String value) – Set the system property

- setSecurityManager(...) – Set a JVM security manager

There are community implementations of properties. See github.com/magiconair/ properties for an example which uses a Java property–like file format.

The *Runtime* class:

- addShutdownHook(...) – Run a thread at the exit of JVM; no direct Go equivalent; Go can trap OS signals; Go can trap panics.

- availableProcessors() – Get CPU (core) count; Go `runtime.NumCPU()`.

- exec(...) – Family of methods to launch external process; Go `exec.Cmd`.

- exit(...) – Exit the JVM with cleanup; no Go equivalent; Go can approx. by using `os.Exit()`.

- freeMemory() – Get free memory available to JVM; Go `runtime. MemStats`.

- gc() – Run a garbage collection; Go `runtime.GC ()`.

- getRuntime() – Get this class's singleton; no Go equivalent.

- halt(...) – Exit JVM with no cleanup; Go `os.Exit(...)`.

- load(...), loadLibrary(...) – Load a foreign code library; no Go equivalent.

- maxMemory()– Get maximum memory available to JVM; Go `runtime.MemStats`.

- removeShutdownHook(...) – Remove the exit hook; no Go equivalent.

- runFinalization() – Force Object finalization; no Go equivalent.

- totalMemory() – Get memory used by JVM; Go `runtime.MemStats`.

- version() – Get the JVM version; Go `runtime.version()`.

Since Go is a complete executable made at build time, there is no need for loading system libraries.

Java IO Package

The JRE has some key classes in the `java.io` package. The following lists describe any Go environment equivalents.

Interface Summary

- Closeable – Can be closed. Used by try with resources; no direct Go equivalent.

- DataInput – Data can be read as a stream of binary encoded values. Some Go encoding libraries provide a similar function.

- DataOutput – Data can be written as a stream of binary encoded values. Some Go encoding libraries provide a similar function.

- Externalizable – Data can be read/written to a stream using non-standard encoding; no direct Go equivalent.

- FileFilter – Select directory paths matching a filter callback; no direct Go equivalent.

- FilenameFilter – Select file names matching a filter callback; no direct Go equivalent.

- Flushable – Can flush (persist buffered data); some Go io package interfaces provide this operation.

- ObjectInput – Can read Java serialized objects (superset of DataInput); no direct Go equivalent.

- ObjectOutput – Can write Java serialized objects (superset of DataOutput); no direct Go equivalent.

- Serializable – Declares a type as serializable by the default encoding; no direct Go equivalent.

Class Summary

- BufferedInputStream – Input stream (on bytes) with buffer; the Go bufio package provides similar support.

- BufferedOutputStream – Output stream (on bytes) with buffer; the Go bufio package provides similar support.

- BufferedReader – Input writer (on characters) with buffer; the Go bufio package provides similar support.

- BufferedWriter – Output writer (on characters) with buffer; the Go bufio package provides similar support.

- ByteArrayInputStream – Read from byte[]; the Go io package provides similar support.

- ByteArrayOutputStream – Write on byte[]; the Go io package provides similar support.

- CharArrayReader – Write on char[]; the Go io package provides similar support.

- CharArrayWriter – Write on char[]; the Go io package provides similar support.

- Console – Abstraction of STDIN, STDOUT, and STDERR; the Go io package provides similar support.

- DataInputStream – Read a stream of binary encoded values; some Go encoding libraries provide a similar function.

- DataOutputStream – Write a stream of binary encoded values; some Go encoding libraries provide a similar function.

- File – Access to a file (or directory); Go io and os packages provide similar support.

- FileDescriptor – Access to host OS files; Go io and os packages provide similar support.

- FileInputStream – Read bytes from a file; Go io and os packages provide similar support.

- FileOutputStream – Write bytes to a file; Go io and os packages provide similar support.

- FilePermission – Access file permissions; Go io and os packages provide similar support.

- FileReader – Read characters from a file; Go io and os packages provide similar support.

- FileWriter – Write characters to a file; Go io and os packages provide similar support.

- InputStream – Read bytes; Go io and os packages provide similar support.

- InputStreamReader – Convert byte input to character input; Go io and os packages provide similar support.

- ObjectInputStream – Read serialized objects; no direct Go equivalent.

- ObjectOutputStream – Write serialized objects; no direct Go equivalent.

- OutputStream – Write bytes; Go io and os packages provide similar support.

- OutputStreamWriter – Convert characters to bytes.

- PrintStream – Formatted byte output; Go `fmt`, `io`, and `os` packages provide similar support.

- PrintWriter – Formatted character output; Go `fmt`, `io`, and `os` packages provide similar support.

- RandomAccessFile – A file that supports seeking; Go `io` and `os` packages provide similar support.

- Reader – Read characters; Go `fmt`, `io`, and `os` packages provide similar support.

- SequenceInputStream – Concatenate input streams; Go `io` and `os` packages provide similar support.

- StreamTokenizer – Tokenize stream input; Go `fmt`, `io`, and `os` packages provide similar support.

- StringReader – Read characters from a string; Go `fmt`, `io`, and `os` packages provide similar support.

- Writer – Write characters; Go `io` and `os` packages provide similar support.

Java also has a NIO (new IO) package with more advanced file (e.g., monitor file changes) and directory services. This book will not cover them. The Go libraries have some functions comparable to those offered by a few of NIO classes.

Java Text Package

The JRE has some key classes in the `java.text` package. This package provides bidirectional iteration over text sequences and message formatting. The following lists describe any Go environment equivalents. Some Go extension libraries and community libraries provide similar support.

Interface Summary

- AttributedCharacterIterator – Bidirectional iteration over attributed text sequences; no direct Go equivalent.

- CharacterIterator – Bidirectional iteration over text sequences; no direct Go equivalent; `utf8` and `utf16` packages have some function.

Class Summary. Unless noted, Go has no direct equivalents.

- Annotation – Annotation-like text attributes.

- AttributedString – String with annotations.

- Bidi – Provides bidirectional traversal rules.

- BreakIterator – Iterates to different types of breaks (word, line, etc.).

- ChoiceFormat – Helps to format messages with varying counts and plurals.

- CollationElementIterator – Walks across characters in under locale rules.

- CollationKey – Key for locale-based collation.

- Collator – Base class for locale-based collation.

- CompactNumberFormat – Decimal format that makes numbers smaller.

- DateFormat – Formats dates and times; Go has a `time` package for a similar function.

- DecimalFormat – Formats decimal numbers.

- Format – Base class for various Format classes.

- MessageFormat – Formats messages with substitutions.

- Normalizer – Normalizes Unicode text to assist with collation.

- NumberFormat – Base class for number formatters.

- RuleBasedCollator – Rules table driver collator.

- SimpleDateFormat – Date format with configurable structures for dates and times; Go has a `time` package for a similar function.

- StringCharacterIterator – Iterates over characters in a string.

Note Go's `fmt` package can be used to do some of the roles of the various Format types. Also, in Java `String.format()` and in Go `fmt.Sprintf()` can do much of what the formatters do.

Java Time Packages

The JRE has some key classes in the `java.time` package and its sub-packages. The following lists describe any Go environment equivalents.

Interface Summary. Go has the `time` package for some of these; mostly as functions, not types; only a small subset of this function is present in Go. Some Go extension libraries and community libraries provide similar support.

- ChronoLocalDate – A Date in some Chronology

- ChronoLocalDateTime<D extends ChronoLocalDate> – A Date Time (timestamp) in some Chronology

- Chronology – A calendar system (say Gregorian)

- ChronoPeriod – A time period

- ChronoZonedDateTime<D extends ChronoLocalDate>> – A time zoned Date Time (timestamp) in some Chronology

- Era – A bounded range in some Chronology (e.g., BCE)

- Temporal – Of Time; following for manipulating dates and times

- TemporalAccessor

- TemporalAdjuster

- TemporalAmount

- TemporalField

- TemporalQuery<R>

- TemporalUnit

Class Summary. Go has the `time` package for some of the behaviors included as follows; mostly as functions, not types.

- Clock – Access to dates and times

- Duration – A span of time; Go has a Duration type

- Instant – A moment in time

- LocalDate – A date in the local time zone

- LocalDateTime – A date and time (aka timestamp) in the local time zone

- LocalTime – A time in the local time zone

- MonthDay – A day in a month

- OffsetDateTime – A date and time (aka timestamp) offset from UTC

- OffsetTime – A time offset from UTC

- Period – A duration in calendar units

- Year – A duration in years

- YearMonth – An instant at month resolution

- ZonedDateTime – A DateTime in a time zone

- DateTimeFormatter – Formats a Date Time

- DateTimeFormatterBuilder – Makes a formatter

- AbstractChronology – Base for Chronologies (calendar system)

- HijrahChronology, HijrahDate, IsoChronology

- JapaneseChronology, JapaneseDate, JapaneseEra

- MinguoChronology, MinguoDate

- ThaiBuddhistChronology, ThaiBuddhistDate

Java Util Packages

The JRE has some key classes in the `java.util` package and its sub-packages. The sub-packages deal with collections of objects, legacy dates, and time processing, concurrent (threaded) processing, and concurrent access to objects. The following lists describe any Go environment equivalents.

Interface Summary. Most have no direct Go equivalents. Much of this function is provided by Go built-in types. Some Go extension libraries and community libraries provide similar support.

- Collection<E> – Iterate able collection of type E.

- Comparator<T> – Compare two comparable objects of type T.

- Deque<E> – Double-ended queue of type E; the Go slice is close.

- Enumeration<E> – Supports forward iteration over a collection of type E.

- EventListener – Formalize the type of an event listener (call back).

- Formattable – Can be formatted.

- Iterator<E> – Supports bidirectional iteration over a collection of type E.

- List<E> – Indexable collection of type E; the Go slice is close.

- Map<K,V>, Map.Entry<K,V> – Associative collection of type V with key K; the Go map is close.

- Queue<E> – A queue (FIFO) of type E; the Go slice is close.

- Set<E> – A set of type K; the Go map is close.

- SortedMap<K,V> – Map with sorted keys.

- SortedSet<E> – Set with sorted elements.

Class Summary. Most have no direct Go equivalents.

- AbstractCollection<E> – The following are base implementations of the type.

- AbstractList<E>

- AbstractMap<K,V>

- AbstractQueue<E>

- AbstractSequentialList<E>

- AbstractSet<E>

- ArrayDeque<E> – Deque on an array.

- ArrayList<E> – List on an array; Go has a slice type.

- Arrays – Helpers for array access.

- Base64.Decoder – Decode Base64 strings; Go has a base64 package.

- Base64.Encoder – Encode Base64 strings; Go has a base64 package.

- BitSet – Set of bits; Go has a `bits` package.

- Calendar – A calendar; Go has a `time` package.

- Collections – Helpers for collections.

- Currency – A currency.

- Date – A date; Go has a `time` package.

- Dictionary<K,V> – A basic map type; Go has a `map` type.

- EnumMap<K extends Enum<K>,V>

- EnumSet<E extends Enum<E>>

- EventListenerProxy<T extends EventListener>

- EventObject

- Formatter

- GregorianCalendar – Western calendar.

- HashMap<K,V> – Default map type; Go has a map type.

- HashSet<E> – Default set type.

- Hashtable<K,V> – Thread-safe HashMap.

- IdentityHashMap<K,V> – Map with Object identities as keys; Go has a map[uintptr] type.

- LinkedHashMap<K,V> – Map iterated in addition order.

- LinkedHashSet<E> – Set iterated in addition order.

- LinkedList<E> – List backed by a linked list.

- Locale – Define locale-sensitive settings and behavior.

- Objects – Helps for all reference types.

- Optional<T> – A null-safe wrapper.

- PriorityQueue<E> – List sorted by priority.

- Properties – A key/value collection with a persistent form.

- Scanner – Reads formatted input; Go `fmt` package.

- SimpleTimeZone – A time zone implementation.

- Stack<E> – List processed in LIFO order.

- StringJoiner – String helper.

- StringTokenizer – Simple string parser; Go `fmt` package.

- Timer – Drive events (callbacks) at intervals.

- TimerTask – Drive events (callbacks) at intervals.

- TimeZone – Base for time zones.

- TreeMap<K,V> – Map sorted by keys.

- TreeSet<E> – Set sorted by keys.

- UUID – UUID type; available from third parties.

- Vector<E> – Thread-safe ArrayList.

- WeakHashMap<K,V> – Map that does not prevent GC of keys.

Interface Summary

- BlockingDeque<E> – Deque with multiple consumer threads.

- BlockingQueue<E> – Queue with multiple consumer threads.

- Callable<V> – A thread can call asynchronously.

- ConcurrentMap<K,V> – Thread-safe high concurrency map.

- ConcurrentNavigableMap<K,V> – Thread-safe high concurrency map.

- Executor – Manager of multiple threads.

- ExecutorService – Manages multiple threads.

- Flow.Processor<T,R> – Reactive programming flow processor.

- Flow.Publisher<T> – Reactive programming flow publisher.

- Flow.Subscriber<T> – Reactive programming flow subscriber.

- Flow.Subscription – Reactive programming flow subscription.

- Future<V> – Asynchronous task that can complete in the future.

- LockSupport – Locking helpers.

- ReentrantLock – Lock implementation.

- ReentrantReadWriteLock

Note locks (and `synchronized` access) in Java is reentrant; the same thread can acquire the lock multiple times. In Go, locks are not reentrant, and the same goroutine trying to reacquire a lock can block (deadlock) itself.

CHAPTER 13

Key Method/Function Comparison

This library survey is not intended to be a programmer reference, but more of an introduction. It will have useful samples of some library functions that should help you to get basic competence in the Go libraries. For a deeper understanding of the mentioned functions and any omitted ones, please see the online Go package documentation. This documentation describes each package and the types in it and the functions they provide. Some examples are also available.

The Go and Java libraries differ significantly since Java is object-oriented and Go is not. In Java, many functions are instance methods on some receiver type (the implied `this` argument). In Go, they are more often general functions that take the receiver type as the first argument. This is more like `static` methods in Java. For example, take the case of a function to convert a string to all uppercase.

In Java, this is

```java
var uc = "some string".toUpperCase();
```

In Go, this is

```go
var uc = strings.ToUpper("some string")
```

These functions differ mostly in the way the receiver is passed to the function. The Java instance methods could have been defined instead as

```java
public class String {
  public static String toUpperCase(String s) {
    :
  }
}
```

© Barry Feigenbaum 2022
B. Feigenbaum, *Go for Java Programmers*, https://doi.org/10.1007/978-1-4842-7199-5_13

Table 13-4. *Key Java String Class Methods*

Java Function	Go Equivalent	Go Package	Notes
s.substr(s,e)	s[s:e]		Go operator
s.charAt(i)	s[i]		Go operator
s.indexOf(s2)	.Index(s, o)	strings	
s.lastIndexOf(s2)		strings	
s.indexOf(c)		strings	
s.lastIndexOf(c)		strings	
s.toUpperCase()	.ToUpper(s)	strings	
s.toLowerCase()	.ToLower(s)	strings	
s.toCharArray()	[]byte(s)		Go conversion
s.length()	len(s)		Go built-in
s.compareTo(o)	s op o		Go operators: < <= == != > >=
s.startsWith(s2)	.HasPrefix(s1, s2)	strings	
s.endsWith(s2)	.HasSuffix(s1, s2)	strings	
s.contains(s2)	.Index(s,s2) >= 0	strings	
s1 + s2	s1 + s2		Go operator
.join(delim,s...)	.join(delim,s...)	strings	
s.getBytes()	[]byte(s)		Go conversion
s.matches(s1)	.matches(s, s1)	regex	
s.repeat(n)	.Repeat(s, n)	strings	
s.replace(c1,c2)			No direct equivalent
s.replace(s1,s2)	.ReplaceAll(s, s1, s2)	strings	
s.replaceAll(p,s2)		regex	
s.replaceFirst(p,s2)		regex	
	.Split(s, s2)	strings	
	.Split(s, s2, n)		

(continued)

Table 13-4. (*continued*)

Java Function	Go Equivalent	Go Package	Notes
s.split(p)			No direct equivalent
s.split(p,n)	.Split(s, n)	regex	
s.trim() s.strip() s.stripLeading() s.stripTrailing()	.TrimSpaces(s)	strings	
s.substring(p) s.substring(p,e) s.substring(0,e) s.substring(0,s.length())	s[p:] s[p:e] s[:e] s[:]		Go operator
.valueOf(x) .format(f, ...)	.Sprintf("%v",x) .Sprintf(f,...)	fmt	

Table 13-5. *Key Java StringBuilder Class Methods*

Java Function	Go Equivalent	Go Package	Notes
sb.append(o)	b.Write String(s)	strings. Builder	
sb.length()	b.Size()	strings. Builder	

Table 13-6. *Key Java List Interface Methods*

Java Function	Go Equivalent	Go Package	Notes
l.add(x)	append(s,x)		Go built-in
l.size()	len(l)		Go built-in
l.get(i)	l[i]		Go operator
l.set(I, x)	l[i] = x		Go operator

Table 13-7. *Key Java Map Interface Methods*

Java Function	Go Equivalent	Go Package	Notes
m.put(k,v)	m[k] = v		Go operator
m.size()	len(m)		Go built-in
m.get(k)	m[k]		Go built-in Test for missing

Table 13-8. *Key Java PrintWriter Class Methods*

Java Function	Java Type	Go Equivalent	Go Package	Notes
pw.println(o)	Print Writer	w.Write(o) w.Write('\n')	io.Writer	

CHAPTER 14

Go Package Survey

This chapter contains brief introductions to several Go packages. Other chapters that follow discuss select packages at a more detailed level.

File Access with Go

A commonly used area where Go and Java differ somewhat is in accessing files and directories. Java's design tends to abstract file access to each more than Go's does. Java provides multiple modes of access:

1. Byte/character streams – Files look like sequences of bytes or characters.

2. Byte/character channels – Support block mode access; oriented toward random and asynchronous access; can share memory across processes.

3. High-level file operation abstractions, like copying a file or walking a directory tree.

Go provides less abstract, but often equivalent, access, especially for the stream-style operation. Go access resembles Unix-style file processing. APIs that closely match Unix file APIs exist. Files are almost always looked at as sequences of bytes. Go also offers lower-level APIs that almost exactly match Unix APIs.

These differences show up in the styles of the Java and Go APIs.

For example, using basic Java streams, one can copy a file like this:

```
public static long copyFile(String fromPath, String toPath)
    throws IOException {
  try (var bis = new BufferedInputStream(new FileInputStream(
    new File(fromPath)))) {
```

399

© Barry Feigenbaum 2022
B. Feigenbaum, *Go for Java Programmers*, https://doi.org/10.1007/978-1-4842-7199-5_14

```
   try (var bos = new BufferedOutputStream(new FileOutputStream(
       new File(toPath)))) {
     return copyContent(bis, bos);
   }
 }
}
```

Note the two try statements can be folded into a single try:

```
public static long copyFile(String fromPath, String toPath)
    throws IOException {
  try (var bis = new BufferedInputStream(new FileInputStream(
        new File(fromPath)));
      var bos = new BufferedOutputStream(new FileOutputStream(
          new File(toPath)))) {
    return copyContent(bis, bos);
  }
}
```

The file data is copied by

```
private static long copyContent(InputStream is, OutputStream os)
    throws IOException {
  var total = 0L;
  var buf = new byte[N]; // N at least several KB
  for (;;) {
    var count = is.read(buf, 0, buf.length);
    if (count == 0)
      break;
    os.write(buf);
    total +=buf.length;
  }
  return total;
}
```

Or more succinctly by use of a JRE library equivalent:

```java
private static long copyContent(InputStream is, OutputStream os)
    throws IOException {
  return is.transferTo(os);
}
```

While in Go, this could be

```go
func CopyFile(fromPath, toPath string) (count int64, err error) {
    var from, to *os.File
    if from, err = os.Open(fromPath); err != nil {
        return
    }
    defer from.Close()
    if to, err = os.Create(toPath)
        err != nil {
        return
    }
    defer to.Close()
    count, err = io.Copy(to, from)
    return
}
```

So, we see the Go tends to use the file type more directly. That is because the `File` type implements the `io.Reader` and `io.Writer` interfaces. We also see how the `try` statements are replaced with multiple `defer` statements.

Both Go and Java can process directories. For example, to output all files and their size starting from some root, in Java one could do this (using Java streams):

```java
public static void PrintAllNames(String path) throws IOException {
  try (var walk = Files.walk(Paths.get(path))) {
    walk.filter(Files::isRegularFile).
        map(p -> String.format("%s %d", p, p.toFile().length())).
        forEach(System.out::println);
  }
}
```

Called like this:

```
PrintAllNames(".")
```

While in Go, this could be

```
var printName = func(path string, info os.FileInfo, xerr error) error{
        if xerr != nil {  // exit fast if entered with an error
                return xerr
        }
        if info.Mode().IsRegular() {
                fmt.Println(path, info.Size())
        }
        return nil
}
func PrintAllNames(path string) (err error) {
        err = filepath.Walk(path, printName)
        return
}
```

Called like this:

```
PrintAllNames(".")
```

The Java code uses Java's functional Streams and method references/lambdas (as a callback). The Go code uses a callback function. In both cases, the callback selects only files and formats the data.

Compression Services

This section provides an overview of some Go packages for compression and archiving.

Archive Packages

Go, like Java, provides functionality to read and write archive files. Java concentrates on the ZIP archive format. Go also supports the TAR format. There are sub-packages for each format:

- tar – Reading and writing tar archives
- zip – Reading and writing ZIP archives

The `archive/tar` package provides these types:

- type Format – Enum representing the supported tar formats USTAR, PAX, and GNU

- type Header – Represents a header in a tar file

- type Reader – Provides read access to a tar

- type Writer – Provides write access to a tar

The Header type has these methods:

- func FileInfoHeader(fi os.FileInfo, link string) (*Header, error) – Make a header from file info

- func (h *Header) FileInfo() os.FileInfo – Get file info from a header

The Reader type has these methods:

- func NewReader(r io.Reader) *Reader – Make a reader

- func (tr *Reader) Next() (*Header, error) – Advance to the next file

- func (tr *Reader) Read(b []byte) (int, error) – Read data from a file

The Writer type has these methods:

- func NewWriter(w io.Writer) *Writer – Make a writer

- func (tw *Writer) Close() error – Flush and close a file

- func (tw *Writer) Flush() error – Write buffered data

- func (tw *Writer) Write(b []byte) (int, error) – Write data with buffering

- func (tw *Writer) WriteHeader(hdr *Header) error – Write a file header

The `archive/zip` package provides these types:

- type Compressor – A function that converts a writer to a compressing writer/closer

- type Decompressor – A function that converts a reader to a decompressing read/closer

- type File – Represents a zipped file; wraps a FileHeader

- type FileHeader – Represents a file in a zip file; has many useful fields

- type ReadCloser – Can read and close

- type Reader – Can read

- type Writer – Can write

The File type has this method:

- func (f *File) Open() (io.ReadCloser, error) – Open a zipped file

The FileHeader type has these methods:

- func FileInfoHeader(fi os.FileInfo) (*FileHeader, error) – Make a file header

- func (h *FileHeader) FileInfo() os.FileInfo

- func (h *FileHeader) ModTime() time.Time

- func (h *FileHeader) Mode() (mode os.FileMode)

- func (h *FileHeader) SetModTime(t time.Time)

- func (h *FileHeader) SetMode(mode os.FileMode)

The ReadCloser type has these methods:

- func OpenReader(name string) (*ReadCloser, error) – Access a zipped entry

- func (rc *ReadCloser) Close() error – Close a zipped entry

The Reader type has this method:

- func NewReader(r io.ReaderAt, size int64) (*Reader, error) – Make a reader

The Writer type has these methods:

- func NewWriter(w io.Writer) *Writer – Make a writer

- func (w *Writer) Close() error – Close a zipped entry

- func (w *Writer) Create(name string) (io.Writer, error) – Add a zipped entry

- func (w *Writer) CreateHeader(fh *FileHeader) (io.Writer, error)

- func (w *Writer) Flush() error – Flush any buffered output

- func (w *Writer) SetComment(comment string) error

Compression Packages

Java supports compression of data in several contexts. It is often done for archive files. Go makes compression a more independent and general-purpose action. It supports several forms of compression. Go supports (by package) these forms of compression:

- `bzip2` – bzip2 decompression

- `gzip` – Reading and writing of gzip compressed data

- `zlib` – Reading and writing of zlib compressed data

- `flate` – DEFLATE compression

- `lzw` – Lempel-Ziv-Welch compression

These can be used to compress/decompress streams of bytes, typically into/from a file. They are used by the archive packages. See the Go package documentation for more details.

As an example of using these packages (and the os package), let us compress a file into another file in GZ format. Here is a possible implementation:

```
func CompressFileToNewGZIPFile(path string) (err error) {
    var inFile, gzFile *os.File
    // access input file
    if inFile, err = os.Open(path); err != nil {
        return
    }
    defer inFile.Close()
    // create output file
    if gzFile, err = os.Create(path + ".gz"); err != nil {
        return
    }
```

```
    defer gzFile.Close()
    // copy input to output, compressing as copied
    w := gzip.NewWriter(gzFile)
    defer w.Close()
    _, err = io.Copy(w, inFile)
    return
}
```

Note the output file may be created with invalid data if this function returns an error. If you replace

```
w := gzip.NewWriter(gzFile)
```

with

```
w := gzFile
```

and remove the last defer statement, you will get an uncompressed file copy.

Image

The image package and its sub-packages provide support for reading, drawing on, and formatting images. The image package contains image representations using colors of various forms/sizes, such as Alpha, Alpha16, CMYK, Gray, Gray16, NRGBA, NRGBA64, NYCbCrA, Paletted, RGBA, YCbCr. It also supports several image types: Image, PalatedImage, and Uniform. It also has some key image-related types such as Point and Rectangle.

For some examples of using this package, see the capstone program.

The image package has these key interfaces and structs:

```
type Image interface {
    ColorModel() color.Model
    Bounds() image.Rectangle
    At(x, y int) color.Color
}
```

The package image has key methods:

- `func Decode(r io.Reader) (Image, string, error)` – Read an image

- `func Encode(w io.Writer, m image.Image) error` – Write an image

```
type Point struct {
    X, Y int
}
type Rectangle struct {
    Min, Max Point
}
```

Point and Rectangle have methods to create, adjust, and compare values:

- func Pt(X, Y int) Point – Make a point

- func (p Point) Add(q Point) Point – Add points

- func (p Point) Div(k int) Point – Divide p by k

- func (p Point) Eq(q Point) bool – Test equal

- func (p Point) In(r Rectangle) bool – Test if p in r

- func (p Point) Mod(r Rectangle) Point – Modulus of p in r

- func (p Point) Mul(k int) Point – Multiply p by k

- func (p Point) Sub(q Point) Point – Subtract a point

- func Rect(x0, y0, x1, y1 int) Rectangle – Make a rectangle

- func (r Rectangle) Add(p Point) Rectangle – Add rectangles

- func (r Rectangle) At(x, y int) color.Color test – Get color at a point

- func (r Rectangle) Bounds() Rectangle – Get bounds

- func (r Rectangle) Canon() Rectangle – Make a canonical version of r

- func (r Rectangle) ColorModel() color.Model – Get a color model

- func (r Rectangle) Dx() int – Get width

- func (r Rectangle) Dy() int – Get height

- func (r Rectangle) Empty() bool – Test if no contained points

- func (r Rectangle) Eq(s Rectangle) bool – Tests equal

- func (r Rectangle) In(s Rectangle) bool – r all in s

- func (r Rectangle) Inset(n int) Rectangle – Returns r inset by n

- func (r Rectangle) Intersect(s Rectangle) Rectangle – Return the largest intersection

- func (r Rectangle) Overlaps(s Rectangle) bool – If intersection not empty

- func (r Rectangle) Size() Point

- func (r Rectangle) Sub(p Point) Rectangle – Translate r by -p

- func (r Rectangle) Union(s Rectangle) Rectangle – Returns rectangle covering r and s

All image forms have, at least, these methods (some beyond the Image interface):

- func (p *<type>) At(x, y int) color.Color – Get value at a point

- func (p *<type>) Bounds() Rectangle – Get image bounds

- func (p *<type>) ColorModel() color.Model – Get an image color model

- func (p *<type>) Opaque() bool – See if an image is opaque (has no transparent cells)

- func (p *<type>) PixOffset(x, y int) int – Get an offset in the pixel list of the point

- func (p *<type>) Set(x, y int, c color.Color) – Set value at a point

- func (p *<type>) SetAlpha(x, y int, c color.Alpha) – Set just the alpha at a point

- func (p *<type>) SubImage(r Rectangle) Image – Get a subset of an image

Input/Output (I/O)

The io and ioutil packages provide basic I/O operations that abstract base operating system (OS)–provided actions. This io package consists mostly of interfaces, not implementations.

Go has several key interfaces that, when combined, allow rich input/output (I/O) functionality. At the most fundamental level, I/O, as in Java, is often done on streams of bytes, sometimes interpreted as UTF-8 characters. Other character encodings are supported.

- Reader – Can read a byte or sequence of bytes

- Writer – Can write a byte or sequence of bytes

- Seeker – Can change the read/write position in a stream (a form of random I/O)

- Closer – Can close access to a stream

- Combinations of the preceding interfaces

Many Go types implement these interfaces, most for bytes, some for characters. For example, the Go File type, which allows an open file instance to be used to access the content of the operating system file it represents.

The ioutil package provides implementations of common file and directory actions.

Both Go and Java support reading and writing to files (or file-like objects). Java supports this via byte or character stream reader/writer access. Java also has higher and often more performant options in its NIO (new I/O) packages. Go's access is generally more low level, but the equivalent of Java's buffered streams is available.

The Go bufio package implements buffered I/O on top of unbuffered I/O. It provides support like the various buffered streams Java supports.

The io package provides these types (mostly interfaces) and functions:

- ByteReader – Read a byte

- ByteScanner – Read and unread a byte

- ByteWriter – Write a byte

- Closer – Close

- LimitedReader – A reader with a limit

- PipeReader – A reader from a pipe

- PipeWriter – A writer to a pipe

- ReadCloser – Can read and close

- ReadSeeker – Can read and seek

- ReadWriteCloser – Can read, write, close

- ReadWriteSeeker – Can read, write, seek

- ReadWriter – Can read, write

- Reader – Can read

- ReaderAt – Read limited at a position

- ReaderFrom – Read remaining

- RuneReader – Read a rune

- RuneScanner – Read and unread a rune

- SectionReader – Read a section (span) of bytes

- Seeker – Can set to a location

- StringWriter – Write a string

- WriteCloser – Can write, close

- WriteSeeker – Can write, seek

- Writer – Can write bytes

- WriterAt – Can write a byte at a location

- WriterTo – Can write limited bytes

The io package has this key value:

```
var EOF = errors.New("EOF")
```

The io package has these functions:

- func Copy(dst Writer, src Reader) (written int64, err error) – Copy bytes src to dst

- func CopyBuffer(dst Writer, src Reader, buf [ ]byte) (written int64, err error) – Copy with a buffer

- func CopyN(dst Writer, src Reader, n int64) (written int64, err error) – Copy with a limit

- func Pipe() (*PipeReader, *PipeWriter) – Copy between pipes

- func ReadAtLeast(r Reader, buf [ ]byte, min int) (n int, err error) – Read with a limit

- func ReadFull(r Reader, buf [ ]byte) (n int, err error) – Read all available

- func WriteString(w Writer, s string) (n int, err error) – Write a string

- func LimitReader(r Reader, n int64) Reader – Make a reader that accepts as most n bytes

- func MultiReader(readers ...Reader) Reader – Make a reader that combines all readers

- func TeeReader(r Reader, w Writer) Reader – Make a reader that copies r to w

- func NewSectionReader(r ReaderAt, off int64, n int64) *SectionReader – Make a section reader

The ioutil package has this key value:

- var Discard io.Writer used to discard anything written to it

The ioutil package defines these functions:

- func NopCloser(r io.Reader) io.ReadCloser – An empty reader

- func ReadAll(r io.Reader) ([ ]byte, error) – Read all remaining bytes

- func ReadDir(dirname string) ([ ]os.FileInfo, error) – Read a directory

- func ReadFile(filename string) ([ ]byte, error) – Read an entire file

- func TempDir(dir, pattern string) (name string, err error) – Create a unique named directory

- func TempFile(dir, pattern string) (f *os.File, err error) – Create a unique named file

- func WriteFile(filename string, data []byte, perm os.FileMode) error – Write an entire file

The bufio package defines these functions (which provide various scanners):

- func ScanBytes(data []byte, atEOF bool) (advance int, token []byte, err error)

- func ScanLines(data []byte, atEOF bool) (advance int, token []byte, err error)

- func ScanRunes(data []byte, atEOF bool) (advance int, token []byte, err error)

- func ScanWords(data []byte, atEOF bool) (advance int, token []byte, err error)

The ReadWriter type implements the Reader and Write interfaces:

- func NewReadWriter(r *Reader, w *Writer) *ReadWriter

The Reader type implements the Reader interface:

- func NewReader(rd io.Reader) *Reader

- func NewReaderSize(rd io.Reader, size int) *Reader

- func (b *Reader) Buffered() int

- func (b *Reader) Discard(n int) (discarded int, err error)

- func (b *Reader) Peek(n int) ([]byte, error)

- func (b *Reader) Read(p []byte) (n int, err error)

- func (b *Reader) ReadByte() (byte, error)

- func (b *Reader) ReadBytes(delim byte) ([]byte, error)

- func (b *Reader) ReadLine() (line []byte, isPrefix bool, err error)

- func (b *Reader) ReadRune() (r rune, size int, err error)

- func (b *Reader) ReadSlice(delim byte) (line [ ]byte, err error)

- func (b *Reader) ReadString(delim byte) (string, error)

- func (b *Reader) Reset(r io.Reader)

- func (b *Reader) Size() int

- func (b *Reader) UnreadByte() error

- func (b *Reader) UnreadRune() error

- func (b *Reader) WriteTo(w io.Writer) (n int64, err error)

The Scanner type implements the Scanner interface:

- func NewScanner(r io.Reader) *Scanner

- func (s *Scanner) Buffer(buf [ ]byte, max int)

- func (s *Scanner) Bytes() [ ]byte

- func (s *Scanner) Err() error

- func (s *Scanner) Scan() bool

- func (s *Scanner) Split(split SplitFunc)

- func (s *Scanner) Text() string

The Writer type implements the Writer interface:

- func NewWriter(w io.Writer) *Writer

- func NewWriterSize(w io.Writer, size int) *Writer

- func (b *Writer) Available() int

- func (b *Writer) Buffered() int

- func (b *Writer) Flush() error

- func (b *Writer) ReadFrom(r io.Reader) (n int64, err error)

- func (b *Writer) Reset(w io.Writer)

- func (b *Writer) Size() int

- func (b *Writer) Write(p [ ]byte) (nn int, err error)

- func (b *Writer) WriteByte(c byte) error

- func (b *Writer) WriteRune(r rune) (size int, err error)

- func (b *Writer) WriteString(s string) (int, error)

As an example of using the os, bufio, and other packages, Listings 14-1 and 14-2 show a function that can count the number of times a word is found in some text file.

Listing 14-1. Word Count Example (Part 1)

```
func CountWordsInFile(path string) (counts map[string]int, err error) {
    var f *os.File
    if f, err = os.Open(path); err != nil {
        return
    }
    defer f.Close()
    counts, err = scan(f)
    return
}

func scan(r io.Reader) (counts map[string]int, err error) {
    counts = make(map[string]int)
    s := bufio.NewScanner(r)
    s.Split(bufio.ScanWords) // make into words
    for s.Scan() {                 // true while words left
        lcw := strings.ToLower(s.Text()) // get last scanned word
        counts[lcw] = counts[lcw] + 1 // missing is zero value
    }
    err = s.Err() // notice any error
    return
}
```

This returns a map of counts per (ignoring case) word in the file. A *scanner* works a lot like a Java *Iterator* (with its hasNext and next methods). The function ScanWords is passed to the scanner to determine how to parse out words. Several other splitting methods are predefined to scan by byte, Rune, or line. The stateful scanner returns its results via the Text() (next scanned string) and Err() (any scanning error) methods. Text is set if there is no error. Scanning stops on the first error.

Listing 14-2. Word Count Example (Part 2)

```
path := `...\words.txt` // point to a real file
counts, err := CountWordsInFile(path)
if err != nil {
    fmt.Printf("Count failed: %v\n", err)
    return
}
fmt.Printf("Counts for %q:\n", path)
for k, v := range counts {
    fmt.Printf("  %-20s = %v\n", k, v)
}
```

with file contents: *Now is the time to come to the aid of our countrymen!*

It produces the following:

```
Counts for ".../words.txt":
  Now                  = 1
  time                 = 1
  come                 = 1
  countrymen!          = 1
  our                  = 1
  is                   = 1
  the                  = 2
  to                   = 2
  aid                  = 1
  of                   = 1
```

Bytes Package

In Go, the type []byte is used often, especially as an input source or output target (I/O). In Java, using a byte array as a target is done less often; instead, streams on byte arrays (or characters) are used. The Go bytes package provides functions to do I/O to byte slices.

The bytes package provides these types and functions. Most are self-explanatory and match the function in the strings package as slices of bytes can often be treated as strings of ASCII or, with a bit more challenge, UTF-8 characters:

- func Compare(a, b []byte) int

- func Contains(b, subslice []byte) bool

- func ContainsAny(b []byte, chars string) bool

- func ContainsRune(b []byte, r rune) bool

- func Count(s, sep []byte) int

- func Equal(a, b []byte) bool

- func EqualFold(s, t []byte) bool – Equals after case folding s and t

- func Fields(s []byte) [][]byte

- func FieldsFunc(s []byte, f func(rune) bool) [][]byte

- func HasPrefix(s, prefix []byte) bool

- func HasSuffix(s, suffix []byte) bool

- func Index(s, sep []byte) int

- func IndexAny(s []byte, chars string) int

- func IndexByte(b []byte, c byte) int

- func IndexFunc(s []byte, f func(r rune) bool) int

- func IndexRune(s []byte, r rune) int

- func Join(s [][]byte, sep []byte) []byte

- func LastIndex(s, sep []byte) int

- func LastIndexAny(s []byte, chars string) int

- func LastIndexByte(s []byte, c byte) int

- func LastIndexFunc(s []byte, f func(r rune) bool) int

- func Map(mapping func(r rune) rune, s []byte) []byte

- func Repeat(b []byte, count int) []byte

- func Replace(s, old, new []byte, n int) []byte
- func ReplaceAll(s, old, new []byte) []byte
- func Runes(s []byte) []rune
- func Split(s, sep []byte) [][]byte – Split at sep, remove sep
- func SplitAfter(s, sep []byte) [][]byte – Split after all sep
- func SplitAfterN(s, sep []byte, n int) [][]byte – Split after sep limited by n
- func SplitN(s, sep []byte, n int) [][]byte
- func Title(s []byte) []byte – Word start to title case
- func ToLower(s []byte) []byte
- func ToTitle(s []byte) []byte – All to title case
- func ToUpper(s []byte) []byte
- func ToValidUTF8(s, replacement []byte) []byte
- func Trim(s []byte, cutset string) []byte
- func TrimFunc(s []byte, f func(r rune) bool) []byte
- func TrimLeft(s []byte, cutset string) []byte
- func TrimLeftFunc(s []byte, f func(r rune) bool) []byte
- func TrimPrefix(s, prefix []byte) []byte
- func TrimRight(s []byte, cutset string) []byte
- func TrimRightFunc(s []byte, f func(r rune) bool) []byte
- func TrimSpace(s []byte) []byte
- func TrimSuffix(s, suffix []byte) []byte

The Buffer type provides these functions. Most are self-explanatory. The Buffer type provides a means to do buffered I/O, often from files or networks:

- func NewBuffer(buf []byte) *Buffer
- func NewBufferString(s string) *Buffer

- func (b *Buffer) Bytes() []byte

- func (b *Buffer) Cap() int

- func (b *Buffer) Grow(n int)

- func (b *Buffer) Len() int

- func (b *Buffer) Next(n int) []byte

- func (b *Buffer) Read(p []byte) (n int, err error)

- func (b *Buffer) ReadByte() (byte, error)

- func (b *Buffer) ReadBytes(delim byte) (line []byte, err error) – Read until delim (often newline)

- func (b *Buffer) ReadFrom(r io.Reader) (n int64, err error)

- func (b *Buffer) ReadRune() (r rune, size int, err error)

- func (b *Buffer) ReadString(delim byte) (line string, err error)

- func (b *Buffer) Reset() – Go back to start

- func (b *Buffer) Truncate(n int)

- func (b *Buffer) UnreadByte() error

- func (b *Buffer) UnreadRune() error

- func (b *Buffer) Write(p []byte) (n int, err error)

- func (b *Buffer) WriteByte(c byte) error

- func (b *Buffer) WriteRune(r rune) (n int, err error)

- func (b *Buffer) WriteString(s string) (n int, err error)

- func (b *Buffer) WriteTo(w io.Writer) (n int64, err error)

The Reader type provides these functions. Most are self-explanatory:

- func NewReader(b []byte) *Reader

- func (r *Reader) Len() int

- func (r *Reader) Read(b []byte) (n int, err error)

- func (r *Reader) ReadAt(b []byte, off int64) (n int, err error)

- func (r *Reader) ReadByte() (byte, error)

- func (r *Reader) ReadRune() (ch rune, size int, err error)

- func (r *Reader) Reset(b []byte)

- func (r *Reader) Seek(offset int64, whence int) (int64, error)

- func (r *Reader) Size() int64

- func (r *Reader) UnreadByte() error

- func (r *Reader) UnreadRune() error

- func (r *Reader) WriteTo(w io.Writer) (n int64, err error)

Format Package

The fmt package provides a formatted string and I/O with functions much like Java's String.format and the *PrintStream/PrintWriter* printf functions.

The scanner package provides text scanning and tokenization.

The tabwriter package provides an easy but low function way to generate tabular (columnized) text output. The community offers higher function support.

The fmt package provides these functions:

- func Errorf(format string, a ...interface{}) error – Makes an error from a formatted string

- func Fprint(w io.Writer, a ...interface{}) (n int, err error) – Outputs to w

- func Fprintf(w io.Writer, format string, a ...interface{}) (n int, err error) – Outputs to w

- func Fprintln(w io.Writer, a ...interface{}) (n int, err error) – Outputs to w with NL added

- func Fscan(r io.Reader, a ...interface{}) (n int, err error) – Scan input from r by type

- func Fscanf(r io.Reader, format string, a ...interface{}) (n int, err error) – Scan input from r by type

- func Fscanln(r io.Reader, a ...interface{}) (n int, err error) – Scan input line from r by type

- func Print(a ...interface{}) (n int, err error) – Outputs to STDOUT

- func Printf(format string, a ...interface{}) (n int, err error) – Outputs to STDOUT

- func Println(a ...interface{}) (n int, err error) – Outputs to STDOUT with NL added

- func Scan(a ...interface{}) (n int, err error) – Scan input from STDIN

- func Scanf(format string, a ...interface{}) (n int, err error) – Scan input from STDIN

- func Scanln(a ...interface{}) (n int, err error) – Scan line input from STDIN

- func Sprint(a ...interface{}) string – Output a string

- func Sprintf(format string, a ...interface{}) string – Output a string

- func Sprintln(a ...interface{}) string – Output a string with NL added

- func Sscan(str string, a ...interface{}) (n int, err error) – Scan input from a string

- func Sscanf(str string, format string, a ...interface{}) (n int, err error) – Scan input from a string

- func Sscanln(str string, a ...interface{}) (n int, err error) – Scan line input from a string

The fmt package provides these types:

- type Formatter – A type that can self-format

- type GoStringer – A type that can support formatting itself with details per %#v

- type Scanner – A type that can customize the Scan methods

- type Stringer – A type that can format itself as a string

The scanner package provides these types and functions.

Scanner reads characters and tokens from an io.Reader:

- func (s *Scanner) Init(src io.Reader) *Scanner – Make a Scanner

- func (s *Scanner) Next() rune – Get the next character

- func (s *Scanner) Peek() rune – Examine the next character

- func (s *Scanner) Pos() (pos Position) – Outputs position information

- func (s *Scanner) Scan() rune – Get the next token

- func (s *Scanner) TokenText() string – Get text of just scanned token

The tabwriter package provides these types and functions.
Writer is an io.Writer with column alignment capabilities:

- func NewWriter(output io.Writer, minwidth, tabwidth, padding int, padchar byte, flags uint) *Writer – Make a Writer

- func (b *Writer) Flush() error

- func (b *Writer) Init(output io.Writer, minwidth, tabwidth, padding int, padchar byte, flags uint) *Writer – Reset a Writer

- func (b *Writer) Write(buf []byte) (n int, err error)

Data Collections

Unlike Java, Go depends less on a set of standard *Collection* (lists, maps, sets, etc.) types and associated implementations. The slice and map types cover most of this need. But Go includes (by package) a few special-purpose container libraries. See the Go online package documentation for more details:

- heap provides operations for any heap interface implementer; interface only.

- list provides a doubly linked list.

- ring provides a circular list.

The package heap provides these types and functions that some implementing type must provide:

- func Fix(h Interface, i int) – Fix after element values change
- func Init(h Interface) – Initialize
- func Pop(h Interface) interface{} – Get the lowest value
- func Push(h Interface, x interface{}) – Add a new value
- func Remove(h Interface, i int) interface{} – Remove the ith value

The package list provides these types and functions.
An element is a list member:

- func (e *Element) Next() *Element – Get any predecessor
- func (e *Element) Prev() *Element – Get any successor

List contains elements. The methods are self-explanatory:

- func New() *List – Make a list
- func (l *List) Back() *Element – Move backward
- func (l *List) Front() *Element – Get first
- func (l *List) Init() *List – {Re}initialize (empty) a list
- func (l *List) InsertAfter(v interface{}, mark *Element) *Element
- func (l *List) InsertBefore(v interface{}, mark *Element) *Element
- func (l *List) Len() int – Get length
- func (l *List) MoveAfter(e, mark *Element)
- func (l *List) MoveBefore(e, mark *Element)
- func (l *List) MoveToBack(e *Element)
- func (l *List) MoveToFront(e *Element)
- func (l *List) PushBack(v interface{}) *Element
- func (l *List) PushBackList(other *List)
- func (l *List) PushFront(v interface{}) *Element

- func (l *List) PushFrontList(other *List)

- func (l *List) Remove(e *Element) interface{}

For example, to output, in reverse order, all elements in a list:

```
var l = list.New()
for _, x := range []int{1,2,3,4,5} {
    l.PushFront(x)
}
for v := l.Front(); v != nil; v = v.Next() {
    fmt.Print(v.Value)
}
fmt.Println()
```

which produces 54321.

The package ring provides the Ring type with these functions. Each Ring element has a Value field. No element is special:

- func New(n int) *Ring – Make a ring of n elements

- func (r *Ring) Do(f func(interface{})) – Run a function on each element

- func (r *Ring) Len() int – Get length

- func (r *Ring) Link(s *Ring) *Ring – Insert s into r

- func (r *Ring) Move(n int) *Ring – Advance n elements

- func (r *Ring) Next() *Ring – Advance one element

- func (r *Ring) Prev() *Ring – Retreat one element

- func (r *Ring) Unlink(n int) *Ring – Make the next n elements into a ring

Here is an example that prints a ring of integers:

```
N := 5
ring := ring.New(N)  // some capacity
count := ring.Len()
```

```go
// set each element to square root the element index cubed
for i := 0; i < count; i++ {
    ring.Value = math.Sqrt(float64(i * i * i))
    ring = ring.Next()
}
// now output the values; now back at start
x := 0
ring.Do(func(v interface{}) {
    fmt.Printf("Root of cube %v = %v\n", x, v)
    x++
})
```

which produces

```
Root of cube 0 = 0
Root of cube 1 = 1
Root of cube 2 = 2.8284271247461903
Root of cube 3 = 5.196152422706632
Root of cube 4 = 8
```

Sorting

The sort package provides means to sort slices of comparable types and user-defined collections that support certain interfaces.

The sort package provides these types and functions:

- func Float64s(a []float64) – Sort []float64

- func Float64sAreSorted(a []float64) bool – Test if []float64 is already sorted

- func Ints(a []int) – Sort []int

- func IntsAreSorted(a []int) bool – Test if []int is already sorted

- func IsSorted(data Interface) bool – Test if already sorted

- func Search(n int, f func(int) bool) int – Binary search 0...N-1 for a value with f true

- func SearchFloat64s(a []float64, x float64) int – Binary search sorted []floats64 for x

- func SearchInts(a []int, x int) int – Binary search sorted []ints for x

- func SearchStrings(a []string, x string) int – Binary search sorted []string for x

- func Slice(slice interface{}, less func(i, j int) bool) – Sort []? using the less function

- func SliceIsSorted(slice interface{}, less func(i, j int) bool) bool – Test if already sorted

- func SliceStable(slice interface{}, less func(i, j int) bool) – Stable sort []? using the less function

- func Sort(data Interface) – Sort data

- func Stable(data Interface) – Stable sort data

- func Strings(a []string) – Sort []string

- func StringsAreSorted(a []string) bool – Test if already sorted

- func Reverse(data Interface) Interface – Reverses data

Type *Interface* (an interface, not the best name choice) defines methods used for sorting. Types need to implement this interface to be sortable. This is like Java's `Comparable` interface:

- Len() int – Length of backing collection

- Less(i, j int) bool – Compares elements at i and j

- Swap(i, j int) – Exchange elements at i and j

Float64Slice acts as []float64 that implements the `Interface` interface:

- func (p Float64Slice) Search(x float64) int

- func (p Float64Slice) Sort()

IntSlice acts as []int that implements the `Interface` interface:

- func (p IntSlice) Search(x int) int

- func (p IntSlice) Sort()

StringSlice acts as []string that implements the Interface interface:

- func (p StringSlice) Search(x string) int

- func (p StringSlice) Sort)

For example, to sort a slice of strings:

```
in :=[...]string{"32", "-1", "0", "a"}
out :=[...]string{"32", "-1", "0", "a"}
var xout = sort.StringSlice(out[:])
xout.Sort()
fmt.Printf("in:  %v\nout: %v\n", in, xout)
```

which produces

```
in:  [32 -1 0 a]
out: [-1 0 32 a]
```

A simpler special case alternate to sort a slice of strings:

```
var sortable = []string{"32", "-1", "0", "a"}
sort.Strings(sortable)
fmt.Printf("out: %v\n", sortable)
```

which produces

```
out: [-1 0 32 a]
```

Context Package

Go has different support for asynchronous behavior than Java does. Java has no standard way to watch or cancel such actions; each library does it differently. Also, in Java, similar support is provided by libraries and/or frameworks, such as the Spring framework, not included in the standard library.

In Go, the context package gives support to do this where the *Context* type carries timeouts, interrupts, and scoped values across both local and possibly remote API boundaries and possibly processes. Many long-running Go APIs (generally expecting to be running in a goroutine) accept a context argument to allow them to be asynchronously cancelled or notify the caller, via a channel, when they are done.

The context package has these types and functions:

- func WithCancel(parent Context) (ctx Context, cancel CancelFunc) – Add a cancel function

- func WithDeadline(parent Context, d time.Time) (Context, CancelFunc) – Add a deadline

- func WithTimeout(parent Context, timeout time.Duration) (Context, CancelFunc) – Add a timeout

where

- Cancel function – Call this function to (by a client) cancel an operation or (by self) release resources when the operation is complete; should have been called "CancelOrDoneFunc" as that better reflects its role.

- Deadline – Set time in the future to abort an incomplete operation.

- Timeout – Set delay after which to abort an incomplete operation (alternate to Deadline).

A Context holds a context state. It provides these functions:

- func Background() Context – Return a basic context used as first input to With... operations; most often used.

- func TODO() Context – Return a TODO (needs more work) context; usage is rare.

- func WithValue(parent Context, key, val interface{}) Context – Add a value to the context.

A Context has these special functions:

- Done() – Returns a channel that will receive a message when the operation is completed

- Err() – Returns any error that occurred in the operation; often nil

Listing 14-3 demonstrates a simple use of a context to cancel an infinite value generator.

Listing 14-3. Random Int Generator (Part 1)

```go
func generateIntValues(ctx context.Context, values chan<- int) {
    loop: for {
            v, err := genIntValue()
            if err != nil {
                    fmt.Printf("genIntValue error: %v\n", err)
                    close(values)
                    break
            }
            select {
            case values <- v: // output value
                    fmt.Printf("generateIntValues sent: %v\n", v)
            case <-ctx.Done():
                    break loop // done when something received
            }
    }
}
func genIntValue() (v int, err error) {
    test := rand.Intn(20) % 5
    if test == 0 {
            err = errors.New(fmt.Sprintf("fake some error"))
            return
    }
    v = rand.Intn(100)
    fmt.Printf("genIntValue next: %d\n", v)
    return
}
```

Run by the code shown in Listing 14-4.

Listing 14-4. Random Int Generator (Part 2)

```go
values := make(chan int, 10)
ctx, cf := context.WithTimeout(context.Background(), 5 * time.Second)
go generateIntValues(ctx, values)
```

```
for v := range values {  // get all generated
    fmt.Printf("generateIntValues received: %d\n", v)
}
cf()
fmt.Printf("generateIntValues done\n")
```

It produces results like this:

```
genIntValue next: 87
generateIntValues sent: 87
genIntValue next: 59
generateIntValues sent: 59
genIntValue next: 18
generateIntValues sent: 18
genIntValue error: fake some error
generateIntValues received: 87
generateIntValues received: 59
generateIntValues received: 18
generateIntValues done
```

Note the timeout makes sure the generation ends sometime; it does not occur in this example. Note because the channel has many (say 100) slots, the generation all happens before a value is processed. If the channel capacity is set to zero, the processing order becomes more intermixed:

```
genIntValue next: 87
generateIntValues sent: 87
genIntValue next: 59
generateIntValues received: 87
generateIntValues received: 59
generateIntValues sent: 59
genIntValue next: 18
generateIntValues sent: 18
generateIntValues received: 18
genIntValue error: fake some error
generateIntValues done
```

Cryptography and Hashing and Data Encoding

Go has significant cryptography and hashing function built in. This includes support for multiple algorithms and functions. Each is in its own package. This book will not detail these sub-packages. See the Go online package documentation.

- `adler32` provides Adler-32 checksum.

- `aes` provides AES encryption.

- `cipher` provides standard block cipher modes that wrap lower-level cipher implementations.

- `crc32` provides 32-bit cyclic redundancy check checksum.

- `crc64` provides 64-bit cyclic redundancy check checksum.

- `crypto` provides cryptographic constants.

- `des` provides Data Encryption Standard and the Triple Data Encryption Algorithm.

- `dsa` provides Digital Signature Algorithm.

- `ecdsa` provides Elliptic Curve Digital Signature Algorithm.

- `ed25519` provides Ed25519 signature algorithm.

- `elliptic` provides several standard elliptic curves over prime fields.

- `fnv` provides FNV hash functions.

- `hash` provides interfaces for hash functions.

- `hmac` provides Keyed-Hash Message Authentication Code.

- `maphash` provides hash functions on byte sequences.

- `md5` provides MD5 hash algorithm.

- `pkix` provides for ASN.1 parsing.

- `rand` provides cryptographically secure random number generator.

- `rc4` provides RC4 encryption.

- `rsa` provides RSA encryption.

- `sha1` provides SHA hash algorithm.

- sha256 provides several SHA hash algorithms.

- sha512 provides several SHA hash algorithms.

- subtle provides helper functions for cryptographic code.

- tls provides TLS 1.2 and TLS 1.3.

- x509 provides X.509-encoded keys and certificates.

Encoding Packages

The encoding package provides interfaces that define how to convert data between byte-level and string-like representations. There are several sub-packages for different support. This book will only detail a few of these sub-packages:

- ascii85 provides ascii85 data encoding.

- asn1 provides parsing of the ASN.1 data structure.

- base32 provides base32 encoding.

- base64 provides base64 encoding.

- binary provides a translation between numbers and byte sequences.

- csv reads and writes comma-separated values (CSV) files.

- gob manages streams of gobs, a form of binary interchange.

- hex provides hexadecimal encoding and decoding.

- pem provides PEM data encoding.

- json provides JSON encoding and decoding.

- xml provides an XML parser with XML namespace support.

The csv package has these types and functions.
Reader parses CSV input:

- func NewReader(r io.Reader) *Reader – Make a reader

- func (r *Reader) Read() (record []string, err error) – Read one line

- func (r *Reader) ReadAll() (records [][]string, err error) – Read all lines

Writer generates CSV output:

- func NewWriter(w io.Writer) *Writer – Make a writer

- func (w *Writer) Flush() – Commit what is written

- func (w *Writer) Write(record []string) error – Write one line

- func (w *Writer) WriteAll(records [][]string) error – Write many lines

The hex package has these functions:

- func NewDecoder(r io.Reader) io.Reader – Make a reader

- func NewEncoder(w io.Writer) io.Writer – Make a writer

- func Decode(dst, src []byte) (int, error) – src hex string to dst bytes

- func DecodeString(s string) ([]byte, error) – src hex string to dst bytes

- func DecodedLen(x int) int – Always x / 2

- func Dump(data []byte) string – Formats hex dump

- func Dumper(w io.Writer) io.WriteCloser – Formats hex dump

- func Encode(dst, src []byte) int – src bytes to dst hex string

- func EncodeToString(src []byte) string – src bytes to hex string

- func EncodedLen(n int) int – Always n * 2

The json package has these types and functions:

- func Compact(dst *bytes.Buffer, src []byte) error – Removes insignificant whitespace

- func HTMLEscape(dst *bytes.Buffer, src []byte) – Makes safe to embed in HTML

- func Indent(dst *bytes.Buffer, src []byte, prefix, indent string) error – Indents JSON

- func Marshal(v interface{}) ([]byte, error) – Makes JSON based on passed type

- func MarshalIndent(v interface{}, prefix, indent string) ([]byte, error) – Makes indented JSON based on passed type

- func Unmarshal(data []byte, v interface{}) error – Parses JSON into passed type

- func Valid(data []byte) bool – Tests a JSON string for validity

Decoder decodes/parses JSON strings. It provides these functions:

- func NewDecoder(r io.Reader) *Decoder – Make a decoder

- func (dec *Decoder) Decode(v interface{}) error – Decodes the next JSON value

- func (dec *Decoder) DisallowUnknownFields() – Causes an error on unknown keys

- func (dec *Decoder) InputOffset() int64 – Position in input text

- func (dec *Decoder) More() bool – Test if more data to parse

- func (dec *Decoder) Token() (Token, error) – Get the next token

Encoder encodes/builds JSON strings. It provides these functions:

- func NewEncoder(w io.Writer) *Encoder – Make an encoder

- func (enc *Encoder) Encode(v interface{}) error – Format a value as JSON

- func (enc *Encoder) SetEscapeHTML(on bool) – Escape HTML control characters

- func (enc *Encoder) SetIndent(prefix, indent string) – Set indent whitespace

See the capstone program for examples of using JSON and XML encoders.

Unicode Encoding Packages

The unicode package provides functions to examine and manipulate *Unicode* characters (i.e., Runes) in popular encodings. This package has constants and variables that define the major Unicode character categories such as Letter, Digit, Punct, Space, and many others.

It has the following functions. Many test a Rune's type by Unicode classification. This is like the Java `Character.isXxx(...)` methods.

- func In(r rune, ranges ...*RangeTable) bool – Tests a Rune for membership
- func Is(rangeTab *RangeTable, r rune) bool – Tests a Rune for membership
- func IsControl(r rune) bool
- func IsDigit(r rune) bool
- func IsGraphic(r rune) bool
- func IsLetter(r rune) bool
- func IsLower(r rune) bool
- func IsMark(r rune) bool
- func IsNumber(r rune) bool
- func IsOneOf(ranges []*RangeTable, r rune) bool
- func IsPrint(r rune) bool
- func IsPunct(r rune) bool
- func IsSpace(r rune) bool
- func IsSymbol(r rune) bool
- func IsTitle(r rune) bool
- func IsUpper(r rune) bool
- func SimpleFold(r rune) rune
- func ToLower(r rune) rune
- func ToTitle(r rune) rune
- func ToUpper(r rune) rune

The `unicode` package has sub-packages:

- `utf8` provides encoding and decoding runes to/from UTF-8.
- `utf16` provides encoding and decoding runes to/from UTF-16.

The utf8 package provides these functions:

- func DecodeLastRune(p []byte) (r rune, size int) – Get the last rune and length

- func DecodeLastRuneInString(s string) (r rune, size int) – Get the last rune and length

- func DecodeRune(p []byte) (r rune, size int) – Get the first rune and length

- func DecodeRuneInString(s string) (r rune, size int) – Get the first rune and length

- func EncodeRune(p []byte, r rune) int – Make a rune into UTF-8

- func FullRune(p []byte) bool – Test if p starts with a valid UTF-8 rune

- func FullRuneInString(s string) bool – Test if s starts with a valid UTF-8 rune

- func RuneCount(p []byte) int – Count runes in p

- func RuneCountInString(s string) (n int) – Count runes in s

- func RuneLen(r rune) int – How many bytes in rune UTF-8

- func RuneStart(b byte) bool – Is b a valid rune started

- func Valid(p []byte) bool – Test p is a value rune sequence

- func ValidRune(r rune) bool – Can a rune be represented as UTF8

- func ValidString(s string) bool – Test s is a valid rune sequence

The utf16 package provides these functions:

- func Decode(s []uint16) []rune – Convert to runes

- func DecodeRune(r1, r2 rune) rune – Convert a pair to a rune

- func Encode(s []rune) []uint16 – Convert from runes

- func EncodeRune(r rune) (r1, r2 rune) – Convert to a pair

- func IsSurrogate(r rune) bool – Test if a rune needs a pair

CHAPTER 15

SQL Database Access

Java provides multiple levels of SQL-based database access, referred to as *JDBC* (aka Java Database Connectivity), in the `java.sql` and `java.sqlx` packages. Go does much the same thing but with less function with the `sql` and `driver` packages. The `sql` package provides a generic framework of functions like `java.sql` does for SQL databases, while the driver package is a *Systems Programming Interface* (SPI) to allow pluggable drivers to be consumed. Most SQL actions are done by the drivers. Unlike with Java, most of the Go drivers come from community sources, not the database vendors.

Java has community support (e.g., *Hibernate*[1] or *Java Persistence Architecture*[2] (JPA) implementations) for *Object-Relational Mappers* (ORMs)[3] that make saving persistent objects (or *Entities*; classes in Java, structs in Go) in relational databases much easier. Many Java developers use these ORMs instead of the more basic CRUD[4] SQL[5] access provided by JDBC.

The following packages offer low-level JDBC-like access. There are community packages, such as GORM, that add ORM support to Go.

The `sql` package is large and has several types and functions.

The key types are

- ColType – Defines the type of a table column

- Conn – Represents a single database connection

- DB – Represents a pool of connections

- Row – Represents a single returned table row (subcase of Rows)

- Rows – Represents multiple returned table rows

---

[1] https://en.wikipedia.org/wiki/Hibernate_(framework) and https://hibernate.org/
[2] https://en.wikipedia.org/wiki/Jakarta_Persistence
[3] https://en.wikipedia.org/wiki/Object%E2%80%93relational_mapping
[4] CRUD – Create, Read (aka Query), Update, Delete.
[5] Structured Query Language – The standard API for relational database systems.

B. Feigenbaum, *Go for Java Programmers*, https://doi.org/10.1007/978-1-4842-7199-5_15

- Scanner – An interface to access columns of a row

- Stmt – Represents a prepared SQL statement

- Tx – Represents a database transaction

The `sql` package has these functions:

- func Drivers() []string – Get registered driver names

- func Register(name string, driver driver.Driver) – Register a driver

ColumnType provides these functions. They are self-explanatory:

- func (ci *ColumnType) DatabaseTypeName() string

- func (ci *ColumnType) DecimalSize() (precision, scale int64, ok bool)

- func (ci *ColumnType) Length() (length int64, ok bool)

- func (ci *ColumnType) Name() string

- func (ci *ColumnType) Nullable() (nullable, ok bool)

- func (ci *ColumnType) ScanType() reflect.Type

Conn provides connection-level access functions:

- func (c *Conn) BeginTx(ctx context.Context, opts *TxOptions) (*Tx, error) – Start a transaction

- func (c *Conn) Close() error – Close the connection; return it to a pool

- func (c *Conn) ExecContext(ctx context.Context, query string, args ...interface{}) (Result, error) – Execute non-query SQL

- func (c *Conn) PingContext(ctx context.Context) error – See if the connection can work

- func (c *Conn) PrepareContext(ctx context.Context, query string) (*Stmt, error) – Prepare a SQL statement

- func (c *Conn) QueryContext(ctx context.Context, query string, args ...interface{}) (*Rows, error) – Execute a SQL query that can return many rows

- func (c *Conn) QueryRowContext(ctx context.Context, query string, args ...interface{}) *Row – Execute a SQL query that will return <= 1 row

DB provides database-level access functions:

- func Open(driverName, dataSourceName string) (*DB, error) – Open the DB by name

- func OpenDB(c driver.Connector) *DB – Open the DB

- func (db *DB) Begin() (*Tx, error) – Start a transaction

- func (db *DB) BeginTx(ctx context.Context, opts *TxOptions) (*Tx, error) – Start a transaction with options

- func (db *DB) Close() error – Close the DB

- func (db *DB) Conn(ctx context.Context) (*Conn, error) – Get a connection to the DB

- func (db *DB) Driver() driver.Driver – Get a driver for the DB

- func (db *DB) Exec(query string, args ...interface{}) (Result, error) – Exec generic SQL

- func (db *DB) ExecContext(ctx context.Context, query string, args ...interface{}) (Result, error) – Exec generic SQL

- func (db *DB) Ping() error – Test DB is available

- func (db *DB) PingContext(ctx context.Context) error – Test DB is available

- func (db *DB) Prepare(query string) (*Stmt, error) – Prepare SQL

- func (db *DB) PrepareContext(ctx context.Context, query string) (*Stmt, error) – Prepare SQL

- func (db *DB) Query(query string, args ...interface{}) (*Rows, error) – Execute a generic SELECT

- func (db *DB) QueryContext(ctx context.Context, query string, args ...interface{}) (*Rows, error) – Execute a generic SELECT

- func (db *DB) QueryRow(query string, args ...interface{}) *Row – Execute a query

- func (db *DB) QueryRowContext(ctx context.Context, query string, args ...interface{}) *Row – Execute a query

- func (db *DB) Stats() DBStats – Get various DB access statistics

Row is a single SELECT result row:

- func (r *Row) Err() error – Get any execution error

- func (r *Row) Scan(dest ...interface{}) error – Copy returned data to variables

Rows is a set of SELECT result rows:

- func (rs *Rows) Close() error – Indicate now finished processing the rows

- func (rs *Rows) ColumnTypes() ([]*ColumnType, error) – Get column metadata

- func (rs *Rows) Columns() ([]string, error) – Get column names

- func (rs *Rows) Err() error – Get any execution error

- func (rs *Rows) Next() bool – Advance to the next row

- func (rs *Rows) NextResultSet() bool – Advance to the next result set

- func (rs *Rows) Scan(dest ...interface{}) error – Copy returned data to variables

Stmt provides SQL statement–level access functions:

- func (s *Stmt) Close() error

- func (s *Stmt) Exec(args ...interface{}) (Result, error)

- func (s *Stmt) ExecContext(ctx context.Context, args ...interface{}) (Result, error)

- func (s *Stmt) Query(args ...interface{}) (*Rows, error)

- func (s *Stmt) QueryContext(ctx context.Context, args ...interface{}) (*Rows, error)

- func (s *Stmt) QueryRow(args ...interface{}) *Row

- func (s *Stmt) QueryRowContext(ctx context.Context, args ...interface{}) *Row

Tx provides transaction-level access functions. See similar descriptions earlier.

- func (tx *Tx) Commit() error – Commit any changes

- func (tx *Tx) Exec(query string, args ...interface{}) (Result, error)

- func (tx *Tx) ExecContext(ctx context.Context, query string, args ...interface{}) (Result, error)

- func (tx *Tx) Prepare(query string) (*Stmt, error)

- func (tx *Tx) PrepareContext(ctx context.Context, query string) (*Stmt, error)

- func (tx *Tx) Query(query string, args ...interface{}) (*Rows, error)

- func (tx *Tx) QueryContext(ctx context.Context, query string, args ...interface{}) (*Rows, error)

- func (tx *Tx) QueryRow(query string, args ...interface{}) *Row

- func (tx *Tx) QueryRowContext(ctx context.Context, query string, args ...interface{}) *Row

- func (tx *Tx) Rollback() error – Roll back (cancel) any changes

- func (tx *Tx) Stmt(stmt *Stmt) *Stmt – Get a statement in this transaction

- func (tx *Tx) StmtContext(ctx context.Context, stmt *Stmt) *Stmt

As an example of using the sql package, Listing 15-1 shows a program that CRUDs a simple table.

Listing 15-1. Sample DB Access (Part 1)

```
// Table row entity
type DBEntity struct {
    name  string
    value string
}
```

```go
// Do in a DB context.
func DoInDB(driverName, datasourceParams string, f func(db *sql.DB) error)
(err error) {
    db, err := sql.Open(driverName, datasourceParams)
    if err != nil {
        return
    }
    defer db.Close()
    err = f(db)
    return
}

// Do in a connection.
func DoInConn(db *sql.DB, ctx context.Context, f func(db *sql.DB, conn
*sql.Conn, ctx context.Context) error) (err error) {
    conn, err := db.Conn(ctx)
    if err != nil {
        return
    }
    defer conn.Close()
    err = f(db, conn, ctx)
    return
}

// Do in a transaction.
func DoInTx(db *sql.DB, conn *sql.Conn, ctx context.Context, txOptions
*sql.TxOptions, f func(tx *sql.Tx) error) (err error) {
    if txOptions == nil {
        txOptions = &sql.TxOptions{Isolation: sql.LevelSerializable}
    }
    tx, err := db.BeginTx(ctx, txOptions)
    if err != nil {
        return
    }
```

```go
        err = f(tx)
        if err != nil {
            _ = tx.Rollback()
            return
        }
        err = tx.Commit()
        if err != nil {
            return
        }
        return
    }

    var ErrBadOperation = errors.New("bad operation")

    // Execute a SQL statement.
    func ExecuteSQL(tx *sql.Tx, ctx context.Context, sql string, params
    ...interface{}) (count int64, values []*DBEntity, err error) {
        lsql := strings.ToLower(sql)
        switch {

        // process query
        case strings.HasPrefix(lsql, "select "):
            rows, xerr := tx.QueryContext(ctx, sql, params...)
            if xerr != nil {
                err = xerr
                return
            }
            defer rows.Close()
            for rows.Next() {
                var name string
                var value string
                if err = rows.Scan(&name, &value); err != nil {
                    return
                }
                data := &DBEntity{name, value}
                values = append(values, data)
            }
```

```
        if xerr := rows.Err(); xerr != nil {
            err = xerr
            return
        }

    // process an update
    case strings.HasPrefix(lsql, "update "), strings.HasPrefix(lsql,
    "delete "), strings.HasPrefix(lsql, "insert "):
        result, xerr := tx.ExecContext(ctx, sql, params...)
        if xerr != nil {
            err = xerr
            return
        }
        count, xerr = result.RowsAffected()
        if xerr != nil {
            err = xerr
            return
        }

    default:
        err = ErrBadOperation  // INSERT and DELETE not demo'ed here
        return
    }
    return
}
```

The library is driven by this test function (Listing 15-2).

Listing 15-2. Sample DB Access (Part 2)

```
func testDB() {
    values := make([]*DBEntity, 0, 10)
    values = append(values, &DBEntity{"Barry", "author"},
        &DBEntity{"Barry, Jr.", "reviewer"})

    err := DoInDB("postgres", "postgres://postgres:postgres@localhost:5432/
                postgres?sslmode=disable",
```

```
        func(db *sql.DB) (err error) {
            err = DoInConn(db, context.Background(), func(db *sql.DB,
            conn *sql.Conn,
                    ctx context.Context) (err error) {
                err = createRows(db, conn, ctx, values)
                if err != nil {
                    return
                }
                // must be done in separate transaction to see the change
                err = queryRows(db, conn, ctx)
                return
            })
            return
        })
    if err != nil {
        fmt.Printf("DB access failed: %v\n", err)
    }
}

// Create data rows.
func createRows(db *sql.DB, conn *sql.Conn, ctx context.Context, values
[]*DBEntity) (err error) {
    err = DoInTx(db, conn, ctx, nil, func(tx *sql.Tx) (err error) {
        // first remove any old rows
        count, _, err := ExecuteSQL(tx, ctx, `delete from xvalues`)
        if err != nil {
            return
        }
        fmt.Printf("deleted %d\n", count)
        // insert new rows
        for _, v := range values {
            count1, _, xerr := ExecuteSQL(tx, ctx, fmt.Sprintf(`insert
            into xvalues(name, value) values('%s', '%s')`, v.name,
            v.value))
```

```
                if xerr != nil || count1 != 1 {
                    err = xerr
                    return
                }
                fmt.Printf("inserted %q = %q\n", v.name, v.value)
            }
            // update a row
            v := &DBEntity{"Barry", "father"}
            _, _, xerr := ExecuteSQL(tx, ctx, fmt.Sprintf(`update xvalues set
            value='%s' where name='%s'`, v.value, v.name))
            if xerr != nil {
                err = xerr
                return
            }
            fmt.Printf("updated %q = %q\n", v.name, v.value)
            return
        })
        return
}

// Query and print all rows.
func queryRows(db *sql.DB, conn *sql.Conn, ctx context.Context) (err error)
{
    err = DoInTx(db, conn, ctx, nil, func(tx *sqB.Tx) (err error) {
        _, xvalues, err := ExecuteSQL(tx, ctx, `select name, value from
        xvalues`)
        if err != nil {
            return
        }
        for _, v := range xvalues {
            fmt.Printf("queried %q = %q\n", v.name, v.value)
        }
        return
    })
    return
}
```

Note the nested approach to ensuring database resources is closed. Releasing resources is important, especially for long-running programs such as servers. At the top level is access to the database connection pool. Then there is access to a single connection from the pool. Finally, there is a transaction to perform SQL statements in. In this example, multiple transactions are done in a single connection, which is typical. Also, multiple statements are often done in a single transaction.

The program outputs the following:

```
deleted 2
inserted "Barry" = "author"
inserted "Barry, Jr." = "reviewer"
updated "Barry" = "father"queried "Barry, Jr." = "reviewer"
queried "Barry" = "father"
```

Note two records were deleted because this output is from a secondary execution of the program.

When the program ends, the database has the data shown in Figure 15-1.

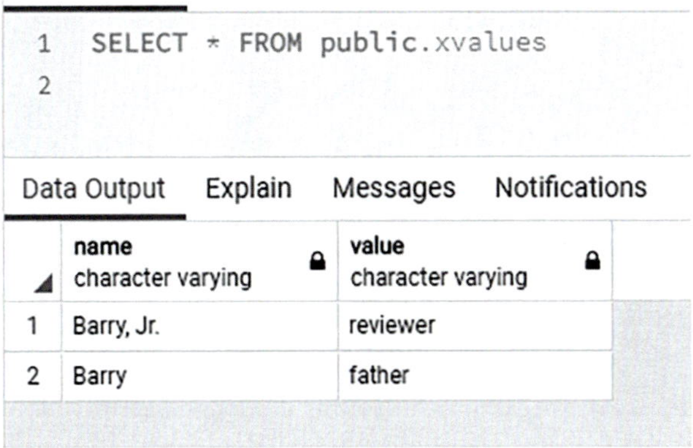

Figure 15-1. *DB example results (in PostgreSQL)*

CHAPTER 16

Client and Server Support

The html package provides functions for processing HTML text. Java Standard Edition (JSE) has little similar support; the Java community provides most of this capability. The Go template packages provide templates for generating text output with value insertions. It has support for plain text and extension for hack-resistant HTML text.

MIME Packages

The mime package provides support for MIME types. It has sub-packages:

- Multipart provides MIME multipart parsing.

- Quotedprintable provides quoted-printable encoding via readers and writers.

Network Packages

The net package provides interfaces to use TCP/IP with socket-level access and UDP. It has several sub-packages, but only the http sub-package is covered in this book. The http package provides the ability to create HTTP clients and servers. It has several commonly used sub-packages:

- Cgi provides support for the Common Gateway Interface (CGI) process per request server.

- Fcgi provides support for "fast" Common Gateway Interface (CGI) servers.

- Cookiejar provides support for HTTP cookies.

© Barry Feigenbaum 2022
B. Feigenbaum, *Go for Java Programmers*, https://doi.org/10.1007/978-1-4842-7199-5_16

- Httputil provides HTTP helper utility functions.

- Textproto provides help for protocols with text headers and sections like HTTP and SMTP.

The Net Package

The net package is large. It provides basic services for access TCP/IP networks using sockets and datagrams and for select protocols, such as HTTP. The net package has many types and functions. They will not be listed in this book, but they are available online. The following sample shows how a small subset (Dial, Listen, Accept, Read, and Write) of the APIs can be used.

Before we go into Go's HTTP package, we should briefly discuss TCP/IP and HTTP vs. REST vs. RPC.

The *Terminal Control Protocol* (TCP),[1] combined with the *Internet Protocol* (IP),[2] is the primary foundation of the Internet. Together they allow low-level and unreliable datagram transmission or reliable socket/conversational exchanges between hosts on a network.

The *HyperText Transfer Protocol* (HTTP)[3] is a popular protocol, delivered over TCP sockets, that, combined with the *HyperText Markup Language* (HTML)[4] (and *Cascading Style Sheets* (CSS)[5] and JavaScript and other MIME types), creates the *World Wide Web* (WWW or just the Web)[6] as we know it today.

HTTP allows for data in many formats to be interchanged between servers and clients (often browsers). It supports many verbs, but mostly it allows GET (to read), PUT (to create or replace), POST (to create or append to), and DELETE, aka CRUD,[7] of resources.

---

[1] https://en.wikipedia.org/wiki/Transmission_Control_Protocol

[2] https://en.wikipedia.org/wiki/Internet_Protocol

[3] https://en.wikipedia.org/wiki/Hypertext_Transfer_Protocol

[4] https://en.wikipedia.org/wiki/HTML

[5] https://en.wikipedia.org/wiki/CSS

[6] https://en.wikipedia.org/wiki/World_Wide_Web

[7] https://en.wikipedia.org/wiki/Create,_read,_update_and_delete

REpresentational State Transfer (REST, sometimes ReST)[8] builds on HTTP but restricts it to improve both ease of use and scale. REST is not an implementation but a set of design guidelines. It reflects the most desirable qualities of WWW support. It limits the server operations to only CRUD applied to resources identified by URLs. REST done to the maximum implements HATEOAS,[9] which reflects the WWW organization. Most RESTful APIs do not reach the level. RESTful services are an alternative to RPC-based services. Go has a lot of support for such services.

Remote Procedure Call (RPC)[10] is an alternative way to use HTTP (or other protocols) with less restrictions (and typically better performance) than REST has by allowing one to create arbitrary operations (procedures) that a server provides to its clients (almost always programs, not humans).

Web Services (WS),[11] a form of RPC, are often implemented over *SOAP*,[12] an XML-based protocol, using HTTP. Such services have fallen out of favor vs. RESTful services. Go has little standard library support for SOAP-based WS.

Go has limited standard RPC support in the net/rpc/jsonrpc package. A more powerful and popular community option is *gRPC*[13] from Google.

Go's http and rpc sub-packages of the net package allow one to develop programs at any of these levels. This book deals mostly with REST-style access.

All these are built on lower-level TCP/IP[14] *Socket*[15]–based communication. Go also has support for working at this level in the net package.

Included in the following is a simple TCP socket client/server pair. They demonstrate basic communications over a socket. Note how more involved (more code needed) using the socket approach is when contrasted to doing HTTP communications (as shown in other examples in this book). The following code is inefficient as only one request per connection is allowed (this is like HTTP version 1). It is also inefficient as it reads/writes data one byte at a time.

---

[8] https://en.wikipedia.org/wiki/Representational_state_transfer
[9] https://en.wikipedia.org/wiki/HATEOAS
[10] https://en.wikipedia.org/wiki/Remote_procedure_call
[11] https://en.wikipedia.org/wiki/Web_service
[12] https://en.wikipedia.org/wiki/SOAP
[13] https://en.wikipedia.org/wiki/GRPC
[14] https://en.wikipedia.org/wiki/Internet_protocol_suite
[15] https://en.wikipedia.org/wiki/Network_socket

As a demonstration, we will run a configuration that starts a server and makes multiple requests (all normally launched in different machines but simulated via multiple goroutines here). This demonstration starts sending ten requests in the background at random intervals with some overlapped and then quickly (before any requests can be lost) launches a server to process them. The demonstration is hardcoded to use localhost:8080 for the server. Note the server processes concurrent requests (the nest value is sometimes greater than one; three is observed in the example output).

The server works in two parts:

1. A long-running loop accepting connections.

2. A goroutine to process a request on an accepted connection; there can be any number of such processors running concurrently.

The preceding pattern is typical for server request processing. In other languages, such as Java, an OS thread (often from a limited thread pool) is generally used for each request; in Go, a goroutine is used instead. This can allow for better request scale using Go.

As shown in Listing 16-1, the client sends commands, and the server sends responses. Commands are strings with a message end marker ('~' that must not be part of the message text).

See the log package section for the definition of getGID().

Listing 16-1. Sample TCP/IP Socket Usage

```go
var xlog = log.New(os.Stderr, "", log.Ltime+log.Lmicroseconds)

func main(){
    var wg sync.WaitGroup
    wg.Add(1)
    go SocketClientGo(&wg)
    ss := NewSocketServer()
    go func() {
        gid := getGID()
        err := ss.AcceptConnections(8080)
        if err != nil {
            xlog.Printf("%5d testSocketServer accept failed: %v\n", gid, err)
            return
        }
    }()
```

```go
        wg.Wait()
        ss.Accepting = false
}
func SocketClientGo(wg *sync.WaitGroup) {
        defer wg.Done()
        gid := getGID()
        cmds := []string{TODCommand, SayingCommand}
        max := 10

        var xwg sync.WaitGroup
        for i := 0; i < max; i++ {
            xwg.Add(1)
            go func(index, max int) {
                defer xwg.Done()
                time.Sleep(time.Duration(rand.Intn(5)) * time.Second)
                sc := newSocketClient("127.0.0.1", 8080)
                xlog.Printf("%5d SocketClientGo request %d of %d\n", gid,
                index, max)
                resp, err := sc.GetCmd(cmds[rand.Intn(len(cmds))])
                if err != nil {
                    xlog.Printf("%5d SocketClientGo failed: %v\n", gid, err)
                    return
                }
                xlog.Printf("%5d SocketClientGo response: %s\n", gid, resp)
            }(i+1, max)
        }
        xwg.Wait()
}

// allowed commands
const (
        TODCommand    = "TOD"
        SayingCommand = "Saying"
)
```

```go
var delim = byte('~')

// some saying to return
var sayings = make([]string, 0, 100)

func init(){
    sayings = append(sayings,
     `Now is the time...`,
     `I'm busy.`,
     `I pity the fool that tries to stop me!`,
     `Out wit; Out play; Out last!`,
     `It's beginning to look like TBD!`,
     )
}

// a Server
type SocketServer struct {
    Accepting bool
}

func NewSocketServer() (ss *SocketServer) {
    ss = &SocketServer{}
    ss.Accepting = true
    return
}

// Accept connection until told to stop.
func (ss *SocketServer) AcceptConnections(port int) (err error) {
    gid := getGID()
    xlog.Printf("%5d accept listening on port: %d\n", gid, port)
    listen, err := net.Listen("tcp", fmt.Sprintf("127.0.0.1:%d", port))
    if err != nil {
        return
    }
    for ss.Accepting {
        conn, err := listen.Accept()
        if err != nil {
            xlog.Printf("%5d accept failed: %v\n", gid,err)
```

```go
                continue
            }
            xlog.Printf("%5d accepted connection: %#v\n", gid, conn)
            go ss.handleConnectionGo(conn)
        }
        return
}

var nesting int32

// Process each connection.
// Only one command per connection.
func (ss *SocketServer) handleConnectionGo(c net.Conn) {
        defer c.Close()
        nest := atomic.AddInt32(&nesting, 1)
        defer func(){
            atomic.AddInt32(&nesting, -1)
        }()
        gid := getGID()
        data := make([]byte, 0, 1000)
        err := readData(c, &data, delim, cap(data))
        if err != nil {
            xlog.Printf("%5d handleConnection failed: %v\n", gid, err)
            return
        }
        cmd := string(data)
        xlog.Printf("%5d handleConnection request: %s, nest: %d, conn: %#v\n",
        gid, cmd, nest, c)
        if strings.HasSuffix(cmd, string(delim)) {
            cmd = cmd[0 : len(cmd)-1]
        }
        xlog.Printf("%5d received command: %s\n", gid, cmd)
        time.Sleep(time.Duration(rand.Intn(500)) * time.Millisecond)
        // make request take a while
        var out string
```

```go
    switch cmd {
    case SayingCommand:
        out = sayings[rand.Intn(len(sayings))]
    case TODCommand:
        out = fmt.Sprintf("%s", time.Now())
    default:
        xlog.Printf("%5d handleConnection unknown request: %s\n", gid, cmd)
        out = "bad command: " + cmd
    }
    _, err = writeData(c, []byte(out+string(delim)))
    if err != nil {
        xlog.Printf("%5d %s failed: %v\n", gid, cmd, err)
    }
}

// a Client
type SocketClient struct {
    Address    string
    Port       int
    Connection net.Conn
}

func newSocketClient(address string, port int) (sc *SocketClient) {
    sc = &SocketClient{}
    sc.Address = address
    sc.Port = port
    return
}
func (sc *SocketClient) Connect() (err error) {
    gid := getGID()
    xlog.Printf("%5d attempting connection: %s:%d\n", gid, sc.Address,
    sc.Port)
    sc.Connection, err = net.Dial("tcp", fmt.Sprintf("%s:%d", sc.Address,
    sc.Port))
```

```go
    if err != nil {
        return
    }
    xlog.Printf("%5d made connection: %#v\n", gid, sc.Connection)
    return
}
func (sc *SocketClient) SendCommand(cmd string) (err error) {
    gid := getGID()
    c, err := sc.Connection.Write([]byte(cmd + string(delim)))
    if err != nil {
        return
    }
    xlog.Printf("%5d sent command: %s, count=%d\n", gid, cmd, c)
    return
}
func (sc *SocketClient) ReadResponse(data *[]byte, max int) (err error) {
    err = readData(sc.Connection, data, delim, 1000)
    return
}

// send command and get response.
func (sc *SocketClient) GetCmd(cmd string) (tod string, err error) {
    err = sc.Connect()
    if err != nil {
        return
    }
      defer sc.Connection.Close()
    err = sc.SendCommand(cmd)
    data := make([]byte, 0, 1000)
    err = readData(sc.Connection, &data, delim, cap(data))
    if err != nil {
        return
    }
    tod = string(data)
    return
}
```

```go
func readData(c net.Conn, data *[]byte, delim byte, max int) (err error) {
    for {
        xb := make([]byte, 1, 1)
        c, xerr := c.Read(xb)
        if xerr != nil {
            err = xerr
            return
        }
        if c > 0 {
            if len(*data) > max {
                break
            }
            b := xb[0]
            *data = append(*data, b)
            if b == delim {
                break
            }
        }
    }
    return
}
func writeData(c net.Conn, data []byte) (count int, err error) {
    count, err = c.Write(data)
    return
}
```

This produces the following output (can vary per run). Each line has a timestamp and a goroutine id. This allows you to sort out which message is coming from which goroutine and when, relatively. The goroutine ids are not important, but they are the same in each line from a certain goroutine. New goroutines can reuse prior ids of completed goroutines. Note that the requests are sent in an apparently random order.

A customized logger is used to remove the date normally output:

```
09:32:57.910516    20 accept listening on port: 8080
09:32:57.911512    19 SocketClientGo request 7 of 10
09:32:57.911512    19 SocketClientGo request 9 of 10
```

```
09:32:57.911512    19 SocketClientGo request 8 of 10
09:32:57.912507    13 attempting connection: 127.0.0.1:8080
09:32:57.912507    11 attempting connection: 127.0.0.1:8080
09:32:57.912507    12 attempting connection: 127.0.0.1:8080
09:32:57.914499    11 made connection: &net.TCPConn{conn:net.conn{fd:(
                      *net.netFD)(0xc000298000)}}
09:32:57.914499    12 made connection: &net.TCPConn{conn:net.conn{fd:(
                      *net.netFD)(0xc00021a000)}}
09:32:57.914499    20 accepted connection: &net.TCPConn{conn:net.conn{fd:(
                      *net.netFD)(0xc0000cc000)}}
09:32:57.914499    13 made connection: &net.TCPConn{conn:net.conn{fd:(
                      *net.netFD)(0xc000198000)}}
09:32:57.914499    12 sent command: TOD, count=4
09:32:57.914499    11 sent command: TOD, count=4
09:32:57.914499    13 sent command: Saying, count=7
09:32:57.914499    20 accepted connection: &net.TCPConn{conn:net.conn{fd:(
                      *net.netFD)(0xc000298280)}}
09:32:57.914499    15 handleConnection request: TOD~, nest: 1, conn: &net.
                      TCPConn{conn:net.conn{fd:(*net.netFD)(0xc0000cc000)}}
09:32:57.914499    15 received command: TOD
09:32:57.914499    20 accepted connection: &net.TCPConn{conn:net.conn{fd:(
                      *net.netFD)(0xc000316000)}}
09:32:57.914499    51 handleConnection request: TOD~, nest: 2, conn: &net.
                      TCPConn{conn:net.conn{fd:(*net.netFD)(0xc000298280)}}
09:32:57.914499    51 received command: TOD
09:32:57.914499    82 handleConnection request: Saying~, nest: 3,
                      conn: &net.TCPConn{conn:net.conn{fd:(*net.netFD)
                      (0xc000316000)}}
09:32:57.914499    82 received command: Saying
09:32:58.004647    19 SocketClientGo response: 2020-12-29
                      09:32:58.0046474 -0800 PST m=+0.097117101~
09:32:58.150718    19 SocketClientGo response: 2020-12-29
                      09:32:58.150718 -0800 PST m=+0.243187101~
09:32:58.190435    19 SocketClientGo response: I'm busy.~
09:32:58.925744    19 SocketClientGo request 1 of 10
```

```
09:32:58.925744      19 SocketClientGo request 2 of 10
09:32:58.925744      19 SocketClientGo request 5 of 10
09:32:58.925744       6 attempting connection: 127.0.0.1:8080
09:32:58.925744       5 attempting connection: 127.0.0.1:8080
09:32:58.925744       9 attempting connection: 127.0.0.1:8080
09:32:58.925744       5 made connection: &net.TCPConn{conn:net.conn{fd:(
                         *net.netFD)(0xc00014cc80)}}
09:32:58.925744      20 accepted connection: &net.TCPConn{conn:net.conn{fd:(
                         *net.netFD)(0xc000298780)}}
09:32:58.925744       6 made connection: &net.TCPConn{conn:net.conn{fd:(
                         *net.netFD)(0xc000316280)}}
09:32:58.925744       9 made connection: &net.TCPConn{conn:net.conn{fd:(
                         *net.netFD)(0xc000298500)}}
09:32:58.925744       5 sent command: Saying, count=7
09:32:58.925744       6 sent command: Saying, count=7
09:32:58.925744       9 sent command: TOD, count=4
09:32:58.925744      20 accepted connection: &net.TCPConn{conn:net.conn{fd:(
                         *net.netFD)(0xc000298a00)}}
09:32:58.925744      53 handleConnection request: TOD~, nest: 1, conn: &net.
                         TCPConn{conn:net.conn{fd:(*net.netFD)(0xc000298780)}}
09:32:58.925744      53 received command: TOD
09:32:58.925744      54 handleConnection request: Saying~, nest: 2,
                         conn: &net.TCPConn{conn:net.conn{fd:(*net.netFD)
                         (0xc000298a00)}}
09:32:58.925744      54 received command: Saying
09:32:58.925744      20 accepted connection: &net.TCPConn{conn:net.conn{fd:(
                         *net.netFD)(0xc00021a280)}}
09:32:58.925744      35 handleConnection request: Saying~, nest: 3,
                         conn: &net.TCPConn{conn:net.conn{fd:(*net.netFD)
                         (0xc00021a280)}}
09:32:58.925744      35 received command: Saying
09:32:58.954615      19 SocketClientGo response: Out wit; Out play; Out last!~
09:32:59.393099      19 SocketClientGo response: I pity the fool that tries
                         to stop me!~
09:32:59.420974      19 SocketClientGo response: 2020-12-29
                         09:32:59.4209749 -0800 PST m=+1.513438801~
```

```
09:32:59.921948    19 SocketClientGo request 10 of 10
09:32:59.921948    19 SocketClientGo request 3 of 10
09:32:59.921948    14 attempting connection: 127.0.0.1:8080
09:32:59.921948     7 attempting connection: 127.0.0.1:8080
09:32:59.921948    14 made connection: &net.TCPConn{conn:net.conn{fd:(
                      *net.netFD)(0xc0000cc280)}}
09:32:59.921948     7 made connection: &net.TCPConn{conn:net.conn{fd:(
                      *net.netFD)(0xc000298c80)}}
09:32:59.921948    20 accepted connection: &net.TCPConn{conn:net.conn{fd:(
                      *net.netFD)(0xc00021a500)}}
09:32:59.921948    14 sent command: Saying, count=7
09:32:59.921948     7 sent command: Saying, count=7
09:32:59.921948    56 handleConnection request: Saying~, nest: 1,
                      conn: &net.TCPConn{conn:net.conn{fd:(*net.netFD)
                      (0xc00021a500)}}
09:32:59.921948    56 received command: Saying
09:32:59.921948    20 accepted connection: &net.TCPConn{conn:net.conn{fd:(
                      *net.netFD)(0xc00021a780)}}
09:32:59.921948    36 handleConnection request: Saying~, nest: 2,
                      conn: &net.TCPConn{conn:net.conn{fd:(*net.netFD)
                      (0xc00021a780)}}
09:32:59.921948    36 received command: Saying
09:33:00.219828    19 SocketClientGo response: Now is the time...~
09:33:00.314614    19 SocketClientGo response: I'm busy.~
09:33:00.924919    19 SocketClientGo request 6 of 10
09:33:00.924919    10 attempting connection: 127.0.0.1:8080
09:33:00.924919    20 accepted connection: &net.TCPConn{conn:net.conn{fd:(
                      *net.netFD)(0xc00021ac80)}}
09:33:00.924919    10 made connection: &net.TCPConn{conn:net.conn{fd:(
                      *net.netFD)(0xc00021aa00)}}
09:33:00.924919    10 sent command: TOD, count=4
09:33:00.924919    38 handleConnection request: TOD~, nest: 1, conn:
                      &net.TCPConn{conn:net.conn{fd:(*net.netFD)
                      (0xc00021ac80)}}
09:33:00.924919    38 received command: TOD
```

```
09:33:01.316527      19 SocketClientGo response: 2020-12-29 09:33:01.
                        3165274 -0800 PST m=+3.408983501~
09:33:01.911216      19 SocketClientGo request 4 of 10
09:33:01.911216       8 attempting connection: 127.0.0.1:8080
09:33:01.911216      20 accepted connection: &net.TCPConn{conn:net.conn{fd:(
                        *net.netFD)(0xc000316780)}}
09:33:01.911216       8 made connection: &net.TCPConn{conn:net.conn{fd:(
                        *net.netFD)(0xc000316500)}}
09:33:01.911216       8 sent command: Saying, count=7
09:33:01.911216      85 handleConnection request: Saying~, nest: 1,
                        conn: &net.TCPConn{conn:net.conn{fd:(*net.netFD)
                        (0xc000316780)}}
09:33:01.911216      85 received command: Saying
09:33:02.349666      19 SocketClientGo response: I'm busy.~
```

Note the volume and complexity of the output, even for this simple scenario. The amount of information from logging can quickly get out of hand. This is typical of logs from server programs that handle many requests, especially at cloud scale. One often uses specialized search programs, such as *Elasticsearch* and *Kibana*,[16] often combined with tools like *Fluentd*,[17] to view such logs.

The HTTP Template Package

The template package provides services to generate HTML text safely (HTML escapes are added as needed) and including dynamic values. The template sub-package in the text package can be used for simpler text, like an email message. Go has a default template engine. Java does not have a standard template engine, but the Java community provides several.[18]

A template is a string with some embedded replacements in it. All other text in the template is output as is. A replacement (aka *directive*) has this form: {{ ... }}, where

---

[16] www.elastic.co/guide/en/kibana/current/introduction.html

[17] https://en.wikipedia.org/wiki/Fluentd

[18] Some are described here: https://dzone.com/articles/template-engines-at-one-spring-boot-and-engines-se. Also, any JEE Java Server Page (JSP) engine such as Apache *Tomcat* (http://tomcat.apache.org/).

the ... is replaced with one of several options including conditional or repeated output and calling Go code to generate output. One can even format an embedded template. The possibilities are rich. Fully explaining template capabilities is beyond the scope of this book. See the Go package documentation for a deeper explanation.

Templates evaluate in some context, often provided by a struct or map instance. This is best demonstrated by an example:

```go
var tformat = time.RFC850

type Purchase struct {
    FirstName, LastName string
    Address string
    Phone string
    Age float32
    Male bool
    Item string
    ShipDate string
}

var purchases = []Purchase{
    {LastName:"Feigenbaum", ShipDate: time.Now().Format(tformat),
        Male:true, Item:"Go for Java Programmers"},
      //...
}

const purchaseTemplate = `
Dear {{ if .Male}}Mr.{{ else }}Ms.{{ end }} {{.LastName}},
Your purchase request for "{{ .Item }}" has been received.
It will be shipped on {{ .ShipDate }}.
Thank you for your purchase.
`

func runTemplate(p *Purchase, f *os.File, t *template.Template) (err error)
{
    err = t.Execute(f, *p)
    return
}
```

```go
func genTemplate(prefix string)  {
    t := template.Must(template.New("purchases").Parse(purchaseTemplate))
    for i, p := range purchases {
        f, err := os.Create(fmt.Sprintf("%s-%d.tmpl",prefix, i) )
        if err != nil {
            log.Fatalf("failed to create file, cause:", err)
        }
        err = runTemplate(&p, f, t)
        if err != nil {
            log.Fatalf("failed to run template, cause:", err)
        }
    }
}
```

Here, the input purchase value provides the values to replace in the various replacements. Calling genTemplate with a path prefix generates a file (/tmp/example-0. tmpl) with content:

```
Dear Mr. Feigenbaum,
Your purchase request for "Go for Java Programmers" has been received.
It will be shipped on Friday, 07-May-21 06:19:24 PDT.
Thank you for your purchase.
```

It is important to note that templates can be in memory or stored externally, such as in files. This makes them act much like the *Java Server Page*[19] (JSP) templates defined in Jakarta Enterprise Edition. JSPs get dynamically converted to Java *Servlets*[20] and then run. Go templates are always interpreted. This can make the Java (servlet) way more efficient for large volumes of work but more costly for small volumes.

As an example, here is a complete HTTP server that can render a single template. It can be easily extended to render multiple templates, say one per request handler.

Assume there is a file "tod.tmpl" with the following HTML-like text as its content:

```
<!DOCTYPE HTML>
<html>
```

---

[19] https://en.wikipedia.org/wiki/Jakarta_Server_Pages
[20] https://en.wikipedia.org/wiki/Jakarta_Servlet

```
<head><title>Date and Time</title></head>
<body>
<p>Date and Time:</p>
<br><br>
<sl>
<li>The date is <big>{{ .TOD | formatDate }}</big>
<li>The time is <big>{{ .TOD | formatTime }}</big>
</sl>
</body>
</html>
```

The complete code to consume it is shown in Listing 16-2.

Listing 16-2. Time Server Implementation

```go
package main
import (
    "fmt"
    "io/ioutil"
    "log"
    "net/http"
    "text/template"
    "time"
)
var functionMap = template.FuncMap{
    "formatDate": formatDate,
    "formatTime": formatTime,
}
var parsedTodTemplate *template.Template

func loadTemplate(path string) {
    parsedTodTemplate = template.New("tod")
    parsedTodTemplate.Funcs(functionMap)
    data, err := ioutil.ReadFile(path)
    if err != nil {
        log.Panicf("failed reading template %s: %v", path, err)
    }
```

```go
    if _, err := parsedTodTemplate.Parse(string(data)); err != nil {
        log.Panicf("failed parsing template %s: %v", path, err)
    }
}
func formatDate(dt time.Time) string {
    return dt.Format("Mon Jan _2 2006")
}
func formatTime(dt time.Time) string {
    return dt.Format("15:04:05 MST")
}

type TODData struct {
    TOD time.Time
}

func processTODRequest(w http.ResponseWriter, req *http.Request) {
    var data = &TODData{time.Now()}
    parsedTodTemplate.Execute(w, data) // assume cannot fail
}

var serverPort = 8085

func timeServer() {
    loadTemplate( `C:\Temp\tod.tmpl`)
    http.HandleFunc("/tod", processTODRequest)
    spec := fmt.Sprintf(":%d", serverPort)
    if err := http.ListenAndServe(spec, nil); err != nil {
        log.Fatalf("failed to start server on port %s: %v", spec, err)
    }
    log.Println("server exited")
}

func main() {
    timeServer()
}
```

Note error handling is not complete.

A request like http://localhost:8085/tod produces output as shown in Figure 16-1.

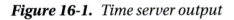

Date and Time:

- The date is Mon Jul 19 2021
- The time is 07:03:48 PDT

Figure 16-1. *Time server output*

The Net.HTTP Package

The net.http package is very large. It provides basic services for HTTP access over TCP/IP. It makes creating HTTP clients and servers, especially REST-like servers, relatively easy. As demonstrated earlier, combined with Go templates, it can make serving variable HTML content (much like servlets in Java can do) easy. Static HTML, CSS, JS, etc. content in files can also be easily served. Go 1.16 adds the ability to access static content bundled within the executable; this allows a full-featured web server to be built into a single distributable file. See the Go 1.16 release notes for more details.

The http package provides constants for the various HTTP methods and status codes. It has these key variables:

- var DefaultClient – Used by built-in Head, Get, and Post methods

- var DefaultServeMux – ServeMux used by the Serve method when no override is provided

- var NoBody – An empty body

The http package provides these functions. Some are self-explanatory:

- func CanonicalHeaderKey(s string) string – Return a canonical header name

- func DetectContentType(data []byte) string – Educated guess at the content type

- func Error(w ResponseWriter, error string, code int) – Return an HTTP error

- func Handle(pattern string, handler Handler) – Register a request handler

- func HandleFunc(pattern string, handler func(ResponseWriter, *Request)) – Register a handler function

- func ListenAndServe(addr string, handler Handler) error – Begin accepting HTTP requests

- func ListenAndServeTLS(addr, certFile, keyFile string, handler Handler) error – Begin accepting HTTP and HTTPS requests

- func MaxBytesReader(w ResponseWriter, r io.ReadCloser, n int64) io.ReadCloser – Make a limited reader

- func NotFound(w ResponseWriter, r *Request) – Return an HTTP 404

- func ParseHTTPVersion(vers string) (major, minor int, ok bool)

- func ParseTime(text string) (t time.Time, err error)

- func ProxyFromEnvironment(req *Request) (*url.URL, error) – Return a proxy URL if any

- func Redirect(w ResponseWriter, r *Request, url string, code int) – Return a redirect response

- func Serve(l net.Listener, handler Handler) error – Accept HTTP requests; process each in a new goroutine

- func ServeContent(w ResponseWriter, req *Request, name string, modtime time.Time, content io.ReadSeeker) – Return supplied content (often a file's content)

- func ServeFile(w ResponseWriter, r *Request, name string) – Read and serve a file/directory

- func ServeTLS(l net.Listener, handler Handler, certFile, keyFile string) error – Serve HTTP and HTTPS

- func SetCookie(w ResponseWriter, cookie *Cookie) – Set a response cookie

- func StatusText(code int) string – Get text of HTTP status code

Client supports HTTP clients. It provides these functions. Some are self-explanatory:

- func (c *Client) CloseIdleConnections()

- func (c *Client) Do(req *Request) (*Response, error) – Send/receive a request

- func (c *Client) Get(url string) (resp *Response, err error) – Do a GET

- func (c *Client) Head(url string) (resp *Response, err error) – Do a HEAD

- func (c *Client) Post(url, contentType string, body io.Reader) (resp *Response, err error) – Do a POST with a body

- func (c *Client) PostForm(url string, data url.Values) (resp *Response, err error) – Do a POST with 0+ form values

CloseNotifier allows notification when a connection is closed.

ConnState allows observation of a connection.

Cookie represents an HTTP cookie.

CookieJar represents a set of cookies.

Dir allows access to directories.

- func (d Dir) Open(name string) (File, error)

File allows access to a file.

FileSystem allows access to multiple static files. It makes implementing a static content (say images, HTML, CSS, etc.) server easy.

Handlers respond to HTTP requests. They provide these functions:

- func FileServer(root FileSystem) Handler

- func NotFoundHandler() Handler

- func RedirectHandler(url string, code int) Handler

- func StripPrefix(prefix string, h Handler) Handler

- func TimeoutHandler(h Handler, dt time.Duration, msg string) Handler

HandlerFuncs respond to HTTP requests. They provide these functions:

- func (f HandlerFunc) ServeHTTP(w ResponseWriter, r *Request)

Header represents an HTTP request/response header:

- func (h Header) Add(key, value string)

- func (h Header) Clone() Header

- func (h Header) Del(key string)

- func (h Header) Get(key string) string

- func (h Header) Set(key, value string)

- func (h Header) Values(key string) []string

- func (h Header) Write(w io.Writer) error

- func (h Header) WriteSubset(w io.Writer, exclude map[string]bool) error – Writes selected headers

Request represents a client request. It provides these functions. Many use the request's fields:

- func NewRequest(method, url string, body io.Reader) (*Request, error) – Make a request

- func NewRequestWithContext(ctx context.Context, method, url string, body io.Reader) (*Request, error) – Make a request with a context

- func ReadRequest(b *bufio.Reader) (*Request, error) – Parse a request

- func (r *Request) AddCookie(c *Cookie) – Add a cookie

- func (r *Request) BasicAuth() (username, password string, ok bool) – Get credentials from a request using basic authentication

- func (r *Request) Clone(ctx context.Context) *Request – Make a clone in a new context

- func (r *Request) Context() context.Context

- func (r *Request) Cookie(name string) (*Cookie, error)

- func (r *Request) Cookies() []*Cookie

- func (r *Request) FormFile(key string) (multipart.File, *multipart. FileHeader, error)

- func (r *Request) FormValue(key string) string

- func (r *Request) MultipartReader() (*multipart.Reader, error)

- func (r *Request) ParseForm() error – Sets fields form data

- func (r *Request) ParseMultipartForm(maxMemory int64) error – Sets fields form data

- func (r *Request) PostFormValue(key string) string – Sets fields form data

- func (r *Request) ProtoAtLeast(major, minor int) bool – Test a protocol version at least

- func (r *Request) Referer() string

- func (r *Request) SetBasicAuth(username, password string)

- func (r *Request) UserAgent() string

- func (r *Request) WithContext(ctx context.Context) *Request

- func (r *Request) Write(w io.Writer) error

- func (r *Request) WriteProxy(w io.Writer) error

Response represents a server response and HTTP operations:

- func Get(url string) (resp *Response, err error) – Do a GET request

- func Head(url string) (resp *Response, err error) – Do a HEAD request

- func Post(url, contentType string, body io.Reader) (resp *Response, err error) – Do a POST request with a body

- func PostForm(url string, data url.Values) (resp *Response, err error) – Do a POST request with form data

- func ReadResponse(r *bufio.Reader, req *Request) (*Response, error) – Do a HTTP request; make a response

- func (r *Response) Cookies() []*Cookie

- func (r *Response) Location() (*url.URL, error)

- func (r *Response) ProtoAtLeast(major, minor int) bool

- func (r *Response) Write(w io.Writer) error – Send a response

RoundTripper encapsulates send/receive transactions based on different protocols:

- func NewFileTransport(fs FileSystem) RoundTripper

ServeMux decodes incoming requests:

- func NewServeMux() *ServeMux – Make a decoder

- func (mux *ServeMux) Handle(pattern string, handler Handler) – Decode a request

- func (mux *ServeMux) HandleFunc(pattern string, handler func(ResponseWriter, *Request)) – Decode a request

- func (mux *ServeMux) Handler(r *Request) (h Handler, pattern string) – Receives a request

- func (mux *ServeMux) ServeHTTP(w ResponseWriter, r *Request) – Starts an HTTP server

Server provides basic HTTP server behavior:

- func (srv *Server) Close() error – Stop request processing

- func (srv *Server) ListenAndServe() error – Start serving HTTP

- func (srv *Server) ListenAndServeTLS(certFile, keyFile string) error – Start serving HTTP and HTTPS

- func (srv *Server) RegisterOnShutdown(f func()) – Register a shutdown callback

- func (srv *Server) Serve(l net.Listener) error – Start serving HTTP

- func (srv *Server) ServeTLS(l net.Listener, certFile, keyFile string) error – Start serving HTTP and HTTPS

- func (srv *Server) Shutdown(ctx context.Context) error – Shut down request processing

Transport provides a round-trip data movement. It manages the state of connections between clients and servers. It configures TCP connections:

- func (t *Transport) CancelRequest(req *Request)

- func (t *Transport) Clone() *Transport

- func (t *Transport) CloseIdleConnections()

- func (t *Transport) RegisterProtocol(scheme string, rt RoundTripper) – Register a protocol handler

- func (t *Transport) RoundTrip(req *Request) (*Response, error)

An example of a complete but low function HTTP REST-like server is shown in Listing 16-3.

Listing 16-3. Basic Hello World, Time and File HTTP Server

```go
package main

import (
    "fmt"
    "io"
    "log"
    "net/http"
    "strings"
    "time"
)

func greet(w http.ResponseWriter, req *http.Request) {
    if req.Method != "GET" {
        http.Error(w, fmt.Sprintf("Method %s not supported",
        req.Method), 405)
        return
    }
    var name string
    if err := req.ParseForm(); err == nil {
        name = strings.TrimSpace(req.FormValue("name"))
    }
```

```go
    if len(name) == 0 {
        name = "World"
    }
    w.Header().Add(http.CanonicalHeaderKey("content-type"),
        "text/plain")
    io.WriteString(w, fmt.Sprintf("Hello %s!\n", name))
}

func now(w http.ResponseWriter, req *http.Request) {
    // request checks like in greet
    w.Header().Add(http.CanonicalHeaderKey("content-type"),
        "text/plain")
    io.WriteString(w, fmt.Sprintf("%s", time.Now()))
}

func main() {
    fs := http.FileServer(http.Dir(`/temp`))

    http.HandleFunc("/greet", greet)
    http.HandleFunc("/now", now)
    http.Handle( "/static/", http.StripPrefix( "/static", fs ) )
    log.Fatal(http.ListenAndServe(":8088", nil))
}
```

This provides two paths:

1) Greet – Returns a greeting for the supplied name

2) Now – Returns the server's current time

And it serves them on port 8080.

Some sample results are shown in Figures 16-2, 16-3, and 16-4.

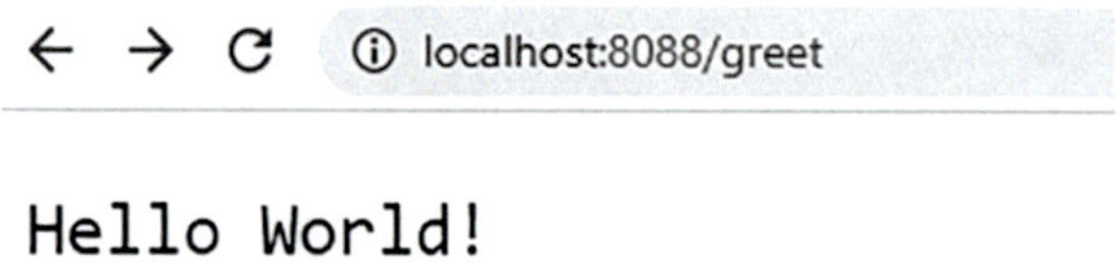

Hello World!

Figure 16-2. *Hello server response*

← → C ⓘ localhost:8088/now

`2021-07-20 13:33:56.2099208 -0700 PDT m=+0.111657601`

Figure 16-3. *Time server response*

← → C   ⓘ localhost:8088/static/show.txt

`Now is the time.`

Figure 16-4. *File server response 1*

Or for an unknown file, see Figure 16-5.

← → C   ⓘ localhost:8088/static/x

`404 page not found`

Figure 16-5. *File server response 2*

But if an invalid HTTP method is used, see Figure 16-6.

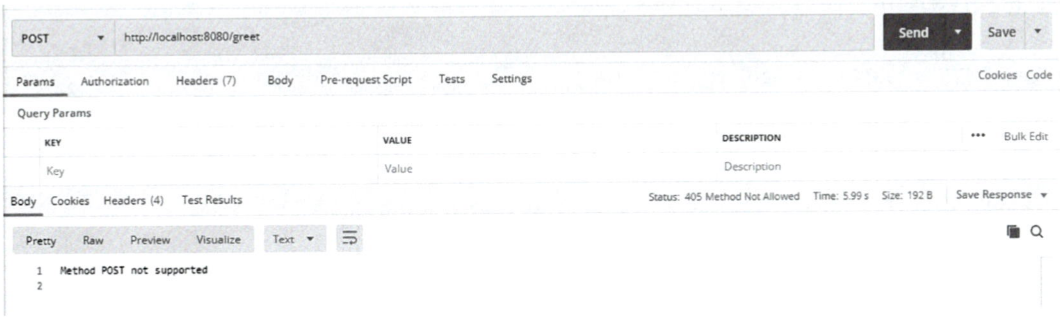

Figure 16-6. *Bad request response*

The handlers (by default) return HTTP 200 responses with a `text/plain` content type. The handlers are saved by `HandleFunc` in a global list that the `nil` value passed to `ListenAndServer` (LnS) uses. If the server cannot start (say port 8080 is already in use), the server program ends with an error; otherwise, the LnS function does not return.

The server will process incoming requests until terminated by the operating system. Each request is run in its own goroutine, so the server is highly performant, and the server can handle many concurrent requests.

The http package offers a simple-to-use file server. One has been included in the preceding sample server code with the static route. It can be used as shown in Figure 16-7.

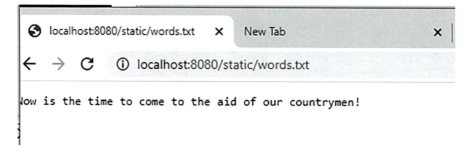

Figure 16-7. *File server sample output; service the content of a text file*

This feature can be used to serve static content like HTTP, CSS, images, JavaScript, etc. Care must be taken to not share data that is private to the server.

As a sample of the similarity of Go to Node.js, consider this similar (only one function and with no error checking) equivalent, which is run by the Node.js engine. The following is written in JavaScript:

```
const http = require('http');
const os = require('os');
var todHandler = function(req, resp) {
    resp.writeHead(200);
    resp.end(new Date().toString());
}
var server = http.createServer(todHandler);
server.listen(8080);
```

URL Package

The url package is a net sub-package that provides URL parsing and processing.

It has these functions and types:

- func PathEscape(s string) string – URL escape a path

- func PathUnescape(s string) (string, error) – Reverse an escape

- func QueryEscape(s string) string – URL escape a query string

- func QueryUnescape(s string) (string, error) – Reverse an escape

URL provides functions on a URL. Most functions get/test parts of a parsed URL:

- func Parse(rawurl string) (*URL, error) – Parse any URL

- func ParseRequestURI(rawurl string) (*URL, error) – Parse a URL; no fragment allowed

- func (u *URL) EscapedFragment() string

- func (u *URL) EscapedPath() string

- func (u *URL) Hostname() string

- func (u *URL) IsAbs() bool

- func (u *URL) Parse(ref string) (*URL, error) – Parse in context of this URL

- func (u *URL) Port() string

- func (u *URL) Query() Values

- func (u *URL) Redacted() string

- func (u *URL) RequestURI() string

- func (u *URL) ResolveReference(ref *URL) *URL – Resolve in context of this URL

Userinfo provides user credentials:

- func User(username string) *Userinfo

- func UserPassword(username, password string) *Userinfo

- func (u *Userinfo) Password() (string, bool)

- func (u *Userinfo) Username() string

Values provides functions to get/use path and query parameters:

- func ParseQuery(query string) (Values, error) – Parse query params into values

- func (v Values) Add(key, value string) – Add a value to a key's values

- func (v Values) Del(key string) – Remove a key

- func (v Values) Encode() string – URL encode values

- func (v Values) Get(key string) string – Get the first value of a key

- func (v Values) Set(key, value string) – Reset a key's value

CHAPTER 17

Go Runtime

This chapter surveys several Go packages related to the Go runtime.

Errors Package

The errors package provides functions to help create and select errors. Many community extensions, some drop-in replacements, exist.

There is a built-in error type. All errors implement this predefined interface:

```
type error interface {
    Error() string
}
```

This means any type that conforms to this interface (i.e., has the Error method) can be used as an error. This means many custom errors can be created. Many Go packages provide custom errors, often including supplemental information about the failure. For example, consider the os.PathError type:

```
type PathError struct {
    Op string     // failed operation
    Path string   // failed on path
    Err error     // root cause, if any
}
```

All custom errors need to implement the error interface, such as this possibility for the preceding error:

```
func (pe *PathError) Error() string {
    if pe.Err == nil {
        return fmt.Sprintf("PathError %s:%s", pe.Op, pe.Path)
    }
```

479

© Barry Feigenbaum 2022

B. Feigenbaum, *Go for Java Programmers*, https://doi.org/10.1007/978-1-4842-7199-5_17

```
    return fmt.Sprintf("PathError %s:%s:%v", pe.Op, pe.Path, pe.Err.
    Error())
}
```

Custom error types can be any base type, not just structs, such as strings. For example:

```
type MyError string

func (me MyError) Error() string {
    return string(me)
}
```

The errors package has these functions:

- func As(err error, target interface{}) bool – Convert to the target type if of target type; a target is a pointer to a location to receive the cast error.

- func Is(err, target error) bool – Test if err of target type.

- func New(text string) error – Makes an error.

- func Unwrap(err error) error – Get a wrapped error cause if available; err must have an Unwrap() method.

Often, errors are declared as top-level values. This lets them be tested for equality or used with the preceding functions against returned errors. For example:

```
var (
    ErrSystem = errors.New("System Error")
    ErrIO = errors.New("I/O Error")
    ErrOther = errors.New("Other Error")
        :
)
```

Flag Package

The flag package implements a simple but standardized means to parse command lines. Often, parameters are binary switches (aka *flags* and thus the package name). Many community extensions exist.

The flag package works mostly as a global library as it assumes there is a single command line to parse. Various possible command-line values are defined, then the command line is parsed to look for these values, and any found are set. Also provided is a help feature to describe the arguments. There are several options in the way values are defined. In general, don't mix the Xxx and XxxVar (where Xxx is a type name) styles; use them consistently.

Some example flag definitions:

```go
var iflag int
var fflag float64
var sflag string
func init() {
    flag.IntVar(&iflag, "IntFlag", 1, "IntFlag sets ...")
    flag.Float64Var(&fflag, "FloatFlag", 1.0, "FloatFlag sets ...")
    flag.StringVar(&sflag, "StringFlag", "", "StringFlag sets ...")
}
```

Note the flags are defined in an init function and thus are defined before the Parse function is called, typically in a main function.

Flags look like one of these options on a command line:

- -flag

- -flag=x

- -flag x - flag must not be of Boolean type

The flag package provides this key variable:
var CommandLine – Default access to os.Args
The flag package provides these types:

- ErrorHandling – Enums to control how errors are handled

- Flag – The state of a flag, including the current value

- FlagSet – A collection of flags, generally one per possible flags

The flag package provides these functions. They access a global flag set:

- func Arg(i int) string – Returns the ith non-flag argument

- func Args() []string – Returns all non-flag arguments

- func Bool(name string, value bool, usage string) *bool – Make a Boolean flag

- func BoolVar(p *bool, name string, value bool, usage string) – Wrap p as a flag

- func Duration(name string, value time.Duration, usage string) *time.Duration – Make a duration flag

- func DurationVar(p *time.Duration, name string, value time.Duration, usage string) – Wrap p as a flag

- func Float64(name string, value float64, usage string) *float64 – Make a float flag

- func Float64Var(p *float64, name string, value float64, usage string) – Wrap p as a flag

- func Int(name string, value int, usage string) *int – Make an int flag

- func Int64(name string, value int64, usage string) *int64 – Make an int64 flag

- func Int64Var(p *int64, name string, value int64, usage string) – Wrap p as a flag

- func IntVar(p *int, name string, value int, usage string) – Wrap p as a flag

- func NArg() int – Number of non-flag arguments

- func NFlag() int – Number of flag arguments

- func Parse() – Parse the command line and set args and flags after all flags are defined

- func Parsed() bool – Test if parsed

- func PrintDefaults() – Describe defaults to the user

- func Set(name, value string) error – Sets value for a flag

- func String(name string, value string, usage string) *string – Make a string flag

- func StringVar(p *string, name string, value string, usage string) – Wrap p as a flag

- func Uint(name string, value uint, usage string) *uint – Make a uint flag

- func Uint64(name string, value uint64, usage string) *uint64 – Make a uint64 flag

- func Uint64Var(p *uint64, name string, value uint64, usage string) – Wrap p as a flag

- func UintVar(p *uint, name string, value uint, usage string) – Wrap p as a flag

- func UnquoteUsage(flag *Flag) (name string, usage string) – Get a flag's description

- func Var(value Value, name string, usage string) – Make a generic flag

- func Visit(fn func(*Flag)) – Apply f to all set flags

- func VisitAll(fn func(*Flag)) – Apply f to all flags

A Flag has this function:

- func Lookup(name string) *Flag – Get defined flag by name

A FlagSet has these functions. Many are the same as described earlier and will not be redescribed:

- func NewFlagSet(name string, errorHandling ErrorHandling) *FlagSet

- func (f *FlagSet) Arg(i int) string

- func (f *FlagSet) Args() []string

- func (f *FlagSet) Bool(name string, value bool, usage string) *bool

- func (f *FlagSet) BoolVar(p *bool, name string, value bool, usage string)

- func (f *FlagSet) Duration(name string, value time.Duration, usage string) *time.Duration

- func (f *FlagSet) DurationVar(p *time.Duration, name string, value time.Duration, usage string)

- func (f *FlagSet) ErrorHandling() ErrorHandling

- func (f *FlagSet) Float64(name string, value float64, usage string) *float64

- func (f *FlagSet) Float64Var(p *float64, name string, value float64, usage string)

- func (f *FlagSet) Init(name string, errorHandling ErrorHandling)

- func (f *FlagSet) Int(name string, value int, usage string) *int

- func (f *FlagSet) Int64(name string, value int64, usage string) *int64

- func (f *FlagSet) Int64Var(p *int64, name string, value int64, usage string)

- func (f *FlagSet) IntVar(p *int, name string, value int, usage string)

- func (f *FlagSet) Lookup(name string) *Flag

- func (f *FlagSet) NArg() int

- func (f *FlagSet) NFlag() int

- func (f *FlagSet) Name() string

- func (f *FlagSet) Output() io.Writer

- func (f *FlagSet) Parse(arguments []string) error

- func (f *FlagSet) Parsed() bool

- func (f *FlagSet) PrintDefaults()

- func (f *FlagSet) Set(name, value string) error

- func (f *FlagSet) SetOutput(output io.Writer)

- func (f *FlagSet) String(name string, value string, usage string) *string

- func (f *FlagSet) StringVar(p *string, name string, value string, usage string)

- func (f *FlagSet) Uint(name string, value uint, usage string) *uint

- func (f *FlagSet) Uint64(name string, value uint64, usage string) *uint64

- func (f *FlagSet) Uint64Var(p *uint64, name string, value uint64, usage string)

- func (f *FlagSet) UintVar(p *uint, name string, value uint, usage string)

- func (f *FlagSet) Var(value Value, name string, usage string)

- func (f *FlagSet) Visit(fn func(*Flag))

- func (f *FlagSet) VisitAll(fn func(*Flag))

The Go flags package is opinionated. It supports a restricted style of flags. Different operating system (OS) types may have different flag styles. Especially Windows that typically uses the forward slash ("/") character instead of the dash ("-") to introduce flags.

To make your programs match the OS styles, you may need to write code to parse the command line differently. The runtime.GOOS value can be used to determine the OS type. You may find community packages that can help here.

Log Package

The log package provides a simple logging feature. Many community extensions exist. Some are drop-in replacements, while others use different styles. Many community offerings consume (or façade) this logging feature. This package is something like the Java *Log4J*[1] or similar logging frameworks.

This package provides package-level logging functions. It also has a *Logger* interface with similar functions that any code can implement. It provides a formatted log prefix for any messages directed to some io.Writer, such as STDOUT. The details, such as date and time format, source file reference, etc., of the prefix string can be configured. Some log actions can raise a panic or exit the program.

---

[1] https://en.wikipedia.org/wiki/Log4j

In Java using Log4J, one would do this:

```
import ...Log4J.Logger;
static Logger log = Logger.getLogger(<myclass>.class);
:
log.trace("Program running...")
:
log.trace("Program done")
```

A basic Go log sequence is

```
import "log"
:
log.Print("Program running...")
:
log.Print("Program done")
```

Note this predefined logger logs to STDERR.

Similarly, if you have a Logger instance, you can configure it:

```
import "log"
var logger = log.New(<someWriter>, "<someLinePrefix>", <flags>)
:
logger.Print("Program running...")
:
logger.Print("Program done")
```

Either might output a line like the following depending on the configuration:

```
2021/01/01 00:00:00.123456 /x/y/x.go:100: Program running...
```

Note that there is no severity provided. Many third-party logging offerings add this and other statistics. See the following example.

Since logger creation takes a Writer as an argument, logging can be to many targets, including persistent ones like files. Clients (creators) of the Logger need to open and close such targets. For example, to log the output of a complete program:

```
var DefaultLogger log.Logger
var DefaultLoggerTarget os.File
```

```go
var DefaultLoggerTargetPath = "main.log"
    :
func main() {
        var f *os.File
        if f, err := os.Create(DefaultLoggerTargetPath); err != nil {
                log.Fatalf("Cannot create log file: %s\n",
                        DefaultLoggerTargetPath)
        }
        defer f.Close()
        DefaultLoggerTarget = f
        DefaultLogger = log.New(f, "main ", log.LstdFlags)
        defer DefaultLogger.Flush()
        DefaultLogger.Println("main starting...")
            :
        DefaultLogger.Flush()
            :
        DefaultLogger.Println("main done")
}
```

Note the logger is made a public top-level value so it can be accessed from all functions in the program. This is easier than passing the logger instance around the programs as a function argument. This example recreates the log each time the program is run. One can use the Open function (vs. Create) to (say) append to an existing log.

The log output may not be written until the program exits. If one exposes the created file as a public top-level value (as done in the example), a coder could use the Flush function on it to force the data to be written at other times.

As an example of using Go logging, Listing 17-1 shows a simple extension/wrapper to it as the Go community might provide. It provides a *Logger* interface that outputs leveled logging messages that any logging engine needs to implement. This logger is not API equivalent to the standard logger and is thus not a drop-in replacement.

The example provides a default engine implementation called DefaultLoggerImpl. There are helper functions that access the current state, including getting the id of the calling goroutine; this is something that the Go runtime does not provide a function to directly access.

Listing 17-1. Sample Logger Implementation

```go
type Logger interface {
        Error(format string, args ...interface{})
        Warn(format string, args ...interface{})
        Info(format string, args ...interface{})
        Debug(format string, args ...interface{})
        Trace(format string, args ...interface{})
}

type DefaultLoggerImpl struct{
        logger log.Logger
}
func (l *DefaultLoggerImpl) output(level, format string, args
...interface{}) {
        l.logger.Printf(fmt.Sprintf("%s %s %s\n",getCallerDetails(2,
        "-"),level, fmt.Sprintf(format, args...)))
}
func (l *DefaultLoggerImpl) Error(format string, args ...interface{}) {
        l.output("ERROR", format, args...)
}
func (l *DefaultLoggerImpl) Warn(format string, args ...interface{}) {
        l.output("WARN ", format, args...)
}
func (l *DefaultLoggerImpl) Info(format string, args ...interface{}) {
        l.output("INFO ", format, args...)
}
func (l *DefaultLoggerImpl) Debug(format string, args ...interface{}) {
        l.output("DEBUG", format, args...)
}
func (l *DefaultLoggerImpl) Trace(format string, args ...interface{}) {
        l.output("TRACE", format, args...)
}
```

```go
var DefaultLogger  *DefaultLoggerImpl

func init(){
    DefaultLogger = &DefaultLoggerImpl{}
    DefaultLogger.logger = log.New(os.Stdout, "GoBook ",
    log.LstdFlags|log.Lmicroseconds|log.LUTC)
}

// get details about the caller.
func getCallerDetails(level int, lead string) string {
    level++
    if pc, file, line, ok := runtime.Caller(level); ok {
        file = getName(file)
        goId := getGID()
        xlineCount := atomic.AddUint64(&lineCount, 1)
        lead = fmt.Sprintf("%7d go%-5d %08X %-40v@%4v", xlineCount,
        goId, pc, file, line)
    }
    return lead
}

var lineCount uint64

// Get the current goroutine id.
func getGID() (n uint64) {
    b := make([]byte, 64)
    b = b[:runtime.Stack(b, false)]
    b = bytes.TrimPrefix(b, []byte("goroutine "))
    b = b[:bytes.IndexByte(b, ' ')]
    n, _ = strconv.ParseUint(string(b), 10, 64)
    return
}

// Get the file name part.
func getName(file string) string {
    posn := strings.Index(file, src)
    if posn >= 0 {
        file = file[posn+len(src):]
```

```
        if strings.HasSuffix(file, goExtension) {
                file = file[0 : len(file)-len(goExtension)]
        }
    }
    return file
}

const src = "/src/"
const goExtension = ".go"
```

It can be used like this where logging is done in different goroutines, as shown in Listing 17-2.

Listing 17-2. Sample Logger Implementation Client

```
DefaultLogger.Trace("Hello %s!", "World")
var wg sync.WaitGroup
for i := 0; i < 10; i++ {
    wg.Add(1)
    go func(id int) {
        defer wg.Done()
        DefaultLogger.Info("Hello from goroutine %d!", id)
        time.Sleep( time.Duration(rand.Intn(2000)) * time.Millisecond)
        DefaultLogger.Info("Goodbye from goroutine %d!", id)
    }(i)
}
wg.Wait()
DefaultLogger.Trace("Goodbye %s!", "World")
```

This example produces an output like this:

```
GoBook 2020/12/18 15:21:57.365337        1 go1      004D6AE7 main/main
@ 122 TRACE Hello World!
GoBook 2020/12/18 15:21:57.366333        3 go15     004D6D97 main/main
@ 128 INFO  Hello from goroutine 9!
GoBook 2020/12/18 15:21:57.366333        5 go9      004D6D97 main/main
@ 128 INFO  Hello from goroutine 3!
```

```
GoBook 2020/12/18 15:21:57.366333          4 go6      004D6D97 main/main
@ 128 INFO  Hello from goroutine 0!
GoBook 2020/12/18 15:21:57.366333          2 go7      004D6D97 main/main
@ 128 INFO  Hello from goroutine 1!
GoBook 2020/12/18 15:21:57.366333          7 go10     004D6D97 main/main
@ 128 INFO  Hello from goroutine 4!
GoBook 2020/12/18 15:21:57.366333          9 go14     004D6D97 main/main
@ 128 INFO  Hello from goroutine 8!
GoBook 2020/12/18 15:21:57.366333          8 go11     004D6D97 main/main
@ 128 INFO  Hello from goroutine 5!
GoBook 2020/12/18 15:21:57.366333         10 go12     004D6D97 main/main
@ 128 INFO  Hello from goroutine 6!
GoBook 2020/12/18 15:21:57.366333          6 go8      004D6D97 main/main
@ 128 INFO  Hello from goroutine 2!
GoBook 2020/12/18 15:21:57.366333         11 go13     004D6D97 main/main
@ 128 INFO  Hello from goroutine 7!
GoBook 2020/12/18 15:21:57.426070         12 go7      004D6E84 main/main
@ 130 INFO  Goodbye from goroutine 1!
GoBook 2020/12/18 15:21:57.447973         13 go15     004D6E84 main/main
@ 130 INFO  Goodbye from goroutine 9!
GoBook 2020/12/18 15:21:57.447973         14 go10     004D6E84 main/main
@ 130 INFO  Goodbye from goroutine 4!
GoBook 2020/12/18 15:21:57.792721         15 go11     004D6E84 main/main
@ 130 INFO  Goodbye from goroutine 5!
GoBook 2020/12/18 15:21:57.822589         16 go8      004D6E84 main/main
@ 130 INFO  Goodbye from goroutine 2!
GoBook 2020/12/18 15:21:57.917368         17 go12     004D6E84 main/main
@ 130 INFO  Goodbye from goroutine 6!
GoBook 2020/12/18 15:21:58.674824         18 go13     004D6E84 main/main
@ 130 INFO  Goodbye from goroutine 7!
GoBook 2020/12/18 15:21:58.684779         19 go14     004D6E84 main/main
@ 130 INFO  Goodbye from goroutine 8!
GoBook 2020/12/18 15:21:59.228337         20 go6      004D6E84 main/main
@ 130 INFO  Goodbye from goroutine 0!
```

```
GoBook 2020/12/18 15:21:59.254222        21 go9      004D6E84 main/main
@ 130 INFO  Goodbye from goroutine 3!
GoBook 2020/12/18 15:21:59.254222        22 go1      004D6C2E main/main
@ 134 TRACE Goodbye World!
```

Note the different goroutine ids (go##). Having the goroutine id present in logging helps a lot when looking at traces of code that uses multiple goroutines. Otherwise, the logging can seem very jumbled and confusing.

The records are assigned line numbers when created, not when written to the console by the Go logger; thus, the line numbers do not always come out in sequential order because the goroutines do not run in any predictable order. Line numbers are generally sequential within a single goroutine.

The actual code location inside the executable is shown (in hexadecimal) of the logging caller. This can help in crashes. If the logging calls had come from different packages, that would be shown. In this case, all the logging called were done from the same package (main) and function (main). The calling line number is included.

The result of runtime.Stack(b, false) starts like the following text. This is how getGID() can access the id:

```
goroutine 1 [running]:
:
```

Note it is not guaranteed that the Stack method's output will not change in the future, thus rendering this code obsolete.

Math Package

The math package provides functions similar to the java.math package. Combined with Go's complex number type, that makes Go a stronger numeric processing language relative to Java. It provides useful constants and mathematical functions. The constants are E, Pi, Phi, Sqrt2, SqrtE, SqrtPi, SqrtPhi, Ln2, Log2E (1/Ln2), Ln10, Log10E (1/Ln10). Most are to at least 60 digits of precision.

The math package has several sub-packages:

- big provides a big integer (Int, much like java.math.BigInteger), a big float (Float, similar to but not the same as java.math. BigDecimal), and a Rational (Rat, no Java equivalent) number type.

- `bits` provide functions to count, access, and change bits in unsigned integer types.

- `cmplx` (note the odd name, this is because `complex` is a reserved word) provides useful constants and mathematical functions for the `complex` type.

- `rand` provides random number generation.

The `math` package provides these (self-explanatory) functions:

- func Gamma(x float64) float64

- func Hypot(p, q float64) float64

- func Ilogb(x float64) int

- func Inf(sign int) float64

- func IsInf(f float64, sign int) bool

- func IsNaN(f float64) (is bool)

- func J0(x float64) float64

- func J1(x float64) float64

- func Jn(n int, x float64) float64

- func Ldexp(frac float64, exp int) float64

- func Lgamma(x float64) (lgamma float64, sign int)

- func Log(x float64) float64

- func Log10(x float64) float64

- func Log1p(x float64) float64

- func Log2(x float64) float64

- func Logb(x float64) float64

- func Max(x, y float64) float64

- func Min(x, y float64) float64

- func Mod(x, y float64) float64

- func Modf(f float64) (int float64, frac float64)

- func NaN() float64

- func Nextafter(x, y float64) (r float64)

- func Nextafter32(x, y float32) (r float32)

- func Pow(x, y float64) float64

- func Pow10(n int) float64

- func Remainder(x, y float64) float64

- func Round(x float64) float64

- func RoundToEven(x float64) float64

- func Signbit(x float64) bool

- func Sin(x float64) float64

- func Sincos(x float64) (sin, cos float64)

- func Sinh(x float64) float64

- func Sqrt(x float64) float64

- func Tan(x float64) float64

- func Tanh(x float64) float64

- func Trunc(x float64) float64

- func Y0(x float64) float64

- func Y1(x float64) float64

- func Yn(n int, x float64) float64

As an example of using functions in the math package, Listing 17-3 shows a simple function plotting example:

Listing 17-3. Sample Plotting of a Math Function Client

```
var ErrBadRange = errors.New("bad range")

type PlotFunc func(in float64) (out float64)

// Print (to STDOUT) the plots of one or more functions.
func PlotPrinter(xsteps, ysteps int, xmin, xmax, ymin, ymax float64,
```

```
        fs ...PlotFunc) (err error) {
        xdiff, ydiff := xmax-xmin, ymax-ymin
        if xdiff <= 0 || ydiff <= 0 {
                err = ErrBadRange
                return
        }
        xstep, ystep := xdiff/float64(xsteps), ydiff/float64(ysteps)
        plots := make([][]float64, len(fs))
        for index, xf := range fs {
                plot := make([]float64, xsteps)
                plots[index] = plot
                err = DoPlot(plot, xf, xsteps, ysteps, xmin, xmax, ymin, ymax,
                xstep)
                if err != nil {
                        return
                }
        }
        PrintPlot(xsteps, ysteps, ymin, ymax, ystep, plots)
        return
}

// Plot the values of the supplied function.
func DoPlot(plot []float64, f PlotFunc, xsteps, ysteps int,
        xmin, xmax, ymin, ymax, xstep float64) (err error) {
        xvalue := xmin
        for i := 0; i < xsteps; i++ {
                v := f(xvalue)
                if v < ymin || v > ymax {
                        err = ErrBadRange
                        return
                }
                xvalue += xstep
                plot[i] = v
        }
        return
}
```

```go
// Print the plots of the supplied data.
func PrintPlot(xsteps, ysteps int, ymin float64, ymax float64, ystep
float64,
        plots [][]float64) {
    if xsteps <= 0 || ysteps <= 0 {
        return
    }
    middle := ysteps / 2
    for yIndex := 0; yIndex < ysteps; yIndex++ {
        fmt.Printf("%8.2f: ", math.Round((ymax-float64(yIndex)*yst
ep)*100)/100)
        ytop, ybottom := ymax-float64(yIndex)*ystep, ymax-
        float64(yIndex+1)*ystep
        for xIndex := 0; xIndex < xsteps; xIndex++ {
            pv := " "
            if yIndex == middle {
                pv = "-"
            }
            for plotIndex := 0; plotIndex < len(plots); plotIndex++ {
                v := plots[plotIndex][xIndex]
                if v <= ytop && v >= ybottom {
                    pv = string(markers[plotIndex%len(markers)])
                }
            }
            fmt.Print(pv)
        }
        fmt.Println()
    }
    fmt.Printf("%8.2f: ", math.Round((ymax-float64(ysteps+1)*yst
ep)*100)/100)
}

const markers = "*.^~-=+"
```

It is driven by this test function:

```go
func testPlotPrint() {
    err := PlotPrinter(100, 20, 0, 4*math.Pi, -1.5, 4,
        func(in float64) float64 {
            return math.Sin(in)
        }, func(in float64) float64 {
            return math.Cos(in)
        }, func(in float64) float64 {
            if in == 0 {
                return 0
            }
            return math.Sqrt(in) / in
        })
    if err != nil {
        fmt.Printf("plotting failed: %v", err)
    }
}
```

Note that three different function literals, which conform to the PlotFunc type, for different sample equations are passed.

This produces the output shown in Figure 17-1.

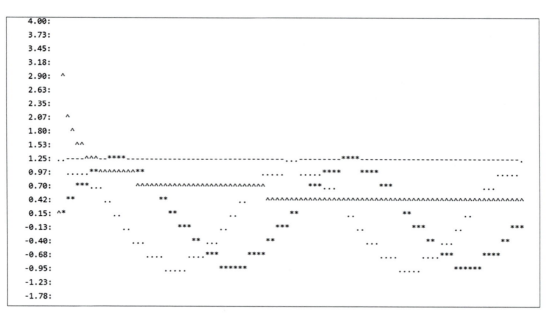

Figure 17-1. *Sample plotting of math functions output*

Note that three plots, using "^", ".", and "*" as markers, are superimposed on the graph. The middle of the graph (not the zero point) is marked with a line of dashes.

The big package provides these types:

- Float – An extended precision floating-point value

- Int – An extended (large) precision integer value

- Rat – A Rational number value composed of an int64 numerator and denominator

A Float type has these functions (most self-explanatory):

- func NewFloat(x float64) *Float

- func ParseFloat(s string, base int, prec uint, mode RoundingMode) (f *Float, b int, err error)

- func (z *Float) Abs(x *Float) *Float

- func (z *Float) Add(x, y *Float) *Float

- func (x *Float) Append(buf []byte, fmt byte, prec int) []byte

- func (x *Float) Cmp(y *Float) int – Compare

- func (z *Float) Copy(x *Float) *Float

- func (x *Float) Float32() (float32, Accuracy)

- func (x *Float) Float64() (float64, Accuracy)

- func (x *Float) Format(s fmt.State, format rune)

- func (x *Float) Int(z *Int) (*Int, Accuracy)

- func (x *Float) Int64() (int64, Accuracy)

- func (x *Float) IsInf() bool

- func (x *Float) IsInt() bool

- func (x *Float) MantExp(mant *Float) (exp int)

- func (x *Float) MinPrec() uint

- func (x *Float) Mode() RoundingMode

- func (z *Float) Mul(x, y *Float) *Float

- func (z *Float) Neg(x *Float) *Float

- func (z *Float) Parse(s string, base int) (f *Float, b int, err error)

- func (x *Float) Prec() uint

- func (z *Float) Quo(x, y *Float) *Float

- func (x *Float) Rat(z *Rat) (*Rat, Accuracy)

- func (z *Float) Scan(s fmt.ScanState, ch rune) error

- func (z *Float) Set(x *Float) *Float

- func (z *Float) SetFloat64(x float64) *Float

- func (z *Float) SetInf(signbit bool) *Float

- func (z *Float) SetInt(x *Int) *Float

- func (z *Float) SetInt64(x int64) *Float

- func (z *Float) SetMantExp(mant *Float, exp int) *Float

- func (z *Float) SetMode(mode RoundingMode) *Float

- func (z *Float) SetPrec(prec uint) *Float

- func (z *Float) SetRat(x *Rat) *Float

- func (z *Float) SetString(s string) (*Float, bool)

- func (z *Float) SetUint64(x uint64) *Float

- func (x *Float) Sign() int

- func (x *Float) Signbit() bool

- func (z *Float) Sqrt(x *Float) *Float

- func (x *Float) String() string

- func (z *Float) Sub(x, y *Float) *Float

- func (x *Float) Text(format byte, prec int) string

- func (x *Float) Uint64() (uint64, Accuracy)

An Int type has these functions (most self-explanatory):

- func NewInt(x int64) *Int

- func (z *Int) Abs(x *Int) *Int

- func (z *Int) Add(x, y *Int) *Int

- func (z *Int) And(x, y *Int) *Int

- func (z *Int) AndNot(x, y *Int) *Int

- func (x *Int) Append(buf []byte, base int) []byte

- func (z *Int) Binomial(n, k int64) *Int

- func (x *Int) Bit(i int) uint

- func (x *Int) BitLen() int

- func (x *Int) Bits() []Word

- func (x *Int) Bytes() []byte

- func (x *Int) Cmp(y *Int) (r int) – Compare

- func (x *Int) CmpAbs(y *Int) int – Compare absolute

- func (z *Int) Div(x, y *Int) *Int

- func (z *Int) DivMod(x, y, m *Int) (*Int, *Int)

- func (z *Int) Exp(x, y, m *Int) *Int

- func (x *Int) FillBytes(buf []byte) []byte

- func (x *Int) Format(s fmt.State, ch rune)

- func (z *Int) GCD(x, y, a, b *Int) *Int

- func (x *Int) Int64() int64

- func (x *Int) IsInt64() bool

- func (x *Int) IsUint64() bool

- func (z *Int) Lsh(x *Int, n uint) *Int

- func (z *Int) Mod(x, y *Int) *Int

- func (z *Int) ModInverse(g, n *Int) *Int

- func (z *Int) ModSqrt(x, p *Int) *Int

- func (z *Int) Mul(x, y *Int) *Int

- func (z *Int) MulRange(a, b int64) *Int

- func (z *Int) Neg(x *Int) *Int

- func (z *Int) Not(x *Int) *Int

- func (z *Int) Or(x, y *Int) *Int

- func (x *Int) ProbablyPrime(n int) bool

- func (z *Int) Quo(x, y *Int) *Int

- func (z *Int) QuoRem(x, y, r *Int) (*Int, *Int)

- func (z *Int) Rand(rnd *rand.Rand, n *Int) *Int

- func (z *Int) Rem(x, y *Int) *Int

- func (z *Int) Rsh(x *Int, n uint) *Int

- func (z *Int) Scan(s fmt.ScanState, ch rune) error

- func (z *Int) Set(x *Int) *Int

- func (z *Int) SetBit(x *Int, i int, b uint) *Int

- func (z *Int) SetBits(abs []Word) *Int

- func (z *Int) SetBytes(buf []byte) *Int

- func (z *Int) SetInt64(x int64) *Int

- func (z *Int) SetString(s string, base int) (*Int, bool)

- func (z *Int) SetUint64(x uint64) *Int

- func (x *Int) Sign() int

- func (z *Int) Sqrt(x *Int) *Int

- func (x *Int) String() string

- func (z *Int) Sub(x, y *Int) *Int

- func (x *Int) Text(base int) string

- func (x *Int) TrailingZeroBits() uint

- func (x *Int) Uint64() uint64

- func (z *Int) Xor(x, y *Int) *Int

As an example of using the Int type, consider the N! (N factorial) function. N! is defined:

- N < 0: undefined

- N == 0: 1

- N > 0: N * (N-1)!

Note that N!, as implemented in Listing 17-4, gets large very quickly as N increases. Even with small N (<< 100), the value exceeds what can be held in an uint64 (the biggest machine integer) type.

Listing 17-4. N! Function

```go
var ErrBadArgument = errors.New("invalid argument")

func factorial(n int) (res *big.Int, err error) {
    if n < 0 || n >= 1_000 {  // limit result and time
        err = ErrBadArgument
        return    // or raise panic
    }
```

```
    res = big.NewInt(1)
    for i := 2; i <= n; i++ {
        res = res.Mul(res, big.NewInt(int64(i)))
    }
    return
}
```

The sequence:

```
fact, _ := factorial(100)
fmt.Println("Factorial(100):", fact)
```

produces this output:

```
Factorial(100):  933262154439441526816992388562667004907159682643816214685
92963895217599993229915608941463976156518286253697920827223758251185210916
86400000000000000000000000000
```

A Rat type has these functions (most self-explanatory):

- func NewRat(a, b int64) *Rat
- func (z *Rat) Abs(x *Rat) *Rat
- func (z *Rat) Add(x, y *Rat) *Rat
- func (x *Rat) Cmp(y *Rat) int – Compare
- func (x *Rat) Denom() *Int
- func (x *Rat) Float32() (f float32, exact bool)
- func (x *Rat) Float64() (f float64, exact bool)
- func (x *Rat) FloatString(prec int) string
- func (z *Rat) GobDecode(buf []byte) error
- func (x *Rat) GobEncode() ([]byte, error)
- func (z *Rat) Inv(x *Rat) *Rat
- func (x *Rat) IsInt() bool
- func (z *Rat) Mul(x, y *Rat) *Rat

- func (z *Rat) Neg(x *Rat) *Rat

- func (x *Rat) Num() *Int

- func (z *Rat) Quo(x, y *Rat) *Rat

- func (x *Rat) RatString() string

- func (z *Rat) Scan(s fmt.ScanState, ch rune) error

- func (z *Rat) Set(x *Rat) *Rat

- func (z *Rat) SetFloat64(f float64) *Rat

- func (z *Rat) SetFrac(a, b *Int) *Rat

- func (z *Rat) SetFrac64(a, b int64) *Rat

- func (z *Rat) SetInt(x *Int) *Rat

- func (z *Rat) SetInt64(x int64) *Rat

- func (z *Rat) SetString(s string) (*Rat, bool)

- func (z *Rat) SetUint64(x uint64) *Rat

- func (x *Rat) Sign() int

- func (x *Rat) String() string

- func (z *Rat) Sub(x, y *Rat) *Rat

The cmplx package provides these (self-explanatory) functions:

- func Abs(x complex128) float64

- func Acos(x complex128) complex128

- func Acosh(x complex128) complex128

- func Asin(x complex128) complex128

- func Asinh(x complex128) complex128

- func Atan(x complex128) complex128

- func Atanh(x complex128) complex128

- func Conj(x complex128) complex128

- func Cos(x complex128) complex128

- func Cosh(x complex128) complex128

- func Cot(x complex128) complex128

- func Exp(x complex128) complex128

- func Inf() complex128

- func IsInf(x complex128) bool

- func IsNaN(x complex128) bool

- func Log(x complex128) complex128

- func Log10(x complex128) complex128

- func NaN() complex128

- func Phase(x complex128) float64

- func Polar(x complex128) (r, θ float64)

- func Pow(x, y complex128) complex128

- func Rect(r, θ float64) complex128

- func Sin(x complex128) complex128

- func Sinh(x complex128) complex128

- func Sqrt(x complex128) complex128

- func Tan(x complex128) complex128

- func Tanh(x complex128) complex128

The rand package provides these types:

- Rand – A random number generator.

- Source – A 63-bit seed source for random numbers; defaults to the same value on all executions, resulting in repeated "random" sequences; this differs from Java behavior.

The rand package provides these functions:

- func ExpFloat64() float64 – Get exponentially distributed value

- func Float32() float32 – Get [0.0, 1.0)

- func Float64() float64 – Get [0.0, 1.0)

- func Int() int

- func Int31() int32

- func Int31n(n int32) int32 – Get [0, n)

- func Int63() int64

- func Int63n(n int64) int64 – Get [0, n)

- func Intn(n int) int – Get [0, n)

- func NormFloat64() float64 – Get normally distributed value

- func Perm(n int) []int – Get permutation of [0.0, 1.0)

- func Read(p []byte) (n int, err error) – Read n bytes into p

- func Seed(seed int64)

- func Shuffle(n int, swap func(i, j int)) – Shuffle n items. Items access via swap closure

- func Uint32() uint32

- func Uint64() uint64

Note do not depend on the preceding generator functions to seed the generator randomly (say by process start time). You must do this yourself if needed. Without seeding, each execution of a Go program will repeat the same sequence of random values.

The Rand type provides these functions. See the previous list for explanations:

- func New(src Source) *Rand

- func (r *Rand) ExpFloat64() float64

- func (r *Rand) Float32() float32

- func (r *Rand) Float64() float64

- func (r *Rand) Int() int

- func (r *Rand) Int31() int32

- func (r *Rand) Int31n(n int32) int32

- func (r *Rand) Int63() int64

- func (r *Rand) Int63n(n int64) int64

- func (r *Rand) Intn(n int) int

- func (r *Rand) NormFloat64() float64

- func (r *Rand) Perm(n int) []int

- func (r *Rand) Read(p []byte) (n int, err error)

- func (r *Rand) Seed(seed int64)

- func (r *Rand) Shuffle(n int, swap func(i, j int))

- func (r *Rand) Uint32() uint32

- func (r *Rand) Uint64() uint64

The Source type provides this function:

- func NewSource(seed int64) Source

Operating System Support Packages

The os package provides access to operating system (OS) functionality in an OS-agnostic way. This is the preferred way to access these functions. This package has sub-packages:

- exec provides the ability to launch external processes as command-line style programs.

- signal provides the ability to watch for and capture operating system originated signals (aka interrupts).

- user provides access to operating system user and group accounts.

The path package provides utility functions to process operating system file system paths. It has one sub-package:

- filepath provides utility functions to parse and process operating system file paths.

The syscall package provides access to low-level operating system functions not provided by other packages. It is somewhat operating system type dependent, and thus its functions may not work the same on all OS types.

The os package has these types:

- File – Represents access to a file

- FileInfo – Represents metadata about a file

- FileMode – File access modes (as bit flags)

- Process – Represents an external process

- ProcessState – Represents a process exit status

The os package has these useful constants:

- PathSeparator – OS-specific file path separator

- PathListSeparator – OS-specific shell path list separator

The os package has these useful values:

- Stdin – File for/dev/stdin.

- Stdout – File for standard out.

- Stderr – File for standard err.

- Args – []string of command-line arguments; unlike in Java, argument 0 is the command that launched the program.

The os package has these functions. These are based on the Unix functions of the same name. Some functions may not work (say return useful values) on all operating system types, especially Microsoft Windows:

- func Chdir(dir string) error – Change the current directory

- func Chmod(name string, mode FileMode) error – Change file mode

- func Chown(name string, uid, gid int) error – Change the file owner

- func Chtimes(name string, atime time.Time, mtime time.Time) error – Change file times

- func Clearenv() – Clear the process environment

- func Environ() []string – Get the process environment

- func Executable() (string, error) – Get the active program path

- func Exit(code int) – Force exit of this process

- func Expand(s string, mapping func(string) string) string – Replace ${var},$vaR in string

- func ExpandEnv(s string) string – Replace ${var},$vaR in string using the environment

- func Getegid() int – Get the effective group id

- func Getenv(key string) string – Get the environment value by key

- func Geteuid() int – Get the effective user id

- func Getgid() int – Get the group id of the user

- func Getgroups() ([]int, error) – Get group ids the user belongs to

- func Getpagesize() int – Get the virtual memory page size

- func Getpid() int – Get the current process id

- func Getppid() int – Get the current process's parent id

- func Getuid() int – Get the user id

- func Getwd() (dir string, err error) – Get the working directory

- func Hostname() (name string, err error) – Get the system's hostname

- func IsExist(err error) bool – Tests error for "exists"

- func IsNotExist(err error) bool – Tests error for "not exists"

- func IsPathSeparator(c uint8) bool – Is c a path separator

- func IsPermission(err error) bool – Tests error for "permission issue"

- func IsTimeout(err error) bool – Tests error for "timeout"

- func Lchown(name string, uid, gid int) error – Change the owner of the file/link

- func Link(oldname, newname string) error – Create a hard link between files

- func LookupEnv(key string) (string, bool) – Get an environment value by key (name)

- func Mkdir(name string, perm FileMode) error – Make a directory

- func MkdirAll(path string, perm FileMode) error – Make all needed directories

- func Pipe() (r *File, w *File, err error) – Create a pipe between files

- func Readlink(name string) (string, error) – Reads a link

- func Remove(name string) error – Removes (deletes) a file or empty directory

- func RemoveAll(path string) error – Remove a directory tree

- func Rename(oldpath, newpath string) error – Change a file/directory name

- func SameFile(fi1, fi2 FileInfo) bool – Tests for the same file

- func Setenv(key, value string) error – Set an environment value

- func Symlink(oldname, newname string) error – Create a symbolic link between names

- func TempDir() string – Get the current temporary directory

- func Truncate(name string, size int64) error – Extend/shorten a file

- func Unsetenv(key string) error – Remove an environment key

- func UserCacheDir() (string, error) – Get the user cache directory

- func UserConfigDir() (string, error) – Get the user configuration directory

- func UserHomeDir() (string, error) – Get the user home directory

A File provides these functions:

- func Create(name string) (*File, error) – Create/truncate a file

- func Open(name string) (*File, error) – Open a file with default access

- func OpenFile(name string, flag int, perm FileMode) (*File, error) – Open a file

- func (f *File) Chdir() error – Make directory f the current directory

- func (f *File) Chmod(mode FileMode) error – Change file mode

- func (f *File) Chown(uid, gid int) error – Change the file owner

- func (f *File) Close() error – Close an open file

- func (f *File) Name() string – Get a file name

- func (f *File) Read(b []byte) (n int, err error) – Read from the current location in a file

- func (f *File) ReadAt(b []byte, off int64) (n int, err error) – Read from a location in a file

- func (f *File) Readdir(n int) ([]FileInfo, error) – Read directory entries

- func (f *File) Readdirnames(n int) (names []string, err error) – Read directory names

- func (f *File) Seek(offset int64, whence int) (ret int64, err error) – Set the current location

- func (f *File) Stat() (FileInfo, error) – Get file info

- func (f *File) Sync() error – Flush pending changes

- func (f *File) Truncate(size int64) error – Set the file length

- func (f *File) Write(b []byte) (n int, err error) – Write bytes at the current location

- func (f *File) WriteAt(b []byte, off int64) (n int, err error) – Write bytes at the location

- func (f *File) WriteString(s string) (n int, err error) – Write a string

A FileInfo provides these functions:

- func Lstat(name string) (FileInfo, error) – Get link/file info

- func Stat(name string) (FileInfo, error) – Get file info

A FileMode provides these functions:

- func (m FileMode) IsDir() bool – Test m represents a directory

- func (m FileMode) IsRegular() bool – Test m represents a regular file

- func (m FileMode) Perm() FileMode – Gets file mode

A Process provides these functions:

- func FindProcess(pid int) (*Process, error) – Find by process id

- func StartProcess(name string, argv []string, attr *ProcAttr) (*Process, error) – Create and start

- func (p *Process) Kill() error – Kill a running process

- func (p *Process) Release() error – Release resources if Wait not used

- func (p *Process) Signal(sig Signal) error – Send a signal (interrupt) to a process

- func (p *Process) Wait() (*ProcessState, error) – Wait for a process to end

A ProcessState provides these functions to access the state:

- func (p *ProcessState) ExitCode() int

- func (p *ProcessState) Exited() bool

- func (p *ProcessState) Pid() int

- func (p *ProcessState) Success() bool

- func (p *ProcessState) SystemTime() time.Duration

- func (p *ProcessState) UserTime() time.Duration

The exec package has these types and functions:

- func LookPath(file string) (string, error) – Look for an executable in the OS path; return a path

- func Command(name string, arg ...string) *Cmd – Make a command

- func CommandContext(ctx context.Context, name string, arg ...string) *Cmd – Make with context

The Cmd type has these functions:

- func (c *Cmd) CombinedOutput() ([]byte, error) – Run and get stdout and stderr

- func (c *Cmd) Output() ([]byte, error) – Run and get stdout

- func (c *Cmd) Run() error – Run

- func (c *Cmd) Start() error – Start

- func (c *Cmd) StderrPipe() (io.ReadCloser, error) – Connect a pipe to stderr

- func (c *Cmd) StdinPipe() (io.WriteCloser, error) – Connect a pipe to stdin

- func (c *Cmd) StdoutPipe() (io.ReadCloser, error) – Connect a pipe to stdout

- func (c *Cmd) Wait() error – Wait for the started command to end

Operating systems can send "signals" (asynchronous event notifications) when asked to by a user or program. Some programs may want to detect/intercept these signals. Go supports this via channels which are sent a message whenever a signal occurs.

These signals are always supported. Others may also be:

```
var Interrupt Signal = syscall.SIGINT
var Kill     Signal = syscall.SIGKILL
```

The signal package has these functions:

- func Ignore(sig ...os.Signal) – Ignore the signal

- func Ignored(sig os.Signal) bool – Test if ignored

- func Notify(c chan<- os.Signal, sig ...os.Signal) – Enable the signal to the channel

- func Reset(sig ...os.Signal) – Undoes a notify action

- func Stop(c chan<- os.Signal) – Similar to reset but by the channel

The user package allows access to users and user groups. Not all operating system types support these functions.

The group provides these functions:

- func LookupGroup(name string) (*Group, error) – Find by group name

- func LookupGroupId(gid string) (*Group, error) – Find by group id

The user provides these functions:

- func Current() (*User, error) – Get the current user

- func Lookup(username string) (*User, error) – Find by user name

- func LookupId(uid string) (*User, error) – Find by user id

- func (u *User) GroupIds() ([]string, error) – Get the groups a user belongs to

As an example of using the os package, here is a function to read the contents of a file and return it as a string:

```go
func ReadFile(filePath string) (text string, err error) {
    var f *os.File
    if f, err = os.Open(filePath); err != nil {
        return
    }
    defer f.Close()  // ensure closed
    var xtext []byte // accumulate result
    buffer := make([]byte, 16*1024)
    for { // read file in chunks
        n, xerr := f.Read(buffer)
        if xerr != nil {
            if xerr == io.EOF {
                break // EOF is OK error
            }
            err = xerr
            return
        }
        if n == 0 {
            continue
        }
        xtext = append(xtext, buffer[0:n]...)
    }
    text = string(xtext) // want as string
    return
}
```

Invoked by

```
text, err := ReadFile(`.../words.txt`)
if err!=nil {
      fmt.Printf("got: %v" , err)
      return
}
fmt.Printf("testFile: %q" , text)
produces:
```

```
testFile: "Now is the time to come to the aid of our countrymen!\r\n"
```

Reflection Package

The reflect package provides *reflection* (runtime type and data introspection and/or creation) capabilities that allows the processing of data of arbitrary type. It is similar in concept to the java.lang.reflect package.

Reflection is a complex subject (it could have its own book), and the detailed usage is beyond the scope of this text.

In Go, each discrete value (not necessarily each array, slice, or map element) has a runtime type associated with it. Go provides functions to query the type at runtime. It also allows values to be created and/or changed dynamically at runtime. In most cases, the value being queried is declared as an interface{} type and thus could be many different types at runtime:

```
var x interface{}
:
fmt.Printf("%v is of type %T\n", x, x)
```

This prints the current value and runtime type of the value in x.

A common thing to do via reflection is to test the type of a value. Functions like fmt.Sprintf() do this. Given

```
var values = []interface{}{0, 0.0, 0i, "", []int{}, map[int]int{},
    func() {}, }
```

one can test the types as follows:

```
for _, v := range values {
        switch v := reflect.ValueOf(v); v.Kind() {
        case reflect.Int, reflect.Int8, reflect.Int16, reflect.Int32,
        reflect.Int64:
                fmt.Println(v.Int())
        case reflect.Float32, reflect.Float64:
                fmt.Println(v.Float())
        case reflect.String:
                fmt.Println("-", v.String() , "-")
        default:
                fmt.Printf("other type %v: %v\n", v.Kind(), v)
        }
}
```

This produces the following:

```
0
0
other type complex128: (0+0i)
-  -
other type slice: []
other type map: map[]
other type func: 0x81baf0
```

The ValueOf() method is used to dereference a potential *T type into a T type (*T and T are considered different when testing types). A *kind* is an integer (enum) form of the type of the value.

The reflect package has two main types:

1. Type – Represents a type at runtime; returned by the reflect. TypeOf(interface{}) function

2. Value – Represents the value of an interface type at runtime; returned by the reflect.ValueOf(interface{}) function

To get the value of a Value, one must call one of the Value methods based on the value's kind. Asking for a value of the wrong kind can result in a panic.

516

Regular Expression Package

The regexp package provides an implementation of a *Regular Expression* (RE) parser and matcher. It is assumed the reader understands the concept of an RE. The particulars of the RE syntax and function are explained in the Go package documentation. Note many languages support REs, but most have subtle differences in how they work. This is true for Java vs. Go.

There are several variants of RE matching, using this (RE-like) pattern:

```
Xxxx(All)?(String)?(Submatch)?(Index)?
```

where when present

- All – Match all non-overlapping segments

- String – Match a string (vs. []byte)

- Submatch – Return capture groups per (...) in the pattern

- Index – Augment Submatch with the position of the match in the input

It provides these functions and types:

- func Match(pattern string, b []byte) (matched bool, err error)

- func MatchReader(pattern string, r io.RuneReader) (matched bool, err error)

- func MatchString(pattern string, s string) (matched bool, err error)

- func QuoteMeta(s string) string – Quote RE meta characters (e.g., * . ? +) in s

The Regexp type provides a regular expression engine:

- func Compile(expr string) (*Regexp, error) – Compile Go regex

- func CompilePOSIX(expr string) (*Regexp, error) – Compile POSIX regex

- func MustCompile(str string) *Regexp – Compile or panic

- func MustCompilePOSIX(str string) *Regexp – Compile or panic

- func (re *Regexp) Copy() *Regexp

- func (re *Regexp) Expand(dst []byte, template []byte, src []byte, match []int) []byte

- func (re *Regexp) ExpandString(dst []byte, template string, src string, match []int) []byte

- func (re *Regexp) Find(b []byte) []byte

- func (re *Regexp) FindAll(b []byte, n int) [][]byte

- func (re *Regexp) FindAllIndex(b []byte, n int) [][]int

- func (re *Regexp) FindAllString(s string, n int) []string

- func (re *Regexp) FindAllStringIndex(s string, n int) [][]int

- func (re *Regexp) FindAllStringSubmatch(s string, n int) [][]string

- func (re *Regexp) FindAllStringSubmatchIndex(s string, n int) [][]int

- func (re *Regexp) FindAllSubmatch(b []byte, n int) [][][]byte

- func (re *Regexp) FindAllSubmatchIndex(b []byte, n int) [][]int

- func (re *Regexp) FindIndex(b []byte) (loc []int)

- func (re *Regexp) FindReaderIndex(r io.RuneReader) (loc []int)

- func (re *Regexp) FindReaderSubmatchIndex(r io.RuneReader) []int

- func (re *Regexp) FindString(s string) string

- func (re *Regexp) FindStringIndex(s string) (loc []int)

- func (re *Regexp) FindStringSubmatch(s string) []string

- func (re *Regexp) FindStringSubmatchIndex(s string) []int

- func (re *Regexp) FindSubmatch(b []byte) [][]byte

- func (re *Regexp) FindSubmatchIndex(b []byte) []int

- func (re *Regexp) LiteralPrefix() (prefix string, complete bool) – Is prefix all of RE

- func (re *Regexp) Longest() – Modify RE to match longest

- func (re *Regexp) Match(b []byte) bool

- func (re *Regexp) MatchReader(r io.RuneReader) bool

- func (re *Regexp) MatchString(s string) bool

- func (re *Regexp) NumSubexp() int

- func (re *Regexp) ReplaceAll(src, repl []byte) []byte

- func (re *Regexp) ReplaceAllFunc(src []byte, repl func([]byte) []byte) []byte

- func (re *Regexp) ReplaceAllLiteral(src, repl []byte) []byte

- func (re *Regexp) ReplaceAllLiteralString(src, repl string) string

- func (re *Regexp) ReplaceAllString(src, repl string) string

- func (re *Regexp) ReplaceAllStringFunc(src string, repl func(string) string) string

- func (re *Regexp) Split(s string, n int) []string

- func (re *Regexp) SubexpIndex(name string) int

- func (re *Regexp) SubexpNames() []string

Go Runtime Packages

The runtime package contains functions that expose the Go runtime system. It is similar in role to the java.lang.System and java.lang.Runtime types. The runtime package has several sub-packages not covered in this text.

The runtime package has these functions:

- func Caller(skip int) (pc uintptr, file string, line int, ok bool) – Get caller info

- func GC() – Run garbage collection

- func GOMAXPROCS(n int) int – Set the number of goroutine processors

- func GOROOT() string – Get the Go install root

- func Goexit() – Exit the calling goroutine

- func Gosched() – Run another ready goroutine

- func NumCPU() int – Get the number of CPU cores

519

- func NumGoroutine() int – Get the active goroutine count

- func SetFinalizer(obj interface{}, finalizer interface{}) – Set the finalizer func for an object

- func Version() string – Get the Go version

Unlike in Java, where each Object has a `finalize` method, most Go data has no associated finalizer. If you have a value that needs finalization (i.e., resource cleanup at the time of garbage collection), you should use the `SetFinalizer` function on it, perhaps in a constructor function for the data type.

String Processing Packages

The `strconv` provides conversion functions that convert from and to (i.e., parse and format) the `string` type. The `fmt` package is also often used to format values.

The `strconv` package has this key constant:

`const IntSize` – The size in bits of the `int` (and `uint` and pointers) type; this can vary based on HW architecture (32/64-bit).

The `strconv` has these functions:

- func AppendBool(dst []byte, b bool) []byte – Append a Boolean to dst

- func AppendFloat(dst []byte, f float64, fmt byte, prec, bitSize int) []byte – Append a float to dst

- func AppendInt(dst []byte, i int64, base int) []byte – Append a signed integer to dst

- func AppendQuote(dst []byte, s string) []byte – Append quoted s to dst

- func AppendQuoteRune(dst []byte, r rune) []byte – Append quoted r to dst

- func AppendUint(dst []byte, i uint64, base int) []byte – Append an unsigned integer to dst

- func Atoi(s string) (int, error) – Parse a string to an integer

- func FormatBool(b bool) string – Boolean to string

- func FormatComplex(c complex128, fmt byte, prec, bitSize int) string – Complex to string

- func FormatFloat(f float64, fmt byte, prec, bitSize int) string – Float to string

- func FormatInt(i int64, base int) string – Signed integer to string in base

- func FormatUint(i uint64, base int) string – Unsigned integer to string in base

- func IsGraphic(r rune) bool – True if a Unicode graphic char

- func IsPrint(r rune) bool – True if a printable character

- func Itoa(i int) string – Integer to string in base 10

- func ParseBool(str string) (bool, error) – Parse a string to a Boolean

- func ParseComplex(s string, bitSize int) (complex128, error) – Parse a string to a complex

- func ParseFloat(s string, bitSize int) (float64, error) – Parse a string to a float

- func ParseInt(s string, base int, bitSize int) (i int64, err error) – Parse a string to a signed integer

- func ParseUint(s string, base int, bitSize int) (uint64, error) – Parse a string to an unsigned integer

- func Quote(s string) string – Wrap a string in quotes with escapes if needed

- func QuoteRune(r rune) string – Wrap a rune in quotes with escapes if needed

- func Unquote(s string) (string, error) – Remove quotes and escapes

The strings package provides functions and types to ease the processing of strings. Note that in Go, like in Java, strings are immutable, so all these functions return new, not modified, strings. In Java, most of these functions are methods on the String or StringBuilder/Buffer types:

- func Compare(a, b string) int – Compares a and b, returns -1, 0, 1; alternative to <, <=, ==, !=, >, >=

- func Contains(s, substr string) bool – True if a string in s

- func ContainsAny(s, chars string) bool – True if any char in chars is in s

- func ContainsRune(s string, r rune) bool – True if r in s

- func Count(s, substr string) int – Count of substr in s

- func EqualFold(s, t string) bool – True if s == t after Unicode folding

- func Fields(s string) []string – s split at whitespace

- func FieldsFunc(s string, f func(rune) bool) []string – s split at chars where f returns true

- func HasPrefix(s, prefix string) bool – True if s starts with a prefix

- func HasSuffix(s, suffix string) bool – True if s ends with a suffix

- func Index(s, substr string) int – >= 0 if substr in s

- func IndexAny(s, chars string) int – >=0 if any char in chars in s

- func IndexByte(s string, c byte) int – >= 0 if c in s

- func IndexFunc(s string, f func(rune) bool) int – >= 0 if f true on any char

- func IndexRune(s string, r rune) int – >=0 if r in s

- func Join(elems []string, sep string) string – Concatenate items in elems with sep between

- func LastIndex(s, substr string) int – >= 0 if substr in s from end

- func LastIndexAny(s, chars string) int – >= 0 if any char in chars in s from end

- func LastIndexByte(s string, c byte) int – >0 if c in s from end

- func LastIndexFunc(s string, f func(rune) bool) int – >= 0 if f true on any char in s from end

- func Map(mapping func(rune) rune, s string) string – Chars of s replaced with the mapping result or removed if rune < 0

- func Repeat(s string, count int) string – s repeated count times

- func Replace(s, old, new string, n int) string – Occurrences of old in s replaced with new up to n times

- func ReplaceAll(s, old, new string) string – All occurrences of old in s replaced with new

- func Split(s, sep string) []string – s split at occurrences of sep

- func SplitAfter(s, sep string) []string – s split after occurrences of sep

- func SplitAfterN(s, sep string, n int) []string – s split after occurrences of sep up to n times

- func SplitN(s, sep string, n int) []string – s split at occurrences of sep up to n times

- func Title(s string) string – Convert each word initial letter to title case

- func ToLower(s string) string – Convert to all lowercase

- func ToTitle(s string) string – Convert to all title case

- func ToUpper(s string) string – Convert to all uppercase

- func Trim(s, cutset string) string – Remove s leading/trailing chars in cutset

- func TrimFunc(s string, f func(rune) bool) string – Remove s leading/trailing chars where f is true

- func TrimLeft(s, cutset string) string – Remove s leading chars in cutset

- func TrimLeftFunc(s string, f func(rune) bool) string – Remove s leading chars where f is true

- func TrimPrefix(s, prefix string) string – Remove from s any prefix

- func TrimRight(s, cutset string) string – Remove s trailing chars in cutset

- func TrimRightFunc(s string, f func(rune) bool) string – Remove s trailing chars where f is true

- func TrimSpace(s string) string – Remove s leading/trailing whitespace

- func TrimSuffix(s, suffix string) string – Remove from s any suffix

Type Builder – Used to build strings (like Java's *StringBuilder*)
Type Reader – Used to read text from a string as a source
The Builder type has these methods:

- func (b *Builder) Cap() int – Current builder capacity

- func (b *Builder) Grow(n int) – Add to builder capacity

- func (b *Builder) Len() int – Current content length

- func (b *Builder) Reset() – Sets length to 0

- func (b *Builder) Write(p []byte) (int, error) – Add bytes

- func (b *Builder) WriteByte(c byte) error – Add a byte

- func (b *Builder) WriteRune(r rune) (int, error) – Add a rune

- func (b *Builder) WriteString(s string) (int, error) – Add a string

The Reader type has these methods:

- func NewReader(s string) *Reader – Make a reader on a string

- func (r *Reader) Len() int – Get unread count

- func (r *Reader) Read(b []byte) (n int, err error) – Read up to n bytes into b

- func (r *Reader) ReadAt(b []byte, off int64) (n int, err error) – Read at position

- func (r *Reader) ReadByte() (byte, error) – Read a byte

- func (r *Reader) ReadRune() (ch rune, size int, err error) – Read a rune

- func (r *Reader) Reset(s string) – Set to start

- func (r *Reader) Seek(offset int64, whence int) (int64, error) – Set to position

- func (r *Reader) Size() int64 – Get original (total) length

- func (r *Reader) UnreadByte() error – Reverse read

- func (r *Reader) UnreadRune() error – Reverse read

- func (r *Reader) WriteTo(w io.Writer) (n int64, err error) – Copy to writer

Concurrency and Goroutines

The sync package provides goroutine synchronization support such as mutual exclusion functions. This is often used as replacement for the synchronized statement and select methods in Java. It has a function similar to the java.util.concurrent.locks package. The atomic sub-package provides atomic access to certain data types. It is similar to the java.util.concurrent.atomic package. The Go community provides many more concurrent types and serialization functions.

The sync package provides these types:

- Cond – Provides a conditional variable; like Java's Object.wait/notify{All} pairs.

- Map – Provides behavior like Java ConcurrentHashMap.

- Mutex – Provides access control to shared values; see java.util.concurrent packages.

- RWMutex – A Mutex with multiple concurrent readers; see java.util.concurrent packages.

- Once – Does a code block only one time; useful for singleton creation.

- Pool – Like a cache of the same type values; members can be removed spontaneously.

- WaitGroup – Used to wait for multiple goroutines to exit (like Thread.join() in Java).

Note that a `synchronized` block can be reentered by the same thread but not by other threads. Go has no predefined library that offers this behavior; Go locks will block the same goroutine that owns them (a deadlock).

Many of the preceding types have no direct analogue in Java, but they can often be approximated. Often, the reverse is also true; many Java concurrency functions can be easily emulated in Go. For example, the *Once* type could be emulated in Java as

```
@FunctionalInterface
public interface Onceable {
    void doOnce(Runnable r);
}
public class Oncer implements Onceable {
    private AtomicBoolean once = new AtomicBoolean(false);
    public void doOnce(Runnable r) {
      if(!once.getAndSet(true)) {
        r.run();
      }
    }
}
```

This is used as

```
Onceable oncer = new Oncer();
  for(var i = 0; i < N; i++) {
    oncer.doOnce(()->System.out.println("Hello World!"));
  }
}
```

In Go, this is done:

```
var once sync.Once
for i := 0; i < N; i++ {
    once.Do(func(){
            fmt.Println("Hello World!");
    })
}
```

Given:

```
type Locker interface {
    Lock()
    Unlock()
}
```

The Cond type has these methods:

- func NewCond(l Locker) *Cond – Make a Cond

- func (c *Cond) Broadcast() – Like `Object.notifyAll`

- func (c *Cond) Signal() – Like `Object.notify`

- func (c *Cond) Wait() – Like `Object.wait`

The (concurrent) Map type has these methods (generally self-explanatory – load => get; store => put):

- func (m *Map) Delete(key interface{})

- func (m *Map) Load(key interface{}) (value interface{}, ok bool)

- func (m *Map) LoadAndDelete(key interface{}) (value interface{}, loaded bool)

- func (m *Map) LoadOrStore(key, value interface{}) (actual interface{}, loaded bool)

- func (m *Map) Range(f func(key, value interface{}) bool) – For range over keys

- func (m *Map) Store(key, value interface{})

The Mutex type has these methods (generally self-explanatory) and thus is a `Locker`:

- func (m *Mutex) Lock()

- func (m *Mutex) Unlock()

The RWMutex type has these methods (generally self-explanatory) and thus is a `Locker`:

- func (rw *RWMutex) Lock()

- func (rw *RWMutex) RLock()

- func (rw *RWMutex) RLocker() Locker

- func (rw *RWMutex) RUnlock()

- func (rw *RWMutex) Unlock()

The Once type has these methods (generally self-explanatory):

- func (o *Once) Do(f func()) – f called only one time

The Pool type has these methods (generally self-explanatory):

- func (p *Pool) Get() interface{} – Get and remove an arbitrary instance (all should be of type returned from New)

- func (p *Pool) Put(x interface{}) – (Re)add an instance

- Pool has a member function value New used to create entries if none is found.

The WaitGroup type has these methods (generally self-explanatory):

- func (wg *WaitGroup) Add(delta int)

- func (wg *WaitGroup) Done() – Same as Add(-1)

- func (wg *WaitGroup) Wait() – Wait for count to go to 0

Testing Package

This section is a condensation of Chapter 17, "Go Unit Tests and Benchmarks."

Java itself has no built-in testing framework, but good community testing frameworks exist. Many authors use the main method of a class as a test case. Because creating a main function is more overhead (not per class as in Java) in Go, this method of creating tests is not often used in Go. Similarly, since a package can have many init() functions, they can be used to conveniently contain test cases, but they must be manually enabled/disabled in code.

The Go testing package provides support and a framework for doing *JUnit*[2]-like repeatable testing of Go code. This package is reflection driven and has many types used to run test suites and benchmarks and is not generally used directly by testers.

---

[2] https://en.wikipedia.org/wiki/JUnit

In Go, a test suite is any Go source file with a name of the form *xxxx*_test.go (where xxxx is the suite name) that contains one or more test functions (aka test cases). The test code is often placed in the same package as the *code under test* (CUT), so it can access non-public names. These types of tests are called "white-box"[3] tests. By placing the test code in a different package from the CUT, "black-box"[4] tests can be made.

A test function has this form:

```go
func TestXxx(*testing.T) {
    :
}
```

where *Xxx* is the name of the test case. There can be any number of such test cases in a test suite. The "go test" command will run them and the CUT and report the results. Note that the test suite has no main function. The test case interacts with the test runner via the T argument.

The typical structure of a test is like

```go
func TestSomething(t *testing.T) {
    got := <run some test>
        want := <expected value>
    if got != want {
        t.Errorf("unexpected result %v (vs. %v)", got, want)
    }
}
```

Like test cases, benchmarks have a consistent form:

```go
func BenchmarkXxx(*testing.B) {
    :
}
```

where *Xxx* is the name of the benchmark. There can be any number of such benchmarks in a test suite. The "go test" command with the benchmark option (off by default as

---

[3] https://en.wikipedia.org/wiki/White-box_testing. No intent to use racial implications, these are just the traditional names.

[4] https://en.wikipedia.org/wiki/Black-box_testing. No intent to use racial implications, these are just the traditional names.

benchmarks often take significant elapsed time) will run them and report the results. The benchmark interacts with the benchmark runner via the B argument.

The typical structure of a benchmark is like

```
func BenchmarkSomething(b *testing.B) {
    : do some setup which may take time
    b.ResetTimer()
    for i := 0; i < b.N; i++ {
        : some code to time
    }
}
```

The benchmark runner will determine a good N value (often quite large) to use. Thus, running benchmarks can take a lot of time and probably should not be done on each build.

The key types are B and T:

- B – Context/helpers for benchmark functions

- BenchmarkResult – Struct with benchmark results as fields

- PB – Supports running benchmarks in parallel

- T – Context/helpers for test case functions

- TB – Methods in both type T and type B

The testing package has these functions:

- func AllocsPerRun(runs int, f func()) (avg float64) – Get average allocation per call of f

- func Short() bool – Reports short options

- func Verbose() bool – Reports verbose options

The B (benchmark) type has these functions:

- func (c *B) Cleanup(f func()) – Call f to clean after benchmarks

- func (c *B) Error(args ...interface{}) – Log and then fail

- func (c *B) Errorf(format string, args ...interface{}) – Formatted log and then fail

- func (c *B) Fail() – Mark failed

- func (c *B) FailNow() – Fail and exit

- func (c *B) Failed() bool – Test failed

- func (c *B) Fatal(args ...interface{}) – Log and then fail now

- func (c *B) Fatalf(format string, args ...interface{}) – Formatted log and then fail now

- func (c *B) Helper() – Mark a caller as a helper (not traced)

- func (c *B) Log(args ...interface{}) – Log values

- func (c *B) Logf(format string, args ...interface{}) – Formatted log

- func (c *B) Name() string – Get benchmark name

- func (b *B) ReportAllocs() – Enable allocation tracking

- func (b *B) ReportMetric(n float64, unit string) – Sets report scales

- func (b *B) ResetTimer() – Reset benchmark timer and counts

- func (b *B) Run(name string, f func(b *B)) bool – Run benchmarks sequentially

- func (b *B) RunParallel(body func(*PB)) – Run benchmarks concurrently

- func (c *B) Skip(args ...interface{}) – Skip benchmark and log

- func (c *B) SkipNow() – Skip and stop now

- func (c *B) Skipf(format string, args ...interface{}) – Skip benchmark and formatted log

- func (c *B) Skipped() bool – Test skipped

- func (b *B) StartTimer() – Start timing

- func (b *B) StopTimer() – Stop timing

- func (c *B) TempDir() string – Get temp directory

Type BenchmarkResult

- func Benchmark(f func(b *B)) BenchmarkResult – Benchmark f
- func (r BenchmarkResult) AllocedBytesPerOp() int64 – Get info
- func (r BenchmarkResult) AllocsPerOp() int64 – Get info
- func (r BenchmarkResult) MemString() string – Get info
- func (r BenchmarkResult) NsPerOp() int64 – Get info

The T (test) type has these functions. Many are the same as for the B type and not redescribed:

- func (c *T) Cleanup(f func())
- func (t *T) Deadline() (deadline time.Time, ok bool) – Get test deadline
- func (c *T) Error(args ...interface{})
- func (c *T) Errorf(format string, args ...interface{})
- func (c *T) Fail()
- func (c *T) FailNow()
- func (c *T) Failed() bool
- func (c *T) Fatal(args ...interface{})
- func (c *T) Fatalf(format string, args ...interface{})
- func (c *T) Helper() – Marks a caller as a helper; it is not included in reports
- func (c *T) Log(args ...interface{})
- func (c *T) Logf(format string, args ...interface{})
- func (c *T) Name() string
- func (t *T) Parallel() – Set to run a test in parallel with other tests
- func (t *T) Run(name string, f func(t *T)) bool
- func (c *T) Skip(args ...interface{})
- func (c *T) SkipNow()

- func (c *T) Skipf(format string, args ...interface{})

- func (c *T) Skipped() bool

- func (c *T) TempDir() string

Time and Date Package

The time package provides functions to display and manipulate dates, times, and durations. It has one sub-package:

- tzdata provides support for time zones without reliance on operating system support.

The time package has these time formats (really templates – actual values are formatted to look like the template) built-in:

- ANSIC = "Mon Jan _2 15:04:05 2006"

- UnixDate = "Mon Jan _2 15:04:05 MST 2006"

- RubyDate = "Mon Jan 02 15:04:05 -0700 2006"

- RFC822 = "02 Jan 06 15:04 MST"

- RFC822Z = "02 Jan 06 15:04 -0700"

- RFC850 = "Monday, 02-Jan-06 15:04:05 MST"

- RFC1123 = "Mon, 02 Jan 2006 15:04:05 MST"

- RFC1123Z = "Mon, 02 Jan 2006 15:04:05 -0700"

- RFC3339 = "2006-01-02T15:04:05Z07:00"

- RFC3339Nano = "2006-01-02T15:04:05.999999999Z07:00"

- Kitchen = "3:04PM"

- Stamp = "Jan _2 15:04:05"

- StampMilli = "Jan _2 15:04:05.000"

- StampMicro = "Jan _2 15:04:05.000000"

- StampNano = "Jan _2 15:04:05.000000000"

Note the preceding patterns are not arbitrary. The values (like month name/abbreviation and day of month) are keywords. For example, one cannot use May instead of January or 03 instead of 02.

Time is measured in nanosecond precision, but the computer may not be able to measure time passing at this resolution, so steps in time may happen in multiple nanoseconds. The time package has these durations built-in:

- `Nanosecond Duration = 1`
- `Microsecond = 1000 * Nanosecond`
- `Millisecond = 1000 * Microsecond`
- `Second = 1000 * Millisecond`
- `Minute = 60 * Second`
- `Hour = 60 * Minute`

The time package has these functions and types:

- func After(d Duration) <-chan Time – Returns a channel that fires after a duration

- func Sleep(d Duration) – Sleeps/suspends caller goroutine for a duration

- func Tick(d Duration) <-chan Time – Returns a channel that fires each duration

- type Duration – Represents a span of time

- type Location – Represents a time zone

- type Month – Enum for month

- type Ticker – Wraps a channel getting ticks; used to do actions repeatedly

- type Time – Represents an instant in time with nanosecond resolution

- type Timer – Fires a channel at periodic intervals

- type Weekday – Enum for weekday

The Duration type has these methods (generally self-explanatory):

- func ParseDuration(s string) (Duration, error)
- func Since(t Time) Duration
- func Until(t Time) Duration
- func (d Duration) Hours() float64
- func (d Duration) Microseconds() int64
- func (d Duration) Milliseconds() int64
- func (d Duration) Minutes() float64
- func (d Duration) Nanoseconds() int64
- func (d Duration) Round(m Duration) Duration
- func (d Duration) Seconds() float64
- func (d Duration) Truncate(m Duration) Duration

Type Location

- func FixedZone(name string, offset int) *Location
- func LoadLocation(name string) (*Location, error)

Type Ticker

- func NewTicker(d Duration) *Ticker – Make and start a ticker
- func (t *Ticker) Reset(d Duration) – Change interval
- func (t *Ticker) Stop()

Type Time

- func Date(year int, month Month, day, hour, min, sec, nsec int, loc *Location) Time
- func Now() Time
- func Parse(layout, value string) (Time, error)
- func ParseInLocation(layout, value string, loc *Location) (Time, error)

- func Unix(sec int64, nsec int64) Time – Time from Epoch

- func (t Time) Add(d Duration) Time

- func (t Time) AddDate(years int, months int, days int) Time

- func (t Time) After(u Time) bool

- func (t Time) Before(u Time) bool

- func (t Time) Clock() (hour, min, sec int)

- func (t Time) Date() (year int, month Month, day int)

- func (t Time) Day() int

- func (t Time) Equal(u Time) bool

- func (t Time) Format(layout string) string

- func (t Time) Hour() int

- func (t Time) ISOWeek() (year, week int)

- func (t Time) In(loc *Location) Time

- func (t Time) IsZero() bool

- func (t Time) Local() Time

- func (t Time) Location() *Location

- func (t Time) Minute() int

- func (t Time) Month() Month

- func (t Time) Nanosecond() int

- func (t Time) Round(d Duration) Time

- func (t Time) Second() int

- func (t Time) Sub(u Time) Duration

- func (t Time) Truncate(d Duration) Time

- func (t Time) UTC() Time

- func (t Time) Unix() int64

- func (t Time) UnixNano() int64 – Time since Epoch

- func (t Time) Weekday() Weekday

- func (t Time) Year() int

- func (t Time) YearDay() int

- func (t Time) Zone() (name string, offset int)

Type Timer

- func AfterFunc(d Duration, f func()) *Timer – Call func in goroutine after duration

- func NewTimer(d Duration) *Timer – Make a timer

- func (t *Timer) Reset(d Duration) bool

- func (t *Timer) Stop() bool

On Ticker vs. Timer, Tickers supply multiple events at periodic intervals, while a Timer supplies just one event. Both work on time durations. Consider this simple version of a clock that outputs the time of day every minute:

```
func startClock(minutes int) {
    minuteTicker := time.NewTicker(time.Minute)
    defer minuteTicker.Stop() // cleanup ticker when done
    fmt.Println("Clock running...")
    complete := make(chan bool) // notifies end
    go func() { // trigger the clock to stop eventually
        time.Sleep(time.Duration(minutes) * time.Minute)
        complete <- true
    }()
    count := 0
loop:
    for {
        select { // blocks while waiting for an event
        // ticker has a channel that fires every minute
        case tod := <-minuteTicker.C:
            fmt.Println(tod.Format(time.RFC850))
            count++
```

```
        case <-complete:
                break loop
        }
    }
    fmt.Println("Clock stopped; final count:", count)
}
```

This is run by use of startClock(5) in some main with this result:

```
Clock running...
Friday, 07-May-21 14:16:07 PDT
Friday, 07-May-21 14:17:07 PDT
Friday, 07-May-21 14:18:07 PDT
Friday, 07-May-21 14:19:07 PDT
Friday, 07-May-21 14:20:07 PDT
Clock stopped; final count: 5
```

Contrast this with a timer that triggers a function when it is done. The timer is created with the Tick() function. The timer() function returns before the timeout:

```
func timer(seconds int, f func(t time.Time)) {
    ticks := time.Tick(time.Duration(seconds) * time.Second)
    go func() {
        // only iterates once as only one value sent before closure
        for t := range ticks {
            f(t)
        }
    }()
}
```

This is driven by the following code in main:

```
var wg sync.WaitGroup
wg.Add(1)
start := time.Now()
fmt.Println("Running...")
```

```
timer(5, func(t time.Time) {
    defer wg.Done()
    trigger := time.Now()
    fmt.Println("Trigger difference:", trigger.Sub(start))
})
wg.Wait()
fmt.Println("Done")
```

That produces this output:

```
Running...
Trigger difference: 5.0041177s
Done
```

APPENDIX A

Installing Go

To install Go, go to the Go site at `https://golang.org/dl/`. It will look something like (the appearance may change over time) what you see in Figure A-1. While not shown in this text, this site supports downloading many Go versions, starting with the latest. You can download the Go development kit for different operating systems and HW architectures. Select the appropriate one.

Also included at the site are installation instructions with the supported operating system types. In general, they are simple to follow (e.g., run some installer program and answer a few simple questions). This text will not repeat them for each operating system type.

© Barry Feigenbaum 2022
B. Feigenbaum, *Go for Java Programmers*, https://doi.org/10.1007/978-1-4842-7199-5

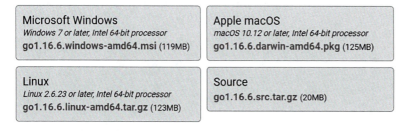

Figure A-1. *Go download page*

A sample installation sequence on the Windows operating system is shown in Figures A-2 through A-6. Installers for another operating system may be different.

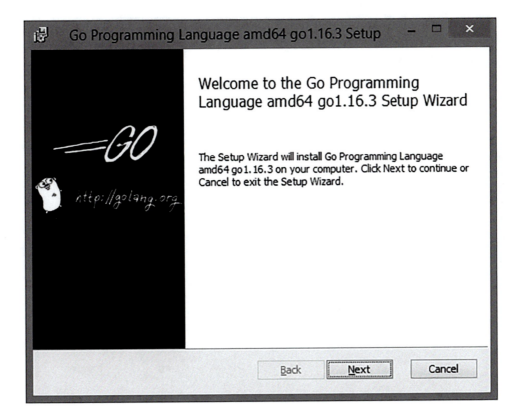

Figure A-2. *Go install for Windows (part 1)*

Set the Go runtime installation directory.

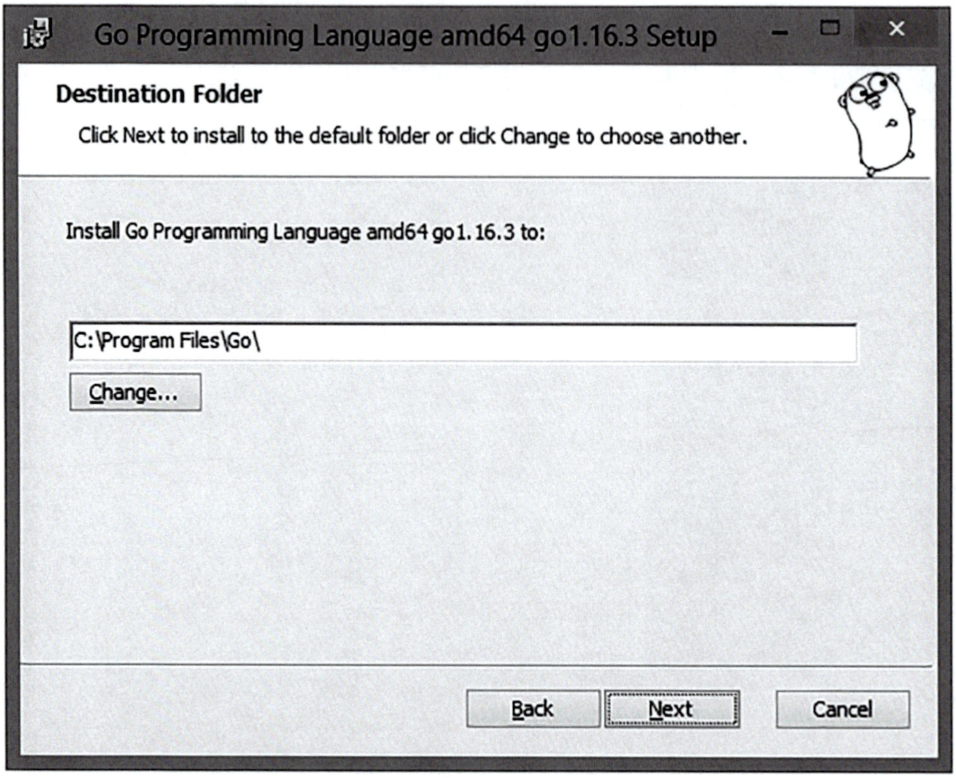

Figure A-3. *Go install for Windows (part 2)*

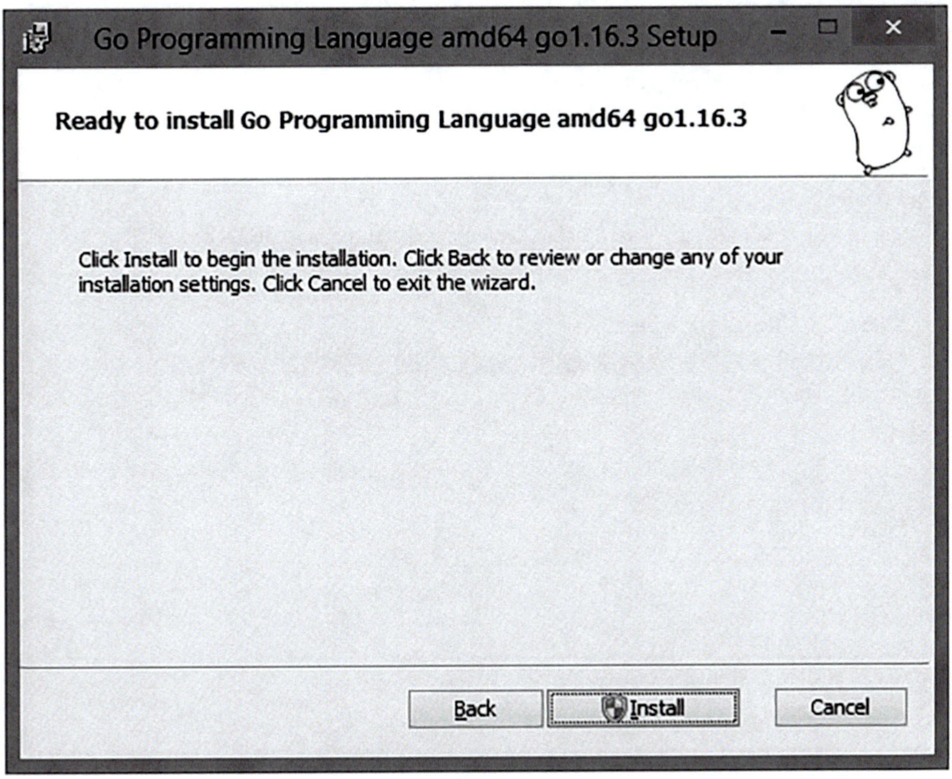

Figure A-4. *Go install for Windows (part 3)*

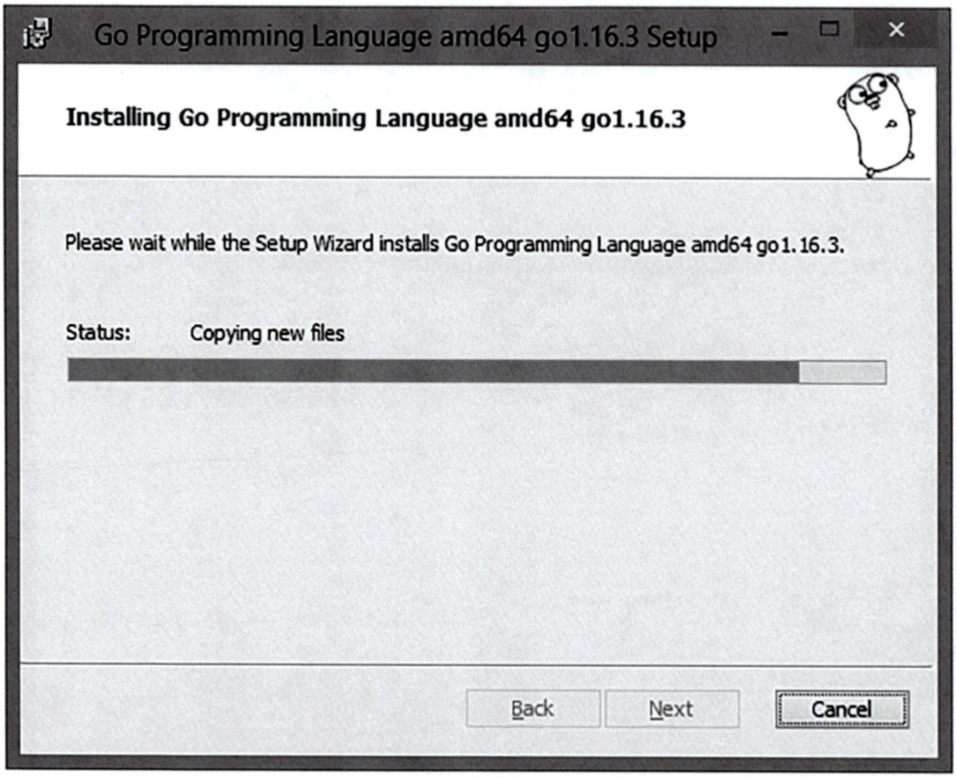

Figure A-5. *Go install for Windows (part 4)*

Wait for the installation to complete.

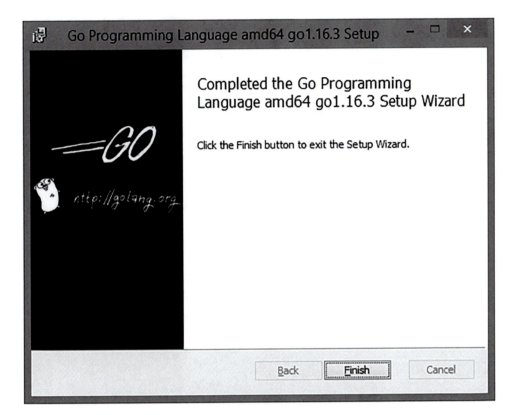

Figure A-6. *Go install for Windows (part 5)*

Once installed, you may need to add the go program's executable location to your operating system path (or PATH) variable, usually an environment variable. How this is set is operating system dependent. For Windows, this is done through the Control Panel, as shown in Figure A-7.

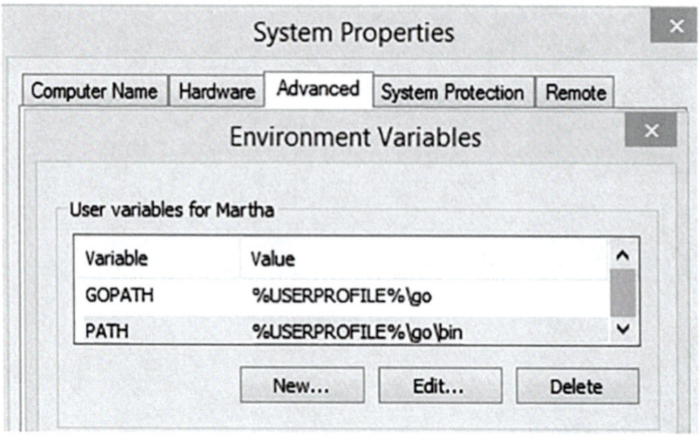

Figure A-7. *Setting the PATH in Windows*

The PATH is the location where the Go runtime is installed (often called the GOROOT). The GOPATH is where your workspace (or workspaces) is located. You can confirm the installation by using the go command. It will produce output like this:

$>go
```
Go is a tool for managing Go source code.
```

```
Usage:
```

```
        go <command> [arguments]
```

The commands are as follows:

```
        bug             start a bug report
        build           compile packages and dependencies
        clean           remove object files and cached files
        doc             show documentation for package or symbol
        env             print Go environment information
        fix             update packages to use new APIs
        fmt             gofmt (reformat) package sources
        generate        generate Go files by processing source
        get             add dependencies to current module and install them
        install         compile and install packages and dependencies
        list            list packages or modules
        mod             module maintenance
```

run	compile and run Go program
test	test packages
tool	run specified go tool
version	print Go version
vet	report likely mistakes in packages

Use "go help <command>" for more information about a command.
Additional help topics:

buildconstraint	build constraints
buildmode	build modes
c	calling between Go and C
cache	build and test caching
environment	environment variables
filetype	file types
go.mod	the go.mod file
gopath	GOPATH environment variable
gopath-get	legacy GOPATH go get
goproxy	module proxy protocol
importpath	import path syntax
modules	modules, module versions, and more
module-get	module-aware go get
module-auth	module authentication using go.sum
packages	package lists and patterns
private	configuration for downloading non-public code
testflag	testing flags
testfunc	testing functions
vcs	controlling version control with GOVCS

Use "go help <topic>" for more information about any topic.
The following command shows an example location for an installed Go runtime:

```
$>where go
C:\Program Files\Go\bin\go.exe
```

You should set up a *workspace* to enter your Go code. Many installers create one as the go directory in your user home (as shown earlier). If not already created, you should add the src (for Go source), bin (for generated executables and tools), and pkg (for package archives) directories under the workspace directory. You can have multiple workspaces, but you may need to use chdir to switch between them.

When the Go runtime is installed and as dependencies get installed, Go builds up a module cache, typically in the go subdirectory of the user home directory. Typically, Gophers do not need to interact with this cache directly, but the Go builder does. These resources are distinct from any project workspace and may be shared between workspaces. The cache speeds up building as the dependency is downloaded only once (unless the dependency version is changed). The following screen captures show such a cache snapshot's pkg and src subdirectories, with content depending on the installed dependencies. The structure shown will vary, but Figures A-8 and A-9 illustrate an example.

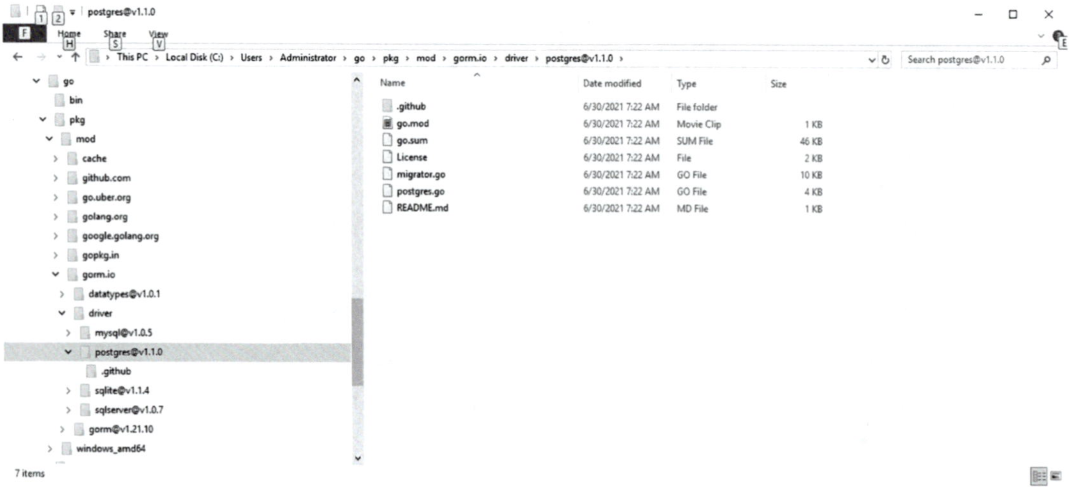

Figure A-8. *Go dependency cache, pkg subdirectory*

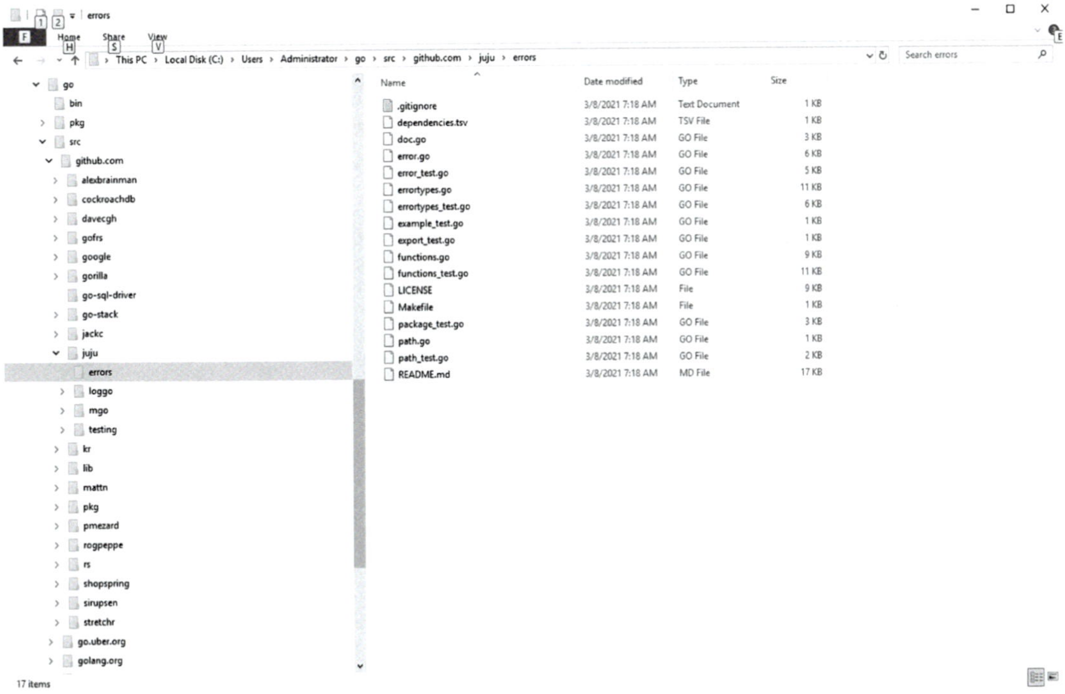

Figure A-9. *Go dependency cache, src subdirectory*

APPENDIX B

Some Go FAQs

More on the Frequently Asked Questions (FAQ) in this appendix and many others can be found at the Go FAQ[1] site. At the time of this text's creation, the following FAQs are excerpts from the more general topics covered and questions answered at the Go site.

The questions themselves give some insight into the nature of Go as a language and a runtime. It is hoped that this text also addresses many of these questions. A brief answer is provided with each question.

General Go questions

- *Java has a runtime. Does Go?* Yes. The runtime gets built into each generated executable, so it is not separate as it is with Java (i.e., the Java Runtime Environment (JRE)).

- *Java allows Unicode characters in identifiers. Does Go?* Go allows any Unicode identifier character in Go identifiers, not just ASCII letters and digits. They must be entered as UTF-8 characters by the source editor, not Unicode escapes (e.g., \u1234) as is possible in Java. This is because Go lacks the compiler preprocessor pass javac has that converts such escapes into UTF-8.

- *Go has far fewer features than Java does. Why?* In most cases because the feature is redundant with another feature or not consistent with the designed simplicity of the Go language. Go features exist because the three Go lead designers, Robert Griesemer, Rob Pike, and Ken Thompson, all agreed they should be present.

---

[1] https://golang.org/doc/faq

B. Feigenbaum, *Go for Java Programmers*, https://doi.org/10.1007/978-1-4842-7199-5

- *Java has Generic types. Go does not. Why?* Originally, they were believed to be overly complex and not needed. This decision is changing, and a future Go language definition will (Generics is an approved enhancement) include them.

- *Java has Exceptions. Go has panics. Why the difference?* Exceptions represent an often-misused means to implicitly force alternative flow paths. Go uses error returns for simple/typical cases and panics for situations like Java Errors. Work is in progress to reduce the source repetition of error processing. Go has *panics* for truly exceptional circumstances.

- *Java has compile-time assertions. Go does not. Why?* Go panics provide much of the function of assertions (`assert` statements) but are not conditionally generated as assertions can be. Conditional assertions, when omitted, often leave bad situations undetected in code (producing unexpected failures). Go wants such situations always tested.

- *Java bases its concurrency model on threads. Go builds* concurrency *on the ideas of goroutines and channels (or CSP). Why?* CSP is a well-known and understood approach to concurrency with relatively low complexity. Combined with goroutines, it hides creation and management of threads as is done in Java.

- *Why does Go use goroutines instead of operating system threads like Java does?* Goroutines are much less resource intensive than operating system threads and can thus be used for more situations (e.g., high scale needed) than threads can be and in greater numbers. This is considered by many to be a major advantage of Go over Java. Go does use threads under the covers to implement goroutines.

- *Why is the map type not thread-safe?* Doing so on all map access is not required and thus adds overhead. Cases where atomic access is needed can be provided explicitly by the Map type. Java also makes this distinction (`HashMap` vs. `Hashtable` types; Go maps are like `HashMap`).

- *Why does a small Go program generate a large executable?* The Go runtime is included in all programs. If used, the generated code of many libraries may also be included. This is in addition to the generated code of your application. In Java, the separate JRE holds the runtime and many libraries. They are not part of the application JAR (the Java binary), but they do take computer resources when your application is running.

Questions on types

- *Java is highly object-oriented. Is Go?* Not really. It is best described as an object-based (the struct type) language. It does support a reduced level of encapsulation and polymorphism.

- *Java supports dynamic (polymorphic) method dispatch. Can Go do this too?* This is possible by using Go interfaces which provide dynamic dispatch something like Java interfaces do.

- *Java supports type inheritance as part of being object-oriented. Go does not. Why?* Go does not force source time inheritance hierarchies to be declared. It uses interfaces to allow different types to behave in a common way, so they can be used in an abstract way. Go uses composition (vs. inheritance) to compose complex types from simpler types.

- *Why are some Go functions, like* len, *built-in and not methods on types like they would be in Java?* They are generic functions for many types. Thus, the compiler must know its implementation based on the type. This is true of several other built-in functions, such as make.

- *Java has overloaded operators and methods. Go does not support this. Why?* Because it makes Go simpler and thus faster to compile. Alternates (via name mangling[2]) can generally be used with little loss of functionality.

---

[2] How the C++ compiler created non-overloaded versions of function names for C runtimes. Often done by adding type suffixes.

- *Java types implement interfaces explicitly (*`implements` *clause). Go does not do this. Why?* The Go interface design does not need the source time binding `implements` implies. Structs implement (or satisfy) interfaces implicitly.

- *Java uses the* `abstract` *modifier to indicate if a class fully implements an interface or not. Go does not do this. Why?* In Go, one simply implements all the methods in the interface. No special syntax is needed. This can be tested at runtime via type assertions.

- *In Go, an interface type, such as* `error`, *value may not always be nil when expected. Why?* For `error` (or any interface type), the value is a (internal) struct which points to the current runtime type and the current runtime value (either of which could be `nil`). The struct will be not `nil` even if the pointer to the value in it is. This can be a confusing aspect of Go interface types.

Questions about values

- *Java often implicitly converts values, especially numeric values. Go does not. Why?* With the ability to derive user types from built-in types, such implicit conversions often would be inappropriate (or even wrong); thus, Go makes them required even in cases where it could judge them to be safe. For example, there can be *Apple* and *Orange* types both based on an `int` type. It would be possibly wrong to allow automatic conversions between these types.

- *How do Go constants differ from Java's* `static final` *values?* They are a compile-time construct only. They are mapped to a language type at the point of usage. For example, the constant 1 can be mapped to an `int`, `uint`, `float64`, etc. as needed. In Java, a constant is simulated by a `static final` value. Such values exist at runtime and must be declared with a type.

- *Why is the Go* `map` *type built-in vs. supplied by libraries as in Java?* Unlike with Java, they need to be generic, and since Go does not support library generic types yet, maps must be built-in. Similar for slices and channels.

- *Why does Go restrict the type of map keys? For example, slices cannot be keys.* Like with Java maps, map keys must be hashable, and the hash value needs to be stable over time. It is difficult for a mutable type, like slice (or map or channel) and many custom types, to meet these conditions.

- *In Go, slices, maps, and channels often act as references while arrays act like values. Why?* They themselves are values, but their contents are accessed via (internal) pointers. This is because they are mutable in size (where arrays are not). To make this practical, they internally contain a pointer to the backing store (often an array). Thus, they act much like a pointer themselves.

Questions about best coding practices

- *Java uses JavaDoc to document types and APIs. How should types and APIs be documented in Go?* Like with Java, mostly by commentary included in the Go source. Generally, by comments that immediately proceed a declaration of any public types, functions, or values in the source. There is no special (say *JavaDoc*) syntax for these comments. The godoc server offers library documentation formatting like the HTML generated by the JavaDoc tool.

- *Java has idiomatic code style. Does Go have anything similar?* Yes, see the Go site. The go fmt tool and many IDEs offer source formatting that complies with these guidelines. Thus, in Go, style conventions are enforced more strongly than in Java.

- *How is module and package versioning done in Go?* Similar to Java modules, Go modules (a collection of related package sources) can be given version numbers. The go tool, much like using Maven or Gradle in Java, allows one to select any available version of any module for use in an application.

Questions on pointers and memory allocation

- *Java passes method parameters and return values by value. Does Go?*
  Like in Java, they are always *passed by value* (which means they are
  copied into the function; same for return values). But the value can
  be a pointer (or a pointer wrapper, such as a slice is) which gives
  effective *pass by reference*.

- *Is it safe to use a pointer to an interface?* While not enforced by the
  Go compiler, for best practice never do this. The use of a pointer
  to an interface vs. a direct interface can be very confusing. Note an
  interface argument will accept a pointer to a value implementing the
  interface as well as a value implementing the interface directly.

- *Go method receivers can be a type (T) or a pointer to a type (*T).
  Which is better?* If you need to modify the value received by the
  method or the type is complex so making a copy of it is inefficient,
  then pass a pointer. Best practice is to use pointers or non-pointers
  consistently across all methods of a type.

- *Java has the new operator. Go has new and make functions. Why?* In Go,
  new creates the space to hold the value (with the zero value implied).
  Go's make does additional initialization (like a default constructor
  would in Java). New returns a pointer to the created value. Make
  returns the value itself.

- *Java has no architecture-dependent data type sizes. Go does for
  integers. Why?* Go is a lower-level language than Java. Thus, in
  rare cases, the size of an integer can vary based on the machine
  architecture the code runs (and is compiled to) against. The `int/
  uint` type can vary, but the `int32/uint32` or `int64/uint64` types
  cannot. Use the varying types when the range of the values can be
  contained in either size.

- *How can one determine if a variable is located on the* heap *or the
  stack?* For all cases, you cannot. And mostly you do not care.

- *Some Go programs use a lot of computer memory. Why?* Like with Java, the program's binary code uses memory. The data the program uses takes memory. The Go runtime may reserve additional memory for future heap allocations in advance. The rate of memory consumption per line of code differs between Go and Java.

Questions on concurrency

- *What Go data types are implicitly thread-safe?* Several data types, like channels, offer implicit atomic actions. Most do not. The Go standard library offers several atomic data access functions and synchronization types to manage this need. The use of CSPs (channels) can greatly reduce the need to use synchronization.

- *Go programs often do not get faster when more CPUs are added. Why?* Like in Java, not all programs are implicitly scalable to exploit more CPUs (or cores). Often, to get better use of more CPUs, the program needs to be written to use multiple goroutines and use them well (say with CSPs).

- *Java threads have an identity. Goroutines do not. Why?* Goroutine identity is an internal construct. In general, Go code has no need for this value; Go library APIs are provided that hide the need to know these ids. There are techniques that can access it if you must have it (say for logging), but they may not be supported in future releases. This text includes an example of one of these techniques that looks at a call stack to extract the goroutine id.

Questions on functions

- *Why do the types T and pointer to T (*T) have a different set of methods?* It has to do with how interfaces are processed. The methods of *T are generally a superset of T.

- *Closures can sometimes capture the wrong values, especially when using goroutines. Why?* Closures identify the variables defined in their lexical context when they are defined, not when they are called. One must make sure the captured value is the intended one. Surrounding a closure in a loop or goroutine can cause the value to not be what is expected. In general, avoid implicitly (via context) passing context values; use explicit goroutine parameters instead.

559

- *Java has a ternary (?:) operator. Go does not. Why?* Its use (especially when nested) can be confusing, and the use case for it is less compelling than in (say) Java or C, so it was omitted. In the author's opinion, this was a mistake.

In addition to scanning the FAQs, it is recommended you also review *Effective Go*.[3] Many of the code samples in this book reflect guidance this document provides. Some of the samples in this book are based on the samples from that source and from examples in the Go runtime library documentation.

---

[3] https://golang.org/doc/effective_go.html

APPENDIX C

Go *Gotchas* to Look Out For

Go behavior and corresponding Java behavior can sometimes differ. Go has some *gotchas*[1] (often initially surprising and sometimes subtle differences) for experienced Java programmers. When encountered, often compiler errors occur, but sometimes runtime errors result. Many of these gotchas are mentioned throughout the various chapters of this book. Some key ones, in no special order, are summarized as follows:

- Because of semicolon insertion, opening braces (of `{...}`) must be on the same line as the introducer (often a statement such as `if`, `for`, or `switch`).

- All imported packages must be used in the importing source file, unless imported with the override name of underscore (_).

- All declared variables must be read by some code in the same scope; only assigning a value to them is not enough.

- Either a type or an initial value must be provided with `var` declarations; an initial `nil` value requires a type be provided.

- The combined (aka short assignment) declaration and assignment statement (`x := 1`) can only be used inside functions.

- Short assignments must always declare at least one new variable. Short assignments can redeclare (replace) multiple variables, resulting in sometimes confusing hidden variables. Short assignments generally cannot target fields of structs.

---

[1] Based on the gotchas listed in `http://devs.cloudimmunity.com/gotchas-and-common-mistakes-in-go-golang/`

© Barry Feigenbaum 2022
B. Feigenbaum, *Go for Java Programmers*, https://doi.org/10.1007/978-1-4842-7199-5

- There is no binary (integer) not (inverse) operator; the exclusive-or (^) operator must be used instead.

- Arrays are fixed in size; slices are not. Array and slice syntax are similar so they can be confused.

- Arrays and slices are one-dimensional; multiple dimensional source forms are represented by nested forms. This is also true in Java.

- Arrays are copied when assigned or passed to/from functions. Slices are also, but any backing array is not copied.

- Unless passed by a pointer, a function cannot change the value of variables that are passed into the function because they are copied in the function. Some types, like structs and maps, act much like pointer types when passed to functions.

- Arrays, slices, and maps are not safe for concurrent write access. Read-only access is safe.

- The `for-range` clause on slices and maps always returns both an index/key and a value; use underscore (_) to ignore at most one of these values.

- A slice is a mapping on top of some base slice or array. It is a form of alias, or view, of the base data, so updates to a slice can have impacts on all such views.

- Appending to a slice may create a new slice. Always save the resulting slice, often back in the input slice. For example, `var x []int; x = append(x, 1)`.

- The `for-range` clause on maps may return the keys in an apparent random order with different maps, but this is not always true when repeating the range against the same map.

- The `for-range` clause makes a copy of values, so changes to any values are local and not reflected in the source. For example, you can delete a key from a map while iterating over the map. In Java, this often results in a runtime exception.

- A string variable cannot be assigned a `nil` value. Empty values are allowed.

- Structs are comparable (`==`/`!=`) to other structs of the same type only if their members are comparable. Structs are not orderable (`<, >, <=, >=`).

- A `string` often stores UTF-8 (vs. fixed length) characters; thus, characters may not be directly indexable. The `range` iterator walks over a string by individual characters (Rune), not bytes.

- Take care when storing non-UTF-8 content in strings; unexpected failures may occur. Remember all ASCII text is UTF-8 text.

- The `len()` of a string returns the count of bytes, not characters.

- The go statement does not wait for the target goroutine to end (or maybe even to start).

- The go statement requires a function call, not just a function definition.

- The `defer` statement requires a function call, not just a function definition.

- The `recover()` function returns `nil` if called outside a deferred function or when no panic is active. It can return a value of any data type, not just `error` types. Avoid returning the `nil` value. It is best practice to only use `error` instances as panic values.

- A receive on an unbuffered channel implicitly blocks (waits) for a send to occur.

- A send on an unbuffered channel implicitly blocks (waits) for a receiver to be active.

- One cannot send anything to a closed channel; a panic will result.

- A map returns the zero value (not `nil`) for undefined keys. Since they can also store the zero value, this can cause confusion.

- The ++ and -- prefix and postfix operators are not supported. A ++ and -- postfix action as a statement is provided.

- Multiline initializer sequences (`{x, y, ..., z, }`) must end in a comma (if on one line, the last comma can be omitted).

- Go does not guarantee zero-sized objects have distinct addresses. Use care when comparing addresses of such objects (e.g., an empty struct or string).

- The `iota` operator is reset in new `var` or `const` groups, not each time `iota` is referenced. The iota value is incremented for each declaration in the group.

- All switch cases automatically `break`; use the `fallthrough` statement to drop to the next case. This works on value/expression switch statements, not type testing switch statements.

- A `nil` slice can be appended to, but a `nil` map cannot have keys added. Always `make` a map.

- Conversion expressions between `[]byte` and `string` types act as a cast, not a conversion.

- Visibility is determined by the first character of a name, not a visibility keyword. Names starting with capital letters are public; others are not. Visibility on function locals is always private to the function or nested blocks. Avoid using capitalized local names.

- Variables captured by closure functions used as goroutines, especially in `for-range` clauses, may not be unique; make a copy of the variable or pass it to the closures as a parameter (which copies it).

- Only public fields are processed by encoders (e.g., JSON or XML); private names are skipped. Thus, to use a lowercase name in the encoded object, an appropriate tag must be used.

- Not all expressions are addressable (can have their address taken by the & operator). For example, map index expressions (e.g., `names["barry"]`) are not addressable, while the map itself is. Slice elements (like array elements) are addressable.

- Testing an interface type expression, especially on interface types returned from a function, against `nil` can have confusing results.

- Passing a pointer to an interface type into a function can cause confusing behavior. Avoid doing this, especially for the universal interface type. For example, do not declare a function like this: `func(xxx *interface{})`. A function declared as `func(xxx interface{})` may actually receive a pointer as the xxx value.

- Go's standard library random number generator uses the same seed on all runs. This produces an identical random number sequence on each run. This can be useful for testing and certain use cases, but typically a different random sequence is desired on each run. To achieve this, you must randomly seed the generator, say with a function of the current Epoch (in nanoseconds), to get more randomness.

Note the preceding list is not intended to be all inclusive. Other gotchas not listed almost certainly exist.

APPENDIX D

Mark-Sweep Pseudocode

The basic process to allocate a heap object of size N is summarized[1] in pseudo-Go as follows:

```go
// Allocate size bytes from the heap.
func Allocate(size uint64) (result *Datum) {
    result = allocate(size)
    if result != nil {
        return
    }
    gc() // failed; try to free garbage and retry once
    result = allocate(size)
    if result == nil {
        panic(ErrOutOfMemory)
    }
    return
}

var ErrOutOfMemory = errors.New("out of memory")

func allocate(size uint64) (result *Datum) {
    heapLock.Lock()
    defer heapLock.Unlock()
    for _, datum := range heap.items {
        if !datum.allocated && datum.size >= size {
            datum.allocated = true
            result = datum
```

---

[1] Based on an example from www.educative.io/courses/a-quick-primer-on-garbage-collection-algorithms/jy6v

© Barry Feigenbaum 2022
B. Feigenbaum, *Go for Java Programmers*, https://doi.org/10.1007/978-1-4842-7199-5

```
                    return
            }
        }
        return
    }

func gc() {
    runtime.PauseOtherGoroutines()       // not provided
    defer runtime.ResumeOtherGoroutines() // not provided
    markRoots()
    sweep()
}

func GetRoots() *Collection {
    // currently known root Datums; not detailed how known but at least
    // all global Datums
    // all Datums on each go routine's call stack
    return NewCollection()
}

type Datum struct {
    marked    bool
    allocated bool
    size      uint64   // allocated size
    fields    []*Datum // other referenced datums
    data      []byte   // holds used (<= size) local data
}

func (d *Datum) GetReferences() []interface{} {
    // all heap objects referenced by this object; not detailed how known
    return nil
}

type Collection struct {
    items []*Datum
}
```

```go
func NewCollection() *Collection {
      return &Collection{items:make([]*Datum, 0, 100)}
}

var heap Collection
var heapLock sync.Mutex

func (c *Collection) Push(f *Datum) {
      c.items = append(c.items, f)
}
func (c *Collection) Pop() (f *Datum) {
      lenm1 := c.Len() - 1
      if len(c.items) == 0 {
            panic(ErrEmptyCollection)
      }
      f = c.items[lenm1]
      c.items = c.items[:lenm1-1]
      return
}
func (c *Collection) Get(index uint64) (f *Datum) {
      lenm1 := c.Len() - 1
      if len(c.items) == 0 {
            panic(ErrEmptyCollection)
      }
      f = c.items[lenm1]
      c.items = c.items[:lenm1-1]
      return
}
func (c *Collection) Len() int {
      return len(c.items)
}

var ErrEmptyCollection = errors.New("pop from empty collection")

func markRoots() {
      for _, datum := range heap.items {
            datum.marked = false
      }
```

```
        var candidates Collection
        for _, root := range GetRoots().items {
                for _, dataum := range root.fields {
                        if dataum != nil && !dataum.marked {
                                dataum.marked = true
                                candidates.Push(dataum)
                                mark(candidates)
                        }
                }
        }
}

func mark(candidates Collection) {
        for len(candidates.items) > 0 {
                dataum := candidates.Pop()
                for _, field := range dataum.fields {
                        if field != nil && !field.marked {
                                field.marked = true
                                candidates.Push(dataum)
                        }
                }
        }
}

func sweep() {
        for _, datum := range heap.items {
                if !datum.marked {
                        datum.allocated = false
                }
                datum.marked = false
        }
}
```

The preceding code is not real Go code and is not a general-purpose memory allocator, just an example of how mark-sweep collection might be done. In a real memory allocator, the Datum blocks would start as one big object that can be split during allocations and rejoined (concatenated) when freed to keep as many free large datum instances available as possible.

APPENDIX E

ASCII vs. UTF-8

American Standard Code for Information Interchange (ASCII)[1] is a limited (128) set of characters, including upper- and lowercase English letters and punctuation, that can be represented by a single-byte integer value. ASCII is limited as it cannot represent all the characters of the world's languages nor many of the special characters used. Most Go programs can be written entirely (except perhaps for string or character literals, but escapes exist for these) in ASCII characters. Some ASCII characters act as control characters, such as New Line. Table E-1 shows the full[2] ASCII set.

Table E-1. *The Full ASCII Set*

Dec	Char	Dec	Char	Dec	Char	Dec	Char
0	NUL (null)	32	SPACE	64	@	96	`
1	SOH (start of heading)	33	!	65	A	97	a
2	STX (start of text)	34	"	66	B	98	b
3	ETX (end of text)	35	#	67	C	99	c
4	EOT (end of transmission)	36	$	68	D	100	d
5	ENQ (enquiry)	37	%	69	E	101	e
6	ACK (acknowledge)	38	&	70	F	102	f
7	BEL (bell)	39	'	71	G	103	g
8	BS (backspace)	40	(	72	H	104	h
9	TAB (horizontal tab)	41	)	73	I	105	i

(continued)

---

[1] American Standard Code for Information Interchange – https://en.wikipedia.org/wiki/ASCII

[2] www.cs.cmu.edu/~pattis/15-1XX/common/handouts/ascii.html

© Barry Feigenbaum 2022

B. Feigenbaum, *Go for Java Programmers*, https://doi.org/10.1007/978-1-4842-7199-5

Table E-1. (*continued*)

Dec	Char	Dec	Char	Dec	Char	Dec	Char
10	LF (NL line feed, new line)	42	*	74	J	106	j
11	VT (vertical tab)	43	+	75	K	107	k
12	FF (NP form feed, new page)	44	,	76	L	108	l
13	CR (carriage return)	45	-	77	M	109	m
14	SO (shift out)	46	.	78	N	110	n
15	SI (shift in)	47	/	79	O	111	o
16	DLE (data link escape)	48	0	80	P	112	p
17	DC1 (device control 1)	49	1	81	Q	113	q
18	DC2 (device control 2)	50	2	82	R	114	r
19	DC3 (device control 3)	51	3	83	S	115	s
20	DC4 (device control 4)	52	4	84	T	116	t
21	NAK (negative acknowledge)	53	5	85	U	117	u
22	SYN (synchronous idle)	54	6	86	V	118	v
23	ETB (end of trans. block)	55	7	87	W	119	w
24	CAN (cancel)	56	8	88	X	120	x
25	EM (end of medium)	57	9	89	Y	121	y
26	SUB (substitute)	58	:	90	Z	122	z
27	ESC (escape)	59	;	91	[	123	{
28	FS (file separator)	60	<	92	\	124	|
29	GS (group separator)	61	=	93	]	125	}
30	RS (record separator)	62	>	94	^	126	~
31	US (unit separator)	63	?	95	_	127	DEL

Some of the control characters have Go escapes to ease entry into string or character literals, as shown in Table E-2.

Table E-2. Special Control Characters

Name (Acronym)	Escape
Backspace (BS)	\b
Carriage Return (CR)	\r – Generally ignored in Go
New Line (NL or LF)	\n – Generally used to mark the end of a line (especially on Unix systems; use CR + NL (not NL + CR) on Windows systems)
Form Feed (FF)	\f – Generally used to mark a section break
Horizontal Tab (TAB)	\t – Often used instead of a space as a delimiter between fields or to align text for display/printing
Null (NUL)	\0 – Often used as a delimiter between fields or a logical string end

Unicode[3] is a large (> 100,000) set of characters that can be represented by a four-byte integer value called a *Rune*. It can represent almost every possible character in use today. Often, a character representation that can represent all the defined characters but is generally smaller than a Rune is desired. UTF-8 fills this need.

UTF-8[4] is a variable-length representation (more frequent characters, at least in English, tend to have shorter lengths) of a character. It is a superset of (i.e., overlaps) ASCII. UTF-8 can be difficult to deal with in strings as any embedded UTF-8 characters do not always start at fixed offsets in the string. Alternate Unicode representations, such as UTF-16 (typically used for a high-frequency subset of Unicode; as in Java) or UTF-32 (1 per rune), are fixed length and thus easier to deal with. For example:

- []rune and string are similar, but the characters are fixed length.

- []byte and string are similar but not necessarily in UTF-8; good for ASCII strings.

---

[3] https://en.wikipedia.org/wiki/Unicode
[4] https://en.wikipedia.org/wiki/UTF-8

Index

A

American Standard Code for Information Interchange (ASCII), 571

AnnimatedGifWriter.java, 281, 320–322

Annotation, 10, 21, 28, 63, 164, 237, 249, 262

Apache Software Foundation, 26, 363

API outputs
  DELETE /history, 358, 359
  history action, 358
  JSON, 355, 356
  XML, 357

Architecture, 58, 59, 61, 66, 124, 373

Archive packages, 402–405

ASCII, 89, 125, 416, 553, 563, 571, 573

Aspect Oriented Programming (AOP), 244

Atomic, 96, 105, 372

Atomic values, 12, 105

B

Benchmark, 249, 253, 258, 259, 262, 528–531

Biannual release cycle, 14

Blank field, 167, 180

Built-in error type, 199

Built-in functions, 120, 208, 555

Bytecode, 55, 56, 59

Bytes package
  Buffer type, 417, 418
  functions, 416, 417
  Reader type, 418, 419

strings package, 416

types, 416, 417

uses, 415

C

Capstone, 406
  API paths, 278, 279
  command-line arguments, 278
  game rules, 275
  go doc output, 353
  GoL, 275–277, 279
  grid size, 275
  image formats, 278

Cascading Style Sheets (CSS), 65, 364, 450, 467, 469, 476

CGo command, 64, 123, 158, 364

Channels, 12, 20, 23, 94, 96–98, 100, 102, 104, 108, 109, 175–177, 179, 230, 231, 399, 513

C++ language, xvii, 2, 6, 27, 29, 56, 60, 65, 73, 94, 150

C language, 5, 6, 19, 25, 27, 29, 44, 54, 56, 60, 64, 65, 73, 94, 123, 124, 150, 158, 163, 372, 549, 560

Class-based language, 9

Classes, 7–9, 12, 13, 17–19, 22, 26, 27, 34, 36, 41, 43, 56, 66, 72, 76, 78, 81, 128, 132, 134, 159, 162, 165, 167–169, 211, 376

575

© Barry Feigenbaum 2022
B. Feigenbaum, *Go for Java Programmers*, https://doi.org/10.1007/978-1-4842-7199-5